POLITICS AND PERSONALIT

Politics and Personalities

Dennis Kavanagh
Professor of Politics, University of Nottingham

MACMILLAN

First published 1990

Published by
MACMILLAN ACADEMIC AND PROFESSIONAL LTD
Houndmills, Basingstoke, Hampshire RG21 2XS
and London
Companies and representatives
throughout the world

Printed in Great Britain by
Billing & Sons Ltd,
Worcester

British Library Cataloguing in Publication Data
Kavanagh, Dennis
Politics and personalities.
1. Great Britain. Politics
I. Title
320.941
ISBN 0–333–51579–X (hardcover)
ISBN 0–333–51530–3 (paperback)

To J

Contents

List of Figures and Tables

Figures

Tables

Acknowledgements

I am grateful to April Pidgeon, my secretary in the Politics Department at Nottingham, for her skill and patience in coping with my handwriting and dictation. I have also been greatly helped by the comments on previously unpublished papers of my colleague Peter Morris and my daughter Jane.

The author and publishers acknowledge with thanks permission from the following to reproduce copyright material:

Pergamon Press, for the data in Table 7.3, from A. Heath, R. Jowell and J. Curtice, *How Britain Votes* (1985).

Department of Employment *Gazette*, for the data in Table 7.4.

Gallup Polls, for the data in Tables 9.1 and 9.2 and for Figures 9.1 and 9.3.

Allen & Unwin, for the data in Table 14.3, from D. Kavanagh (ed.), *The Politics of the Labour Party* (1982).

Fontana, for Figure 9.2, from H. Pelling, *Britain in the Second World War* (1970).

Electoral Studies (1982), for Chapter 1.

West European Politics (1985), for Chapter 2.

Political Studies (1985), for Chapter 3.

Government and Opposition (1971), for Chapter 12.

Political Studies (1974), for Chapter 13.

Cambridge University Press (1989), for Chapter 15.

Comparative Politics (1976), for Chapter 16.

American Enterprise Institute, for Chapter 17, from D. Butler, H. Penniman and A. Ranney, *British Democracy at the Polls* (1981).

DENNIS KAVANAGH

Introduction

This book of essays draws on some of my articles and conference papers, published and unpublished, on topics in British politics. They cover problems of contemporary history, political personalities, elections and political parties. With few exceptions I have resisted the temptation to update the articles or insert second thoughts.

The ideas in the opening chapter, 'On Writing Contemporary Electoral History', were first presented at a conference on the study of elections at Nuffield College in 1976. They were subsequently rewritten and published in the journal *Electoral Studies* in 1982. I have taken the liberty of adding some paragraphs covering my experience of the 1987 election study.

A personal note may be relevant concerning my interest in the. Nuffield studies of British general elections. I was an undergraduate between 1960 and 1963 at Manchester University, studying politics and modern history, and at the time both departments were outstanding. The government department was being built up by W.J.M.MacKenzie and the new subject of psephology was attracting much interest at the time. One of my tutors was Richard Rose and he had just co-authored *Must Labour Lose?* with Mark Abraham and *The British General Election of 1959* with David Butler. He fired my interest in political behaviour. In the 1960s David Butler and Robert McKenzie were 'telly academics' and dominated BBC coverage of elections. Some years later, in December 1973, David Butler was searching for a co-author for the next Nuffield election study (on the February 1974 election). I had never met him before when out of the blue he invited me to lunch and to co-author the next study. We have collaborated on every general election study since.

Butler had a youthful interest in election statistics. It was first turned to more serious purposes in 1945. A committee of the new Oxford college of Nuffield was seeking a research topic that would advance understanding of the contemporary world. The Oxford historian R.B.McCallum had the idea of studying the 1945 general election and was invited by the committee to do so. The 21-year-old Butler was sent to see him and commissioned to produce 'some statistics for my book'. Butler was able to show that there were certain mathematical relationships between changes of votes and changes of seats.

Butler developed his work and on Christmas night 1949 anonymously published a piece on the cube law for the *Economist*. This showed that if votes between political parties are divided in the ratio A:B then the seats will divide in the ratio $A^3:B^3$, so exaggerating the majority in seats of the winning party. The article was read in the New Year by the Conservative opposition leader, Winston Churchill, then vacationing in Madeira. The young Butler was duly summoned to Chartwell to explain his findings. The great man lay in bed and puzzled over the matter for some hours but the elementary arithmetic about the relationship between seats and votes passed him by. (The cube law operated as a 'law' of British elections until 1970). In 1951 Butler took over the authorship of the Nuffield election studies and since then has co-authored every one.

Contemporary history still has the air of a bastard subject. Its critics say that it has more in common with journalism and current affairs than with serious history. 'It is old men drooling over their youth', A.J.P.Taylor once remarked. 'Serious' historians rely on proper documents. The passage of time, it is claimed, cultivates a more detached outlook and an awareness of how events evolve over the long term. The claim has merits. But all history is in some degree a product of its own time. Nicholas Cox, a PRO archivist, notes that British governments today produce over 100 miles of documents each year; of these only about 1 mile finds its way to the PRO. Cox warns: 'We can only find on file what was put there at the time. If an official transacted a piece of business on the telephone or did not take the trouble to note what has been said, then we shall have no record of it'.[1] And since official British papers are released only after a 30-year gap, this would leave the recent past a void.

If, however, historians vacate the field, then economists, sociologists and political scientists will proceed without them. Outside academe, politicians and commentators are ready to grind their axes. In Britain and the United States a flood of largely self-serving memoirs and diaries bears witness to the attempt by many political participants to manage history. No party conference is without its crop of recently published diaries and memoirs. Today political leaders are not content to wait for the verdict of history; they seek accolades in their own lifetimes. In the United States retiring presidents even build their own libraries. As I note in the essay,

Butler and I have not escaped attempts to 'manage' what we write about elections.

Chapter 2 – on the significance of the constitutional changes in the Labour Party in 1981 – was written close to the event, and some of its assumptions were soon confounded. Robert McKenzie was more of an all-purpose broadcaster on current affairs than David Butler. His academic reputation rested on his *British Political Parties*, first published in 1955 with a second edition in 1963. The book is an interesting example of how to make a name for oneself in academic as well as other walks of life; attack head on the conventional wisdom of the day. Everybody 'knew' that Labour was a democratic party; its constitution said so and the party's many unruly backbenchers and assertive conference were living proofs of it. Everybody also 'knew' that the Conservative Party was elitist, dominated from the top, and the 'emergence' of its leader, with no pretence at popular consultation or accountability, proved it. So for a young Canadian at the London School of Economics to show that there were actually few differences in the internal operations of the parties caused astonishment. The Labour left in particular was horrified, but for a different reason. It took the myth of inner party democracy – making the leaders accountable to the party conference – seriously. McKenzie argued that the autonomy of party elites – which the Labour left termed 'betrayal' – was inevitable, and that it was a good thing, because it kept at bay the extreme and unrepresentative party activist.

Before he died in 1981, McKenzie had promised a third edition. There had been significant changes in the Conservative Party, underlined by the resignation of Sir Alec Douglas Home and repudiation of Mr Heath as leaders in 1965 and 1975 respectively, and the adoption of rules for the election and re-election of the leader by MPs. In the 1970s an undeniably more assertive National Executive Committee and conference put the PLP leadership on the defensive. In fact McKenzie showed few signs of keeping up with the literature on party organisation and democratic theory and was maddeningly resistant to any ideas, events, and interpretations which did not reinforce his thesis.

Labour's constitutional changes in 1981, its leftward shift in policy and the exit of right-wingers certainly seemed to finish off the McKenzie model. As leader, Michael Foot saw himself as a spokesman for the party conference. Here was Labour's activist democracy alive and well, the gap between myth and reality had been closed, and my paper assumed that the elitist thesis had been conclusively disproved. In fact within a short time of his election as leader in 1983 Neil Kinnock, inevitably for a Labour leader in the 1980s a man of the left, exercised at least as much authority as any other Labour leader in opposition. He bypassed the NEC, setting up a Campaign Committee and hand-picking its representatives, kept control of the manifesto and had his way on most things. Tony Benn and his supporters were furious at the way in which the party machine was being sidelined. The leader proved himself a political 'boss', personally directing NEC meetings to drum out Militant and dump unreliable by-election candidates. Kinnock succeeded largely because he, and a growing section of the party, accepted the importance of winning elections. In no sense has he or the Shadow Cabinet been the creature of the extra-parliamentary groups. Kinnock was in large part a product of the party's surge to the left and the constitutional changes. The 1981 reforms had been seen by Tony Benn as making Labour safe for socialism; the opposite was achieved. Bennery in the 1980s turned off the voters. By the end of the decade Labour was fast dropping many leftist policies, and Benn himself and much of the left had been marginalised.

The article 'Whatever Happened to Consensus Politics?' (Chapter 3) was occasioned by the subject of my inaugural lecture at Nottingham University in May 1984. Inaugurals often deal with the new professor's views on the state of his discipline, or the role he envisages for himself in it, and with his hopes and plans for its future development at his institution. In view of the gloomy state of higher education the timing did not seem appropriate for such a lecture. (Indeed at times I thought of calling it a valedictory lecture.) I therefore chose to address a topic that was of contemporary concern but could be studied in a broader context.

Returning from a trip to London during the 1983 election, I reflected on the fact that I had first started elite interviews for general elections nearly 10 years earlier. Then the February 1974 election was partly forced on Mr Heath (as were the next two, October 1974 and 1979, forced on Mr Wilson because of his lack of a majority and on Mr Callaghan because of his defeat on a no-confidence motion). In 1983 there was a timed election, selected when the opinion polls and economic indicators were favourable for the government, and the governing party was coasting to victory. The issues of February 1974 and 1979 – trade-union power, inflation and the evident inability of government to cope with both incomes policies and social contracts – seemed far away. The lecture was an attempt to describe how the political agenda had changed, and it was subsequently published in *Political Studies* in 1985.

Looking back it appeared that the old framework stemmed from the interaction of three elements: the climate of opinion, incorporating general ideas and specific suggestions for workable policies; events and circumstances which made the ideas acceptable; and 'politics', that is, parties and personalities. Similarly the undermining of the old policy and changes in the old agenda developing through the 1970s framework can be seen as the outcome of shifts in these factors. My book-length study, *Thatcherism and British Politics; the End of Consensus?*, was published[2] in 1987 and a second, revised edition in 1990. The question mark was inserted to cover myself. Essentially, as a reviewer noted, the book was about the development of ideas and politicking in Britain since 1918. In 1989 my Nottingham colleague Peter Morris and I wrote *Consensus Politics from Attlee to Thatcher*,[3] which examined the changes in various issue areas.

Mrs Thatcher and Thatcherism have become big business for the media and academe. The tenth anniversary of her premiership in May 1989 saw an orgy of Maggie mania in the media. I have overcome my own reluctance to add to the noise and written two papers. One tries to make sense of the vast literature on the subject, the other asks, not facetiously, if Mrs Thatcher is a Conservative.

Historians are certain to acknowledge that she dominated the British political landscape in the 1980s. They will credit her with reasserting the long dormant free-market, neo-liberal values of her party. Not for her the virtues of the mixed economy, conciliating the unions, a collectivist welfare state and public spending, all celebrated by her Conservative predecessors. She is one of the self-made first-generation Conservative politicians who do not have personal memories of the 1930s and are no longer prepared to share policy-making with the interests or make full employment the main goal of economic policy. She thought that an excess of 'bourgeois guilt' (her expression in New York in 1975) had produced weak leadership and the avoidance of necessary if unpopular policies.

Her government's reforms of trade unions, tax cuts, ruthless centralisation *vis-a-vis* local government, privatisation and sale of council houses, are sure to leave a mark in post-Thatcher Britain. She has also clashed with most of the great interests of 'the Establishment', many of which have been traditional allies of her party. To take on the Church of England, universities, legal and medical professions, and the civil service – in addition to the trade unions and local government – shows quite an appetite for battle. Her attitude towards the EEC shows a similar abrasiveness when confronted with conventional wisdom.

There follow two chapters on the Labour party (Chapters 6 and 7). In 1961 the young student Neil Kinnock would have known the book *Must Labout Lose?*, written in the wake of the party's three successive election defeats in the 1950s. After 1987 Labour was in the same situation and was the subject of the same gloomy forecasts. Could Kinnock be another Harold Wilson? In one respect at least there can be no higher honour: Wilson was the greatest election winner in the party's history. The left of course sees Kinnock following the time-dishonoured path of previous leaders shifting to the right, corrupted by the prospect of power.

Chapter 7, 'Ideology, Sociology and Labour's Strategy', may read as a critical nit pick of the work of the respected and formidable Oxford sociologist, John Goldthorpe. A word of explanation may be appropriate. I was asked to contribute a critical essay on Goldthorpe's work on class and voting; a supportive piece would be written by another Oxford sociologist. Labour's electoral decline in the past two decades has provoked much scholarly analysis as well as polemics. Goldthorpe and his supporters take the view that social class remains an important factor in voting behaviour and that Labour should pursue a class-based electoral strategy. The paper disagrees with the Goldthorpe school's suggested electoral strategy for Labour's recovery.

A major reason for the Conservative dominance in the 1980s has been the division between the Alliance and Labour parties and the prospect of a race between a rising centre force and a declining Labour Party. It took most of the inter-war years for Labour to establish itself as the clear rival to the Conservatives and a credible party of government. For a time, between 1981 and 1983, it appeared that the SDP – Liberal Alliance was in the process of overtaking Labour as one of the two main parties, or at least creating a multi-party system, with a higher probability of coalition or minority government, and consequent changes to the constitution. But the opportunity passed and there followed a series of self-defeating manoeuvres by the Alliance leaders. By the end of the 1980s the centre was further away from being a credible force than it was at the beginning of the decade. Looking back, the prospect of realignment seems to have been little more than a succession of stunning by-election victories and accompanying media hype. (See Chapter 8, 'Do We Need a Centre Party?') That Labour still remains the sole credible alternative to the Conservative party is one of the more remarkable developments of the late 1980s.

But a regular turn-over in government, even in a predominantly two-party system, is not guaranteed. The hegemony of the Democratic Party in the United States between 1932 and the 1960s, the Social Democrats in Sweden since 1932 or the French right between 1958 and 1981, show this. Labour will probably have to become more like a West European Social Democratic party, more of a catch-all party, appealing to the affluent and upwardly mobile people (such as Kinnock, his family, and much of the party's front bench), and more responsive to emerging concerns about the environment, participation, and individualism as well as the quality of public services. The record of Social Democratic parties elsewhere shows that it can be done. But the party will also need help or luck. The Socialists in France have been helped by divisions among the right, as have Social Democrats in Sweden. In Britain in the 1980s the boot has been on the other foot, to the advantage of the Conservative party.

The next three chapters (9–11) deal with politicians, all of whom were 'outsiders' for a good part of their political careers. The paper on Winston Churchill was stimulated by my membership of a panel working on charismatic political leadership, for the International Political Science Association Congress at Montreal in 1973. Most of the other papers dealt with historic figures or third-world leaders and had no doubt of the charisma of their subject. I never assumed that Churchill was charismatic. Instead I decided to regard charisma as a vantage point to analyse the nature of crisis political leadership in Britain.

Enoch Powell still fascinates commentators. Even without a platform in Parliament his utterances continue to command attention. The first time I met him was over lunch, with David Butler, between the 1974 general elections. In October 1988 I gave a lecture to an audience of about 2,000 sixth-formers at the Methodist Central Hall on the topic of the Conservative party since 1979. Mr Powell preceded me and gave a most lucid and dispassionate lecture on the party between 1964 and 1979. I waited for Powell to leave the platform and indeed suggested that he should move on to his next engagement. He replied that he wished to stay: 'I'd like to learn.

But I will leave if you wish me to'. That was a challenge to which I did not rise. Throughout my lecture I was aware of the piercing eyes a few inches behind me. On the train back that day I decided to write the essay.

For a time in the late 1960s Powell seemed to walk with destiny. The cartoons often showed him as a destroyer of Heath. In 1968 *Tribune* showed Powell as an evil genie above the Aladdin-like Mr Heath, who was pleading 'Go Away!' The cartoonist Cummings, shortly before polling day in the February 1974 election showed an exhausted Mr Heath crawling through the desert and close to Number 10. Above was the menacing figure of Mr Powell, portrayed as a buzzard, ready to deny him at the end.[4] Powell is a visionary; his speeches are an invitation to his audiences to share his visions. The subtitle to Chapter 10, 'Vision and Waste', was suggested by a friend who, as a teenager, mixed socially with the Powells. 'What a waste', he commented on reading an early draft of this chapter.

Tony Benn is another figure who has shaken the political foundations. His importance has largely been in terms of internal Labour Party politics. Yet he has also had an impact on the working of the British constitution, notably the referendum, and the right of heirs to renounce their peerages.

The chapter on political deference (Chapter 12) was largely conceived at Stanford University, California. I was the fortunate recipient of a Ford Foundation post-doctoral grant for a year in 1969–70. This enabled me to spend a year at a university of my choice in the United States and work on a number of topics. One day I was asked, by the distinguished American political scientist Gabriel Almond, to lecture to his class about British political culture. In the 1960s deference (and accompanying terms like civility, trust and legitimacy) was used as a catch-all term to explain many features of British politics and society, such as hierarchical authority relations, political stability, the large working-class vote for the Conservative Party, moderation of the Labour Party, continued upper-class presence in politics, and respect for the law. For many Americans deference seemed to be the key to understanding British politics. Many fastened on working-class support for the Conservatives – a form of so-called deviant political behaviour. Eric Nordlinger's *The Working Class Tories*[5] and Robert McKenzie and Allan Silver's *Angels in Marble: Working Class Conservatives in Urban England*[6] were two survey-based studies. A hundred years earlier, in 1868, Engels had expressed his disgust to Marx at so many workers voting

Tory in the 1867 general election. In 1952 the young Peter Shore, then head of the Labour Party's Research Department, wrote in the same vein in a party pamphet: 'How is that so large a proportion of the electorate, many of whom are neither wealthy or privileged, have been recruited for a cause which is not their own?' In preparing the lecture I was struck by the number of authors quoting each other about deference and yet how unimpressive the evidence was. The resulting chapter is a critique of the literature and, I like to think, helped kill off the concept or at least encourage people to use it more carefully.

The paper 'An American Science of British Politics' (Chapter 13) was delivered to the Political Studies Association in 1974 at Lancaster University. The panel invited papers on foreign perceptions of British government. The paper traces a number of recurring themes, in often admiring American views, of the British political system, from the end of the last century down to the present.

Chaper 14, 'From Gentlemen to Players', attempts to link changes in the social composition of British politicians with changes in political style. It was initially read at a conference about change in British politics at Tulane University, New Orleans, 1979, and published in the volume *Britain: Progress and Decline*.[7]

I have added a table from elsewhere on the rise of the 'talking' professions in the Labour Party. The trend to the recruitment of more communicators in the workers' party has continued in the past decade. Front-benchers with a previous occupational background in education include Neil Kinnock, John Cunningham, Michael Meacher, David Clark, Gordon Brown, Robin Cook and Bryan Gould. The lawyers are there too – Kaufman (also a journalist), Dewar, Straw, Blair and John Smith. Of the sixty-nine new Labour MPs who entered the 1987 Parliament, a third of the PLP, only twelve had been former manual workers. The same trend is evident in trade-union sponsorship, originally a device to help working men enter Parliament. In 1987 two-thirds had no prior experience of manual work.

Labour MPs are increasingly drawn from seats in north Britain, Scotland (and Wales), and the inner cities of northern England. Of Labour's 1989 front bench, only Frank Dobson and Bryan Gould sit for constituencies in the south (one an inner London seat). The front-bench team represents the triumph of the 1944 Education Act and the successes of the now virtually extinct 11+ examination; the overwhelming majority went to grammar schools in the 1950s and

1960s, most of which have since gone independent or turned comprehensive. Hull University (with Hattersley, Prescott, and McNamara) has as many representatives as Oxford (Gould, Blair and Kaufman); Edinburgh (Cook and Brown) and Glasgow (Smith and Dewar) outscore Cambridge, which has none.

On the Conservative side the pace of change has been slower but is still evident. The upper middle class and the old Etonians have continued to decline. The title of Norman Tebbit's recent autobiography, *Upwardly Mobile* (1988), is revealing, as is the content when compared with Lord Whitelaw's autobiography, *The Whitelaw Memoirs* (1989). Such ministers as John Major, Chris Patten, John Moore, Cecil Parkinson and Mrs Thatcher represent the new Conservatism, though two of these married into money. A growing number of new Conservative MPs have had experience in local government, and more have to earn nominations rather than inherit safe seats.

In terms of style Mrs Thatcher is clearly a *mobiliser* rather than a *conciliator*. What is more, she has remained so. At the time of writing (1979) I was influenced by the failure of successive British governments and the ineffectiveness of recent political leaders. Many liked to start out as mobilisers but invariably ended up as conciliators or exhausted, and usually both. There was a choice between the power-sharing leadership model, which would have involved quasi-corporatist forms of decision-making in economic management, and a clearer direct form of personal and government leadership. Mrs Thatcher exemplifies the latter, though in the 1970s, many thought that most of the signs pointed to the inevitability of the former.

The paper on the timing of elections (Chaper 15) was read to a conference on the media and the 1987 British general election, held at the University of Essex in October 1987. Norman Tebbit, the Conservative party chairman at the time, may have exaggerated, but he had a good point, when commenting at the conference, 'The timing of an election is as important as the final campaign'. The paper tries to spell out the considerations which affect prime ministers when they are choosing a date for dissolution. The next paper (Chapter 16) was co-authored with Richard Rose of Strathclyde University, and reports the results of a survey into popular attitudes to the monarchy. In fact attitudes were rather shallow: understanding of the monarchy's modest contemporary political role in Britain is best advanced by a comparative study of the melancholy fates of the many European monarchies in this century which refused to adapt. The final paper (Chapter 17) on public opinion polls was first read at a conference organised by the American think tank, the American Enterprise Institute, on national elections in Western Democracies.

NOTES

1. A. Seldon (ed.) *Contemporary History: Practice and Method* (Blackwell, 1988), p. 82.
2. By Oxford University Press.
3. Published by Blackwell.
4. In the *Sunday Express*, 24 February 1974.
5. Published by MacGibbon & Kee, 1967.
6. Published by Heinemann, 1968.
7. Published by Macmillan, 1980.

1 On Writing Contemporary Electoral History*

Since 1945 Nuffield College has sponsored a study** of each British general election. Each volume has combined descriptive writing about the events of the campaign and parties' election strategies with statistical analysis of the characteristics of candidates and aggregate election results. With the publication of the 1979 volume the series has spawned eleven volumes and nearly 4,000 pages. Although the first major national survey of voting behaviour in Britain was not reported until 1969, elections are now perhaps the most studied part of the British political scene and the Nuffield studies have made a major contribution to this situation. To my knowledge, Nuffield-type election studies have so far been undertaken in sixteen other countries as well as of the 1880, 1906 and 1910 British general elections. Yet for no other country has there been such a series of studies mounted on such a scale.

On the assumption that the studies are a contribution to what is called contemporary history, it may be that the problems and issues raised in the exercise are worth some discussion.[1] This chapter is addressed to three of these issues: first, the object of the studies, as understood by the authors; secondly, the methods of collecting data and using sources; and, thirdly, some of the problems involved in conducting such studies close to the time of their occurrence. Apart from David Butler and the present writer, there have been six other authors or co-authors of the election books. Doubtless, each author would address the issues in his own way.[2] What follows

---

* *Electoral Studies* (1982).
** From 1945 onwards, the Nuffield Election Studies have provided comprehensive accounts of general election campaigns in Britain. Such studies have been emulated in other countries, but the series has no counterpart anywhere else. The co-author draws on his personal experiences to discuss how the authors use their sources and research materials in writing contemporary history. Attention is paid to the problems and pitfalls in conducting interviews with political elites.

is inevitably based on my own experience in co-authoring Nuffield studies on the last three British general elections.

OBJECTS

The first, 1945, study was written by R. B. McCallum, of Pembroke College, Oxford, and Alison Readman. There is a charming story about the accidental origins of the series. McCallum was on his way to a meeting of the Nuffield College research committee in March 1945 and searching for a proposal which would justify his membership of the committee. He had the idea of studying the imminent general election, the committee welcomed the idea and persuaded him to do it. Only the previous year, McCallum had published a study of the 1918 election which, he believed, had been widely misunderstood for the previous 25 years by the superficial though influential ('hard faced men') account of J. M. Keynes in *The Economic Consequences of the Peace*. McCallum wanted to kill at birth such myths which quickly grew up about elections. In 1966, looking back on his flash of inspiration, he wrote in a personal letter: 'I thought that when there was an election, after the war it must be photographed *in flight*, studied and analysed (emphasis added).' The original object was to provide a convenient and dispassionate account of an election for future historians, a guide to how contemporaries saw the election. The first authors saw the 1945 election as an historical event and wanted to provide a document for use by future historians. Obviously, historians of an earlier period would regard such accounts of, say, nineteenth-century elections as a useful source. David Butler has often quoted McCallum's hope that his work would achieve 'the immortality of other men's footnotes'. In fact, perusal of works on British politics will show that the Nuffield studies are among the most heavily cited of books on British politics.

An election is a useful vantage point from which to study a political system. The outcome is the end of a long process, and the forces shaping the individual's and the nation's electoral choice are complex and many-sided. But the election itself is a manageable unit of study: it is concentrated in a few weeks; it has a dramatic unity; it relates to many other features of the political system; and many research materials are accessible.

The actual format of the subsequent election studies has not changed greatly from 1945. The set of chapter topics covered (the record of the dissolved Parliament, the histories of the parties and their preparation for the election, the campaign, the mass media, the candidates, the opinion polls, the local campaign and the results) is logical enough and over time a series imposes some constraints on its subject.[3] Within 12 months or so of each election a volume with a comprehensive description of the campaign and aggregate statistics and election results has been published. A change in style did occur in 1964. Before then, the materials had drawn on the public side of the election – leaders' speeches, press reports and party literature. Butler and his co-authors had not talked systematically to London politicians and organisers about campaign strategies.[4] Since 1964, however, this type of interview or 'inside-dopester' material has been a main source for the coverage of the national campaign, and there has been a decline in the coverage of the constituencies. This shift in focus has reflected the growing nationalisation and centralisation of the election.

The commitment to a series format has its dangers, of course. It does inhibit the development of new approaches and, although each election has its distinctive elements, there can be a staleness in description of the election routines. The positive side of having a series of election studies is that the regularity of elections allows the books to become works of reference. Anybody who wants to know, for any of the recent elections, the size of the postal vote, the largest and smallest constituency campaign expenses, the headline of each newspaper of each day of the campaign, which candidates had difficulty getting reselected, the economic trends during the preceding Parliament and so on, knows not only that the information is available, but where in the book to find it. This is one of the real virtues of a series.

SOURCES

The source materials are diverse and over the years they have become more plentiful, particularly in the area of 'haute politique', or the thinking of politicians and officials. The author of the 1951 Nuffield election study lamented:

> One does not know – and if one knew one could not reveal – the arguments [about campaign strategy]. Years will elapse before such information is available. It depends on the publication of

the memoirs of those concerned or, perhaps, more reliable but certainly more distant, the opening of their papers to the research student.

The future historian will have additional sources in the form of private documents, Cabinet papers, diaries and so on. But we have access to radio and television transcripts, press cuttings, face-to-face interviews with participants, postal questionnaires to candidates, public and, sometimes, private opinion polls, and official data on postal votes and expenses. The above provides a substantial body of data that can form the basis for writing an authoritative narrative and informed judgement near to the event. And the contemporary student does have some advantages over the historian of the future. He can check on the press stories at the time, talk to participants before their memories fail and before retrospective wisdom sets in, and can draw on his own impressions. The amount of documentary evidence probably will not satisfy the trained historian. Yet the national and local press, party literature, documents and conference reports, opinion polls and so on, do constitute a useful body of published material. Without wishing to rationalise our relative dearth of accessible historical materials at the present, it may be that documentation will not be as comprehensive a source material for future students of the present as it was in an earlier period. We live in an age of heavily documented government but less documented politics. The telephone has partly replaced the letter as a medium of exchange between politicians compared to 50 years ago. Politicians probably write and speak for the record now even more than their predecessors; they are also more visible on account of more investigative journalism and television coverage.

Secondly, there are the interviews with a large number of politicians, advisers, party officials, and pollsters. In working on each election study in February 1974, October 1974 and 1979, the two authors must have conducted over 400 interviews, talking to some participants six or seven times, over a period of some 2 or 3 years. Refusals to grant an interview have been very rare, though at times it has proved impossible to arrange an interview because of a politician's tight schedule. Our main interview targets cover the chief party spokesmen and/or members of their private office, party officials and regional officers. Access depends partly on personal relationships which have been built up over the years, partly on trust, and partly on the feeling that we are engaged on something serious and not interested in collecting personal gossip. Over the years the party headquarters on both sides of Smith Square have become more generous in providing time and information. In most cases, people are surprisingly direct in answering questions. Sometimes an interview has been unexpectedly rewarding because the respondent has gone off at a tangent and commented on matters which seemed important to him or her.

The reliance on conversation creates some problems. Much information is imparted for background purposes or on condition that the sources are not named, a stipulation which is bound to frustrate the academic reader. Many people are frank – surprisingly so – but how can we be sure that our sources are telling the truth? There are some checks – talking to a large number of participants and comparing different accounts, double-checking on conflicting claims, circulating the manuscript to interested parties and publishing the account so near to the event for it to receive critical reviews. These are all ways of attempting to secure verisimilitude. By writing so close to the event one is exposed to criticism and correction from other observers and from the participants.

It is also important to go on talking to participants after the campaign when they have more time and are less reticent. It was by persistent questioning in the days after the election that we were able to present a reasonably full account of the pressures on Mr Heath to make 'the supreme sacrifice' in the closing stages of the October 1974 election campaign.[5]

We make a practice of taking full notes during an interview and dictating them into a tape recorder soon afterwards, so that we have a reasonably full record.[6] As any experienced interviewer knows, there is no one 'best' way to interview people of different personalities. We tend not to have a set schedule of questions, or anything resembling a questionnaire. Instead we have a list of topics to be covered and this gradually develops into a framework or grid which one adapts to each interview situation. Some respondents are immediately forthcoming, appearing to anticipate our questions and interests. With other interviewees, one has to sketch an explanation and patiently wait for denial or confirmation. I recollect a valuable interview with a party leader who combined direct 'yes' or 'no' answers to questions with digressions, covering evaluations of colleagues, personal philosophy, and other subjects, and would then say: 'I'm sorry. I'm not answering your questions. You must stop me'. Neither of us accepted the challenge.

The interviews tend to be more in the nature of exchanges between reasonably well-informed researchers and participants rather than straight question and answer sessions. Most of the participants are busy and important people and they usually want something out of the interview – self-publicity, an exchange of information and understanding of their work. One must, of course, reassure them that confidences will not be betrayed. Often one has to demonstrate that one already knows a good deal about a subject to encourage the respondent to talk. Perhaps four-fifths of the useful information comes from a very small number of well-placed and reliable sources. Yet different individuals contribute different small pieces of information.

As a result of our interviews we usually compile a set of interview notes, amounting to perhaps 2,000 typed pages for each election. The notes contain a generous amount of trivia, irrelevance and indiscretion, but they also provide hard information and insights into the thinking of politicians (much of which we do not directly use) for any studies of British politics. The notes are useful for us, to refresh our memories about exactly what we thought respondents said at earlier interviews, and to enable us to compare differing claims about what went on.

The third source, on which we rely heavily, is the quality press and television. The media have become more probing and informative in the post-war period, particularly in the development of party strategies. As the campaign has become more concentrated on television, so it has become more essential to follow it there.

The fourth source is the hard data that are already available for collection and analysis. These include the opinion poll findings, audience research data of the BBC and ITV, candidates' election addresses, postal votes, constituency election expenses, backgrounds of candidates, census material and so on. Collection and analysis of this data is perhaps most easily done near to the time of the election.

We have made a point of circulating draft chapters to concerned participants. This is not directly a source material but it is worth discussing in the context. Circulation is a useful way of correcting factual errors, guarding against action for libel or plain misjudgement, and occasionally it generates further material as a participant is prompted to reveal more.

To illustrate our use of sources, it may be useful to refer to the 1979 study. For our chapter on the manifestos we talked to four of the people involved in drafting the two main party manifestos, as well as several other members of the Conservative Inner Shadow Cabinet and the Labour Cabinet NEC working groups. We also saw various documents, minutes and memoranda that participants wrote. The chapter was seen in draft form by the four people involved in writing the manifesto, as well as other participants. The chapter on the Conservative Party drew on interviews with ten Shadow Cabinet ministers, Mrs Thatcher and most of the senior figures in the party organisation. The chapter on the opinion polls drew heavily on the published polls, the parties' private polls, and on interviews with the private pollsters, party officials and politicians. It was read in draft form by the parties' private pollsters, party officials and three other public pollsters. (I might add that the pollsters, as a group, have proved to be the most fastidious and personally sensitive of manuscript readers.) Of course, none of these checks guarantees that our judgements are unchallengeable. It does, however, increase our confidence in what we say.

While exposing oneself to a wide range of sources, it is also vital to travel around the country and not become a prisoner of London-centred views. At each election we have become more and more aware of the separateness of the national campaigns, fought through the mass media, from what happens in the constituencies. The centralisation of the campaign may have diminished the impact of the local candidate and party organisation, but the local ritual continues largely unaltered.

PROBLEMS

We have encountered a number of problems in collecting our material and writing a manuscript. If one writes for different audiences, one is liable to leave each of them dissatisfied, each for different reasons. Journalists and academics each come with different expectations and predispositions. The former often pay little attention to the ample statistical material in the volume – particularly the appendices – while the academic reader may become impatient with the 'who did what?' nature of the early chapters on the making of party strategy and the campaign. The historian looks for documentary evidence and a fuller acknowledgement of sources. These different disappointments and dissatisfactions tend to be reflected in the reviews.

Defence of the studies on the grounds that they are fairly complete
and accurate accounts of the elections and that they are useful for
historians are more persuasive than that they make contributions to
political science as science. A legitimate criticism is that the books
fail to explain an election outcome and range too widely. They
provide information on and analysis of several elements of an
explanation (strategy, broadcasting, the press, issues, patterns in the
results, etc.) but fail to interrelate them. In particular as Ranney
comments:

> . . . the books' main dependent variables (election outcomes,
> interparty distribution of votes and seats, 'swing') are never
> closely and clearly related to the books' main independent
> variables (candidates' characteristics, electioneering, press and
> broadcasting coverage and comment) on which we are given so
> much excellent information.[7]

I happen to be less impressed by complaints about the series' lack
of theory and its concern to describe the campaign and its context
as fully as possible. An election campaign and its antecedents form
an event and, as such, do not easily lend themselves to generalisations
across time or place, or even typological or theoretical frameworks.
What is remarkable is the general lack of academic studies of nation-
wide election campaigns, not least in the United States, where the
subject has largely been left to journalists.[8]

Indeed we have always been aware that in describing and assessing
the strategies and actions of British campaigners, we may be
imposing more rationality and deliberate calculation than the
participants intended. Strategists at the centre frequently draw
analogies with sport or military campaigns to describe their
operations. But campaigns are beset by a fair share of accidents,
ad hoc decisions, misunderstandings, failure of communications and
the unwillingness or inability of participants lower down the line to
comply with decisions. An American politician wisely warned an
academic:

> In campaigns people don't develop a reasoned approach, and the
> trouble with most analyses of political behaviour by political
> scientists is that they attribute a reasoned working out of things
> which are not worked out reasonably.[9]

Another problem relates to the process of interviewing. David
Butler's long involvement with election studies and my own more

modest one have certainly given us a good idea of which respondents are useful and reliable, an opportunity to develop relations with participants and some sense of perspective on each campaign and its events. These are advantages. The faces in Smith Square have changed over the years but the indefatigable David Butler continues as part of the landscape. A danger is not only that one's own reactions become predictable but that those of the people one interviews do also. Because most psephologists are thought to doubt the efficiency of much of the campaign effort, I have suspected that respondents – who genuinely believe that what they are doing may decisively affect the campaign – assume a sceptical or even defensive air about their activities when they speak to us. Again, because David Butler is so visible in the mass media as an expert on elections, I have often felt that there was a 'role reversal' in some interviews; respondents proved more eager to seek his reading of the campaign instead of answering our questions. We have certainly found cases of so-called 'insiders' not knowing of events and people, yet covering up and pretending to be aware of them. These are the dangers of having an interviewer who is well known and is identified with particular views about election campaigns.

One also has to beware of the tendency for some campaign participants to try and 'manage' what is reported. This includes not only what they tell (and do not tell), but also the subtle hints about who else we should see and what lines we might pursue. This is part of a wider, and understandable, pattern of behaviour; politicians have their favoured journalists and television interviewers to whom they grant access or 'leak' stories. People who talk to you have a vested interest in the image presented of themselves.

Attempts at 'management' may be expressed in different ways. Some respondents appear to regard an election book as something akin to a school report, hence you should give a reference to 'x' or 'y' for having done a good job. On at least one occasion, there may have been an attempt to denigrate one party official in the hope that a 'bad report' in the book would speed his demotion. Some people make claims for their own roles which have to be treated with scepticism. In February 1974, we interviewed four people in the Labour camp who each claimed exclusive credit for the decision to replay the controversial Tony Barber Conservative broadcast before a press conference. When taxed with this, the most senior of our sources dismissed the other claimants with the remark that they were 'only out for a mention'.

In 1987 much media attention was directed to the so-called 'Wobbly Thursday' in Downing Street, a week before polling day. Different advertising groups (apart from Saatchi and Saatchi, the agency officially working for the party were linked to different ministers and providing advice about electoral strategy; the agency, Young & Rubicam, were linked to Lord Whitelaw and John Wakeham and their findings were reported to Mrs Thatcher. On that Thursday some leading Conservatives, though not Mr Tebbit, felt that the party was losing its lead over Labour and advocated a change of strategy. After the election victory a number of claims were made by the groups about how they had 'won' the election.

It is not for me to comment on the extent to which we resist such blandishments but it may well be that protecting one's sources and the likelihood that one may have to revisit them for a future election do inhibit our style and lead to a general blandness. In particular, there is some subconscious pressure not to be too critical or revelatory because we will require co-operation next time round. Some well-informed reviewers have commented that it requires an insider to 'code' some of the allusions and read between the lines of some of the passages. For example, the three resignations in the Conservative organisation discussed in the 1979 book were more brutal and occasioned more controversy than our text conveys.

Time is important in two ways. The sheer speed of the operations – particularly the commitment to send a complete manuscript to the publisher within a few months of the election – involves costs. The major costs of writing so close to the event are inadequate time for reading, thinking second and further thoughts, and a blunting of one's judgement. But that is contemporary history and our book is not the last word on the election. Later research and memoirs will undoubtedly add fresh insights and a different perspective, but my own impression is that writing 5 or 10 years after the event would not produce fundamental alterations to our story.

The time factor is perhaps even more important in another respect. One understands the significance of an election more fully only in historical terms. The political (and other) consequences of an election and its immediate aftermath only make themselves felt over time; the *contemporary* historian, however sensitive his historical understanding, can only speculate about the future significance of recent events. Any contemporary study of the 1906 general election, for example, would emphasise the demise of the Conservatives and the Liberal landslide. Twenty or thirty years later, the main significance might lie in the return of 29 Labour MPs – the bridgehead for the party's eventual replacement of the Liberals and realignment of the party system. Who would have placed such an interpretation on the event at the moment of the Liberals' greatest triumph? The historical perspective and passage of time allow the election to be seen as part of a larger subject.

The serialisation of a book by Rodney Tyler on the 1989 election (*Campaign: the Selling of the Prime Minister*) in the *Sunday Times* for three successive weekends and the obvious way in which it promoted the reputations of some people while downgrading those of others certainly produced some interesting reactions. The book reads as though written by his Conservative heroes, the advertiser, Tim Bell, and Lord Young. Although studying the Tory campaign, Tyler never interviewed such key participants as Norman Tebbit, the party chairman, and people concerned with the Young and Rubicam operation. Some of the participants, aggrieved by the book, approached us with a view 'to setting the record straight'. One person close to Mrs Thatcher remarked 'It would be awful if in 30 years time people turned to that book for a history of the election'. We did not accept the validity or truth of all that we were told, but we were unable to present a much fuller account of the tensions inside the Tory campaign.

Writing and publishing the book reasonably close to the event provides the opportunity for others to challenge and possibly correct our account while their memories are still reasonably fresh. When one circulates the manuscript, one often receives suggestions about how passages should be reworded or criticisms toned down, and some readers have a vested interest in what is written. In 1987 it was suggested that we should insert material favourable to a particular organisation or excise material critical of somebody else. We rejected both suggestions. Another participant appealed to us to reconsider our reference to a scandal about him. I am glad to say that we did omit the reference because it was not relevant to the story.

General elections still develop their own myths, notwithstanding the hopes of R. B. McCallum for the Nuffield studies. The competition from partisans and self-interested participants is too intense. An election campaign and its outcome are, after all, highly political. People will disagree in their assessments and evaluations. I would regard as a myth the idea that Mr Heath in 1974 set out on a confrontation with the miners and welcomed the prospect of a 'Who Governs?' election. Some Conservative ministers may have thought along these lines, but Mr Heath was perhaps the last member of the Cabinet to accept the call for an election. He was always worried that the 'Who Governs?' issue – however helpful for the party in the short run – would blur what he regarded as the more important issue of developing understanding of and support for an anti-inflation policy. Another myth that shows signs of sticking is that Mr Callaghan was virtually alone in preferring to continue in office beyond autumn 1978. The decision was his but it was welcomed by senior Transport House officials, regional and local organisers, supported by the main figures in the Cabinet and approved by many MPs. That some of them may have altered their stories later does not affect our memories of *what they said at the time*.

The trade-off is that research conducted close to the event can gain in accuracy because memories of participants and observers have not been affected by retrospective wisdom. Statements, behaviour and events may look very different when you know about their first- and second-order consequences. Such knowledge may equally distort the perspective of the historian as well as the participant. There are both gains and shortcomings from waiting for time to elapse since an event and writing close to the event.

A major academic limitation to our reliance on off-the-record interviews is that footnotes cannot be given to document our claim. It is almost a precondition of holding interviews with British political elites at present that they will be on 'lobby terms'. But it would be the height of methodological purism to dispense with such information, simply because one is not able to identify one's sources. It is possible to point to many other important studies which have drawn largely or in part on interviews without naming sources. These include Richard Rose's *Influencing Voters*, Hugh Heclo and Aaron Wildavsky's *The Private Government of Public Money* and Nigel Lawson and Jock Bruce-Gardyne's *The Power Game*. (The recent authorised biographies of Morrison, MacDonald and Gaitskell have used interview material and identified almost all their sources.)

Over the years, the Nuffield authors have developed informal rules for disguising their interview sources.[10] One may, for example, cite a speculative newspaper article that contained hard information which has been personally confirmed by the participants; where there is an unattributed statement about a politician's views or motives the source is usually the person himself or a member of his private office. Sometimes there is a direct hint ('. . .he often complained that. . . ', 'he felt that. . . '); occasionally permission is sought to use a direct quote or the relevant section of a manuscript is sent to those involved to get clearance.

Perhaps the least serious problem arises from the competition presented by the accounts of some of the participants themselves. In the past decade there seems to have been a flood of memoirs, 'inside views', diaries, and 'records' pouring off the printing presses. All these accounts have the merits and defects of being personal views. A few make a genuine contribution to our understanding of recent events and will be used by future historians. Most are also highly selective, self-serving and remarkably unrevealing about what their subjects were thinking and calculating. They reveal little about the author's thinking on political strategy, on elections, or indeed on many other matters.[11]

The circulation of draft chapters to some participants is an important stage in the process of getting the story right. We have received several useful reactions, largely by writing and circulating the manuscript so close to the event. Some respondents limit their comments to factual errors and explicitly avoid comment on our interpretations; some reply at great length, range widely, and generously provide further inside knowledge and insights; and some reactions are highly partisan, or reflect offence at an innuendo and our use of a less than flattering adjective. One attentive Conservative official acted almost as an attorney for the Tory Party. He seemed to see it as his task to seek to erase from the manuscript any sentence that was in any way critical of the party machine. In 1979 Tony Benn thought our draft chapter on the preparation of the manifesto 'reads as though it was written by Reg Prentice'. His complaints rested almost entirely on matters of interpretation and he had no quarrel with the facts as presented . Our defence is not only that the chapter had been read by six members who attended the Clause 5 meeting but that at least two of them were closely identified with the complainant's own political views. In general, where readers have disagreed on factual matters, we check further to see if we were accurate (more often than not their claims have been verified) or had misinterpreted a point (more often than not we have held to our original position).

Finally, any student of contemporary political events has to recognise the possibility that his work may be seized on by the people whom he is writing about. Instead of describing and analysing he becomes, as it were, an actor. Some practitioners of the genre, particularly if they are still active in politics, may write with this object in mind. One has to recognise the element of personal engagement in such a work as, say, Harold Wilson's *The Labour Government 1964–70*. There have been a few cases of politicians using the Nuffield election studies and other voting studies in internal party debates. Conservative strategists certainly took note of the account of Labour's use of private polls in 1964, and some critics of Mr Wilson in Transport House sought ammunition in the account of his conduct of the 1970 election and his political attitudes.[12] Any account of a political event which is published so close to its occurrence inevitably courts the possibility that it may be so exploited. One has little control over this. The Nuffield studies, as a contribution to contemporary history, have necessarily served various purposes and been addressed to different audiences. But they do, I believe, offer a significant contribution to contemporary history.

NOTES

1. For the view that contemporary government and current events are not suitable subjects for academic study see Maurice Cowling, *The Nature and Limits of Political Science* (London, 1962).
2. See David Butler, 'Instant History', *New Zealand Journal of History*, 2, October 1968, pp. 107–14.
3. For a comprehensive discussion, see Austin Ranney, 'Thirty Years of "Psephology"', *British Journal of Political Science*, 6, April 1976, pp. 217–30.
4. One should add, however, that the authors did travel around the country interviewing candidates, agents and regional and area organisers. The 1959 election study also drew on interviews for the sections dealing with public relations.
5. See *The British General Election of October 1974*, pp. 124–9.
6. A typical record of an interview in 1978–9 amounted to between 1,500 and 2,000 words. An interview with Mrs Thatcher in August 1978 ran to nearly 5,000 words.
    Occasionally respondents suggest that we tape the interviews. We tried it once and the results were unsatisfactory. Some American academics have managed to record interviews with British politicians and civil servants. I suspect, however, that some respondents would be inhibited by the presence of a recorder. For a similar view see the valuable article by Philip Williams, 'Interviewing Politicians. The Life

of Hugh Gaitskell', *Political Quarterly*, July–September 1980.

7. Ranney, *op cit.*, p. 230.
8. But see A. Ranney (editor), *America at the Polls* (Washington and London: American Enterprise Institute, 1981).
9. Quoted by Murray Levin, *The Compleat Politician* (Indianapolis: Bobbs-Merrill, 1962), p. 271.
10. This paragraph draws on 'Interview Sources for the Nuffield Election Series', Michael Pinto-Duschinsky and David Butler, British Politics Group *Newsletter*, Spring 1977.
11. A well-informed political commentator has pointed to the pitfalls of relying on these sources. In *The Times* (10.3.1980), David Wood noted some inaccuracies in Iain Macleod's famous *Spectator* review of Randolph Churchill's *The Fight for Tory Leadership*, and added '. . . the instant histories of principals involved in important or exciting events have to be studied with full allowance for *ex parte* interest; and, if the instant histories are suspect, especially in a day of Cabinet diaries and Prime Minister's memoirs, what of longer range histories that use contemporary records as their sources? Political history is a special form of fiction'.
12. See *The British General Election 1970*, pp. 1–6 and 147–8.

2 Power in British Politics: Iron Law or Special Pleading?*

This chapter analyses the claims advanced by Robert McKenzie about the distribution of power in British political parties. It considers McKenzie's mode of analysis (with particular reference to Labour), his definition of terms, selection of evidence and interpretation of it. The major argument is that McKenzie over-generalised from the events of the 1950s and 1960s and that subsequent events have severely undermined his thesis.

There are few books on British politics which argue a thesis, and even fewer which argue an interesting thesis. It is safe to assume that most would agree to the inclusion of R. T. McKenzie's *British Political Parties* in such a list. The book was first published to critical acclaim in 1955, a second revised edition was issued in 1963, and plans for a third edition were aborted by McKenzie's untimely death in September 1981.[1] The scope of the book was indicated by its sub-title, 'The Distribution of Power Within the Conservative and Labour Parties'. Such a work of political soiology clearly followed in the footsteps of other great European students of political parties – Weber, Michels, Ostrogorski, and Duverger. McKenzie's thesis was that, contrary to the two parties' claims about themselves and their rivals, the distribution of power within the parties was very similar, notably in the domination of the parliamentary leadership over other sections of the parties.

In 1955 such a claim was greeted with astonishment. After all, everybody 'knew' that the Conservative Party was elitist and leader-dominated, and that the mass membership controlled the Labour Party and its leaders were constantly under threat. Here was an

* *West European Politics*, 1985.

'outsider', a young Canadian, who had been active in the Social
Credit Party, assaulting the cherished beliefs of activists and staple
ideas of political scientists. A combination of academic studies and
political events has gradually chipped away at the thesis, and it is
now fair to say that the combined impact of political events and
research since 1955 has qualified McKenzie's original claims.[2] Yet
it remains a testament to the book's importance that students of
British parties have had to confront McKenzie's work. The book is
frequently cited and subsequent works have often related their
contents to McKenzie; the question they faced, to exaggerate a
little, was: ' McKenzie, agree or disagree?'
    McKenzie's thesis was clearly stated:

> . . . whatever the rôle granted in theory to the extra-parliamentary
> wings of the parties, in practice final authority rests in both
> parties with the parliamentary party in its leadership. In this
> fundamental respect the distribution of power within the two
> major parties is the same (p. 582, 1st edition; p. 635, 2nd edition).

In the preface to the second edition McKenzie acknowledged that
he may have glossed over certain differences between the parties,
but

> regardless of the claims the parties themselves may make about
> their own internal organisation, the power structure is determined
> in practice, by their acceptance of the rules and conventions
> which govern the exercise of power by the Prime Minister, the
> Cabinet and Parliament in the British political system. . . The
> distribution of power, as between the Leader and his front-bench
> colleagues, the parliamentary parties, their mass organisations
> and professional machines will be [and is] fundamentally similar
> (p. ix, 2nd edition).

British Political Parties still remains the only book-length study
of the internal workings of the two parties: it has both dominated
the literature and coloured many Anglo-American and West
European views about the British parties. As such, it merits critical
scrutiny after the passage of 30 years.
    The present analysis is in four parts. It begins by noting the
intellectual climate in which the thesis was propounded. It then
examines McKenzie's style of analysis, use of evidence, and the

definition of key terms. It considers the extent to which his claims still stand in the light of subsequent changes in the parties. McKenzie, after all, took for granted the durability of features which buttressed the thesis at the time he was writing. Finally, it relates the book and the debate it has provoked to certain wider features of the British political system. The conclusion is that the analysis was faulty even in 1955, and that subsequent events have further undermined it.

THE CONTEXT OF McKENZIE'S STUDY

It is worth noting that *British Political Parties* is not a comprehensive history or study of the Conservative and Labour Parties. There is, for example, little about the local parties and no acknowledgement of different regional patterns in the operations of the political parties. More serious perhaps, McKenzie at the outset disclaims any concern with the two parties' ideologies and programmes. One should not complain about the book an author has not or might have written. But there is no denying that many disputes about power in the two parties and demands for structural changes have been linked with struggles over policies. One has only to consider the battles in the Labour Party over defence in 1960, or the divisions in the party between the left and right over constitutional reforms in 1979–81 to appreciate the linkage. Rival claims about power in the parties and 'correct' constitutional procedures have frequently been exploited by spokesmen for contrasting values and policies.

The spirited debate the book provoked was almost entirely confined to the Labour Party – in large part because McKenzie challenged more of its fundamental 'myths'. To claim that the realisation of a party's cherished ideal of intra-party democracy was (a) incompatible with the British Constitution, and (b) more honoured in the breach than the observance, not surprisingly rankled with those who took it seriously, particularly on the left. Whereas the first claim was a value judgement, the second could be tested by study of the historical record. Many on the left of the Labour Party might agree with his story of the parliamentary elite's manipulation of conference. But they were appalled by his argument that this was both inevitable and desirable.[3] To support or oppose McKenzie had implications for the distribution of power in the party and the influence of different political factions. If much of the literature on the Labour Party marries scholarship with partisanship, McKenzie's book is a good example of a literature feeding back into the political process. By contrast, his analysis of the Conservative Party has received perfunctory attention, partly because he did not radically challenge existing ideas about the party and clearly regarded its theory and practice as being compatible with the British Constitution. To date there have been only two articles that have dealt with the topic of power in the party.[4] The book has contributed to a certain imbalance, till recently at least, in the study of British political parties.

In orienting his study, McKenzie (pp. 15–17*) borrows Robert Michels' ideas about oligarchy in political parties. In *Political Parties* (first published in 1911), Michels drew on his experience of German trade unions and the Social Democratic Party to argue that direct democracy, in the sense of the mass membership controlling the leaders, was impossible; there was an 'iron law of oligarchy'. Michels had claimed that there were certain consequences of organisation (for example, the specialisation of labour) which, combined with the loyalty of party members to the leaders (parliamentary leaders and bureaucrats) gave the latter a fairly free hand in setting and carrying out the goals of the organisation; oligarchy was 'the inevitable product of the very principles of organisation'. Michels and other elitists were taking account of the growth of mass politics and large-scale organisation during the last years of the nineteenth century. As Geraint Parry notes, these writers recognised the advent of the mass into politics *and* the restriction of leadership to a few. The relationship between leaders and masses was central to elite studies and understanding modern politics.[5] McKenzie wanted to establish whether there was a similar gap between myth and reality about British parties.

In recent years, however, Michels' thesis has been subject to more rigorous scrutiny. Critics have pointed to his inconsistent usage of key terms like 'power', 'embourgeoisement', 'democracy', and the anecdotal style with which he illustrates his points. Michels regarded the conflict as essentially one between different *strata* of the party, the 'ins' who are able to draw on organisational resources and bureaucratic techniques, and the 'outs' who rely on ideas. He refers to the possibility that the party leaders may be divided, with rival members appealing to the followers for support, and that party

* All references are to the second edition of *British Political Parties*.

divisions may be vertical, combining different groups of leaders and followers rather than horizontal, between leaders and followers. It is true that Michels was hostile to professional political leadership and feared for the deradicalising effects on a socialist party of being in government. He wrote about the dangers of oligarchy, and expressed the hope that his book 'will enable us to minimise these dangers, even though they can never be entirely avoided'. The position of leadership automatically separated the leader from the membership in terms of status and wealth. And, over time, the leaders lost their radical élan: 'the revolutionaries of today become the reactionaries of tomorrow'. This was a law which depressed Michels yet, as we shall see, it was a consolation for McKenzie. A different view was expressed by Hands who has claimed that Michels may be read as arguing that there is neither a law nor a tendency to oligarchy.[6] Medding has analysed the text to show that organisation *per se* actually provides checks or counter-leadership tendencies within an organisation,[7] and May claims that Michels' *Political Parties* is actually a theory of democracy rather than oligarchy.[8] For present purposes, this article accepts that *Political Parties* is arguing the thesis of oligarchy though it acknowledges that it has given rise to very different interpretations.

Critics have also taken issue with Michels' concept of democracy. He sought this within the structure of a political party rather than in the interaction of political parties.[9] For Michels, democracy involved the accountability of office-holders to those who elected them. In the Labour Party's idea of intra-party democracy it meant that Members of Parliament were 'the servants of the movement' (i.e. the party conference), not the electorate at large. Yet a number of definitions of liberal democracy in recent years have regarded it as a mechanism which permits popular choice between competing teams of leaders and parties.[10] In other words, liberal democracy in an era of universal suffrage arises out of the electoral competition between political parties, rather than from the quality of the relations between leaders and members within a political party.

McKenzie shared what has come to be termed the elitist view of democracy. He agreed with J. A. Schumpeter that the classical idea of direct democracy was unrealistic because it granted too much initiative and intelligence to the mass and underplayed the role of leadership (pp. 645–6). He also agreed with Conservative objections to the theory and practice of intra-party democracy in the Labour Party on the grounds that it was 'unconstitutional' for MPs to be accountable to an extra-Parliamentary body. Although the Conservatives had come to terms with democratic ideas and the mass suffrage in the twentieth century, the internal operations of the party, and particularly the way the leader 'emerged' (until 1965), hardly reflected this. Social class, or what McKenzie called 'subtle considerations of social deference towards their leading Parliamentarians' (p. 638), and oligarchy, protected the Conservative leadership from the consequences of democratisation. This is an important insight, showing how easy it is to confuse social class and oligarchy. The Conservatives could have both, while Labour was supposed to be different. Class did not work within the Labour Party, but oligarchy did.

Yet two other considerations were relevant to understanding the context of McKenzie's analysis. First, McKenzie was fascinated by the 'puzzle' of how in the world's first industrialised society and the most urbanised and working-class electorate in the west, the Conservatives had been the 'normal' party of government in the twentieth century. The time when he was working on the two editions (1951–63) were years of Conservative electoral dominance. The party won three successive general elections in the 1950s and commentators speculated whether Labour would ever win again. These were also the years in which R. A. Butler and Macmillan had 'modernised' the Conservative Party and accepted the welfare state and mixed economy. He thought that part of its electoral appeal, not least to manual workers, lay in its authoritative leadership, which appealed to working-class deference.[11] Labour's complex structure (its 'incoherence'), however, resulted in a lack of clear and authoritative leadership, promoted disunity, and was an electoral liability.[12]

In taking this position McKenzie was also writing within an important pluralist school of political sociology. This assumed that 'mass politics' or direct political participation was often linked to political extremism, and that the relative autonomy of the elites and the mediated or indirect influence of party members on leaders would better safeguard liberal democratic values. There was some impressionistic evidence at the time that party activists were more extreme than a party's parliamentarians and electoral supporters. Duverger's view, for example, was that the 'parliamentary domination of a party's organisation' was more likely to make it representative of public opinion and win elections than if its activists were influential.[13] McKenzie fully shared this belief in what has been termed the curvilinear law of disparity, i.e. that the political elites are politically and ideologically closer to the voters than the party activists. Labour's constitution, in McKenzie's view, was always a barrier to the leadership adapting itself to the electorate. In his final essay, he returned to this theme, arguing that intra-party democracy was incompatible with democracy.[14] It was because parties, unlike other groups, had a responsibility for governing the country that their leaders could not be subject to dictation from a body outside the elected legislature. This is a different line of argument from that of such party theorists as Neumann and Kirchheimer, who claimed that broader social changes were encouraging parties to be 'catch-all' in their electoral appeals and to downgrade political ideology and the rôle of members. Like Bagehot, and most approving accounts of the British system, McKenzie disapproved of those 'warm partisans' whose influence would produce a worse form of government – 'sectarian government'. Labour could escape from this only by 'living a lie', retaining a constitution and myth, and breaking both when in office.

McKENZIE'S ANALYSIS

An immediate problem is raised by what it is that McKenzie is actually testing. He claims to be testing the 'myth' of extra-parliamentary control of the Parliamentary Labour Party and of the leaders' domination in the Conservative Party. Yet he admits (p.15) that his description of Labour is a caricature, a product of the party's self-portrait in much of the party literature and the self-serving characterisation offered by Conservatives. Now it is extremely difficult to disprove a myth by showing that it is not realised in practice; that is not the test of the power of a myth. A myth is a goal or purpose which may retain its validity, regardless of whether or not it is attained. It may also offer important criteria by which actions are judged.

 McKenzie's hypothesis, as set up, is something of a straw man. If we find a case when the party conference has been defied by Labour leaders or a Conservative leader gave way to grass-roots pressure, then we have disproved the respective 'myth' of each party. W. J. M. Mackenzie claims that McKenzie's approach is tantamount to saying that if 'dictatorship and democracy are disproved, what is left must be oligarchy. Therefore, the Conservative and Labour parties are both oligarchies. . . '.[15]

He has also fairly objected that *British Political Parties* is not helpful as a description of the parties. By demonstrating that the two parties are not as different as their partisans claim, the book tries to argue away the existence of any substantial differences at all, whereas,

> he *knows* by long and intimate experience that they differ in all sorts of other much more interesting respects. He is condemned by his hypothesis to hammer away at tedious resemblances, and to gloss over the interesting differences which the reader can see latent in his material.[16]

Is McKenzie saying that the Labour Party is as elitist as the Conservative Party, or that the Conservative Party is as pluralistic and beset with checks and balances as the Labour Party?

A second difficulty lies in the evidence for the claimed similarity in the distribution of power. McKenzie admits the differences in the formal power of the Conserative and Labour leaders. The former chooses his or her own Shadow Cabinet and has the final authority over party policy and the election manifesto. In practice, however, Labour Prime Ministers have been as free as Conservative ones in deciding to form a government, selecting a Cabinet, dissolving Parliament, defying Annual Party Conference resolutions, and insisting on collective Cabinet responsibility. Constitutionally, the parties, therefore, appear very similar when they are in government. But this view ignores the important differences when the parties are in opposition. An additional 'proof' adduced is that, on average, Labour leaders have enjoyed at least as lengthy a tenure as Conservative leaders. Yet we shall see that holding office is hardly positive proof of the exercise of power.

McKenzie also relies on speeches and writing from commentators, politicians and activists which he regards as supporting his case. But one has to be wary in handling public statements, particularly by politicians, which are occasioned by specific contexts relating to time, audience and purpose. Groups in the Parliamentary Labour Party (PLP) have had an interest in asserting the supremacy of conference when it suited them. It suited the right in the 1950s when it wanted to defeat the Bevanites and it suited the left in the 1970s when it pushed for more left-wing policies. Attlee said one thing in 1937 about the power of conference ('it *issues* instructions which must be carried out. . . ')[17] but behaved very differently years later. In 1937 he was a weak, insecure leader, having been elected as a compromise between Greenwood and Morrison, and when the party, still shamed by MacDonald's 'treachery' in 1931, was suspicious of leaders. In 1957, when he downgraded the rôle of conference, Attlee was speaking as an ex-Prime Minister.[18]

The literature on the conceptualisation and operationalisation of political power has grown immensely since 1955. Awareness of the problems has bred an appropriate caution in usages of the term and a realisation that different methods of research are likely to uncover different power-holders. Most definitions now involve an acknowledgement that an actor is able to realise his will or intentions over another actor and most 'tests' rely to a large degree on studies of actual issues or outcome. In the case of McKenzie's treatment of the Labour Party different 'proofs' of parliamentary domination may take the form of:

(a) conference agreeing to a course of action initiated or favoured by the parliamentary leadership;
(b) the parliamentary leadership successfully defying the conference on one or several issues;
(c) the leadership achieving (a) or (b) above, and also explicitly denying the ultimate authority of the Party Conference.

It is possible to produce evidence in support of all three of these propositions. The first might be illustrated by the formation of the Lib/Lab pact in 1977, in which the NEC and the Party Conference were presented with a *fait accompli* by the Labour Cabinet. The second can be illustrated in the Labour governments between 1966 and 1970 and 1976 and 1978, when conference votes against many of their policies were ignored by Harold Wilson, James Callaghan and the Cabinet. In Wilson's words 'The government must govern'. The third is clearly illustrated in Hugh Gaitskell's defiance of the conference vote for unilateral disarmament in 1960, and less explicitly in Harold Wilson's interpretation of conference votes against his government's policies as constituting 'warnings', not instructions. But it is not immediately clear that any of the above show anything conclusive about power in the party. When the party has been in opposition, the leadership has moderated its support for Britain's application for membership of the EEC, prices and incomes policies and restraint in public expenditure. In other words, the relationship between the party institutions is a variable, and the leader and his front bench are less authoritative when the party is in opposition. It certainly does not mean that a Labour Prime Minister or government has the same amount of latitude *vis-à-vis* the party's extra-parliamentary organs as a Conservative Prime Minister and Cabinet, and particularly so when the parties are in opposition.

McKenzie is so keen to argue that the Labour leadership is autonomous that he neglects the trade unions in his study. Yet on p. 454, he notes how Labour's parliamentary leadership was generally secure, as long as it maintained the support of the leaders of the major trade unions – 'the key to an understanding of the Labour party'. (He might also have noted, however, the traditional restraint which trade union leaders exercised in many policy areas.)[19] But this is an extraordinary give-away, accepting that the autonomy and independence of the PLP are largely conditional on the support of an extra-parliamentary body, namely the major trade unions which dominate conference. The opposition of TUC leaders to the Labour government's package of economic crisis measures in 1931 was important in stiffening the views of some ministers that the government should resign rather than proceed with such a package. The parliamentary leadership paid its respects to the extra-parliamentary organisation largely because the major trade unions assured it of their support. After 1955, as is well known, McKenzie's thesis came under growing strain because this essential condition no longer applied. The major trade unions, for reasons to be discussed below, ceased to operate as 'the Praetorian Guard' of the parliamentary leaders. Moreover, there were also certain political costs attached to this alliance: policy-making on incomes policy and industrial relations was left as the preserve of the trade unions; they were 'not on the agenda' for Labour politicians. As Arthur Deakin, the leader of the Transport and General Workers' Union, bluntly told conference in 1947: 'The question of wages and conditions of employment are questions for the trade unions'. Here is a second, or hidden, face of political power which is neglected in McKenzie's study. In the late 1960s and again in 1978–9, Labour governments transgressed the traditional separation of spheres as questions of incomes policy and industrial relations came to the forefront of the political agenda.

This concern obviously leads on to a consideration of the mechanics of conference management, and the brokerage, horse trading and scheduling of issues involved.[20] This is a major gap in McKenzie's study; its reliance on memoirs, biographies and conference and NEC reports provides a largely public and end-view of the policy process. Minkin's study of how conference outcomes are shaped, which also draws on interviews with participants and looks at policy-making within the affiliated unions and constituency parties, provides a rather different view of power in the party. Minkin, writing from a different political position than McKenzie, is aware of the leaders' attempts to manipulate the agenda through various formulae and mechanisms, by the composing of resolutions, platform requests to activists to remit unwelcome resolutions, the three-year rule, and the vague and generalised platform responses to the floor. But he also shows how partial was the leadership's success in the manipulation.

Another difficulty with McKenzie's mode of analysis is that essentially he posits the existence of two actors, the parliamentary and extra-parliamentary bodies. But these are not unitary actors at all. In the case of the first, it is possible to think of (a) the Party Leader acting fairly independently (e.g. Harold Wilson over the trade-union proposals, *In Place of Strife*, or ruling out discussion of devaluation of the pound between 1964 and 1967), (b) a group of some front-bench leaders, perhaps of the political right or left, and (c) factions within the PLP or *ad hoc* groups (e.g. the sixty-nine Labour MPs who voted for British membership of the EEC against a three-line whip in 1970). The larger point to be made here is that power cannot be seen as a struggle between the parliamentary party and the extra-parliamentary organisation. Many struggles have been between alliances which were formed across these two groups. Alliances for and against proposed reforms of industrial relations in 1969 occurred in the parliamentary leadership, NEC and back-benchers.

The difficulty in viewing the two bodies as unitary actors is reinforced by the overlapping membership of MPs and ministers on the NEC. McKenzie (p. 424) chose to regard this phenomenon as a device whereby PLP could dominate the NEC. In fact in the 1950s and again from the late 1960s most MPs elected to the constituency section of the NEC were left-wing and actually opposed the parliamentary leadership. Similarly, trade-union members were often divided on the NEC. The NEC also provided shelter for a senior Cabinet minister such as James Callaghan to lead the party opposition to his government's trade-union proposals in 1969 and, in 1974, for Tony Benn to defy Harold Wilson. Wilson and, later,

Callaghan, as Prime Ministers, responded by insisting that collective Cabinet responsibility applied to Labour Ministers in their conduct on the NEC.

One also has to take account of the political costs involved in Labour leaders defying the extra-parliamentary party. Why did Hugh Gaitskell and his supporters in the Campaign for Democratic Socialism devote so much energy to reversing the 1960 Conference decision on unilateralism and overcoming the opposition of approximately a third of the PLP, half of the NEC and half of the conference? He must surely have appreciated the importance of the conference vote for his authority, and realised that he might have to resign if he failed to overturn it – a problem which would not face a Conservative leader. It also explains why he backed away from a confrontation with conference and the NEC over his proposals for abandoning or diluting Clause Four in the party constitution in 1960. Similarly, as the conference and the NEC moved to the left and became more assertive and independent in the 1970s and 1980s, there is no doubt that this affected the behaviour of the parliamentary leaders in and out of government.

To show, as McKenzie does, that power does not reside in the Labour Party Conference does not mean that power therefore resides in the PLP. The party's commitment to intra-party democracy has managed to co-exist with the conventions of the autonomy of MPs and sovereignty of Parliament. Apart from the spectacular case of the 1960 conference vote on unilateral disarmament and Gaitskell's rejection of it, the PLP has managed to avoid an outright confrontation with conference. This co-existence depended on a general willingness by the different groups to make the party's constitution work, and the ambiguities, omissions, and room for manoeuvre which are allowed in the party constitution. It is a shortcoming of a number of power studies that they prefer to find one centre of power to a situation of indeterminacy. Saul Rose is persuasive when he writes that Labour leaders operate within parameters which are largely laid down by the extra-parliamentary party, that power in the Labour Party is shared between the institutions, and that 'it is illusory to seek one focus of power, and explain the rest as façade'.[21]

McKenzie also claims that the similarity in the two parties' internal power relationships is largely a product of the British Constitution, particularly the sovereignty of Parliament and collective Cabinet responsibility. Parliament and Cabinet cannot be instructed by an

outside body and Cabinets and Shadow Cabinets dominate because
there is no other way the country can be governed.[22] McKenzie's
'iron law' is as much about the parliamentary domination of parties
as about oligarchy. It is true that the above features, combined with
the unitary system, disciplined parties and a lack of a written
constitution, give the parliamentary leadership great authority. But
when a Labour Cabinet was relatively autonomous (basically up to
1955), this had less to do with an 'iron law' of the British Constitution
than with broad agreement on policy until 1955 and the support of
the leadership by the block vote of the major trade unions. Even
by 1955, or 1963, power relationships within the Labour Party could
be seen to vary over time, and according to the issue, the unity and
attitudes of the major trade unions, and whether the party was in
government or opposition. But even when these factors were
favourable to the leadership, Labour's structure and culture made
it a less parliamentary and elitist party than the Conservatives.

POST-1963

The Conservative Party

In the case of the Conservative Party the story seems to be clearer
and may be dealt with briefly. The extra-parliamentary organisation
was not important in theory or in practice, and McKenzie's focus,
correctly enough, centred on the relations between the one and the
few. Senior appointments to the party bureaucracy (the Central
Office and Research Department) are within the gift of the leader.
The National Union makes no pretence to a policy-making voice
within the party and the leader is the focus of authority in the party
in Parliament.

However, there have been important changes in the formal party
structure since 1963. They confirm McKenzie's contention that the
Conservative party is more pluralistic (in Parliament) and the leader's
tenure of office less secure than caricature suggests. A system of
formal election of the leader by MPs was introduced in 1965. By
1974, following two successive general election defeats, and growing
back-bench criticism of Heath, there was pressure for a formal
system of re-electing the leader. Under the 1965 system the
arrangements dealt only with the election of a leader, not for his
re-election and possible dismissal. Heath gave way reluctantly to

pressures and agreed to a system of annual election of the party
leader.

For the first time Conservative MPs had an established procedure
for displacing a party leader. In the election held in February 1975
Margaret Thatcher defeated Heath on the first ballot and was
eventually elected leader of the party. McKenzie's point about the
greater insecurity of Conservative leaders, compared with their
Labour counterparts, was confirmed. Wilson (1976), Callaghan
(1980) and Foot (1983) went in their own good time. Macmillan
was already under some heavy pressure to resign in 1963, as was
Sir Alec Douglas-Home in 1965, and Heath was voted out.

The election of Mrs Thatcher was an interesting reflection of
other changes which had occurred within the Conservative Party.
She had overthrown the established party leader, had not served in
any of the major offices of state and was, effectively, the product
of a back-bench rebellion against the established leadership. Philip
Norton has demonstrated the greater rebelliousness of Conservative
back-benchers during the 1970s and 1980s.[23] They have been more
willing to defy three-line whips than previous Conservative MPs.
Mrs Thatcher's break with many 'One-Nation' Conservative policies
offended many of her senior colleagues who had served with Heath.
This clash created difficulties not only in managing the parliamentary
party but also made her Cabinet a most disputatious and leaky
body.

The National Union annual conference certainly contained supporters of Enoch Powell and was troublesome in debates on
immigration between 1968 and 1973. But it has not overturned the
platform since the famous resolution on building 300,000 houses in
1950. After 1979 James Prior, on industrial relations, and Willie
Whitelaw, on law and order, also had difficult conferences. In no
sense, however, has the Union attempted to 'instruct' the party
leadership. Platform speakers continue to dominate debates, motions
continue to be bland and self-congratulatory and only a few options
are put to a formal vote. The contrast with the Labour Party
Conference is stark. In essence the Conservative Party is the
parliamentary party, comprising MPs and peers. The party has no
constitution and therefore no formal links between the mass
movement and parliamentary body. The leader is the most obvious
and important link, but he or she is chosen by MPs and can at any
time alter the relationship between the constituent parts of the
party.

The party's election manifesto is firmly in the hands of the parliamentary leadership. There is little or no open debate; and discussion centres in the Shadow Cabinet or a small group of senior ministers in government, with the leader having the final word. The main arena of Conservative Party politics continues to be Parliament, more specifically the leader and senior colleagues.

The Labour Party

The history of the Labour Party since 1963, however, raises major problems for McKenzie's analysis. At first his thesis seemed to be confirmed, as the authority of conference was almost extinguished by 1970. Gaitskell had successfully defied it in 1960 and the Wilson government had virtually ignored it between 1966 and 1970. Policies of incomes restraint and then proposals for trade union reform produced a confrontation between the government and the TUC and the withdrawal of the government's plans for reform. But once the party was in opposition in 1970, conference – particularly in the shape of activists in the constituency parties and trade unions – reasserted itself. The parliamentary leadership had to reverse itself on many policies and a new body, the TUC/Labour Party liaison committee, worked out new policies for a future Labour government. In particular, the trade unions insisted on the exclusion of an incomes policy and on the repeal of the Conservatives' Industrial Relations Act. In government again in 1974, the tone of many speeches and results of votes at the conference made clear the hostility of the movement to many government policies, particularly those on incomes policy, economic strategy and public spending cuts in 1976. Between 1945 and 1969 the platform had rarely lost a vote at conference. But between 1970 and 1979 Minkin shows that the platform lost 32 votes and many of these were against the wishes of the parliamentary leadership. Conference and the NEC had traditionally been used to squash left-wing dissent in the PLP: in the 1970s the two bodies reinforced it. The Labour Conference and Labour government were increasingly speaking with two different voices on many issues between 1976 and 1978. Once again the two wings of the Labour movement collided as the Labour government's incomes policy led to a confrontation with many public sector trade unions in the so-called winter of discontent in 1978–9.

All this seemed to be part of a cycle in the Labour Party. In opposition, the extra-parliamentary bodies, particularly conference,

became more important, the policies often shifted to the left, and
the party leader was no longer also Prime Minister, with authority
and patronage. But in government, the leaders were more concerned
with policies which they judged politically acceptable, administratively practicable and economically affordable. Many of the policies
brought them into conflict with conference, and the NEC. As
members of a 'national' government and with responsibilities to the
electorate, they were less oriented to the party membership.

The lesson which the activists learnt from this recurring pattern
was that there appeared to be little point in winning policy battles
in opposition if Labour governments were going to dilute them in
office. Spearheaded by the Campaign for Labour Party Democracy,
the activists decided to change the structure of the party to ensure
that party policies were carried out and that the parliamentary party
was made subordinate to conference. The call for greater party
democracy was mounted by the left wing to make the PLP more
accountable to conference and MPs more accountable to local party
activists. Shifting the balance of power in the party became the left's
preferred way of closing the gap between conference and PLP and
preventing any alleged 'betrayal' by the latter. It was also a way of
closing the gap between the myth and reality of which McKenzie
had made so much.[24]

Here we have to take account of the power of a myth as a goal
to give rise to patterns of behaviour which go some way to fulfilling
that myth. Revisionism in the Labour Party in the 1960s was a
theory of economic management and of electoral strategy as well
as parliamentary independence of conference. Revisionists argued
that modern managed capitalism had changed, and that it could
provide full employment and economic growth. Its success rendered
irrelevant questions of public owernship and growth, provided funds
for the welfare state and made redistribution easier. But what if
successive Labour governments, while ignoring conference, are
widely thought to be failures, particularly in improving living
standards, promoting economic equality and other goals? What if
they fail to win elections, though defiance of conference has been
justified with a view to cultivating the electorate? What if they
divide the party (for example over *In Place of Strife* or incomes
policies) on the grounds that such policies are economically and
politically necessary? Is there no legacy: do 'victories' have no costs?
In fact, as Labour governments failed to get economic growth,
imposed wage restraint and quarrelled with the unions, so the

influence of the left in the extra-parliamentary party grew, as did that of the extra-parliamentary party.

Pressure for constitutional reform centred on three demands: NEC control of the election manifesto, mandatory reselection of MPs within the lifetime of Parliament, and election of the leader by party members. Between 1979 and 1981 the second two aims were achieved. The PLP, hitherto the exclusive body for electing the leader, has had to share the task with the trade unions and local parties. The changes smashed the old 'rules of the game' in the party.

The new situation in the party was reflected in the preparation of the manifesto for the 1983 General Election. By tradition, as Richard Rose points out, conference resolutions set the terms for negotiations between the NEC and the PLP, under Clause Five of the party constitution these two bodies jointly approve the manifesto.[25] Under Wilson and Callaghan this meeting had been used by the parliamentary leadership to veto proposals which it found objectionable. In 1973, for example, Wilson had boldly rejected the NEC's proposals to nationalise the twenty-five largest companies in Britain, promising to 'veto' them in the Clause Five meeting. In 1979 Callaghan, as Prime Minister, had refused to include in the manifesto a number of policies which were popular with the left and supported by the annual conference.

In 1983 the situation reflected the different balance of power in the party. In March of that year a campaign document entitled *The New Hope for Britain* had been agreed by the NEC and the Shadow Cabinet. It contained many policies approved by conference such as withdrawal from the EEC, commitment to unilateral nuclear disarmament within the lifetime of the next Parliament, plans for an extension of public ownership and increased public spending, and no commitment to an incomes policy which were known to be an anathema to many in the parliamentary leadership. On the eve of the general election, Michael Foot suggested to the Shadow Cabinet that the document be largely accepted as the manifesto. There was little discussion on the draft document in the Clause Five meeting and it was forced through in an hour or so, virtually undiscussed. It was the shortest Clause Five meeting ever and showed no evidence of parliamentary domination. The memory of Callaghan's behaviour in 1979 – and the rows it led to – served as a warning symbol. That legacy and the shift in the balance of power greatly weakened the hands of the parliamentary leaders.[26]

McKenzie clearly understood the impact of the constitutional reforms and new balance of power in the party. In a letter to *The Times* on 2 March 1981 he commented on 'the virtual obliteration of Clause V of the Labour party constitution'. He was referring to remarks made by Tony Benn in 1980 stating that the policy of the party was decided by conference and that spokesmen in the House of Commons should reflect that policy. McKenzie concluded that, 'The consequences of the achievement will in themselves almost certainly ensure that any future Labour government is fundamentally unlike any of its predecessors'. Was this an admission that his thesis was no longer valid?

It would be a formidable undertaking to explain why Labour has undergone such a change in recent years. It would have to explore the performance of Labour governments, the behaviour of party leaders, changes in the role and structure of trade unions, and changes in electoral behaviour. Perhaps one can refer to four particular factors which were at work in the internal politics of the Labour Party. First, there was the myth of 'betrayal' by the parliamentary leadership. The most articulate spokesman for the view that successive Labour governments had betrayed the policies and ideals of the movement was, of course, Tony Benn. The leadership could point to many reasons for its failures, but the charge of 'betrayal' became a potent one. A second factor was the role of party activists. Impressionistic evidence and survey data suggest that they became more middle-class, articulate, ideological and assertive.[27] Yet this change occurred at a time when party membership was actually falling. With fewer than 300,000 members in 1979, the party had the smallest ratio of members to voters of any West European socialist party. Thirdly, there were changes within the trade unions. Callaghan, like earlier Labour leaders, tried to rely upon the major unions to control conference. But the union activists became more politicised and their executives moved to the left. Trade-union leaders were no longer able to control their delegations on behalf of the parliamentary leaders as they had 20 or 30 years earlier. McKenzie, however, had been developing his argument when the 'Big Three' trade unions (Transport, Miners' and General Workers' Unions) still dominated conference and early studies by Ben Roberts, Vic Allan and Joseph Goldstein exposed the oligarchical tendencies in the unions. Another change was that the parliamentary leadership had interfered with the unions' sacred preserve of free collective bargaining. Finally, though the PLP was to the political right of other party organisations, it was slowly shifting to the left, as a result of retirements and replacements, apart from the split to the Social Democrats during 1981. Mandatory reselection has added a further pressure. The view that revisionist and consensus policies had been tried and failed also gained ground – as it did in the Conservative Party. There were very few defenders of the economic records of the Labour governments of 1964–70 and 1974–9.

CONCLUSION

The main challenge to the authority of the Conservative leader comes from parliamentary colleagues, to that of the Labour leader from the NEC and leaders of the major trade unions, and from parliamentary colleagues who can count on the support of these groups. In recent years, the balance has shifted between the Conservative leader and the MPs because the leader is now elected by the parliamentary party. In the Labour Party the constitutional changes have shifted the balance from the parliamentary leadership and PLP to the extra-parliamentary organs. The power relationships in each party, particularly Labour, vary over time with the issues, personalities, events and whether or not the party is in office. Differences of party structure and values are much more important than McKenzie allowed. Labour's more pluralistic structure, its anti-elitist ethos and factionalism all combine to produce a different pattern of management and leadership compared with that in the Conservative Party. Leadership in the Labour Party is more a matter of managing and bargaining with the different power centres in the party.

   Some conclusions about the party structures and how they operate do seem to be warranted. Firstly, the parties outside Parliament may be seen as lobbies or even pressure groups on the parliamentary leadership. This connection is more apparent for Labour because of the position granted to the trade unions in policy-making bodies like the annual party Conference and the NEC. But small business and farming also operate as lobbies in the Conservative Party. Secondly, possession of office tends to produce a pattern of authoritativeness – loyalty in the party which is more marked than when it is in opposition. For most of the twentieth century, the Conservative leader has been Prime Minister and his colleagues

Cabinet ministers, while Labour leaders have spent more time out of government. Labour, unlike its rival, was created by an extra-parliamentary body, and for its first 20 years the trade unions were a more substantial and influential body than the small number of Labour MPs. The party and movement acquired a marked extra-parliamentary character early on, which it has never entirely lost. The historical factors are reflected in the different tone and atmosphere of the two party conferences. Delegates to Labour's conferences and many members of the NEC believe that they should have a major say in making party policy, and party leaders are expected to explain and defend themselves. There are no such expectations in the Conservative organisation. No longer is it rare for the Labour leader and the platform to be voted down in conference.

Thirdly, it is clear that Labour's structure, with its separate centres of decision-making, has facilitated political divisions and factionalism in the party. The parliamentary wing is only one element in the Labour movement; a group of MPs defeated on an issue in the PLP can carry its case to the NEC and conference and try to overturn the majority view of MPs or vice versa. The political and structural divisions in the Labour Party mean that the leaders face a complicated task in managing the diverse strands and keeping the party together.

British Political Parties presented a view of British political parties that itself became something of a myth. I have argued that the thesis was flawed at the time it was presented in 1955. Subsequent developments in the Labour Party in the 1970s and the changes in the party constitution in 1981 have certainly shattered the validity of McKenzie's thesis. Features that he took as permanent – namely, right-wing trade union support for the parliamentary leaders and Labour MPs on the NEC also supporting the PLP – proved to be contingent. Increasingly, in the 1970s, the party's left-wing activists and constitutional reformers were able to invoke the myth of conference supremacy and the values of intra-party democracy to promote their demands. They used the language of party democracy and constitutionalism to shift the party's policies to the left and to achieve a radical redistribution of power between the different institutions of the party.

McKenzie's later arguments in his letter to *The Times* in 1981 and in an article written the same year suggest that, had he lived, he would have acknowledged the changed nature of the Labour Party, while more vigorously restating his value judgement that Labour's intra-party democracy was incompatible with the ideas and practice of representative democracy and parliamentary sovereignty. If the party conference really did 'instruct' Labour MPs, then how could the latter be accountable to the voters? Where there were differences in policy choices between voters and activists, then which group should the MP represent? There need not be a major difference, of course! But, as the activists gained more power in the party, surveys in 1970 indicated that many of their policy preferences were out of line with those of Labour voters. This 'gap' between the party's policies, increasingly shaped by conference, and the views of labour voters widened in 1979 and 1983. Invariably, the party policies were to the left of what the voters wanted. On six of eight important issues in the 1979 general election – unemployment, industrial relations, incomes policy, public ownership, social services, race relations, taxation and the European Community – the Conservatives were more representative than Labour not only of the electorate but also of the working class.[28] In his last published work on the subject McKenzie attacked the claims of the activists, and asserted this value judgement. 'The process by which the leaders of political parties escape the control of their party members is *functional* for the working of democracy.'[29] This might be restated: 'If my model (as a description of how the Labour Party works) has broken down, this is electorally damaging for the Labour Party and validates my model.'

McKenzie's book belongs to the elitist school of British political science, a tradition which stretches from Bagehot to L. S. Amery. Like them, his thesis of centralised political power and independent parliamentary leadership is 'proved' by historical analysis and selective illustrations rather than statistical association. The thesis is implicit in McKenzie's description of the Labour Party as adhering to what he calls the 'bourgeois model' of a political party:

> No emphasis on the auxiliary functions of the mass organization outside Parliament can be allowed to obscure the basic proposition that the mass parties are primarily the servants of their respective parliamentary parties; that their principal function is to sustain teams of parliamentary leaders between whom the electorate is periodically invited to choose.

Thus the leader was elected by MPs and became leader of the whole party; MPs were free from the pressures of mandatory reselection by the constituency parties; the extra-parliamentary bodies were not in practice able to instruct the parliamentary party; and the parliamentary leadership managed to keep control of the party manifesto.

This view sees political power being concentrated in Parliament, Cabinet and Whitehall, and buttressed by traditions of political practice and usage, the cohesiveness of the political parties. Treasury control, ministerial responsibility and the prerogative of the Crown. As part of the school of 'strong British government' it fits easily with theories of the dominance of the Prime Minister, the deferential political culture and the political consensus. A reason for the acceptance of McKenzie's thesis was that it so obviously formed a part of the dominant view of the British politics. But it was also convenient for the analyses of those on the political left who argued that Labour's reliance on parliamentary methods, the leadership's willingness to trim and compromise, and the extra-parliamentary bodies' ultimate loyalty to the leaders, account for the failure of Labour to promote socialism.[30] The structural and role-socialising effects of the Cabinet and parliamentary system have turned aside what Crossman called the 'battering ram' of outside pressures for political changes.[31]

McKenzie's other claim, derived from Michels – that popular control of party leaders, particularly when they are in government, is not really possible in a complex modern democracy – still stands, even if some detailed points need qualification. But his more controversial claim about the similarity between Labour and Conservative Parties in their internal power relationships is no longer true. Over 20 years ago an admiring anonymous reviewer of *British Political Parties* claimed that '. . . affronted critics have steadily dwindled. The second edition of his book should extinguish them altogether'.[32] If the epitaph was only partly true in 1963, it is surely no longer valid in 1985.

NOTES

An earlier version of this chapter was read as a paper at an Anglo-German Conference on 'Current Challenges to Government' at Munich University in July 1984. I am grateful to participants for comments on the paper and to Vernon Bogdanor, D. E. Butler, Peter Morris, Richard Rose and L. J. Sharpe for further suggestions.

1. McKenzie had talked about a third edition for at least 10 years before his death.
2. An important study which qualified McKenzie was M. Harrison, *Trade Unions and the Labour Party since 1945* (London: Allen & Unwin, 1960).
3. See, for example, R. Miliband, 'Party Democracy and Parliamentary Government', *Political Studies*, 1958.
4. M. Pinto-Duschinsky, 'Central Office and "Power" in the Conservative Party', *Political Studies*, 1972; and P. Seyd, 'Factionalism within the Conservative Party: The Monday Club', *Government and Opposition*, 1972.
5. *Political Elites* (London: Allen & Unwin 1969), p. 20.
6. G. Hands, 'Roberto Michels and the Study of Political Parties', *British Journal of Political Science*, 1971.
7. P. Medding, 'Power in Political Parties', *Political Studies*, 1970.
8. J. D. May, 'Democracy, Organisation, Michels', *American Political Science Review*, 1965.
9. R. Michels, *Political Parties* (New York: Anchor Books, 1962), p. 400.
10. G. Sartori, *Democratic Theory* (New York: Praeger, 1967), pp. 123–4.
11. He explored this later with Allen Silver, in *Angels in Marble* (London: Heinemann, 1968).
12. See his 'Policy Decision in Opposition: A Rejoinder', in *Political Studies*, 1957.
13. M. Duverger, *Political Parties* (London: Methuen, 1954), pp. 182–92.
14. R. T. McKenzie, 'Power in the Labour Party: The Issue of "Intra-Party Democracy"', in D. Kavanagh (ed.) *The Politics of the Labour Party* (London: Allen & Unwin, 1982), p. 158.
15. W. J. M. Mackenzie, 'Mr. McKenzie on British Political Parties', *Political Studies*, 1955, p. 158.
16. *Ibid.*, p. 158.
17. C. Attlee, *The Labour Party in Perspective* (London: Odhams, 1937), p. 93.
18. F. Williams, *A Prime Minister Remembers* (London: Heinemann, 1965).
19. L. Minkin, 'The Trade Unions Have Not Hi-jacked the Labour Party', *New Society*, 6 October 1977.
20. L. Minkin, *The Labour Party Conference* (London: Allen Lane, 1978).
21. S. Rose, 'Policy Decision in Opposition', *Political Studies*, 1956.
22. For an explicit statement of this, see G. Loewenberg. 'The British Constitution and the Constitution of the Labour Party'. *American Political Science Review*, 1958. See the interesting letter in reply by R. Rose in the same journal, 1959, pp. 501–5.
23. P. Norton. *Conservative Dissidents* (London: Temple Smith, 1978).
24. See D. Kogan and M. Kogan, *The Battle for the Labour Party* (London: Fontana, 1982).
25. R. Rose, *The Problem of Party Government* (London: Macmillan, 1974), p. 162.
26. See D. Butler and D. Kavanagh, *The British General Election of 1983* (London: Macmillan, 1984).

27. P. Whiteley, *The Labour Party in Crisis* (London: Methuen, 1983).
28. I. Crewe, 'Labour and the Electorate', in D. Kavanagh (ed.), *The Politics of the Labour Party* (London: Allen & Unwin, 1980); and I. Crewe, 'How to Win a Landslide Without Really Trying', in A. Ranney and H. Penniman (eds.), *Britian at the Polls 1983* (Washington DC: A. E. I., 1984).
29. R. McKenzie, 'Power in the Labour Party: The Issue of "Intra-Party Democracy"', p. 201.
30. For two such accounts, see R. Miliband, *Parliamentary Socialism* (London: Allen & Unwin, 1977), and D. Coates, *The Labour Party and the Struggle for Socialism* (Cambridge: Cambridge University Press, 1975).
31. As argued by R. Crossman, *Inside View* (London: Cape, 1972).
32. *Times Literary Supplement*, 7 November 1963, p. 869.

3 Whatever Happened to Consensus Politics?*

The term 'consensus politics' has frequently been used to describe post-war British politics. More recently it appears to have been overtaken by 'the end of consensus politics'. The first part of this paper examines the different meanings of consensus in British politics, and analyses the concept with reference to the mixed economy and welfare. The second part examines the salient features of the consensus and how they emerged. The third section analyses the forces that have undermined the consensus and the conclusion considers evidence about the nature of the political agenda in the 1980s.

For much of the 20th century the expression 'The British Consensus' had readily been invoked as an outstanding and enviable feature of British politics. One had only to look at the experiences of such other West European states as France, Italy and Germany in the inter-war period to understand this envy. Those states were bitterly divided between political extremes of left and right over questions of policy and, more importantly, over the nature of the régime, and then defeated or occupied in the Second World War. The British system had survived intact the rigours of two great wars and mass unemployment and had entered the post-war era of peace and affluence. Many other states veered between an excess of opposition on the one hand, and authoritarianism on the other, inhibiting the operation of 'normal' politics. The British, by contrast, combined agreement on procedures and broad policy goals with contained disagreements about methods and means.

Yet for some time now there has been much talk of the end of consensus in Britain. The personalities of Tony Benn and Margaret Thatcher, of the new left and the new right, have represented rising forces. They have been scathing about the post-war consensus and,

* *Political Studies* (1985); an earlier version of the paper was presented as an inaugural lecture at Nottingham University in May 1984. The author would like to thank his colleagues Peter Morris and John McClelland, Hugh Berrington and Richard Rose, for their comments and advice on the earlier version.

by implication, have charged their predecessors with a form of 'betrayal', the one of true socialism, the other of true conservatism. Witness Sir Keith Joseph's confession that it was only when he left government in 1974 that he became a Conservative.[1] In her rhetoric, the present Prime Minister scorns consensus politics and proclaims her determination to scrap many aspects of it.

In a prepared speech in the 1979 General Election Mrs Thatcher compared herself to the Old Testament Prophets who did not say 'Brothers I want a consensus'. Instead, she proclaimed the importance of conviction and principle in politics – as if these were incompatible with consensus. In 1981, from Australia, she replied to criticisms from Mr Heath that she was abandoning consensus politics: 'For me, consensus seems to be the process of abandoning all beliefs, principles, values and policies'. Consensus has long been a 'hooray' word, along with 'moderate', 'centrist' and 'reasonable', and opposed to 'ideological' or 'extreme'. Some part of the explanation for her hostile reaction is that she realizes that it is a code-word for criticism of her own political style and policies. The consensus has also protected a set of policies and values, and a style that she has wanted to abandon. What is remarkable, however, is her negative definition of consensus politics and her disavowal, in contrast to most other leaders, of seeking such a goal.

This paper examines the nature of the British consensus and the forces that have helped to undermine it, and speculates on what a new settlement might look like. The term itself presents a problem. The *Oxford English Dictionary* defines it as 'collective unanimous opinion'; but this is clearly an impossibility in politics. Trevor Smith has objected to the loose use of the term consensus, which he associates with agreement by deliberation or conscious bipartisanship.[2] He thinks a more accurate term in this context is policy coincidence. However, it seems that consensus is a firmly established and wide-ranging concept. In referring to political consensus, students have usually had in mind one or all of the following:

1 A high level of agreement across the political parties and governing elites about the substance of public policy. There have been many areas – defence, foreign affairs, regional aid, Northern Ireland and so on – where this has often been obtained. But for most of the post-war period the term has referred to broad agreement on the mixed economy and the welfare state.

2 A high level of agreement between the elites about the nature of the régime, or the rules of the political game. Institutional change in Britain has been incremental and even over the last 60 years there has been little popular support for proponents of comprehensive, far-reaching constitutional change.

3 The political style in which policy differences are resolved, namely a process of compromise and bargaining and a search for policies which are acceptable to the major interests. Disagreements have rarely been pushed to breaking point, and the legitimacy of the government rarely called into question. The elites have managed to make timely concessions to new interests. 'Consensus' has also referred to the tendency of a new government to accept its predecessor's legislation – even when, in opposition, it had derided it. The classic example of this is that of the Conservative governments in the 1950s and 1960s which substantially accepted the 1945 Labour government's initiatives in the fields of public ownership, welfare and the retreat from Empire.

The shared ideas were largely confined to the political elites – politicians, senior civil servants, business and trades union leaders and opinion formers. It is at this level that one has to explore the forces of continuity and change. Of course most of the public were in favour of full employment, welfare, consultation with interests, and so forth. But there is no evidence that more than a fraction of the public thought in a systematic way about these matters and its influence was in any case mediated and brokered by elites.

'Political consensus' and associated concepts like 'hegemony', 'folkways', 'political culture', 'rules of the game' and so on, also represent a mobilisation of bias. Political consensus favours certain interests, and directs attention to certain issues and procedures, while neglecting others. Here is what social scientists now call 'a second face of power', one that shapes the political agenda.[3] One has only to think of the negative receptions given to the ideas of many of the free-market wing of the Conservative party until recently and to the Alternative Economic Strategy ideas of Labour's left wing today. In economic management, the lengthy dominance of Keynesian ideas led to only a perfunctory hearing for proponents of monetarism. This paper suggests, nevertheless, that changes in policies and the climate of opinion over time are not a reflection of the power of ideas alone. Ideas do count, but usually when they conspire with circumstances, as John Stuart Mill observed.[4]

There is an important strand in political and social theorizing which is apolitical and/or antipolitical. The tendency to reduce politics to matters of technique or to the promotion of a single purpose is an old story in political theory. Aristotle warned against Plato's quest for unity; he feared that if everything in the *polis* were reduced to unity, there would cease to be a *polis* at all. From the eighteenth century onwards the quest for a social science has often involved a wish to eliminate uncertainty, indeterminacy, and conflicts of values, all of which are associated with the political realm. As Sheldon Wolin observes, the approach sublimated the political by claiming that reality was socioeconomic.[5] In Marx's future society, for example, man would be a *social* not a *political* animal. In the twentieth century the approach has given rise to the claims of new elites – the bureaucracy, technostructure, managers, planners and the scientific/educational estate. But planners and social engineers have often, whether consciously or not, been hostile to politics and, *ergo*, to political activity. The elimination of the political is a consistent strand in this type of thinking; the actual experience of attempts in the present century to implement it have invariably been disastrous.

Yet politics is the activity of reconciling, not eliminating, differences. It arises from diversity, depends upon freedom, and, as such, is found in a minority of societies. Bernard Crick expressed this well when he wrote that '. . . politics represents at least some tolerance of differing truths, some recognition that government is possible, indeed best conducted, amid the open canvassing of rival interest'.[6] Crick's book, *In Defence of Politics*, contains essays critical of the advocates of technology, nationalism, ideology and even consensus. In these approaches political truth is invariably assumed to be known – the task of government is to implement it.

Britain has long been admired as the home of responsible party government. The Conservative and Labour Parties dominated the political right and left; in contrast to most West European states there were no significant votes for communist, rural or religious-oriented parties to fragment a simple choice between left and right. The multi-party systems in many other western states resulted in coalitions and in the blurring of electoral responsibility. The British parties aggregated preferences and interest into meaningful alternatives for voters. They organised and channelled disagreements and yet also promoted consensus.

But two qualifications are in order. First, the parties are coalitions. There have been important policy divisions within the parties and at times many Labour Members of Parliament have had more in common with some Conservative Members than with their own party's MPs. One has only to think of the divisions in attitudes to British membership of the European Community, incomes policies, defence and the American alliance, devolution, and electoral reform, to see the cross-party combinations. Samuel Brittan has plausibly argued that the reduction of choice to two parties and the division between left and right is a 'bogus dilemma'.[7]

Second, there is also a tradition of the national interest, or a hankering for a government of national unity, particularly at a time of crisis, which will decide issues free from politics.[8] In other countries in the twentieth century this has sometimes taken totalitarian forms, and the case is still officially propounded in one-party states and military dictatorships. In Britain the tradition has obviously been seen in the resort to coalition government in wartime and in the economic crisis of 1931. It has also been reflected in the bipartisanship over foreign and defence policies and in the recent critique of adversary politics. It is observable in calls for coalition, referendums, the adoption of a written constitution, and a greater role for the judiciary, royal commissions, or the civil service. In 1906 Lord Milner, one of the self-avowed non-party proponents of a more efficient government, argued: 'The only cause for right thinking people was to resolve to withdraw first one, then another, national problem from the arena of party strife and to tackle them from the national point of view'.[9] Note the assumption that there is a national interest which is easily recognisable by men and women of good will. Note also the hostility to partisanship and the belief in the existence and feasibility of policies which are 'above politics'.

For much of the first half of the twentieth century the problem for the political elites in Britain was what to do about the 'passion of labour'. This issue became clearer after 1918, with the removal of the pre-war constitutional conflicts over the role of the House of Lords, women's suffrage, and Home Rule for Ireland. The removal from the United Kingdom of the twenty six counties simplified British society in terms of nationality, occupation and religion. This event also coincided with the last great realignment of the party system. From the early 1920s onwards it was a Labour versus Conservative party system and the electorate was more clearly divided on lines of social class. It is most unlikely that the Labour

Party or trades union leaders ever wanted to overturn the political system. But this does not mean to say that the governors were not alarmed by labour unrest, particularly in 1919, 1921 and 1926. Leaving aside larger historical theories, one may point to three different explanations for the difference between Britain's experience and that of her West European neighbours in the inter-war years, in particular in achieving social and political stability.

One school singles out for credit the role of Baldwin and moderate Conservatives in the 1920s. The private and rarely stated concern of the small world of English 'high politics' was what to do about the 'red menace'. The leaders, it is said, inducted the Labour Party into the British constitution and Conservative moderation begot similar Labour moderation. This explanation parallels the analysis of those critics of 'Labourism' who claim that the trades union leaders and the Labour Party, partly by organising working-class demands, partly by relying on Parliament, partly by negotiating and bargaining with employers, and partly by acting 'responsibly', have 'tamed' genuine radical pressures from below. The great achievement of capitalist democracy in Britain has been to transmute and deradicalise working-class pressures.[10] In neighbouring European states, however, parties of the left denied legitimacy to those of the right and vice-versa, and an exaggerated stance produced an exaggerated response.

Another view, which refers back to 1916 and Lloyd George's premiership, claims that the wartime government, faced by the need to mobilise organised labour, accepted the trades unions as an estate of the realm. Governments recognised the powers of unions and business, gradually sucked them into Whitehall, and appointed their spokesmen to various government advisory and consultative committees. The British style of decision-making came to resemble a form of neo-corporatism in which the government bargained with the leaders of the major interest. Keith Middlemas claims that over time the role and influence of Parliament and of the political parties declined while those of senior civil servants and the producer interests grew.[11] It was a case not of the aristocratic or bureaucratic embrace but of the consultative hug weakening pressures from outside for radical change. The new system, it is claimed, was successful in avoiding crisis until recently.

A third, and perhaps more accepted, view dates the pattern of elite agreement back to the coalition government between 1940 and 1945, particularly to the Cabinet Committee on Reconstruction, on which both parties were represented.[12] A number of ideas about economic planning, social welfare and Keynesian economics were already current in the 1930s. The Second World War – especially because it boosted state management and control of the economy, and because of the notion of a 'contract' in which the people deserved social reconstruction after victory – forged the new understanding between the parties.

The package of policies in this consensus is familiar enough: full employment budgets; the greater acceptance, even conciliation, of the trades unions, whose bargaining position was enhanced through a larger membership and the achievement of full employment; public ownership of basic or monopoly services and industries; state provision of social welfare, requiring in turn high public expenditure and taxation; and economic planning of a sort via a large public sector and a reduced role for the market. This is the vocabulary, as it were, of modern capitalism and of social democracy. Many of these features were already in place in wartime, reinforced by Attlee's government, and then accepted by Churchill in 1951 and by his successors. Indeed, the war experience was a good example of how outstanding events can alter the expectation of policy-makers, particularly their perception of what is politically and administratively possible. Middlemas notes that 'Slowly but inevitably the state came to be seen as something vaster and more beneficent than the political parties'.[13]

The central figure in this story is John Maynard Keynes. Keynesian techniques of economic management reconciled political control over the economy with political freedom. This was the great choice of the inter-war years – planning versus freedom, both in the political and economic sectors. Keynes was the genius who reconciled freedom with planning, by curbing the risks and uncertainties of the market. As a tool of economic management Keynesianism lent itself to Labour and Conservative interpretations. And it worked. Large-scale unemployment disappeared from Western societies for the 30 years after the war. Perhaps no other feature marks such a dramatic social change between the inter-war and post-war years.

The consensus appeared to render irrelevant the old debate between capitalism and socialism. It also had consequences for the two main political parties. In the Conservative Party 'One Nation' defenders of active government and welfare became dominant and the neo-liberal wing was effectively routed by the late 1940s. In 1956 Prime Minister Anthony Eden wrote to Harold Macmillan, then Chancellor of the Exchequer, of his worry about rising prices and wages. In considering ways to cope with the pressure of trades unions for higher wages he noted the possible role of unemployment but went on to dismiss this as 'politically not tolerable'.[14] Harold Macmillan, a rather isolated prophet of *The Middle Way* in the 1930s, was able to look back in 1960 on how much of his programme had been accomplished. Edward Heath faced a similar dilemma when unemployment threatened to reach the 1 million mark in 1972, and he abandoned his neo-liberal economic policies.

Among many Labour Party leaders there was a more pragmatic, instrumental, attitude towards public ownership, explicitly under Hugh Gaitskell, covertly under Harold Wilson. The term 'Butskellism', coined by The Economist in 1954, reflected the general view that the economic policies of the two major parties were converging. Socialism, or collectivism, was overtaking capitalism, as J. A. Schumpeter had forecast.[15] But, Marx notwithstanding, it was coming, peacefully. In many large firms ownership was divorced from managerial control; large firms were hostile to the free market; and distinctions between public and private enterprise were blurred. Socialism appeared to be based more on demand management and efficiency than state ownership and planning.

One should not over-stress the uniqueness of the British experience in this respect. Broadly similar policy packages were emerging in other West European states in the same period. The growth of scientific thought and expertise, exemplified not least in Keynesian economics, appeared to weaken the appeal and relevance of the ideologies of left and right. Affluence softened social and class polarisation and narrowed policy differences between the parties of the left and right. So-called 'catch-all', voter-oriented, political parties sought support from most sections of the electorate. Parties relied more on public relations techniques and played down distinctive sectional and ideological appeals in elections. Trends in socioeconomic distribution, state intervention, provision of welfare, all moved in similar directions in Western states, in spite of their different histories, party systems and forms of government.[16] The literature about the end of ideology between political parties and convergence across industrial states, not surprisingly, prompted the question 'Does Politics Matter?' According to one observer 'This ideological agreement, which might best be described as 'conservative socialism' has become *the* ideology of the major parties in the developed states of Europe and America'[17]

In the case of Britain the salient themes of social democracy were as follows:

1 The purposive rôle of government. Keynes obviously provided the most important justification for active government in economic management. The larger rôle of government as employer, taxer and distributor of benefits seemed to be a useful tool for mobilizing popular consent. In a study of Western states, Douglas Hibbs demonstrated that countries with highly socialised patterns of consumption and distribution and a large social wage (or a high level of state-provided benefits) had fewer strikes and industrial disputes than those which ranked low on these criteria. Processing issues though the political arena rather than the free market seemed to produce greater social peace, at least in the 1950s and 1960s.[18]

2 The provision of the welfare state, and what was eventually termed 'the social wage'. During the war there was greater acceptance of the claim that citizenship encompassed not only political rights but also a range of social rights. The welfare state acquired an ideological life of its own, incorporating ideas of fairness, a common society, and collectivism.[19]

3 The commitment to economic growth to provide social welfare and protect the take-home pay of workers. In his classic work, *Modern Capitalism*, published in 1965, Andrew Shonfield took for granted continuing steady economic growth and the provision of social welfare in Western states. Parties competed in their ability to make the economy grow faster and then distribute the fiscal dividend of economic growth.

4 The conscious pursuit of full employment as a goal of economic policy. This was expressed in the famous 1944 White Paper on employment. It was accepted that such a goal would have priority, in cases of conflict, over stable prices or the balance of payments.

5 Optimism about the goals described above and the belief that the relevant knowledge for social engineering was available. After all, since it had worked with employment, why should it not work with education, housing, regional policy and so on.?

There is some evidence to show that the public supported these goals. David Robertson has shown how the political parties' programmes at elections gradually converged.[20] and Gallup found a steady increase until 1964 in the proportion of voters who regarded

the political parties as 'much of a muchness', and who agreed that
it did not make much difference which party won the election. All
this appeared to confirm Anthony Downs' analysis, advanced in *An
Economic Theory of Democracy*, that two evenly matched parties
in a largely consensual electorate would converge in their policies
to win the decisive votes of the floating voters.[21] Moreover, a
number of commentators argued that if modern government were
interventionist and engaged in promoting far-reaching social and
economic objectives, then there *should* be a large measure of
consensus and continuity between the parties. According to
Mannheim:

> The reduction of the political element is essential to any form of
> planning. . . The task of straightening out its [*the trade cycle's*]
> booms and slumps and repairing the damage it has done, is only
> partly a political problem; it is largely a matter of science and
> technique.[22]

Parties and elections, in other words, should not make much
difference.

It is difficult to date the precise point at which the sense of relative
political and economic decline developed. There was a growing
awareness of Britain's loss of international influence, reflected in
the Suez fiasco in 1956 and in the application to join the European
Community in 1961. There was also awareness that other West
European states were achieving much faster rates of economic
growth. During the remainder of the 1960s, there was a plethora
of investigative Royal Commissions and committees, and many
institutions were reformed. These were 'reforms without improvement'. In 1967 there was devaluation; inflation and unemployment
both rose; in 1973 there was the first explosive increase in Arab oil
prices, and the onset of economic recession. Governments were
regularly turned out of office, ignominiously in February 1974 and
1979, and support for alternative political parties grew.
    Gradually the stock of ideas and policies identified with the post-
war consensus came to be regarded as part of the problem. By the
mid-1970s there was a rash of literature on such themes as
the 'Bankruptcy of Government', the 'Second Great Crash',
'Governability', 'Pluralistic Stagnation', 'Overloaded Government',
'The Disease of Government', 'Adversary Politics', and so on. Much

of this literature concentrated on the British experience. What a change this was from the Whiggish assumption that the British had an unmatched capacity for government, and from the almost universal admiration for the British system. From being the examplar of stable representative democracy, indeed the exporter of institutions, Britain was widely regarded as a country on the verge of political breakdown.

Defenders of Keynes have made various claims on his behalf. One tactic has been to rescue him from vote-seeking politicans. His most recent biographer has argued that post-war British politicians have overloaded the economy. Keynes was an elitist; his early years, home background at Eton and Cambridge, and then his working life at the Treasury and as a university don led him to take for granted the authority of government and disinterested political leadership. Like Beveridge and the Webbs, he assumed 'the agency of a benevolent state serviced by a technocratic elite.'[23]

A second tactic has been to say that his ideas have been misused. Sir Keith Joseph and Mrs Thatcher have tried to distinguish Keynes from the neo-Keynesians. Politicans were indeed selective in their interpretation of Keynes (surely the fate of most theories which are vulgarised when used in the real world by civil servants and politicians). Keynes had argued that in boom times they should budget for a surplus of revenue over expenditure and that they should do the opposite when demand exceeded supply, threatening inflation. In fact deficit financing became the rule, as politicians in Western states practised what Rose and Peters called 'One-eyed Keynesianism'.[24] Politics, particularly democratic politics, and politicians, had let Keynes down.

Both Keynes and Beveridge were worried about the potentially inflationary effects of free collective bargaining in a situation of nearly full employment. Keynes claimed that this (now called 'the trade-union problem') was an 'essentially political problem'. The 1944 White Paper was also aware of the difficulty. It stated:

> . . . if we are to operate with success a policy for maintaining a high and stable level of employment, it will be essential that employers and workers should exercise moderation in wage matters so that increased expenditure provided at the outset of a depression may go to increase the volume of employment.[25]

Each of the main ideas of that Social Democratic consensus has been in retreat for some time now. It is possible to comment only briefly on some orienting features of the new mood. One is the call to roll back the government. It is difficult to quantify this. If one looks at the Thatcher government's record since 1979 in presiding over an increase in spending and taxation as proportions of Gross National Product, the thesis does not stand up at all. Some part of the attack on 'big government', 'bureaucracy', and taxation is rhetoric and has been a regular theme of Conservative election manifestos. But the call for retreat is in part a reaction to the recession and slow-down of economic growth, and the resulting problems of funding government programmes, particularly in the welfare state. In a slow-growth economy, like Britain's, pressures for increases in public spending have collided with pressures to protect take-home pay. Governments have sought to cope with the inflationary pressure by using various forms of incomes policies. There is some evidence that the 'capping' effect was resented by well-organised groups of workers and led to industrial disruption. There is also evidence in Western Europe that political protest movements have been strongest and that industrial disruption has been most marked where direct or visible taxes have increased most – the tax backlash phenomenon.[26] In Britain, Conservative promises of tax cuts in the 1979 election were important in converting former Labour voters.[27]

The litany of the new political economy is now well known – tax cuts, reductions in public spending, cash limits, encouragement of market forces, and privatisation of state services and industries. Apart from privatisation, this is the régime introduced by Denis Healey in 1976 – a classic case of an opportunist finding the Whigs bathing and running off with their clothes. The present government has been concerned to appear to stand aside from industrial disputes and from private-sector wage negotiations, and has abandoned the commitment to full employment. The arguments in favour of such a retreat are based partly on the belief that government cannot solve these problems and partly on the view that it is a way of protecting governments from political trouble.

There has also been a new modesty about the possibility of social engineering. This is not just the traditional conservative respect for the *status quo*, the Burkeian view of the complexity and interdependence of society and scepticism about its malleability by reason or naked intellect. Rather the new modesty claims to be born of experience. In Britain the experience of wages policies, economic planning, regional policy, high-rise council estates and policies for economic growth did not inspire confidence. In the United States there was similar disillusionment with the results of the various Great Society programmes to promote educational standards and equality and to combat poverty. Part of the negative reaction to these policies is to 'inputism', or the belief that complex social problems may be amenable to the investment of yet more resources. In the United States the massive Coleman report demonstrated that differences in the input of resources and facilities had little, nil, or even, sometimes, an inverse relationship to student achievements.[28] One can readily see how this research has fuelled fiscal conservatism in many countries. It is an interesting case of the monitoring rôle of social science being used to confute the problem-solving claims of 'techfix' and professionalism

More important perhaps has been the greater self-doubt among decision-makers about their problem-solving abilities. Richard Rose has observed that at the beginning of this century governments were mainly concerned with the defining activities of the modern state, namely diplomacy, defence, law, finance and public order.[29] Governments had reasonably well-established technologies for carrying out these functions. By contrast, many activities of contemporary government are not only more complex (be they the promotion of social and economic equality, health, economic growth or educational standards) but also governments lack a social engineering capability for many of these tasks. Moreover, much of the data about social conditions or the consequences of policies are ambiguous or indeterminate. When a policy appears to have failed – be it public ownership or monetarism – there will be as many advocates calling for more of the same policy as for its abandonment. And even where the information and policy knowledge are available, the means may be politically unacceptable. There is indeed an ignorance about social intervention, in the sense that the person intervening knows what he is doing and can predict that his actions will have intended effects.

The position of the trades unions has also changed. In 1974 Labour won two elections, largely on the claim that it could get on with the unions. At the time this seemed to be the key to social and political stability in Britain. But the power of the unions, as it was termed, was more accurately described by Peter Jenkins as the Social Democratic Dilemma.[30] In other words, how was the Labour movement to reconcile the political objectives of the trades unions, i.e. maintaining full employment, the welfare state, and stable prices, with their industrial objective, i.e. free collective bargaining? In 1946 J. A. Schumpeter, while anticipating the eventual replacement of capitalism by socialism, noted that 'the real problem' for socialism would be the position of labour. He wrote, 'A government that means to socialise to any great extent, will have to socialise the trade unions. And, as things actually are, labour is of all things the most difficult to socialise'.[31]

In Britain, governments have tried various approaches over the past 20 years – voluntary and statutory incomes policies, greater legal regulation, bargaining or a social contract, and, finally, abandoning the commitment to full employment. They have oscillated between burden sharing, social and political partnership, persuasion, and clobbering. It was the attempt from 1961 onwards to prop up Keynesian policies by various incomes policies that led the parties in government to seek the co-operation of the unions and general agreement on economic policy. Since 1979 the onset of mass unemployment has not only given bite to Conservative rhetoric about self-reliance but has also enabled the government to disregard the unions, as their power has declined.

One route to redistribution is via social policy and welfare expenditure – the Beveridge package. Another is via free collective bargaining. The Labour movement in Britain has been reluctant to acknowledge the tensions between these two routes. A good example is seen in the trades' union leaders' objections to the introduction of a scheme of child benefits in 1977, when it was realised that the benefits would be paid to the mother and deducted from the wage packet. On the whole the results of free collective bargaining have not been kind to those who want to promote greater equality of incomes. And the experience of the 1974-9 Labour government dashed the belief that the unions would or could trade off wage claims for the social wage. In various ways, the so-called 'winter of discontent' in 1979 may have spelt the bankruptcy of a political tradition and style of government in Britain.

It is interesting to consider two statements of what went wrong. One regards it as the failure of capitalism, the other as the failure of social democracy. Both statements concern the political economy; that is, they deal with the failure of the economy to grow sufficiently to meet the expectations of the public and politicians, and how this 'gap' interacts with political behaviour. The failure of politicians to carry out their promises fed back into the political system, as disappointed voters gradually withdrew their approval from one party, and then the other. This is now called the politics of economic decline, and spills over generally to reduce the effectiveness of government. Depending upon which analysis is more persuasive, different sets of policies are called for.

The 'crisis of capitalism' school is largely Marxist. Ever-hopeful of cataclysm and counterposed to the revisionists, it claims that capitalism is inevitably prone to breakdown. It also argues that profits are squeezed to pay for wages and welfare, that is, to purchase legitimacy, but at the cost of creating an investment crisis. Fulfilling the consent function of the modern capitalist state creates a fiscal crisis and obstructs its effectiveness.[32]

The 'crisis of social democracy' school, of both the political left and right, notes that social democrats had claimed that modern managed capitalism had changed and could deliver economic growth. In addition, economic growth lessened demands for state ownership, while funding public services and making redistribution and the promotion of equality easier. But, the left could ask: what would happen if there were no economic growth? On past form there would be policies of deflation, 'sound' finance, wage restraint, and probably conflict with the unions. From a different political viewpoint Samuel Brittan argued, in 1975, that excessive popular expectations were produced by competing political parties and pressure groups and might result in political breakdown, because of 'excessive burdens being placed on the "sharing out" function of government'.[33] Other free-market critics also agreed that the interventions of the government in the economy risked transforming economic and industrial disputes into potential constitutional crises.

Of these two analyses the second appears to have been the more persuasive to date. James Alt found in the 1970s that low economic growth, far from promoting solidarity or radicalising people, has actually dented altruism – a crucial motive for values of socialism and redistribution.[34] It has also added to the Labour Party's problems. Programmes of government intervention and public spending depend to some degree upon public confidence in the beneficence of government. As Labour found, in 1983, this was not widespread, in spite of survey evidence that more people are prepared to pay higher taxes for more welfare benefits. The sectional nature of trade unionism has also militated against redistribution and industrial modernisation. The working class itself is divided into the affluent and non-affluent, public and private sectors of employment, skilled and unskilled occupations, home-owners and council tenants. For all the sociological theorising about the British working class being the most 'mature' in Europe (third generation, integrated and so on) the class is highly differentiated. This has increased Labour's problem of how to offer policies which do not divide the working class. In the three general elections of 1974 and 1979 Labour averaged less than 50 per cent of the working-class vote. In 1983 it collapsed to 38 per cent of the working-class vote, only fractionally more than the Conservative Party obtained. And among the growing section of the working class, that is, those living in the south, working in the private sector, who are also owner-occupiers or mortgagees, the Conservatives had a commanding lead.[35]

We can now see how much the advance of the welfare state depended upon economic growth. Yet Karl Marx, Ramsay MacDonald, Anthony Crosland and Harold Wilson (pre-1964) all assumed that the problem of production was about to be solved. In *The Future of Socialism*, in 1956, Anthony Crosland, the most influential theorist of modern social democracy, envisaged a period two decades later when this might indeed be the case. Then, he wrote, he might be prepared to 'stop worrying about hard work and economic matters and to relax into greater leisure and more cultural pursuits'.[36] As a labour minister he later realized the indispensability of growth for the realisation of his goals.

But the abandonment of the consensus must also be connected with the internal dynamics of the two main political parties. In both parties in the past decade the traditional policy minorities made major advances, partly in response to the alleged failures of earlier governments, and they identified the post-war consensus with those failures. The personalities of Tony Benn, Sir Keith Joseph and Margaret Thatcher are an essential part of this story. The revisionists had dominated Labour governments and pursued policies, even in defiance of the party conference, on the grounds that these policies were (a) economically necessary and (b) the way to win elections. Revisionism was as much a theory about electoral sociology as about economic management. The Labour leaders, however, did not deliver economic growth, lost general elections in 1970 and 1979, and spectacularly divided the movement in 1969 and 1978–9. Constitutional reformers, invoking the language of accountability, the authority of the annual party conference, and the values of intra-party democracy, overturned the party's constitution in 1980 and 1981, and moved the party's policies sharply to the left.

Throughout the Labour movement the charges of 'betrayal' were heard and supported. The only significant response to this from the right was not 'voice' but 'exit', in the form of the creation of the Social Democratic Party.

Mrs Thatcher similarly challenged many of the operating ideas and practices of her Conservative predecessors.[37] They had been accommodating and defensive, believing it to be politically necessary to maintain the welfare state, full employment, high levels of public expenditure, and to conciliate the trades unions. It is not that her ideas and values – individualism, thrift, self-reliance, the superiority of the market over socialism and over neo-corporate deals with the major interests – are very different from those of Mr Heath in 1970, but her sense of conviction is. Government, she believes, has a limited capacity to do good, but a great capacity to do harm, not least by distorting or interfering with the 'natural' working of society and the market economy. In contrast to Baldwin and the immediate post-war generation of Conservative leaders, she lacks the sense of what she terms 'bourgeois guilt' for the mass unemployment of the 1930s.

When Mrs Thatcher became leader in 1975, the Conservatives, for long the natural party of government, had lost four of the previous five general elections and appeared to have no politically acceptable answer to the problems of inflation and trades union power. Monetarism appeared to provide a means of avoiding incomes policies and the need for bargains with the unions. She was incvitably a divisive leader for her party, given that so many of her senior colleagues had been closely involved in the policies of earlier Conservative governments. In terms of programmes the two main parties in 1979 and 1983 were further apart than for many elections.[38] The emergence of a 'new left' was matched by a 'new right' and a 'new centre' party in the form of the SDP. During the post-war period, until 1979, successive Prime Ministers had felt that electoral advantage lay in leading their parties from the centre of the party. The art was to persuade their parties that they were being true to their principles while convincing the electorate that they were following policies which were non-doctrinaire and in the national interest.

What do we know about the public mood over this period? First, notwithstanding the economic recession and increase in unemployment, there was no revival of working-class consciousness or, in terms of voting, of solidarity. Second, the conventional wisdom about the effects of the economy on political behaviour has been confounded. How else do we account for the re-election of the government in 1983, with 3 million out of work, and for the general lack of political protest? After two decades of disappointment there are signs that British voters' expectations have been gradually scaled down in line with the reduction in economic growth. James Alt, in *The Politics of Economic Decline*, has argued, with impressive survey evidence, that changes in popular perceptions of the British government's influence over the economy have lessened the instrumental value of voting. Voters became increasingly sceptical of the political parties' ability to do much about unemployment, inflation or economic growth, and more willing to look elsewhere than the government when allocating blame for high inflation or high unemployment. If this is true, Mrs Thatcher's government was probably the first post-war ministry to profit from the unwillingness of voters to hold governments largely responsible for economic conditions. And of course the reduction of popular expectations has been a major goal of both parties in government since 1976.

But what evidence is there for the emergence of a new set of values, Thatcherite or otherwise? We know that for several elections now people have voted Labour in spite of its policies. What has contributed to the sharp fall in Labour's electoral fortunes is that declining identification with the party and diminishing working-class loyalty have left the party exposed on policies, many of which fail to find a response among voters. In 1979 and 1983 clear majorities of voters agreed with many of the Conservative policies. Indeed, majorities of Labour voters were more in agreement with a number of Conservative policies and divided on many of the policy planks of the Labour party.[39]

But this is not to say that there has been a ringing endorsement of the ideas of Thatcherism. It is true that there has long been clear support for Conservative positions on populist – authoritarian issues, like law and order and immigration. Crewe's analysis of survey data on attitudes shows only qualified support for a number of would-be Thatcherite values.[40] Many voters, however, did not think the election of either a Conservative or Labour government would make much difference. Of twelve issue areas surveyed by Gallup in the 1983 election a majority thought that the election of one or other party would make much difference to the outcome in only two cases – public ownership and trades-union power.[41] But surveys show that the major programmes of the welfare state still attract strong support and that more prefer to see their expansion even at the cost of rising taxes, while generalised attacks on the market or on the state, by Labour or Conservative respectively, find little favour. It is not a case of the public being divided between approval of a state economy and state welfare on the one hand, and approval of the free market and private provision of welfare on the other. The public support the market for generating wealth while wanting the government to use a share of the wealth for social purposes, particularly welfare. It is a case of two and a half cheers for the market and for the welfare state.[42] Mrs Thatcher has been a mobiliser in a country still reluctant to be mobilised.

Overall, the survey evidence indicates that the electorate has become even more Conservative over the past decade, even as that party has moved to the right. David Robertson has recently monitored changes of opinion on many questions that were asked in identical form in October 1974 and May 1979. Of seventeen questions that can be directly compared the electorate moved to a more right-wing average position on fifteen and to the left only on the question of increasing cash to the National Health Service. He claims 'the brute evidence is that the rightwards shift of the Conservative policy in the 1970s was at least matched by a similar shift in mass opinion'.[43] This is paralleled by a significant decline in support for many estabished Labour policies among party voters between 1964 and 1979.[44]

Two rival views about the effects of parties on public policy have been advanced by academics and politicians. The first claims that the 'adversary' form of two-party system, combined with the all-or-nothing nature of the electoral system, one-party government and with the growing polarisation of parties, produces abrupt reversals of policy as one set of partisans replaces another in government.[45] This view claims that parties do influence government, though, regrettably, for short-term and ideological motives, and that they may misrepresent widely held views among the electorate. It is also a thesis about the interaction of the two parties in which the adoption of radical policies in one party stimulates a radical response from the other. Critics of these abrupt changes have recommended the adoption of proportional representation. The coalitions which will probably result will, it is claimed, be a means of slowing down abrupt changes translating excessive partisanship into public policy. In the 1970s, as Sammy Finer notes, the argument for electoral reform shifted from electoral justice to efficient government.[46]

A different view is that the same recurring problems and similar constraints force parties, regardless of their ideological leanings, into following a broadly similar set of policies. Richard Rose has demonstated that if one relates party incumbency to various economic outputs – rates of inflation, unemployment, economic growth, prosperity, changes in the distribution of income and wealth, and the size of government deficits – it is striking how slight are the differences which are associated with party control of government. If parties do not have much impact, this is not, Rose adds, because of agreement but because 'necessity more than ideological consensus is the explanation for similarities in behaviour'.[47] Stop-go economic policies, attempts at reforms of trades unions and industrial relations, incomes policies, public spending cuts and cash limits have not been the prerogative of any one party in office. We may also observe that nearly as many discontinuities in economic policies have taken place within the lifetime of a government as when governments change. The more relevant point, however, is that these continuities occurred in spite of the parties' attempts to try different policies. The adversarial critique has some relevance to explaining the early stages of a government, but Rose's 'moving consensus' helps more in understanding the long-term trends.

We can advance various reasons for the moving consensus: the conservatising impact of the civil service and the political wisdom it conveys; the role of the established lobbies and interests represented in the terms 'pluralist democracy' and 'group politics'; the pressures of international factors; the poor preparation of parties in opposition;. the limited turnover of elites in the commanding heights of the economy and society when a new government assumes office; the long-term commitment of resources in advance and the inertia effects of so many statutory expenditures and policy routines. This is all summed up in the late Sir William Armstrong's reference to 'ongoing reality', as a great limitation on what any government can do. However powerful modern government is thought to be, a great deal of continuity flows from the political limits and checks and balances on government in any pluralistic society. We may also explain the limited differences in terms of political office and opposition in which the balance of ideas and personalities within a party changes as it moves between government and opposition; it is a cycle of radicalism in opposition giving way to caution in government.

It is difficult to argue, however, in the light of experience since 1979, that a determined government still makes little difference in Britain. Many observers have been impressed at how radical the present government has remained in practice. Mrs Thatcher has certainly challenged many of the assumptions of those who participate, either as actors or observers, in the British political process. The reduction in the legal immunities and rights of trades unions, rejection of the tripartite style of decision-making, according priority to the abatement of inflation, even with unemployment at over 3 million, introduction of privatisation and the changing framework in which traditionally public services are carried out, interventions in local government structure and far-reaching controls over its finance, open hostility to the civil service and large parts of the public sector and service, and attacks on some professions' monopoly of services, amount to a major change of style. It is more difficult to demonstrate a durable change in the popular mood, operating assumptions of decision-makers, and terms of public debate. But it would be surprising if these have not moved in response to the above changes. Her challenge is to attitudes and it is, in the last resort, attitudes that create a consensus. A radical government, in power for some 10 years, and faced by a weak opposition in Parliament and defensive trade unions, is well placed to answer positively the question 'Do Parties (and Leaders) Make a Difference?'

The political agenda is always in a state of transition and any climate of opinion contains contrary trends. Like a paradigm, the old Butskellite optimism, and Social Democratic and Keynesian policies, have gradually been abandoned, as more and more anomalies have crept in. The old consensus had its admirers among various lobbies. Senior civil servants, front-benchers and opinion-formers grew up with it. It would be quite wrong to assume that the leaders lacked conviction or belief in the policies they pursued. In recent years the political party, political groups, economic interests, and social class associated with the collectivist consensus have all declined. And, of course, the country's economic failure has also gnawed at the foundations. Although governments can govern in a fashion without consensus or consent – look at Northern Ireland – the normal British mode of government has rested on consensus. But the post-war consensus had its critics too – particularly among Labour's left and the free-market wing of the Conservative party. What has happened since the mid-1970s is that these have come to the fore. An increase in political polarisation and adversarial politics between the parties has been an inevitable consequence of the new situation,

A new agenda is likely to incorporate some elements of the old one and, like it, will emerge from the interaction of events, ideas, positions of parties and election outcomes. It is too early to say that there will be a new 'Thatcherite' consensus: most economic outcomes and survey evidence about attitudes show that the present government has fallen far short of its declared objectives in these two areas. The expectation is that, over time, there will be an uneasy synthesis between some elements of the old consensus and some parts of present economic thinking, one that will have more to do with holding the line on state welfare provision and government intervention in industry, than with 'rolling back the state'. In particular, it will include the social and welfare elements of the old consensus and some of the economic thinking of Thatcherism.

NOTES

1. Sir Keith Joseph, *Reversing the Trend* (London, Barry Rose: 1975), p. 4.
2. T. Smith, *The Politics of the Corporate Economy* (Oxford: Martin Robertson, 1979), p. 127.
3. See R. Bachrach and M. Baratz, 'The Two Faces of Power', *American Political Science Review,* 56, 1962.
4. J. S. Mill, 'The Claims of Labour', *Edinburgh Review*, April 1845, p. 503.
5. S. Wolin, *Politics and Vision* (London: Allen & Unwin, 1961), pp. 414–16.
6. B. Crick, *In Defence of Politics* (Harmondsworth: Penguin, 1964), p. 18.
7. S. Brittan, *Left or Right: the Bogus Dilemma* (London: Secker & Warburg, 1968).
8. R. Skidelsky, 'Politics is not Enough', *Encounter*, January 1969.
9. Quoted in G. R. Searle, *The Quest for National Efficiency* (London: Blackwell, 1971), p. 167.
10. For such an analysis, see R. Miliband, *Capitalist Democracy in Britian* (Oxford, Oxford University Press, 1983).
11. K. Middlemas, *The Politics of Industrial Society* (London: Deutsch, 1979).
12 C. Addison, *The Road to 1945* (London, Cape, 1976).
13. Middlemas, *op. cit.* p. 272.
14. Cited in S. Beer, *Modern British Politics* (London, Faber, 1965), p. 360.

15. J. A. Schumpeter (ed.), *Capitalism, Socialism and Democracy* (London, Allen & Unwin, 1946).
16. On this see O. Kirchheimer, 'The Transformation of Western Europe Party Systems', in J. La Palombara and M. Weiner (eds), *Political Parties and Political Development* (Princeton, NJ: Princeton University Press, 1964), and S. M. Lipset. 'The Modernisation of Contemporary European Politics', in S. M. Lipset (ed.), *Revolution and Counter-Revolution* (London: Heinemann, 1964).
17. Lipset *op. cit.* pp. 244–5.
18. See D. Hibbs, 'On the Political Economy of Long-Run Trends in Strike Activity', *British Journal of Political Science*, 8, 1978, 153–76.
19. See H. Heclo, 'Welfare: Progress and Stagnation', in W. Gwynn and R. Rose (eds), *Britain: Progress and Decline* (London: Macmillan, 1980).
20. D. Robertson, *The Theory of Party Competition* (London, Wiley, 1976).
21. A. Downs, *An Economic Theory of Democracy* (New York: Harper & Row, 1957).
22. K. Mannheim, *Man and Society* (London: Kegan Paul, 1946), p. 360.
23. R. Skidelsky, 'The Decline of Keynesian Politics', in R. Skidelsky (ed.), *The End of the Keynesian Era* (London: Macmillan, 1977), p. 62.
24. R. Rose and B. G. Peters, *Can Government Go Bankrupt?* (New York: Basic Books, 1978).
25. *Employment Policy* (London, HMSO, 1944), Cmnd 6527, p. 18, para. 49.
26. H. Wilensky, *The 'New Corporatism, Centralisation and the Welfare State'* (London: Sage, Political Sociology series, Vol. II, 1976).
27. I. Crewe, 'Why the Conservatives Won', in H. Penniman (ed.), *Britain at the Polls* (Washington DC: American Enterprise Institute, 1981).
28. J. S. Coleman, *Equality and Educational Opportunity* (Washington DC: Government Printing Office, 1966); and C. Jencks, *Inequality: A Reassessment of the Effects of Family and Schooling in America* (London: Allen Lane, 1973).
29. R. Rose, 'On the Priorities of Government: a Developmental Analysis of Public Policies', *European Journal of Political Research*, 4, 1976, 247–89.
30. P. Jenkins, 'The Social Democratic Dilemma', *New Statesman*, 20 September 1974.
31. Schumpeter (ed.), *Op. cit.*, p. 379.
32. J. O'Connor, *The Fiscal Crisis of the Capitalist State* (New York: St. Martins Press, 1973).
33. S. Brittan, 'The Economic Contraditions of Democracy', *British Journal of Political Science*, 5, 1975, 129–59. Also see A. Wright, 'What Sort of Crisis?', *Political Quarterly*, 1977.
34. J. Alt, *The Politics of Economic Decline* (Cambridge: Cambridge University Press, 1978).
35. I. Crewe, 'How to Win a Landslide Without Really Trying', in H. Penniman and A. Ranney (eds) *Britain at the Polls* (Washington DC: AEI, 1984).
36. A. Crosland, *The Future of Socialism* (London: Cape, 1956), p. 286.

37. On this, see D. Kavanagh, 'Margaret Thatcher, the Mobilising Prime Minister', in H. Clarke and M. Czydnowski (eds), *International Yearbook for Studies of Leaders and Leadership* (Illinois: University of Northern Illinois Press, 1987).
38. M. Laver, 'The 1983 British Party Manifestos', *Parliamentary Affairs*, 1984. Gallup also found a significant increase (to 67 per cent) in the proportion of voters thinking there were important differences between the parties.
39. See I. Crewe, 'Labour and the Electorate', in D. Kavanagh (ed.), *The Politics of the Labour Party* (London: Allen & Unwin, 1982); M. Harrop, 'Labour-Voting Conservatives', in R. Worcester and M. Harrop (eds), *Political Communications* (London: Allen & Unwin, 1982); and I. Crewe, 'How to Win a Landslide Without Really Trying', *op. cit.*
40. Crewe, 'How to Win a Landslide Without Really Trying', *op. cit.*
41. Gallup, June 1983.
42. R. Rose, 'Two and One Half Cheers for the Market', *Public Opinion*, June-July 1983.
43. D. Robertson, 'Adversary Politics, Public Opinion, and Electoral Cleavages', in D. Kavanagh and G. Peele (eds), *Comparative Government and Politics* (London: Heinemann, 1984), pp. 276-7.
44. I. Crewe, B. Sarlvik and D. Robertson, 'Partisan Dealignment in Britain 1964-74', *British Journal of Political Science*, 7, 1977, 129-90.
45. See S. Finer (ed.), *Adversary Politics and Electoral Reform* (London: Anthony Wigram, 1975), and *The Changing British Party System* (London: AEI, 1980).
46. S. Finer, 'Adversary Politics in the Eighties', *Electoral Studies*, 1, 1982, 221-30.
47. R. Rose, *Do Parties Make a Difference?* (second edition) (London: Macmillan, 1984), p. xxv.

4 Is Thatcherism Conservative?*

We are used to Labour leaders being accused of not being socialist or of betraying the workers – such accusations seem to go with the job. Indeed both Mr Callaghan and Mr Foot achieved some fame and internal party legitimacy by expressing such sentiments earlier in their careers. The criticism is usually at its most strident after the party has been voted out of office or when a Labour government has implemented unpopular economic measures. Socialism in Britain has usually meant obeisance to Clause IV, a statement penned by a retired civil servant in 1918 promising large-scale public ownership. More recently, socialism has claimed to promise 'a fundamental and irreversible shift of wealth and power to working people and their families'. Yet no Labour government, with the partial exception of the 1945 administration, has ever been able to convince its own socialists that it has made the word flesh. Ideologists may be doomed to perpetual frustration in politics because of an inevitable shortfall between principle and practice.

Conservative leaders have suffered less often from such charges of betrayal, largely because of the looseness of the party's ideology and because of the *deference* factor in the Tory theory of leadership. Nevertheless there have been examples: Disraeli memorably attacked Peel for betraying 'Conservative principles' (which he was careful not to spell out), Enoch Powell did not regard his leader Mr Heath as a Conservative, and Mr Heath, among others, in turn regards Mrs Thatcher as a betrayer of Conservatism, because she is an exponent of *laissez-faire* liberalism. An admirer of the lady, the Nobel prize winning economist Milton Friedman, asserted in a newspaper interview in 1982 'She is a nineteenth century Liberal'. Many critics and supporters agree: she is not a Conservative. Can such a claim really be made of the greatest election winner in the party's history?

I will argue that Mrs Thatcher represents a strand (that has certainly been in a minority) in the Conservative party in the

* This chapter was specially written for this volume.

twentieth century. Some of her ideas, and the intensity with which she holds and expresses them, also mark her out from her predecessors. It has been the Tories who have written the best history books on the Conservative party. Chris Patten, Sir Ian Gilmour, Robert Rhodes James and John Ramsden have written histories of the party according to the doctrines of R.A. Butler. In a sense they have stolen the best tunes. More recently there has been a reaction by such Thatcherites as Patrick Cosgrave and John Vincent, consigning much of post-war Conservatism before 1979 to the dustbin of betrayal. They argue that Mrs Thatcher has returned the party to its true principles, 1980's style. It is a case of those controlling the present controlling the past.

The subject raises a number of difficulties. Crucially, in answer to the question 'What is a Conservative?' many commentators have said that it is too elusive a term, that it is not possible to distill any essence. Few intellectuals have bothered to elucidate a philosophy of conservatism, and many Conservatives have prided themselves on not being intellectual. John Stuart Mill's label 'the stupid party', has been a long time a-dying. It was the party which found as much merit in fox-hunting as in philosophy. A Conservative disposition in politics was to be acquired: it was not to be imparted by theoretical writing.

Many studies suggest there has been an interplay, historically, between two themes, which cannot be reduced to simple contrasts between 'dry' and 'wet', left and right, or consolidator and radical. The dominant 'Tory' strand sees society as an organic unity, denies the value or possibility of willed societal change and stresses the government's responsibility for managing the economy and providing welfare. Its horror of revolution leads it to be collectivist rather than individualistic in its perception of society and of government's responsibility to society. Burke is the great exponent of such Conservatism. His *Reflections on the French Revolution* was a strong attack on that cataclysmic event. It was also a vehement defence of the *status quo*, and, more importantly for modern Conservatives, established a model of the correct political order and appropriate political behaviour. The follower of Burke respects tradition − 'the general bank and capital of nations and of ages' − makes changes gradually and only in cases of dire necessity, and is suspicious of abstract speculative reasoning. For Burke, a 'disposition to preserve, and an ability to improve would be my standard of a statesman'. He stressed the value of attachment to groups − the 'little platoons' and 'the first principle (the germ as it were) of public affection'. Burke's most celebrated recent disciple, Michael Oakeshott, said that the task of the politician was not to shape society but to pursue 'intimations'. Politics was a matter of keeping the ship afloat on a bottomless and boundless sea, rather than steering for a harbour.

The second and competing strand is that of classical liberalism, nowadays sometimes termed neo-liberalism. In this the individual is the key unit; society and the economy have their own mechanisms, and by and large should be allowed to proceed unhindered by government. Government has a limited, if important, role covering only essential tasks (such as preserving law and order, a stable currency, and maintaining a strong defence) and should allow individuals to work out their own destinies. A hero of the liberal wing, Hayek, finds much of the Tory philosophy objectionable. He complains that Conservatives do not reverse changes: for they 'cannot offer an alternative to the direction in which we are moving'.

Both themes have been influential in shaping Conservative practice. If the Tory tradition has produced paternalist legislation, social reform and accompanying Disraelian One Nation rhetoric, the liberal tradition has preached the virtues of competition, private enterprise, personal freedom and rolling back the state.

Most Conservatives have taken pride in the fact that, unlike Socialists, they are not ideological. One area on which all Conservatives agree is the virtue of holding office − indeed effective exercise of office has been seen as proof of political wisdom. Being in government for two-thirds of the twentieth century has made it easy for Conservatives to identify the national interest with that of the party. Moreover lengthy spells in office impose limits on ideology. Ideas are tested and modified (often destroyed) when set against the criteria of political acceptability and administrative practicality presented by pressure groups, civil servants and public opinion − in short, what a senior civil servant has called 'ongoing reality'. Conservatism becomes what Conservative governments do. It is an instrumental politics: there are no core Conservative ideas. It produces what the American political scientist Samuel Huntington calls a *positional* or *situational* Conservatism, in which the party does what is necessary to preserve existing institutions and the social order. The search for office has, in any case, presented fewer problems of principle for Conservatives than for their rivals. They joined a coalition under Lloyd George in 1915, another under Ramsay MacDonald in 1931 and dominated the one under Churchill in 1940. In October 1974 Mr Heath campaigned on a national unity platform. He sought a Conservative victory so that he could form a government of all good men.

One can see what Conservatives mean when they emphasise freedom, family, monarchy, tradition, rule of law, private property and national unity as party principles. One can also accept that Conservatism is for its followers 'a habit of mind, a mode of feeling, a way of living.'[1] None of this, however, takes us much further. Conservative political thinking, and even practice, have not always been identified with what the Conservative party has done; there are conservatives outside the Conservative party.

If Conservatism is what Conservatives do, then this gives great scope to the leadership at any one time to shape it. Mrs Thatcher would say that providing decisive leadership is clearly in line with Tory traditions of authoritative government. Conservatives have never favoured weakness in the executive. Her rhetoric of duty, authority, discipline and order echo traditional Tory themes. But in one sense at least the choice of Mrs Thatcher as leader in 1975 does mark a change from the record of the party leadership from Baldwin in 1922 down to Heath. Apart from Heath's Selsdon Man period in office (1970–72), many critics and supporters agree that the party's record over time has been one of Tory men and collectivist, or even social democratic, measures. Leaders have often held back from promoting 'Big C Conservatism' (the phrase is Jim Prior's). In 1925 Stanley Baldwin, when faced with a Private Members' bill to abolish the trade unions' political levy (an action which would damage the Labour party), eloquently disarmed his union-bashing back-benchers. Although Baldwin accepted the merits of the bill and was aware of his party's enormous Parliamentary majority, he opposed it, in the higher interests of promoting social cohesion and peace in our time: 'we are not going to push our political advantage home'![2] In 1947 R. A. Butler, in discussion about how the Conservatives could come to terms with socialism, said: 'If they (the people) want that sort of life (welfare and high public spending) they can have it, but under our auspices'. Winston Churchill in 1951 thought the nation needed a rest 'if only to allow for Socialist legislation to reach its full fruition', and his Conservative successors became identified with the policies of the post-war consensus. Adjustment and adaptation have been recurring themes of Conservative statecraft. The records has been a rearguard action, defending but not dying in the last ditch. Peel after 1832 and Disraeli after 1867 persuaded the Conservative party to accept measures initiated by their opponents and which they had bitterly opposed.

The post-war drift of the party upset some Conservatives. Critics on the right, now largely a free-market or liberal right, wanted an alternative to rather than an echo of socialism; if voters favoured economic planning and intervention by the state, conciliation of the unions, high levels of public spending on welfare — social democracy in short — they should vote Labour. The right had to endure the loss of empire, continued public ownership, high taxes and high public spending. Some found objectionable the other liberalism (which increasingly they termed 'permissiveness') in the moral sphere — providing for easier abortion, divorce and homosexuality. Today some Conservatives look back on the 1960s as the decade in which the seeds of permissiveness were sown. Under Macmillan the party turned to economic *dirigisme*, incomes policy and high public spending. Even Mr Heath's Selsdon phase was not entirely reassuring. There was little of the visionary about him. He was an instrumentalist, a technocrat; he wanted things to work more efficiently and the economy to grow faster. Once his free-market strategy failed, he turned to Keynesianism and corporatism. Enoch Powell, preaching monetarism and much of what turned out to be Thatcherite economics, and the Institute of Economic Affairs, canvassing the merits of markets and combating Keynesian ideas, were isolated voices. When the Heath government fell in 1974, it was presiding over record post-war levels of public ownership, government intervention in the economy, public spending as a share of GDP, inflation and the most far-reaching peacetime statutory controls on prices and incomes.

Then came Mrs Thatcher. It is misleading to see her election as leader in February 1975 as the expression of an ideological upsurge in the party. There was a vacuum both in terms of candidates (because none of the obvious contenders would stand against Mr Heath on the first ballot) and of policies. She certainly had admirers and some Conservative free-marketeers saw her as a potential spokeswoman for their cause. Sir Keith Joseph's speeches in late 1974, which called for a major shift of direction in economic policy, and then his support for Mrs Thatcher, lent an ideological flavour to her challenge. Ironically, she and Sir Keith had been the last of the big spenders at Health and at Education respectively in the Heath Government. But it needs emphasising that the Thatcherite ideology came later, in spite of a school of New Conservative historians and commentators who argue otherwise. Indeed Mrs Thatcher may have won the leadership in spite of what her ideas were taken to be. MPs voted for her largely because they wanted a change from Mr Heath, under whom they thought they could not win another election. They were joined by other MPs who were disappointed place-seekers, those who had not received honours they thought they deserved and those who had not received expected courtesies. Mr Heath was niggardly with honours and many back-benchers felt that his reserve with them bordered on rudeness.

Yet in important ways Mrs Thatcher quickly showed that she was prepared to be a mould-breaker. Over time she has increasingly distanced herself from previous Conservative governments. At first she was willing to express some sympathy for Mr Heath's problems in government.[3] However, as he attacked the work of Mrs Thatcher's government, and 'wet' Cabinet ministers in her first government resisted the economic policies, so Mrs Thatcher drew a veil over his record and then counter-attacked. Her supporters were even more vocal in dismissing Mr Heath. The Macmillan government (1959–63) also enjoyed a brief period of official approval, as did the government of 'Winston' (1951–5). That is no longer so. She knew that what she was doing was different from her predecessors. She regarded the problems which she faced – namely, high spending, high taxes, inflation, trade-union power, over-regulated industry and an anti-enterprise culture – as the product of previous post-war governments, both Labour and Conservative. Their policies had helped bring about national decline.

There is an almost sociological explanation for her early rejection of consensus Conservatism. As early as 1975 in a speech in New York she complained about how her predecessors had allowed their 'bourgeois guilt' to prevent them from adopting the tough necessary measures. Worried by the social divisions and mass unemployment of the 1930s, and appreciative of the sacrifices made during the war, they had debased the currency, appeased trade-union power, expanded state welfare and avoided hard decisions. Consensus produced weak leadership and the lowest common denominator in policy. Unlike Macmillan, Butler, even Heath (and Whitelaw, Carrington, Soames, Pym, Gilmour and Prior in her 1979 Cabinet), she had no such guilt. The spirit of 1945 seemed not to have penetrated the corner shop in Grantham.

This social aspect may be significant. The Conservative Party has been part of the British Establishment in the twentieth century.

Britain's dominant social, cultural and economic institutions were tied, via personal links, social and educational background, and shared assumptions, to the party. The press, BBC, Oxbridge, House of Lords, senior civil service, judiciary and Church of England have shared this conservative disposition for much of the century. And leaders of the party were often drawn from this background. As has been well documented by Guttsman, Blondel, Rose and others, Conservative front-benchers were usually of a higher social and educational status than back-benchers, or party activists. In the party Mrs Thatcher – daughter of a grocer, a Methodist, a local grammar school girl, a chemist, a first generation member of a profession – if not quite an upstart, is at least different. Previous leaders (Churchill, Eden, Macmillan, Home) were often socialised among the elite for a long period before becoming leaders. Even Heath, for all his modest family origins, had been a member of the leadership for a decade before he became leader in 1965 and had acquired membership of such elite organisations as the Honourable Artillery Company. Again Mrs Thatcher had not been part of the inner circle before 1975. She was neither part of, nor indebted to, that charmed circle.

Mrs Thatcher accepted Sir Keith's critique of the way in which Conservatives had tried to occupy the middle ground. In the interests of promoting balance and continuity Conservative governments had usually accepted, in spite of some misgivings, the measures of post-war Labour governments. But as socialist governments moved left, so did the middle ground and the Conservatives with it. Pursuit of the middle ground assisted the ratchet of socialism. Hayek claimed that he was not a Conservative, because Conservatives too often compromised with socialism and even borrowed its thinking. His *Road to Serfdom* was written, after all: 'To the socialists in all parties'. He warned that collectivism endangered personal liberty and democracy; free enterprise capitalism was the only system likely to preserve democracy.

Too many of Mrs Thatcher's admirers and detractors describe her as an intellectual. This is not so. Whilst she has passionately held principles and instincts she agrees with Burke and Oakeshott in rejecting abstract thinking. Although she is systematic in her thinking about politics and derives her stances from principles, it is stretching things to say that she is the child of Hayek and Friedman. They may have given some substance and intellectual respectability to her beliefs and instincts, but most of these derive from her own experience and her ideas of what is commonsense. Her beliefs in limited government, widespread ownership as a safeguard for liberty, the need for government to concentrate on its basic tasks, the connection between personal morality and freedom of choice, and the values of thrift, hard work and deferred gratifications, all derive from her own life. In this way she responds to what was once a 'hidden agenda' of Conservatism — the populist authoritarianism of the activists rather than the grandees. In many respects her case was greatly assisted by the events of the 1979 Winter of Discontent — the failure of incomes policies, the weakness of union leaders and the irresponsibility of local officials in some public sector unions. These events followed years of slow economic growth and negligible advances in average living standards. Here was proof that the consensus not only undermined state authority but was economically debilitating.

The writings of Sir Ian Gilmour provide a witty treasure-trove of the One-Nation Conservatism against which Mrs Thatcher rebelled. They are an only half-disguised critique of Thatcherism. For example, in his *Inside Right*,[4] one reads the following:

- On the evidence of Enoch Powell's career, 'an ideological approach does not produce loyalty, consistency, Conservatism or chivalry: and the Tory party should avoid it' (page 139).
- 'The country can only be well governed from the centre . . . Balance and moderation are integral to Toryism' (page 167).
- 'The Tory Party . . . seeks the *via media*' (page 167).
- The Conservative Party should be moderate. 'In the British two party system, moderation in one party is likely to engender moderation in the other, and extremism is likely to breed extremism' (page 130).
- Accepting tradition means accepting much you may not like, including collectivism. The Tory virtues are respect for tradition, distrust of systems and rationalism in politics, approval of balance and suspicion of zeal.

Mrs Thatcher would answer by saying that if she had been concerned with compromise and balance and avoiding zeal, she would have accomplished very little. She denies that she is not a traditional Conservative. In an interview with Michael Charlton on BBC Radio Three, she replied to the charge that, because she was radical and populist, she was not Conservative: 'It [her Conservatism] is radical because at the time when I took over we needed to be radical' (17 December 1985). As far as she is concerned, the problems facing the country in 1979 called for radical action. In the *Observer* 1979 interview she said:

> I felt, and the Conservatives who elected me presumably felt, that the next leader of the party must clearly stand up against the direction in which the country had been moving under both previous governments . . . At the time of the leadership contest which began in November 1974 we were coming to a stage when there really wasn't a party which was clearly standing for the limitation of government.

The case against Mrs Thatcher as a Conservative includes her impatience with the *status quo* and her suspicion, indeed rejection, of so many traditions and institutions. Much of the alleged wisdom that inheres in the institutions and practice is part of what she has regarded as the flabby consensus that dragged the country down. She has not approached the senior civil service, local authorities, universities, trade unions, BBC, Church of England, the legal and medical professions, the public corporations with the reverence − or at least respect − with which Burke recommended that we regard what is handed down by ancestors. In the past some of these institutions were supported by Conservatives because they provided checks on the power of a centralised state and provided independent sources of decision-making. Centralised government was identified with Socialism. But under Mrs Thatcher these institutions, particularly the cultural bloc of universities, churches and BBC, have been regarded as bastions of the left liberalism which she has vanquished in the political arena. Her support for Edmund Burke's 'little platoons' is selective. Although there is much talk in 10 Downing Street of third and fourth-term Thatcherism helping to build up 'mediating' structures between the individual and the state, these must not be public sector intermediary institutions. Some of the professions have been compelled to face up to market discipline. The legal and medical professions have been subject to scrutiny and competition, opticians have lost their exclusive rights to prescribe spectacles, tenure in universities has been abolished, and conditions of work and training of school teachers have been centrally determined by the government.

It is now commonplace to say that the Thatcher governments have had to be highly interventionist to produce an extension of the market and reduction of producer power. They have reduced the claims that groups are able to make on the state. The public sector of the economy has been rolled back. Reliance on monetarism, rather than incomes policy, to curb inflation meant that the government no longer had to compromise its authority in social contracts and wages policies with producer groups, particularly the unions. The government disowned responsibility for full employment. Another tactic has been to give greater scope to consumers *vis-a-vis* public sector groups, e.g. schools and housing associations can opt out of local authority control. A greater voice has been given to parents and governors and head teachers in state schools and to GPs and patients in the health service. Trade-union members have been given more say *via* pre-strike ballots, regular elections of their officials and votes on the unions' political levy. Many nationalised industries, which long posed problems for governments, not least in pay negotiations, were floated to the private sector. The losers have been local authorities, trade unions, health authorities and nationalised industries. The net effect of these measures has been to give greater autonomy to the central government.

But the political record has bitterly disappointed the liberals who regard the constitutional devolution of power as the crucial analogue to the achievement of a free economy. As Vernon Bogdanor points out, it is for this reason that Hayek rejects the notion of parliamentary sovereignty, which he sees as the legal counterpart of omnicompetent government.[5] But in her commitment to a strong state, and her aversion to any reform which might limit its sway, Mrs Thatcher is doing no more than following a well-worn Conservative tradition.

Mrs Thatcher claims that the *status quo* in 1979 was failing to provide what people wanted, and that the balance between the state and society had swung too far in favour of the state. Again, her *Observer* interview in 1979 is interesting: 'We had moved too far towards a society controlled by government, too far towards what wasn't, and isn't, my idea of a society that can flourish'.

Inevitably therefore Thatcherism has involved an attempt at restructuring society and economy – social engineering. Traditional Conservatives would shudder at such an enterprise – social engineering is for sociologists or eugenicists. Altering institutions would cause people's hearts and minds and their own behaviour to alter as well. Extending private home ownership and share ownership, promoting private enterprise, small business and self-employment, encouraging private health, private pensions, and schools to opt out of local authority control, and reducing the privileges and the role of trade unions were relatively easy. A test of Thatcherism's endurance is whether, in time, these reforms breed a set of supportive vaiues.

It is a complex mix. There is the Tory assertion of the national interest against special interest groups (from striking miners to change-resisting barristers), though American multi-national corporations can take over Jaguar or parts of British Leyland. The promotion of consumers' and citizens' interests against the producers of services (most of the housing, trade-union, legal and educational changes) and emphasis on competition, the market and attacks on vested interests comprise a liberal approach. The assertion of moral values (Victorian values are timeless for Mrs Thatcher) contrasts with the wordly scepticism of Churchill or Macmillan. It is neither Liberal nor Tory. The nationalism (Falklands, immigrants are British rather than black, hostility to devolution in Scotland and debunking of many of the schemes of the Europeanists) are in the tradition of Tory imperialism. Thatcherism also seems to envisage the dissolution of the society of special interest groups. Traditionally, Conservatives accepted a major role for interest groups. In France Gaullists appealed to a 'supra-social' nation − not society − of citizens. Mrs Thatcher has more in common with de Gaulle. Above all, Mrs Thatcher is still a pragmatist − bold in talk, cautious in action.

Mrs Thatcher has redefined modern Conservatism. In particular she has emphasised two elements more strongly than before. The perceptive Marxist writer Andrew Gamble says that Thatcherism stands for a *strong state* and *free economy*. Thatcherite Conservatism blends authoritarianism with economic liberalism, and because of the strength with which she defends the two, it is a radical package. Thus the state is strong on defence (e.g. Falklands, and increased defence budget) and national identity (a tougher stand on immigration), resists greater integration in the European Community, and emphasises law and order (legislation for identity cards for soccer crowds, and greater spending on the police) and internal security (treatment of terrorists). Much of this is of course quite alien to nineteenth-century liberalism. It is coupled with a support for authority figures, e.g. teachers, parents and managers, when they defend traditional moral values. In March 1982 she promised 'the old virtues of discipline and self-restraint'. She regularly votes in the Commons for the restoration of capital punishment, even though she is in a minority in her Cabinet. Mr Macmillan once told the journalist Henry Fairlie that if people wanted a sense of purpose they should look to the bishops, rather than the politicians. Mrs Thatcher speaks out partly because she sees this as a rôle of leadership and partly because she feels that the churches are failing in the task of moral leadership. In her controversial address to the Church Assembly meeting in Scotland in 1988 she approvingly quoted St Paul: 'If a man will not work, he shall not eat'.

On the other hand, a number of measures have produced some economic liberalisation. The state, both central and local, has been reduced. Such measures include the ending of exchange controls, the avoidance of prices and incomes laws, privatisation of some central and local services and council house sales. Mrs Thatcher is able to justify these measures by pointing out that there has been a long tradition of Conservative opposition to an excess of bureaucracy, regulation and taxation, and support for the values of self-reliance, enterprise and personal responsibility.

Jim Bulpitt has developed the concept of *high politics* to explain Conservative statecraft. Essentially the party in government has sought to maintain the autonomy of the centre by insulating it from demands and pressures. It did this by restricting the range of issues that were to count as 'high politics'; other issues − of 'low politics' − were delegated to subordinate bodies, to local government, to self-governing groups or to the market. The government wanted autonomy in significant areas, notably economic and foreign policy. By 1979 Mr Heath and his Labour successors had fatally compromised the authority of government in their bargains with trade unions. Government in the 1970s had become 'overloaded' with responsibilities and spending obligations to special interests; it could not carry them out and its authority was sapped. An essential task for the Conservative practitioner of 'high politics' was to regain a substantial area of autonomy for central government by, for example, limiting its responsibilities. Bulpitt's claim, a persuasive one, is that in terms of statecraft there is much continuity between Mrs Thatcher and Churchill and Macmillan. What makes her a novel Conservative is that she is a crusader, and has become more of one over time. Everywhere else the passage of time in office is a force for conservatism. Not so for Mrs Thatcher.

Mrs Thatcher finds her warmest support among two distinct groups in and around the Conservative party. Both can claim to represent significant elements of what is now called the New Right. One is the 'liberal wing', which emphasises the importance of personal freedom and limited government in both economic and non-economic spheres. Understandably such people can be only qualified supporters of the Thatcher government, applauding the measures of economic liberalisation but concerned about the acts of political centralisation and moral authoritarianism.

The other wing centres on the academics and journalists who are associated with the *Salisbury Review*. Roger Scruton and other members of the Peterhouse school of conservatism reject the libertarian approach and instead defend the authority of the state and the prior importance of duties over rights, and emphasise the importance of society *vis-a-vis* the individual. This group is distrustful of too much individualism, permissiveness or liberty. It is concerned about a moral decline, for which it blames the leaders of the 'counter-culture', particularly progressive teachers, social workers, race-relations advisers, social engineers and some of the clergy. Mrs Thatcher feels they owe society an apology for many of the social problems of the 1980s. Mr Tebbit in his 1985 Disraeli lecture spoke for this wing when he inveighed against the permissiveness and 'the valueless values' of the 1960s for sowing the seeds of moral decline. This seems to be what Mrs Thatcher meant by her famous remark 'There is no such thing as society'. She was arguing that it was individuals and families who did things, and society should not be made a scapegoat for bad behaviour and for personal failures. Too often society was invoked as a means of denying individual responsibility. Society is more an effect than a cause. In her address to the General Assembly of the Church of Scotland in May 1988 she said the government should beware of doing so much that it weakened personal responsibility – 'we simply cannot delegate the exercise of money and generosity to others'.

What is remarkable about Mrs Thatcher is the extent to which she has managed to articulate many of the concerns of both these groups. She remains within the Conservative fold but has certainly contributed a distinctive interpretation, alongside that of Disraeli and Butler; what remains to be seen is how much will survive her passing from the scene.

NOTES

1. R. J. White, *The Conservative Tradition*, 1950, p. 1.
2. In 1927, following the General Strike, however, Baldwin did not resist the pressures and The Trades Disputes Act and Trades Unions Act was passed. This imposed new restrictions on the unions' political activities and made sympathetic strikes designed to coerce the government illegal.
3. See the interview which Mrs Thatcher gave to the *Observer* in April 1979. In acknowledging Mr Heath's achievements, she added, 'It is a thousand pities that we didn't win the first 1974 election because what he (Mr Heath) was trying to do would then have been acceptable.
4. Quartet Books.
5. 'The Constitution', in D. Kavanagh and A. Seldon (eds), *The Thatcher Effect* (Oxford: Oxford University Press 1989).

5 Making Sense of Thatcher*

A problem for political scientists is that they can often see their subject changing before their eyes. In the 1970s the received model of the two-party, class-based, consensual and stable British political system was challenged by many of the events in that dismal decade. The rise of nationalism in Scotland, violence in Ulster, inflation, trade-union power and the weakness of government suggested a breakdown. Whether it was a crisis of capitalism (as the left asserted) or a crisis of social democracy (as the right proclaimed), political scientists were forced to search for new models and a new vocabulary. 'Bankruptcy', 'Overload', 'Ungovernability' and 'Britain in Agony' were typical book titles and themes.

Commentators also discerned a crisis of governability in many other Western democracies. But the traditional high regard for Britain's political stability made her case particularly striking. Some expressed doubts that democratic institutions could cope with inflationary pressures, sectional rivalries and the determination and ability of particular groups to dislocate society. Governments seemed unable to cope. It was not just journalists and academics, such as Samuel Brittan, Peter Jay, Anthony King and Richard Rose, who wrote in this vein.[1] One has only to read the accounts of well-placed insiders in governments in the 1970s such as Douglas Hurd, Joel Barnett and Lord Donoughue, or recall Mr Callaghan's remarks that without a Labour government there would be rioting in the streets, to get a sense of the crisis of confidence at the heart of government.[2]

Today such talk has a dated air. People no longer discuss the weaknesses of British government or the crisis of its authority. In France in 1958 General de Gaulle emerged from the ruins of the Fourth Republic and restored the authority of government. Since 1979 Mrs Thatcher may be said to have done something similar in Britain. Of all the changes that have occurred since 1979, perhaps this has been the most significant and least noted.

* This chapter was specially written for this volume.

It is of course dangerous to write so close to events if one is offering interpretations or forecasts about likely developments. Often the contemporary histories by participants take the form of self-exculpatory memoirs and diaries, and are attempts to manage history. Both Harold Macmillan and Harold Wilson spring to mind as practitioners of the art. The passage of time brings a sense of perspective and an awareness of longer-term consequences, as well as access to more documents.

While this is true, it is not the whole truth. All history is a product of its own time. For observers to abstain from the recording and analysis of contemporary events would leave the field free to the participants, often with an axe to grind. No other social science abstains from analysis of its own period. One does not have to wait thirty years to write a first draft of history.

These thoughts are relevant to an attempt to make sense of the impact of Mrs Thatcher. The literature on her is now immense. Perhaps only Churchill and Lloyd George, both at times of national crises, have seized the imagination to the same degree. But few of their biographies were written when they were still in office. In contrast she had been the subject of at least a dozen biographies by late 1988. Another dozen studies were available for the tenth anniversary of her premiership in May 1989. Lord Callaghan and Sir Alec Douglas-Home have each had one biographer and Mr Heath three. Publishers eagerly snap up books on the lady and her works, and usually ensure that her name (and photograph) dominate the jacket. The attention to her personality as a means of understanding public policy is interesting in itself. It was Suetonius, in his *Life of the Caesars*, who warned that such an approach was a symptom of a declining political order.

There is no doubt that Mrs Thatcher will have a secure place in history. She is the only post-war leader to have lent her name to an 'ism'; she is the longest continuously serving Prime Minister this century, and the only one this century to have won three elections in succession; and she has helped change the political agenda. She has also overturned much of the post-war conventional political wisdom: that the Conservatives had to be led from the centre; that a government could not win general elections during mass unemployment; and that it was necessary to co-operate with the major interests to govern the country. History will judge, but in the meantime what do contemporary historians make of her?

Some have argued that there is no such thing as Thatcherism; there have been too many inconsistencies in her policies, rhetoric and goals. Thatcherism is sometimes reduced to the style, personality and approach of the lady herself and will therefore end with her. Like all successful politicians, she is a pragmatist, and has had to adjust to circumstances. Some critics and supporters identify the 'ism' largely with economics, particularly with monetarism and the free market, missing out such important features as the assertion of traditional values and the authority of government. The intellectual (largely Marxist-inspired) left regards Thatcherism as a hegemonic project by the ruling class, reshaping the institutions and procedures which are barriers to its success. The project starts with changing the economy, then tackles institutions, and culminates in the reshaping of behaviour and attitudes. This view credits Thatcherism with higher ambitions – an attempt at social engineering, an assault on so much of the post-war consensus. In an interview[3] she expressed her wish to 'kill off Socialism'. Another school, best represented by Jim Bulpitt of the University of Warwick, regards the post-1979 record as an exercise in Conservative statecraft, one in which the government has adopted radical policies and applied them resolutely to cope with its overload of problems. Bulpitt claims that Mrs Thatcher continues a long line of Conservative statecraft, which he defines as 'the art of winning elections and achieving some necessary degree of governing competence in office'.[4] For Bulpitt politics is more important than economics.

Political scientists, unlike most other academics, face competition from journalists in assessing contemporary political events. A sign of the times is that so many political commentators have already turned their hands to analysing Thatcherism. The *Financial Times*'s Peter Riddell has written a well-regarded commentary (*The Thatcher Government*).[5] The BBC's John Cole has written *The Thatcher Years*[6] and Peter Jenkins has tried to write a 'big' (over 400 pages) book on *Mrs Thatcher's Revolution*[7], placing the rise of Mrs Thatcher in the context of Britain's relative economic decline. Both Riddell and Jenkins are familiar with the relevant political science literature.

Another 'big' (over 500 pages) book is the biography, *One of Us*,[8] by Hugo Young of the *Guardian*. Rather than write an interim book he planned to wait for her retirement. In the end the wait proved too long. He and Anne Sloman had earlier written *The Thatcher Phenomenon*,[9] based on the BBC series of interviews with well-placed observers. A good interim biography is *Thatcher*,[10] by two journalists, Nicholas Wapshott and George Brock. Kenneth

Harris's recent study is disappointing and has the mark of an
'authorised' biography.

The journalists, not surprisingly, are strong on *haute politique*.
Jenkins in particular is quite brilliant at describing political personalities. Readers of the *Independent* know that his standpoint for much
of the 1980s has been that of the disenchanted centrist. He came
to be a reluctant admirer of Mrs Thatcher and at the time of writing
despaired of the Labour party. He would doubtless have wished the
Alliance to have broken the mould, but recognises that it is Mrs
Thatcher who has done so. His broad sweep of political,
economic and social dynamics provides a good understanding of
Mrs Thatcher's work.

Hugo Young eventually replaced Peter Jenkins as the *Guardian*'s
political commentator, having parted from the Murdoch-owned
Sunday Times. Young is always a polished and independent
commentator: the excesses of both the left and right often suffer at
his pen. He mourns the old 'One Nation' Butskellite values, perhaps
now best embodied in the beleaguered BBC and universities. Mrs
Thatcher has not only radicalised politics, she has politicised many
areas in which political considerations were only a minor element,
if one at all. The lady has asked 'Is he one of us?' in making a vast
range of appointments. For Young, Oxford University's decision in
January 1985 not to award its most famous daughter an honorary
doctorate 'perfectly crystallised the cultural change that she has
wrought'.[11]

At times Young's assessment of the success of Mrs Thatcher's
crusade has varied. In September 1986 he was impressed by the
influence of the One Nation ministers and the likelihood that her
legacy could easily be spurned by the election of a different successor:
'. . . we can see clearly that it is the consensualists who are more
likely to come out on top in the post-Thatcher era, whenever that
begins'. Political journalism, however, is as subject to change as the
political weather it reports. A year later he writes:

There is no such thing as moderate Conservatism any more, that
is a Conservatism made different from and at odds with
Thatcherism. Thatcherites have made their compromises but anti-
Thatcherites have made many more: and now they all live happily
on the same terrain where social abrasion, market economics and
welfare cuts are a curse . . . This is the party revolution that Mrs
Thatcher has brought about. Every minister in his fashion wants

82	*Politics and Personalities*

to be another Thatcher, it is quite an achievement: a party approaching its second decade of power more united that it was in its first, crushing all argument beneath the juggernaut of its triumph.[12]

A second category includes books written by advisers and courtiers. Russell Lewis, *Margaret Thatcher. A Personal and Political Biography*;[13] (1975 – 1980); George Gardine, *Margaret Thatcher: From Childhood to Leadership* (Kimber 1975);[14] and Patrick Cosgrove, *Margaret Thatcher: A Tory and Her Party*[15] read like attempts by her supporters to make a quick buck. In 1989 Mrs Thatcher's constituency agent and the indefatigable Lady Porter have added to the hagiography. Indeed Cosgrove, historian and one-time adviser, has actually written two further books on Mrs Thatcher. Apart from the overlaps, the reader wearies of the contrived intimacy, 'As I said to Mrs Thatcher', or the pomposity, 'Mrs Thatcher's position, if I understand it'. A former Treasury Minister, Lord Jock Bruce Gardyne normally writes perceptively, but his *Mrs Thatcher's First Administration*[16] (Macmillan, 1984) is disappointing. Sir Alan Walters', her ex-economic advisor, *Britain's Economic Renaissance: Margaret Thatcher's Reforms 1979–84*[17] is another 'insider' account, which might be entitled *How I Won the War*.

Sympathy does not guarantee quality. *The First Thatcher Government 1979 – 83*[18] is by Martin Holmes, a self-proclaimed Thatcherite. The author is relentlessly hostile to anything to the left of the lady, particularly to 'wet' Tories. He asserts that Mrs Thatcher has transformed her party and the political agenda. On publication the reviewer (an economist) in *The Times Higher Educational Supplement* complained that the book 'does justice to neither the Thatcher Government, nor the discipline of politics'. The book reads more as a contribution to Tory inner party battles.

Some of the above second category books give instant history a bad name. More significantly, they are a crucial part of a revisionism of post-war British history, which sees pre-Thatcher Conservatism as a story of retreat and betrayal. All the books are hostile to the work of the Heath government. It is striking how many students today already identify Thatcherism with Conservatism. A crucial page of history is being confined to the waste bin.

Academics have been reluctant to provide systemic studies of Thatcherism. They have done what they usually do best, case studies in particular policy areas, and historical explanations of the changes in British politics. David Bell has edited a series of studies in his *The Conservative Government 1979–84*.[19] Peter Jackson's *Implementing Government Policy*[20] is an impressive collection of studies on the aims and performances of the first Thatcher government in a number of policy areas. Nicholas Bosanquet's *After the New Right*[21] is good at separating out the different elements of the economic approach – tax cuts for moral and supply side reasons, monetarism for sound money, and the public choice school for moving against the public sector. Essentially the New Right believes in the beneficence of the free market and the deleterious effects of political intervention. Ruth Levitas's collection of essays *The Ideology of the New Right*[22] presents left critiques of the authoritarian features of Thatcherism. What is lacking, however, in such discrete studies is a sense of what it is *all* about.

One attempt to cast such light on the subject is the set of largely admiring essays edited by Professors Kenneth Minogue and Michael Biddis, *Thatcherism, Personality and Politics*.[23] There is much overlap in the lively essays from Sammy Finer, David Marquand, Peter Hennessy and the editors. They correctly emphasise that Thatcherism is a matter of style (no nonsense, abrasive and self-confident) and values ('you can't spend more than you earn' and, for Minogue, 'morality without bourgeois guilt').

The collection of essays called simply *Thatcherism*,[24] edited by Robert Skidelsky, promises much. Skidelsky, an original and accomplished historian and biographer, collected a team of distinguished professors. But if he gave them a remit to outline and evaluate Thatcherism they did not hear him. Instead the good and the great do their own thing. Skidelsky places her rise firmly in the context of the breakdown of government authority in the 1970s. Frank Kahn is very good on economic ideas, Brian Barry stimulating on the case for socialism, and Ivor Crewe presents a wealth of survey data on the failure of Thatcherite ideas to strike a chord with the electorate. Sensibly he concludes that all this may not matter much when compared with the poor standing of the opposition, the mood of prosperity and the perceived competence of the government.

Skidelsky's book makes Thatcherism a bit like the modern dance – everybody's doing it. Everybody is expected to have a view on the subject – as a sociologist, historian, economist, political partisan and so forth. The editorial injunction, judging by the result, unfortunately seems to have been: say what you want, it will be interesting because of the nature of the subject.

If it is true that the political views of most academic social scientists range from a 'wet' Tory to a social democratic (incorporating centrist and leftist political views) persuasion, it is understandable that they have been uncomfortable with Mrs Thatcher. But she has now been around so long and some of the changes so marked that they have had to take notice. Among the first to appreciate that something was going on was the journal *Marxism Today*, as well as the *New Left Review* and *New Socialist*. Stuart Hall and Elliot Jacques were early in the field with their *The Politics of Thatcherism* (1982). They have been followed by Andrew Gamble, *The Free Economy and the Strong State*,[25] Bob Jessop, with K. Bonnett, S. Bromley and T. Linz, *Thatcherism*,[26] and Stuart Hall, *The Hard Road to Renewal*.[27]

As these authors try to carve out distinct left-wing interpretations of Thatcherism, so there is a good deal of intellectual gymnastics and verbal hair-splitting. The studies are suffused with the insights and models of grand sociological theory, of Claus Offe, Gramsci, and Nicos Poulantzas. It is a classic case of intellectuals taking in each other's washing. Jessop and his co-authors claim that Hall attributes too much coherence to Thatcherism, credits it with too much success, and too readily accepts that it has broken the old consensus. They doubt that there is much of a coherence and see Thatcherism as a rag-bag of policies serving different groups. Hall in turn asserts that this misunderstands what he said. Professor Julius Gould, in the Minogue essays, fairly claims that the idea of Thatcherism is the product of her opponents and that Marxist intellectuals have 'Thatcher on the brain'. So many of the changes in local government, education, health and even privatisation were the consequences of frustration with earlier reforms rather than a well-worked-out strategy.

This literature has many strengths. Not surprisingly the left is aware of the role of the state, and how Mrs Thatcher has used it. An exercise in reshaping society and restructuring the economy has required an interventionist state. The strong state has been able to weaken the veto of interest groups and reimpose the market on institutions such as local government, engaged in delivering welfare and collective services. Quasi-corporatist bodies such as the NEDC and wages councils have been reduced and privatisation has 'recommodified' parts of the former state sector. Jessop *et al.* (pp.

26–8) are also persuasive in their critique of what they regard as conventional political science. 'Business as usual' studies of public opinion and measures of macro-economic indicators may suggest that not much has changed. But the undoubted changes in policy-making, the role of the state and political representation may not be amenable to such approaches.

Hall and Jacques regard Mrs Thatcher's combination of populism and authoritarianism as mould-breaking. Free-market ideas are fused with 'tough' positions on law and order, patriotism, standards in schools and restrictions on immigration. The programme is populist because it exploits unpopular features of the old consensus. It is authoritarian because of its centralising tendencies. In early 1983 they wrote that Thatcherism should be judged in terms of its success or failure 'in disorganising the labour movement and progressive forces, in shifting the terms of political debate, in reorganising the political terrain and in changing the balance of political forces in favour of capital and the right. In that sense, Thatcherism has already achieved a great deal' (p. 13). 'Thatcherism' was originally coined as a term of abuse by her critics – who identified it with unemployment, monetarism, cuts in services, racism and Cold War rhetoric ('Thatcherism' is now accepted with pride by Mrs Thatcher and her supporters). In 1958 the cartoonist, Vicky, ridiculed Harold Macmillan as 'Supermac'. The joke bounced on him, as Macmillan was widely seen as a successful leader.

How to assess the considerable literature? The policy consensus in terms of the breakdown of the old consensus and the loss of government authority is well covered. The New Right's ideas on the economy and on social ideas have also been analysed, in large part by critics from the centre (Bosanquet) and left (Held and Levitas). But to have effect ideas must be in tune with circumstances. In terms of describing and analysing Tory political strategy and the collapse of the old order, the work of Bulpitt (on the right) and Hall and Jessop *et al.* (on the left) are excellent.

It may be that we think we already know who the supporters of Thatcherism are. It is the deserving versus the undeserving poor, it is the improving working class, 'doers' versus 'shirkers', finance capital over much of manufacturing, home-owners (the middle-class welfare constituency) over council tenants, the private profit-oriented sector over much of the public sector and the south and the suburbs over much of the north and the cities. Among the main institutional losers have been trade unions, local government and public corporations. Electorally, the affluent working-class (Crewe's 'new' working-class which votes two to one Conservative over Labour) and the private sector middle class form the new Tory constituency. The most Thatcherite (in terms of values) of all is the *petty bourgeoisie*, the self-employed, of whom 70 per cent voted Conservative in 1983 and over 60 per cent in 1987. Jessop and his co-authors write of Thatcherism as a Two-Nation strategy, in which 'the productive core of the market economy' is preferred over the rest. It divides Britain according to region, economic sector and social class, directly contradictory to the old Conservative One-Nation approach.

But who are the carriers of the creed, those who are 'one of us', in Mrs Thatcher's terms? In the business world one can point to Sir Hector Laing, Sir Ralph Halpern, Sir Richard Branson, Sir Jeffrey Sterling and Sir Ian McGregor. In the mass media the editors of the Murdoch press, *Telegraph* stable, and the *Express* and *Mail* spring to mind. Among commentators Brian Walden, Paul Johnson and Bruce Anderson write from a sympathetic stance. In the universities it is monetarist economists (Professors Minford, Griffiths and Budd), Roger Scruton and Peterhouse College, Cambridge, who have lent support. More important have been the 'think tanks', such as the CPS, IEA, Adam Smith Institute, Institute of Directors and several groups concentrating on education. A number of familiar names recur across the groups, Graham Mather, at present Director of the Institute of Economic Strategy, has been a Conservative Parliamentary candidate and formerly headed the Policy Unit at the Institute of Directors. David Willetts, at present Director of Studies at the Centre for Policy Studies, has also worked in the Prime Minister's Policy Unit and in the Treasury as private secretary to Nigel Lawson. The groups have floated many schemes on privatisation, deregulation, contracting-out of local services, personal equity plans and the abolition of ILEA. In early 1987, in the wake of Mrs Thatcher's speech on her views of the EC, the Bruges Group was set up. Rather than a federalist EC, Britain should defend a vision of sovereign states co-operating in those areas in which it was mutually advantageous. Professors Stone, Minford, Minogue and Lord Harris were prominent members.

In the United States a particular target of the New Right has been the 'New Class' – the carriers of a liberal, even 'permissive' culture and an anti-government stance. Their British equivalents are found in the largely professional intelligentsia – the education and welfare salariat, local and central bureaucracy, the BBC and the churches. Many of these groups are *merely* talkers, rather than producers, and in contrast to wealth creators are dependent on the state for finance. Mrs Thatcher spoke of the former in March 1985, shortly after Oxford University refused to award her an honorary doctorate: 'They didn't speak with Oxford accents. They hadn't got what people call the 'right' connections; they had just one thing in common. They were men of action'. She returned to this theme in her 1989 Conference speech: she had been to Oxford University and it had not harmed her!

The bulk of the literature is, interestingly, interdisciplinary, drawing on history, sociology, economics and political science. It is also narrowly nationalist, showing little interest in what was happening in other countries. Yet doubts among policy-makers about state ownership and Keynesianism, and the encouragement of market forces were found in many industrial societies, not just in Britain. Finally, academic students can only welcome the degree to which some of the literature reverses one of the major imbalances in political literature – the greater concern with the Labour rather than Conservative Party, even though the latter has been the usual party of government.

If Mrs Thatcher is what she seems, then the literature does not help us to understand why the spirit of 1945 passed by a corner shop in Grantham. An interview with the psychiatrist Anthony Clare, would concentrate on her close relationship with her Methodist lay preacher father and lack of empathy with her mother. Why did she pursue the male-dominated preserves of chemistry, law and politics? The historian John Vincent, in an essay in *Ruling Performance*,[28] edited by Peter Hennessey and Anthony Seldon, notes that hardly anything is known about her reading and thinking between leaving university in 1947 and entering parliament in 1959. Yet the 1950s was the formative decade. What kind of girl escaped from the Grantham grocer's shop and single-mindedly switched from being a research chemist to law, because that was the way to enter politics, and she wanted to get on to get out of Grantham? Her father, Alderman Roberts, was and probably remains a more potent influence on her basic values than Hayek or Friedman. American journalists and political scientists, by contrast, enjoy a greater intimacy with prominent politicians and are better able to deal with such questions of political personality.

Mrs Thatcher was underrated by many before 1975, and again before 1979. In 1975 she was elected as party leader as an *outsider*, overturning the power structure in the party. Many leading Tories were dismissive of her views, her lack of experience and her talents. Until late 1981 they expected (a few feared) that the collective leadership, clearly Heathite and out of sympathy with the thrust of economic policy, and then Whitehall, would tame her. She has confounded them. In 1986, in the wake of Westland, ministers privately stated that Thatcherism was finished, that it would 'never be glad confident . . . again'. By 1989 the ministerial talk of restoring 'the team' approach to decision-making and of the government playing a more prominent role in protecting the environment and manufacturing industry was a thinly veiled attack on Thatcherism. I have often heard it said that, as a person, she is uninteresting (meaning that she holds commonplace views), rude, and that she has been fortunate. Many of her ideas and policies are not original. What is crucial is the political *push*, will, determination and energy which she has provided. There is no doubt that she has been one of the most remarkable figures of our time. She is not a figure *à la* Hitler, Stalin or Mao Tse Tung, who operates in a centralised political system, but in a highly constitutional system and pluralist society. She is not a de Gaulle, creating her own political regime and standing apart from party. The signposts in the textbooks will have to be rewritten. Familiar chapters on local government, the Whitehall bureaucracy, trade unions and social contracts, public corporations, the post-war consensus and the weakness of party government have to be fundamentally revised. That is appropriate, for, as Mrs Thatcher said in one of her typically self-revelatory interviews, she likes to read 'a *fundamental* book'.

NOTES

1. For example, see Anthony King 'Political Overload', *Political Studies*, 1975; Samuel Brittan, 'The Economic Contradictions of Democracy', *British Journal of Political Science*, 1975; and Richard Rose and B. Guy Peters, *Can Government Go Bankrupt?* (London, Macmillan, 1979).
2. Douglas Hurd, *An End to Promises* (London, Collins, 1979); Joel Barnett, *Inside the Treasury* (London, André Deutsch, 1982); Bernard Donoughue, *Prime Minister* (London, Cape, 1987).
3. *Financial Times*, 14 November 1985.

 4. J. Bulpitt, 'The Thatcher Statecraft', *Political Studies*, 1986.
 5. Blackwell, 1983 and 1987.
 6. BBC, 1987.
 7. Cape, 1987.
 8. Macmillan, 1989.
 9. BBC, 1986.
10. Futura, 1985.
11. *Guardian*, 4 February 1985.
12. *Guardian*, 19 September 1987.
13. RKP, 1975–80.
14. Kimber, 1975.
15. Hutchinson, 1978.
16. Macmillan, 1984.
17. OUP, 1986.
18. Wheatsheaf, 1985.
19. Croom Helm, 1985.
20. RIPA, 1985.
21. Heinemann, 1983.
22. Polity Press, 1986.
23. Macmillan, 1987.
24. Chatto and Windus, 1989.
25. Macmillan, 1988.
26. Polity Press, 1988.
27. Verso, 1989.
28. Blackwell, 1987.

6 Must Labour Lose – Again?*

Party systems are not immutable and parties are not immortal. Who now remembers the RPF, the largest party in France in 1951; the Whigs, a party of government in early nineteenth-century England; or the Federalists, a force in the United States? Parties emerge from complex patterns of social structure (divisions based on class, religion, region and language), formative events or crises in a nation's history, sudden increases in the size of the electorate, or changes in the electoral system. Yet the continuity of parties as institutions in Western states is still impressive. This is in spite of the post-1945 changes in the form of the decline of agriculture and spread of industrialism then the shift to post-industrial economies and the embourgeoisement of society. Successful parties are adaptive, able to outlive the social conditions and issues which attended their birth.

Before 1918 the British party system was dominated by the Liberals and Conservatives, and the Irish Nationalists constituted a large third force. The demand for Home Rule for Ireland not only divided the two major parties, it split the Liberals and at times threatened to paralyse the political system. At the time the Labour Party was small and insignificant. Britain still had a restricted male electorate and the major issues concerned religion and clashes between centre and periphery (Scotland and Wales were solidly Liberal against the English Conservatives, and Ireland apart from Ulster was solidly Nationalist). But after 1918 the withdrawal of twenty-six counties of Ireland (and with it a predominantly peasant, rural-based and Catholic electorate), the splits in and decline of the Liberals, and the achievement of universal suffrage paved the way for Labour/Conservative hegemony and a class-based party system. In spite of massive social and economic changes, the economic depression of the 1930s, the 1939–45 war, and the turnover of the electorate, the system is essentially the same seventy years later.

* This chapter was specially written for this volume.

90

REALIGNMENT

Realignment is an American concept to explain turning-points in the party system. It refers, variously, to a change in the party system in the sense of there being an enduring shift in the balance of strength between the parties, or the emergence of new parties. It may also cover changes in the social or regional bases of parties. Realigning elections are often associated with intense division within the parties or an increase in electoral participation. The present Republican/Democratic party system emerged from the Civil War of 1860–5. The Republicans represented the emerging forces in America – capital, manufacturing industry, the North and the Federal government – in a word, modernisation. The party dominated Presidential and Congressional elections until 1932. The disillusionment with the economic depression and the Republican President, Herbert Hoover, made that a critical or realigning election. The depression and F.D. Roosevelt's skill in adding the big cities, ethnic groups and the labour movement to the white South helped to make the Democrats the new majority party. Between 1932 and 1964 the party lost only two presidential elections.

Since then, the passing of the New Deal generation, the loss of the white southern votes, social change and the growth in economic power and voting strength of the 'sun-belt' states have reversed that Democratic dominance at presidential level. There were bitter divisions within the Democratic Party over Vietnam, race, and law and order. George Wallace was a third-party candidate in 1968 and attracted significant white support in the South. The Republicans have won five of the last six presidential elections, and commentators have wondered whether the United States might be undergoing another realignment. In fact no new party has emerged, and for all the Republican dominance at presidential level, this has not been reflected in comparable Republican strength in state and congressional elections. Commentators are now more inclined to write of a dealignment or a shifting away from the parties.

In Britain there have been tremors in the electorate that suggested there might be a significant change in the system. In 1974 there was an upsurge of support for the Liberals (from 7 per cent in 1970 to 19 per cent in February 1974) in England, and the Nationalists in Scotland (from 11 per cent in 1970 to 30 per cent in October 1974). Both had faded away by 1979. In 1981 the break-away from the Labour party resulted in the formation of the SDP, and, for a time, the Liberal – SDP Alliance seemed to be poised for a break-through. In the 1983 election the Alliance, with 25 per cent of the vote, nearly overtook Labour (27 per cent). In 1987 it failed to consolidate but nevertheless ended with 22 per cent compared to Labour's 30 per cent. That was about the only battle which Labour won – for second place.

The normal 90 per cent of the vote which the two parties gained in post-war elections has fallen steadily – to 73 per cent in 1987. What is equally telling is that if the two party aggregate vote had fallen to 75 per cent in February 1974, it has hovered there since. Yet the two parties still command some 95 per cent of the seats in the House of Commons. In effect, the two main parties were protected by the disproportional first-past-the-post electoral system. After the 1987 election the Liberal and Social Democrat leaders quarrelled bitterly and abandoned the Alliance. The window of opportunity for realignment closed – for the time being at least.

A split within one of the two major parties is still the likeliest means of producing a change in the party system. Essentially, splits arise from disagreement among elites. The split in the Conservative party over Peel's repeal of the Corn Laws in 1846 kept the party out of power for a generation. Joseph Chamberlain's break from Gladstone over Home Rule in 1885 had virtually the same exclusionary effect on the Liberals. The split between Asquith and Lloyd George in 1916 was one among other factors that precipitated the decline of the Liberal party. In 1981 a Gang of Four acted and then found popular support. That was surely important in keeping Labour unelectable in the 1980s.

LABOUR IN DECLINE

The other possible pathway to change is that a party gradually declines, as a result of adverse social and cultural trends; its social base gets smaller and its message appeals to fewer voters. In a late industrial society there is a shift from employment in manufacturing to services and from blue-collar to white-collar occupations. Such a change obviously produces electoral problems for a party of the working class. There is evidence for this above all in the decline of the French Communists. One can see how such a change also connects with the decline of the British Labour Party. The facts of its electoral downturn are not in dispute. Yet the total 'Left' vote in Western

Europe has hardly altered in the past forty or fifty years or in the 1980s, in spite of the decline of the idea of state socialism. The problem is therefore unique to the British Labour Party. For all the talk of the decline of the two-party system, the greater part of the erosion has been suffered by Labour. Compared with the 1950s and 1960s, its average vote in the last five general elections (February 1974 to 1987) has dropped by 10 per cent, and the Conservatives by only 3 per cent. In the ten elections since 1951 its electoral record has been one of steady erosion, punctuated in three elections by an occasional and short-lived recovery. Compared to 1959, its share of the electorate is down by more than a third. This has produced a significant imbalance in support for the Conservative and Labour Parties, which is exaggerated in seats in the House of Commons. In the last three general elections (1979–87) the Conservative lead over Labour in share of votes has averaged 11 per cent.

The thesis of secular decline of the party would not have surprised Sidney Webb. After all he believed in the inevitability of gradualness, though in a socialist direction. Addressing the 1923 Labour conference, he extrapolated from the voting trends, 'from the rising curve of Labour votes', the party would get a majority in 1926.

What is interesting is that Labour's prospects seemed so good for so long. In 1969 the landmark electoral study, *Political Change in Britain*, by David Butler and Donald Stokes, was published. The book explored the ageing of the post-1918 class alignment, demonstrating how Labour was becoming more and more a majority party. The authors showed how this class alignment had reached its height in the late 1940s, but was still operating. The aggregate effects of the growth of the working class, the inheritance for many young voters of parental party loyalties, and the dying off of predominantly Conservative old voters were working in favour of Labour. At the time one Conservative strategist described his party's problems as: 'Death, Youth and the Working-Class'.

The dominant policy assumptions in the 1960s also helped Labour. The role of government in promoting employment and welfare and in managing the economy was expanding in most industrial states. Progressive taxation and welfare were seen as forces promoting greater equality. After 1945 Conservative leaders accepted that history was moving in a social-democratic direction. The party could still win elections but it had to work harder to do so, as the balance of advantage was turning against it. The Conservative Party needed good luck, a poor performance by Labour, or differential turn-out between supporters of the two parties to overcome its demographic disadvantages. In the 1964 and 1966 elections Butler and Stokes found Labour leads of 5 per cent and 11 per cent respectively, when voters were asked which party they identified with. Labour identifiers still outnumbered Conservatives in 1970, though the Conservatives won the election.

A party's response to a series of election defeats is crucial and may lead to changes in the political agenda. Turning-points in the shape of a political agenda are often decided by the outcome. For a few years after 1931 Labour moved sharply left, after 1959 it backpedalled on Clause IV, and after 1979 it moved left again. In the wake of defeat, party strategists have to distinguish between the adverse short-term influences on the electorate (leaders, policies, issues and evaluation of the government record) and the long-term factors. Some Labour optimists discern no trend in the last three election reverses: they regard the defeats as one-off occurrences. In a party whose internal culture is inherently anti-authority, leadership failures are an easy target. Labour's electoral debacle in 1931 could be explained by the leadership's betrayal. The third successive election defeat in 1959 could be explained by social change and the prosperity which worked to the benefit of the Conservative government of the day. The defeats in 1979 and 1983 could be explained by the incompetence of, first, the Labour government and, then, the Labour opposition. In 1987 prosperity again virtually guaranteed a Tory victory.

Sometimes the losing party moves in the direction of the new majority party. In the United States a run of electoral defeats forced the Republicans to accept the New Deal. In 1959 the German Social Democrats, having lost three successive elections, dumped their Marxist baggage at Bad Godesburg. In Britain the Conservatives chose to regard the 1945 election defeat not as a one-off but as a token of more enduring change. They decided to accept the Attlee settlement.

The trick is to know what the voters want − apart from peace and prosperity. In a competitive party system the majority of voters are always right. Parties now have an array of PR techniques and opinion polls to help them gain insights into electoral preferences and also to tailor messages to those concerned.

Since 1979 Labour has faced growing problems of adjusting to a changed electoral situation. Some will say that Labour has been here before – in 1959. Then the party leaders were analysing the significance of a third successive election defeat. Labour's vote had fallen from 49 per cent in 1951 to 44 per cent in 1959 and the party had done particularly badly in the New Towns and affluent working-class areas. Many commentators regarded Labour's continued electoral decline as largely inevitable. The 1960 Penguin special *Must Labour Lose?*, by Mark Abrams and Richard Rose, showed that the party was widely regarded as old-fashioned, the party of the cloth cap, with which fewer voters identified. The electoral crisis coincided with (some would claim was caused by) an ideological crisis. Anthony Crosland, in *The Future of Socialism*, argued that the economy was no longer suitable for 1918 or 1945 forms of Clause IV. Larger firms, on the whole, were serving the nation well: the state had many levers with which to make them behave in a socially responsible way. State ownership was irrelevant as a means. The goal of Socialism should be to promote greater equality.

The contraction of the working class, increase in home ownership and spread of the symbols of affluence (televisions, washing machines, cars and foreign holidays) apparently weakened the sense of working-class solidarity and identification with Labour. Because those trends would continue, it was held, Labour was doomed. The survey was the occasion for a classic left v right battle in the party. Which would best promote electoral advance – more socialism or its dilution, and should Labour anyway regard that as a priority? The Labour leader Hugh Gaitskell tried to free the party from its commitment to sweeping Clause IV style nationalisation. The left attacked the findings and interpretations of the survey because it saw them as an attack on the party's core values and policies. Barbara Castle told the 1959 conference that the party's ethics were too high minded for the voters.

The left seemed to be vindicated, however, when the voters did not play the role mapped out for them by the sociologists. Labour went on to win four of the next five general elections. The revisionists felt vindicated because Labour made an appeal across social classes and identified itself with the theme of modernisation more successfully that the Conservatives under Harold Macmillan or Sir Alec Douglas-Home. Labour could adjust to social change. Under Harold Wilson it looked, for a time, like the natural party of government. Wilson was for a while the British John F. Kennedy – before becoming Labour's Stanley Baldwin!

Labour optimists may point to that experience as a warning

against the gloomy extrapolations from present social and demographic changes. It is worth noting, however, that Labour's post-
1959 election victories were hardly convincing. The 1964 and October
1974 elections were won by a whisker, and in February 1974 the
party actually had fewer votes than the Conservatives. Surveys
showed that even in 1974 many Labour supporters were out of
sympathy with the party's policies of extending public ownership,
increasing trade-union rights and boosting state spending on the
social services. Class and tradition were still the main sources of the
party's appeal, as well as the sheer incompetence of the Conservative
government in 1974. But none of these could be guaranteed to last.

Social change since 1959 has made Labour's position much less
favourable. Then the manual working class was a majority of the
electorate: now it is less than half. In 1959 62 per cent of the
working class voted Labour: in 1987 the figure fell to 42 per cent.
Where 40 per cent were home-owners in 1959, the figures is now
66 per cent. The lead on party identification has been reversed. In
1983 and 1987 Conservative identifiers outnumbered Labour (by 38
per cent to 32 per cent and 36 per cent to 31 per cent).

More important is that the political position in 1987 was very
different from 1959. In 1959 Labour was the only alternative to the
Conservatives, and the Liberals got a miserable 6 per cent of the
vote. In 1987 the Alliance finished second in two-thirds of
Conservative seats, largely in the south. Labour was no longer the
only home for anti-Tory voters. In 1959 Labour's vote was a mere
5 per cent behind the Conservatives, today it is 11 per cent behind.

The social trends and political weaknesses identified after 1959
have been consolidated. The main growth in Conservative support
has been among what Professor Ivor Crewe calls 'the new working-
class', manual workers who live in the south, are home-owners,
work in the private sector and are not members of trade unions.
The scale of Labour's electoral decline and its loss of working-class
support has no parallel in any other West European socialist party.
Must Labour Lose? looked even more persuasive in 1987 than in
1959.

ROAD TO RECOVERY

A number of strategies have been canvassed to try to reverse the apparently inevitable. One is to accept that reliance on class politics does not offer a route to electoral success and that the party therefore needs to identify with a more widely defined constituency of the deprived and neglected. Some invoke the experience of Ken Livingstone of the now deceased GLC, and call for policies which appeal to a coalition of minorities, defined on race, gender and sexual preferences – a so-called 'rainbow coalition'. Such policies, however, have identified Labour in London and elsewhere with the 'loony left' and alienated voters. The policies and personalities associated with that strategy made Labour appear extreme and sectional. In 1987 London was the only city in which Labour lost ground to the Conservatives. In other words, the strategy risks alienating existing Labour support and has plainly scared off potential voters.

A second strategy is for Labour to build on its existing strength and regard 9 million votes in 1987 as votes for socialism. Eric Heffer, for example, makes great play with the swings to Labour in his Liverpool Walton constituency and other Liverpool seats. He sees this as vindication of the Militant Liverpool city council's strategy of defending services and resisting the Conservative government. Recent elections have seen a steady swing to Labour in Scotland, the inner cities and the North, and a steady worsening of its position in the south. The trend has increased in the last three elections. The cumulative party swings from Conservative to Labour in seats in the north of Britain between 1955 and 1987 is 8.6 per cent: in the south the swing is 8.9 per cent *from* Labour to Conservative. The problem with this approach is that it targets the declining areas as Labour's constituency.

It is unlikely, however, that further gains among the working-class will give Labour the extra 3 million votes for the 100 seats necessary for it to gain a majority in Parliament. Three-quarters of Labour's 229 MPs after the 1987 election already sit for seats in North Britain and Wales; 80 per cent of the party's vote already comes from the working-class. The 1983 election survey, *How Britain Votes*, by Heath, Jowell and Curtice, has also suggested that Labour should try to become a more successful working-class party by fighting on working-class issues of redistribution and social justice. The authors believe that 'unrealised potentials for class action may remain within the working-class'. The question remains, in an increasingly bourgeois society – how?

A third strategy is to admit that the game is up. Such a call comes from some of the new Marxist writers found in the journal *Marxism Today*. Professor Eric Hobsbawm in 1978 had already arrived at such a conclusion in *The Forward March of Labour Halted*, on the basis of Labour's long-term electoral decline and the adverse social changes. Both have become even more pronounced since 1978. The left, according to Hobsbawm, had captured the Labour Party when it ceased to be a viable contender for government. Labour, therefore, needs to look beyond itself; it needs to become a party of social reform, part of a progressive alliance. It has to form alliances and electoral pacts with other sympathetic parties, notably the centre parties, in some sort of anti-Thatcher coalition. It has to increase its support among those employed in the public sector, heavily dependent on state-funded services, concerned by the threat to the environment from unregulated enterprises, and women (in recent elections Labour has done badly among women). To the neglected, deprived, trade unions and working-class must be added the frustrated.

The abrupt destruction of the Alliance and decline of the post-Alliance parties after 1987 has increased the appeal of a fourth strategy with the restoration of two-party politics. Labour for the first time since the break-away in 1981 is the sole credible alternative party of government. Labour will have to play down its distinctive ties with the organised working-class and trade unions. The party's 1989 policy review has made friendly noises about the benefits of the free market, acknowledged the need for economic incentives, dropped unilateralism and promised a prudent attitude to public spending. This is an electoral strategy which seeks votes across the board and emphasises non-divisive issues of good public services, investment in training and environmental protections.

WHAT KIND OF PARTY?

Labour's name, origins and culture are inseparable from the trades unions. In Europe only in Belgium and Britain did the unions found political parties. The Labour Party is dependent on the unions for finance, and the unions dominate its decision-making institutions. At times the relationship has been a fruitful one for the Parliamentary leaders. Usually the unions kept clear of 'political' issues and expected the politicans to leave industrial relations issues to the unions. For many years the union block vote was wheeled out at conference to hammer the left wing in the PLP and constituency parties. In 1974 Labour's apparent ability to get on with the union leaders, particularly to coax them into wages moderation, helped to get it elected.

But there were costs from this close relationship. A Labour government in the 1970s was warned off many areas – statutory incomes policy, action against restrictive practices in industry, legislation to limit industrial action in the public sector – and induced to pursue some foolish policies. Yet the alleged power of the unions was more accurately described by Peter Jenkins, a political commentator, as the Social Democratic Dilemma. He posed the question: how was the Labour movement to reconcile the political objectives of the trade unions, that is, the maintenance of full employment, the welfare state, and stable prices with its industrial objective of free collective bargaining? In 1942, J. A. Schumpeter, while anticipating the eventual displacement of capitalism by socialism, had noted that 'the real problem' for socialism would be the position of organised labour. He wrote: 'A government that means to socialise to any great extent, will have to socialise the trade union. And as things actually are, labour is of all things the most difficult to socialise'.[1]

The stability of the union–party relationship was threatened after 1964, as Labour governments increasingly interfered with the unions' cherished free collective bargaining. Labour governments sought to make unions their partners in regulating wages. This process reached its peak in the 'social contract' of the 1974–79 Labour government. In the end the union leaders could not deliver the consent of their members. British trade unions were too decentralised – power was on the shop-floor – to cope with the corporatist style which Labour governments sought.

The miners' year-long strike in 1984–5 was a return to an old tradition – one that it was thought had died with the General Strike. Scargill never disguised his belief that the miners would be the shock troops to overturn capitalism. The struggle would radicalise the miners and force other unions to take sides – against the Thatcher government. He also never disguised that the strike was not against British Coal but against the government. The strike actually embarrassed many Labour leaders and trade unionists; many refused to choose between Scargill and Thatcher.

The precise nature of the party – union connections looks sure to change in the next few years. As the workforce changes its character, the unions no longer organise the majority of employees, and Labour has to broaden its base and move away from its 'macho' image, so the party may prefer to loosen the ties. The unions' dominance at the annual party conference and in the NEC has meant that the party's politics can shift in response to changes in the unions' policy positions. Often the unions' policies have been decided after perfunctory participation by the members. The block vote accentuates the influence of the big unions. Thus Ron Todd, backed by 1 million plus votes of the Transport and General Workers' Union, could veto changes in Labour's defence policy in 1988. It is virtually certain that in the next few years the power of the unions at the annual conference will be significantly reduced.

In the 1970s there emerged a more radical Labour left in urban local government. In London, Manchester, Liverpool and Sheffield, local Labour leaders used their powers in the town hall to practise local socialism. Many of them have been socialised in local community organisation and trade unions, are full-time politicians, and rely on attendance allowances or employment in neighbouring local authorities or public sector trade unions (a 'public service' class). In control, they have taken initiatives in establishing units and support groups for gay rights, womens' rights, race relations, generally campaigning against 'the cuts', and monitoring the local police. The commitment by this new left to a seemingly endless cycle of political activity, campaigning and organising has radicalised Labour and local government. Over the past decade local government has lost many powers over spending and policy and is increasingly by-passed as a provider of local services – in housing, education and development. It is therefore interesting, though not surprising, that Labour, so long a party of centralisation, has discovered the advantages of decentralisation. It now favours the devolution of powers for regional and local authorities – particularly in the north of Britain where it is strong.

LABOUR'S STRENGTH

Some might argue that Labour has been unlucky in recent years; it has suffered from the combination of a number of misfortunes. Thatcherism has won the 1980s by default – the product of ineptitude and division among the opposition parties and the electoral system. Labour's task, they say, remains one of mobilising its natural electoral majority. It can do this by improving its image and its performance. For a number of years now, surveys, notably the *British Social Attitudes* surveys, have demonstrated that Thatcherism has failed to win the hearts and minds of the British people. Though the surveys show widespread approval of the sale of council houses and measures to regulate trade unions, such evidence was available before 1979. There is also support for some aspects of the enterprise culture – approval of profits and small businesses and the widespread wish to work for oneself. By large majorities the Conservatives are regarded as the best party for promoting living standards.

But if one turns to the support for such policies as tax cuts and further privatisation (particularly of water and electricity), then the public has turned against the Thatcher government's policies. Professor Ivor Crewe has recently combed the opinion polls and election surveys and negatively answered the question in his title,'*Has the Electorate become Thatcherite?*'[2] Support for the welfare state and redistribution of income has moved even further to the left since 1979. In 1979 50 per cent thought that welfare benefits had gone 'too far', compared to 13 per cent who thought they had not gone far enough. By 1987 only 17 per cent thought the benefits had gone 'too far', compared to 54 per cent who thought they did not go far enough. In 1979 the public was evenly divided between those who wanted to cut taxes, even if this meant reducing spending on health, education and welfare, and those who wanted to expand spending on services, even if this meant increasing taxes. By 1987 only 10 per cent favoured the tax-cutting options against 71 per cent who wanted more state spending on the services. The Thatcher case for cutting taxes and public spending was partly economic – such spending was regarded as a drag on the productive sector and a hinderance to enterprise – as well as moral, in that these policies would promote personal responsibility and freedom. The Thatcher government has made the reduction of inflation its main economic goal. Gallup, however, has found that by overwhelming majorities the public in the 1980s has wanted the government to pay greater attention to reducing unemployment than curbing inflation.

Such evidence is of course surprising in view of the election results. It may be that values, or at least these values, may not be

important for voting behaviour. John Curtice, one of the Social
Attitudes authors, has made the point that voting in the 1987 general
election was strongly affected by the voters' economic valuations of
the parties. That is not surprising. If the Conservative electoral
success has been largely founded upon the prosperity, then such
support is conditional, and the party may be vulnerable to an
economic downturn.

Another perspective on the survey evidence is to say that many
of the above attitudes may be important but that Labour has been
widely viewed as less competent than the Conservatives and this
has been crucial. At the end of the day people may doubt that
Labour will be able to deliver the improvements in services. Perhaps
parties do not have much to do with values anyway. Many voters
may support a political party out of instrumental or economic
interest reasons. Alternatively, perhaps the survey questions do not
tap values at all. Values are supposed to be deep, enduring and
likely to influence voting behaviour. It is, for example, interesting
that when surveys rephrase the tax and public service question and
ask which matters more to 'you and your family', the response is
rather different. Whereas there is support for the idea of spending
more money *in general* on public services as opposed to cuts in
taxes, more people actually prefer the tax cuts when the question
asks which is best for 'themselves and their families'. There are
problems with questions about issues pitched at a general level,
asked in isolation and questions about tax cuts versus cuts in
spending suffer from offering unpriced trade-offs. The public's
response to a question about economic priorities − curbing inflation
versus reducing unemployment – may tell us more about which
indicator is more salient to voters at the time. For much of the
1970s voters were more concerned about double digit inflation than
relatively low unemployment. In the 1980s, as unemployment soared
and inflation was contained, so unemployment moved to the top of
voters' concerns.

Yet, however qualified, the above evidence of the limited support
for some aspects of Thatcherism is useful in warning us against
being too deterministic about the social trends. Some psephologists
suggest that only about a third of the 13 per cent fall in the Labour
vote between 1964 and 1987 can be explained by social changes.
One has therefore to look elsewhere for a fuller explanation. One
can point to some of the Thatcher government's successes – Falklands
and increased prosperity – and the support of the tabloid press. But

a large part of that explanation must rest in the hands of the Labour Party itself – the choices and policies of its leaders, the performance of the last Labour government and the party's negative image.

Comparison with the fortunes of the left in Western Europe are encouraging for Labour, but also chastening. In the recessionary 1970s most governments were turned out at elections or saw their share of electoral support fall. The misery index (the combined percentages of unemployment and inflation) reached new heights. The 1980s have seen some shift to the political right in the United States and West Germany. But the Socialist share of the vote has hardly changed over the two decades in Austria, Scandinavia, West Germany and Italy. It has increased substantially in France and Spain, and Labour governments have been re-elected in New Zealand and Australia. Only in Britain has the fall in popular support for the left been substantial. Indeed the scale of decline for such a major party of government is virtually unparalleled in any other state in post-war Western Europe.

It is worth adding that, compared to other Socialist parties, Labour has not been handicapped by the opposition to or suspicion of the left by a powerful Catholic Church (as in some West European states), or divided by a powerful communist movement in party politics and in trade unions (as in France and Italy). Moreover, because of the first-past-the-post electoral system and the predominantly two-party system, it has been almost uniquely able to form a government of its own.

Elsewhere socialist parties have had to compete in multi-party and proportional electoral systems and usually share power in government. The question that such analysis suggests is, why has Labour done so badly? Perhaps other parties, simply because they have lacked the British Labour Party's advantages, have necessarily had to be more adaptable and willing to make alliances. More socialism does not seem to be an answer. Apart from Sweden, where the normal governing Social Democrats have achieved a position of virtual hegemony, socialism seems to be in retreat. In France, Mitterrand has abandoned his socialist experiments of 1981: 'We were dreamers then', he explained. Labour governments in Australia and New Zealand have had to pursue a series of economic and social policies that are not too dissimilar from those that Mrs Thatcher's government has pursued since 1979.

The good news for Labour, from a comparative survey, is that such features as wider home ownership, affluence and the *embourgeoisement* of the working class are not necessarily electorally adverse. Perhaps the key distinction is less between left and right than between the 'old' and 'new' Labour Party. 'Old' Labour is associated – negatively for much of the public – with manufacturing industry, union power, inner cities, council housing and in general with the declining forces in Britain. It is on the new issues, such as the environment, training, citizenship and women's rights – as well as public services – which centre left parties elsewhere have scored. Democratic socialist parties can still thrive in prosperous societies, but only if they can shake off their identification with ideologies and interests that no longer appeal.

NOTES

1. *Socialism, Capitalism and Democracy*, p.x.
2. In R. Skidelsky (ed.), *Thatcherism* (London: Chatto and Windus, 1988).

7 Ideology, Sociology and Labour's Strategy*

There is no doubt that the work of John Goldthorpe deservedly commands attention among economists and political scientists, as well as among sociologists. His work is characterised by a concern to define key concepts rigorously, address major substantive problems and to link empirical research with significant issues of theory. He has also shown a refreshing willingness to relate his work to issues which cross disciplinary boundaries. He and his various collaborators have made a major contribution to the study of social class, particularly in clarifying concepts and testing fashionable ideas by empirical research. Not much of Goldthorpe's work on social class addresses itself primarily to political behaviour. Where it does, it is mainly concerned with the nature of change in the working-class and its political implications for the Labour Party.

This chapter is not concerned with the question of whether social class has declined in importance as a shaper of electoral choice. The literature is already immense and I regard the evidence as conclusive and affirmative. Rather, I wish to examine critically Goldthorpe's contribution to the debate. This chapter will consider, first, the work of Goldthorpe on the affluent working class and his recommendations for the Labour Party, and then his recent work on social mobility and, again, his recommendations for Labour.

It is possible to discern a remarkable consistency in Goldthorpe's work on class and political behaviour from *The Affluent Worker* in 1968 to the second edition of *Social Mobility and Social Structure in Modern Britain* in 1987. Three persistent themes are worth noting.:

1 Suggestions of a change in the working class are much exaggerated – be it affluence leading to *embourgeoisement* (or workers becoming middle class in life style, values, or voting Conservative), the reduced propensity of the working-class to vote Labour, the increased rates of social mobility in twentieth-century Britain

* This chapter was specially written for this volume.

proving that Britain is now a more 'open' society, or the working-class acceptance of the 'fairness' of many of the social and economic outcomes in a capitalist society. Goldthorpe has pointed out the shortcomings in these claims and the lack of supporting evidence. He has been an effective demolisher of much conventional wisdom about social structure and political behaviour.

2 Despite the sharp reduction in the size of the manual working-class and in Labour's electoral strength, Labour should not pursue 'the middle ground' or de-emphasise its class orientation. Goldthorpe has consistently argued that by promoting radical egalitarian policies Labour may mobilise a larger electoral coalition.

3 Much discussion of the relationship between social structure and political behaviour has been marred by a 'reverse sociologism', i.e. the tendency to move from the analysis of political events and trends to supposed changes in social structure and processes 'which, it is believed, the events and tendencies must betoken' (Goldthorpe 1987, p. 347). Goldthorpe claims that analyses, particularly by political scientists, of *embourgeoisement* in the early 1960s, of 'class dealignment' in the 1980s and of the consequent decline of Labour as a working-class party, have taken this form. He finds the work of many political scientists on voting behaviour careless, value-laden and technically deficient. They do not meet the Goldthorpe standard.

AFFLUENCE AND LABOUR'S DECLINE

From 1962, in various journal articles and, subsequently, in book form, Goldthorpe and David Lockwood exposed a number of shortcomings in the thesis of *embourgeoisement*. In 1951, 1955 and 1959 the Labour Party had lost three successive general elections, the last two with a reduced share of the vote. The party had done particularly badly in the New Towns and among prosperous workers. A number of commentators argued at the time that because white-collar employment was increasing and the manual working-class was declining in size, then Labour, as the party of that class, would decline with it. It was also claimed that the spread to working-class families of home-ownership and other symbols of affluence would weaken their class consciousness and their propensity to vote Labour. Broader social changes seemed to 'fit' Labour's electoral decline. Although Goldthorpe and Lockwood made a number of pointed observations on the logical and empirical shortcomings of the original *embourgeoisement* thesis, the idea became increasingly important in Labour's internal debates about electoral strategy, policy and political leadership. Revisionism, until then a strategy for managing capitalism rather than replacing it with public ownership, became a strategy for satisfying working-class hopes of middle-class styles of consumption. By implication, the Labour Party had to become a 'catch-all' party rather than one oriented to the working-class, industrial trade unions and council estates.

The Goldthorpe and Lockwood survey of Luton car-assembly workers in 1963 was a *critical* case to test the thesis. Such workers, at the time, were regarded as excellent examples of the newly affluent workers. The authors drew attention to three of their findings. The first was that workers on higher incomes did not adopt middle-class values and middle-class friends. In other words, one had to distinguish the economic from the relational and normative aspects of *embourgeoisement*. Goldthorpe and Lockwood discovered, secondly, a very high level of Labour voting among their sample. At 80 per cent it was appreciably higher than national levels of Labour voting among the C2 workers at the time, 60–65 per cent. These affluent workers were not defecting from Labour. Thirdly, they found no trend to increased Conservative voting in recent elections among their sample of workers. The thesis of *embourgeoisement* was therefore more complex and even doubtful in the light of the Luton study; and when Labour won the 1964 and 1966 general elections, that apparently refuted the claims about *embourgeoisement* and Labour's decline.

But before awarding game, set and match to the affluent worker study, one should enter some reservations. The term *embourgeoisement* was indeed stretched by commentators in the 1960s to encompass a variety of allegedly interrelated features, including higher levels of prosperity for workers, weakening loyalty to Labour, growth of white-collar employment and decline of manual work, and the integration of the working-class into society or the weakening intensity of its loyalty to Labour. One may regret that the term had different usages but it is worth noting that Goldthorpe and Lockwood are tackling only one aspect of the *embourgeoisement* case, namely that prosperous workers are less likely to vote Labour. It can be seen from Table 7.1 that the electoral decline of Labour was only halted, not reversed. Except for the 1966 election Labour has never again come near to reaching the 44.1 per cent it gained

Table 7.1 Labour's share of the
vote in general elections, 1945–87

Year	%
1945	48.3
1950	46.1
1951	48.8
1955	46.4
1959	43.8
1964	44.1
1966	47.9
1970	43.0
1974 (Feb)	37.1
1974 (Oct)	39.2
1979	37.0
1983	27.6
1987	30.8

Source: D. Butler and D. Kavanagh, *The British General Election
of 1987* (London, Macmillan,
1988), p. 283.

then. Labour managed to win the 1964 and 1966 general elections
in defiance of the advice of Goldthorpe and Lockwood, which was
to appeal to the working-class. The landmark survey study by Butler
and Stokes (1969) showed that Labour gained by conveying the
impression of being more 'new' and 'modern' than the Conservatives.
The rhetoric of Labour leaders, particularly of Harold Wilson in
1964 and 1966, was addressed to all classes, and the party's
programme was based on its plan for economic growth and greater
efficiency. Butler and Stokes also found that the major swings to
Labour between the 1964 and 1966 general elections were among
those who felt their economic positions had improved under the
Labour government (p. 405).

The Luton study may also have oversold its findings. The authors
claim: 'The most important single fact to emerge relating to the
politics of the affluent workers we studied was that the large
majorities were, and generally had been, Labour supporters . . . a
notable feature was the *stability* of Labour support.[2] The year in
which the interviews was conducted (1963) was the worst in terms
of public standing for the Conservative party since regular opinion

polls were conducted after 1945. The party was running between ten and fifteen points behind Labour throughout the year and was dogged by the Profumo scandal and divisions over the leadership. This makes it all the more surprising that, in spite of Labour's national popularity in 1963, the Luton study finds that Labour voting among the sample actually fell from 83 per cent in 1955 to 79 per cent in 1963 (Crewe, 1973, p. 32). All the indications would lead one to expect it to have increased.

One of the most striking claims of the study was that a gradual change from *proletarian traditionalism* to *instrumentalism* among workers was taking place. The former, often found in such industries as mining, shipbuilding and docking, is described as voting Labour on the basis of class loyalty, and *instrumentalism* is described as voting Labour on the basis of personal self-interest (Goldthorpe *et al*, 1968, pp 74−80). If *embourgeoisement* was not occurring then, it was claimed, this subtle shift in orientation was. In fact such a shift was included in some of the statements of *embourgeoisement*, which Goldthorpe had attacked. However, neither the distinction nor the *evidence* for the shift are persuasive. As Heath, Jowell and Curtice observe, class loyalty itself may rest on self-interest (1985, p. 9). Indeed many of the responses in the Luton sample show that workers offer a mix of both instrumental and traditional reasons for voting Labour. The evidence for such instrumentalism in the study is anyway hardly conclusive. The authors point to the widespread disapproval among their sample of the party's link with the trade unions as well as the support for the unions' role in gaining workplace benefits (rather than promoting wider social and political change) and the belief that a Labour government is more likely than a Conservative one to provide benefits. The authors claim that such mixed views would 'tend to undermine a genuinely "labour" orientation − or, at least do not readily co-exist with a radical and highly partisan political outlook' (1969, p. 177).

In fact such a statement is more of a very loose interpretation of the data than an actual finding. It is also worth noting that such instrumentalism among the working-class was widely found among the contemporary studies of deferential working-class Conservatives by McKenzie and Silver, by Nordlinger, and in the *Must Labour Lose?* survey (by Abrams and Rose).

POLITICAL AND ELECTORAL STRATEGY: WHAT
SHOULD LABOUR DO?

When working-class parties have performed poorly at the polls,
there have usually been two internal reactions. One (usually on the
right of the party) has been to claim that the party should move to
the 'middle ground' and dilute policies which are regarded as
extremist or sectional. Usually this has meant qualifying or abandoning socialist policies and presenting itself as a national rather than
a class party. The other reaction (usually on the left) has called for
greater socialism, or a programme which advances the interests of
the working-class. After the 1959 election defeat and again after the
election losses since 1979, the working-class-based Labour Party has
faced the problems of coping with socioeconomic change which
appears to weaken support for the party. Should it adapt to such
change (and presumably seek the elusive middle ground) or should
it try even harder to educate the electorate to its socialist values?

John Goldthorpe has argued from the second standpoint in the
debates about Labour's electoral strategy in the early 1960s and
1980s. On the first occasion the growth of affluence was a central
plank of the school of commentators and politicans who envisaged
the end of ideology and a decline of class politics, propositions
which Goldthorpe has rejected. Many of the same themes have
been voiced again in the 1980s, in the wake of the steady decline
in the size of the manual working-class and of Labour's electoral
following. On both occasions Goldthorpe (and co-authors) have
rejected the middle ground strategy. Instead, they have emphasised
the opportunities for creative political leadership which may offset
any adverse social trends:

> that is, to purposive action on the part of elites and organisations,
> aimed at giving a specific and politically relevant meaning to
> grievances, demands and aspirations, which have hitherto been
> of a sub-political kind, and thus mobilising support for a
> programme of movement (1969, p. 189).

Goldthorpe has consistently emphasised active political choice over
passive social determinism, and argued that Labour leaders should
follow a left-wing strategy rather than a centrist one. Thus, 'Far
from reflecting, as is often claimed, a hard-headed recognition of
"the end of ideology", the strategy of winning the middle ground

must been seen as being in fact inspired as much by ideology as by sociology' (1969, p. 191). Ideas of *embourgeoisement* have been a convenient and plausible legitimation for the strategy. Goldthorpe *et al* also argued that Labour should reject 'the – essentially Conservative – doctrine that the efficient management of the economy is the key to electoral success (p.193). That was the enemy's terrain. Instead the party should fight on a radical, egalitarian and class-based programme. It should have a commitment . . . to the interests of the mass of wage-earning, rank-and-file employees, and an endeavour to advance these interests not merely by promoting general economic expansion but also by thorough-going egalitarian measures over a wide-front' (p. 193).

Three points about the recommended strategy are worth making. First, there was hardly any evidence in the Luton survey, or other surveys for that matter, that a significant proportion of the working-class strongly supported such policies. Indeed the authors probably realise this, when they go on to recommend that Labour should not merely respond to wants and expectations already manifest among its potential supporters, ' . . . but expand and diversify such wants and expectations in ways that would carry radical implications' (p. 194). Discussion of these alleged vote-winning policies is unfortunately brief. They include more public provision for recreation and leisure, an improved urban environment, better education, industrial democracy and more democratic decision-making all round. It is all rather thin. There is no acknowledgement that affluent workers, for example, might actually be alienated from Labour by its espousal of 'thorough-going egalitarian measures over a wide front' or that Labour for long has attracted support from highly *conservative* voters (Harrop, 1982). The recommendations also fly in the face of the authors' emphasis on the instrumentalism and the 'pay-off' outlook of many working-class Labour voters. In fact Labour lost much working-class support in 1970 and 1979 because it failed to satisfy such instrumental demands. There was a backlash among skilled workers over tax rates in the 1979 election (and in other Western countries at the time). In spite of Goldthorpe's claims to the contrary, it has been poor management of the economy (and the resultant lack of 'pay-off' for working class voters) that has so often damaged Labour governments at the polls.

Table 7.2 Proportion of skilled working class (C2) voting Labour, 1964–87

	% Voting Labour	Labour lead over Conservative
1964	54.5	20.5
1966	58.5	26.0
1970	55.5	21
1974	49	23
1979	41	0
1983	32	−8
1987	36	−4

Source: Nuffield *British General Election* series, reporting MORI for 1974–87, NOP for 1964–70.

CLASS DEALIGNMENT AND LABOUR'S DECLINE: NOTHING CHANGES

Nearly twenty years later much has changed both in social structure and in electoral behaviour. The scale of Labour's electoral decline (from 44.1 per cent in 1964 to 27.6 per cent in 1983, or 30.8 per cent in 1987) is greater than that suffered by any other major West European socialist party in the post-war period (and is surpassed only by the electoral decline of the PCF, the French Communist Party). Second, there has been a remorseless decline in the size of the manual working-class – from two-thirds to a half of the working population between 1964 and 1983, according to the BMRS social grading, or from 47 per cent to 34 per cent on the Goldthorpe criteria of social class (see below). Finally, in the 1980s there has been a return to mass unemployment, largely affecting the manual working-class.

The social group which has defected most from Labour is the skilled working class, the C2 group. Table 7.2 shows that this group (30 per cent of the electorate) was regularly voting nearly 2–1 for Labour between 1964 and 1974. By 1979 the Conservatives had drawn level with Labour and they have taken a clear lead in the last two general elections. The C2 group has certainly become more *bourgeois* in material terms; between 1979 and 1987 possession of a telephone spread from 35 per cent to 85 per cent, car-ownership from 30 per cent to 60 per cent and home-ownership from 45 per cent to 70 per cent, according to Robert Worcester of MORI. A different way to make the same point is to refer to Labour's long-term decline in the affluent South, and the erosion of its working-class support in the region. In 1987 the Conservatives share of the national vote was almost identical to that of 1964 (42.3 per cent and 43.4 per cent respectively) but Labour has lost substantial ground in such New Towns as Billericay, Epping and Hitchen. In spite of these significant social and electoral changes, Goldthorpe's views have hardly altered. In the 1960s *embourgeoisement* was the dragon to be slain by a sociology of the centre left, in the 1980s it has been *class dealignment*.

At this stage one must refer to the major survey study of the 1983 general election, *How Britain Votes* (1985). The study largely accepts Goldthorpe's ideas about how social class should be conceptualised and measured. Indeed one of the authors, Anthony Heath, had earlier collaborated with Goldthorpe on the Oxford Social Mobility Study, which allocates people to social classes on the basis of their authority and autonomy at work. *How Britain Votes* detaches the self-employed, technicians and foremen from the working-class, so that the working-class amounts to only 34 per cent of the working population. The groups the authors have excluded from the working-class are of course those most likely to be home-owning and affluent. We are left with a smaller and more solidly proletarian working-class, which we would expect to be more solidly Labour. Compared to other surveys, which show working-class support for Labour at 38 per cent in the 1983 election, *How Britain Votes* finds that 49 per cent of its working-class supports Labour. Some of the methodology and arguments of *How Britain Votes* have received a mixed reception. This has been discussed elsewhere and I do not wish to go over this ground again (Crewe, 1986; Dunleavy, 1987; Kavanagh 1986). Goldthorpe, in turn, in the second edition of his *Social Mobility and Class Structure in Modern Britain* approvingly quotes many of the arguments of *How Britain Votes* in support of his views as against those of Crewe and others. It seems justifiable therefore to use this study as a surrogate for some of the views of Goldthorpe.

Goldthorpe (like Heath, Jowell and Curtice) accepts that there has been an *absolute* decline in class alignment, in the sense that the proportions of working-class voting Labour and middle-class

Table 7.3 Labour's share of the manual workers' class vote (BMRS categories)

Year	%
1964	64
1966	69
1970	58
1974	57
1979	50
1983	42
1987	43

Source: For 1964–83 Heath, Jowell and Curtice, 1985, p. 30. See note of explanation in Heath, Jowell and Curtice, p. 40. For 1987 MORI.

voting Conservative has fallen steadily in the last twenty years (Table 7.3). For example, on the BMRS criteria working-class support for Labour fell from two-thirds in 1964−6 to 42 per cent in 1983, and on the Goldthorpe−Heath criteria from 70 per cent to 49 per cent. This decrease in the proportion of manual workers voting Labour and non-manuals voting Conservative is what most scholars have meant in talking about the decline of class politics since 1964. A perceptive critique of *How Britain Votes* by Dunleavy suggests: 'The "intuitive" meaning of class dealignment is simply that non-manual and manual class have become more similar or less contrasting in their voting patterns over time' (Dunleavy, p. 414). Goldthorpe and *How Britain Votes*, however, do not accept that there has been any *relative* decline. Relative class voting is *cross-class* voting, i.e. the combined shares of the working-class voting Conservative and middle-class voting Labour. It is measured by the Conservative–Labour odds in the non-manual group divided by the same odds among manual workers. On this criterion of odds ratios there has been no class dealignment. Class dealignment is spurious, 'an artefact of the inadequate manual non-manual dichotomy', according to Heath, Jowell and Curtice (1985, p. 34). They mean of course that *relative* class dealignment has not occurred. Goldthorpe dismisses the political scientists' claims that there has been a decline in class voting and complains that they do not use the superior analytical techniques and data which are now available (1987, p. 347). *How Britain Votes* argues that Labour's problem is not that it is losing support among the working-class (the argument advanced by most political scientists) but that the working-class has shrunk. If class politics is still alive, Labour has no need to dilute its class policies.

One problem concerns the treatment of those voters who voted for the Alliance. The growth of substantial electoral support for the Alliance in the 1980s was bound to weaken the relationship between two parties and two classes. In four of the last five general elections, support for Conservative and Labour parties has been confined to three-quarters or less of the electorate, compared to the usual 90 per cent for elections between 1950 and 1970. To exclude (as Heath, Jowell and Curtice do) such a large third-party fraction of the electorate in an analysis of social and political change is highly questionable; indeed the rise of third-party voting is surely an important aspect of the decline of class voting and regarded as such by most political scientists.

We are now faced with two different definitions of class dealignment and a clash of statistical techniques. The recent exchanges of views between rival schools reflect the *impasse*. Goldthorpe is roughly dismissive of those who disagree: 'But what is not credible is to seek to maintain the class dealignment thesis on the basis of arguments which either ignore, or show a fundamental lack of understanding of, results achieved via the new techniques' (1987, p. 354). Proponents of other approaches and different statistical techniques continue to disagree. Leaving the scholarly debate aside, surely the electoral decline of Labour, reduction in the size of the working class (however defined) and fall in working-class support for Labour are among the most significant features of British society and politics in the past two decades. In all the rarefied debate over whether we should measure absolute or relative class dealignment, or over the merits of odds-ratios, we are in danger of throwing the baby out with the bathwater, and overlooking the dramatic decline in Labour support.

POLITICAL STRATEGY: NOTHING CHANGES

Scholarly disagreements about dealignment are one thing; consequences for the real world are another. As in the affluent worker
studies, Labour is again warned against accepting claims about an
end to class politics and pursuing the middle ground. In a remarkable
echo of Goldthorpe nearly two decades earlier, Heath, Jowell and
Curtice claim that 'Labour might be able to survive whilst remaining
a class party', and, by pursuing an egalitarian strategy, might 'shape
the social potentials' (1985, p. 174). It could do this by fighting on
the 'working-class issues' of job security, pensions, unemployment
and working conditions, and making an appeal on the basis of social
justice. As evidence of the continuing high level of class consciousness
among the working-class, the authors report the impressive majorities
in 1983 for egalitarian responses on three out of four survey
questions, covering measures to promote redistribution, tackle
poverty and foster industrial democracy. The average positive
response for the three was 74 per cent (1987, p. 276). In optimistic
language, again redolent of the affluent worker studies, the authors
interpret the results as confirmation that 'unrealised potentials for
class action may remain within the working-class'.

I agree with Crewe when he argues that the three attitude
questions are poor indicators of class consciousness or a left-wing
outlook (1986). The values are largely consensual. Who would
declare against redistribution towards ordinary working people, or
spending more money to get rid of poverty or giving more, say, to
people at work? Many One Nation Conservatives would accept such
policies, as would many Liberals and Social Democrats. Although
Labour campaigned on policies which were targetted towards
redistribution and attacking poverty in the 1983 and 1987 general
elections, both elections produced the party's worst results in the
post-war period. It is true that many factors contributed to Labour's
election defeats and perhaps its radical programme made little
difference one way or the other. I would conclude that the electorate
does not doubt that Labour favours such policies but that they are
not major influences on voting behaviour.

Goldthorpe's strategy also assumes that Labour can be a strong
compaigning party, i.e. that it has the resources to 'educate' the
electorate. This is doubtful. The Labour movement as an educational
movement – based on WEAs, Social Sunday Schools, a Labour
press, working men's clubs with libraries, socialist lecture series and

'chapel' – has more or less disappeared. The press is hostile and television neutral. Moreover, it is much easier for parties in government, with their access to information and a civil-service machine, to shift public opinion than it is for an opposition party, which must rely on its own inadequate research staff. The only remaining major vehicle for grassroots campaigning available to the Labour Party is the trade unions and the evidence so far is that they are singularly unsuccessful (Minkin, 1986).

The issue once again becomes that of the relative importance of the voters' perceptions of a party in terms of its competence in managing the economy or its egalitarianism. According to a survey conducted in 1971–2, 'the greater part of Labour supporters would appear to have been broadly satisfied with its existing degree of commitment to egalitarian objectives' (Gallie, 1983, pp. 137–8). The same study found that the number who criticised Labour for being too moderate were balanced by those who thought it was too dependent on the trade unions and discouraged individual effort. Above all there was dissatisfaction based on the perception that the party was economically incompetent. Surveys after the 1983 and 1987 elections found a similar concern. More recently Rose and McAllister (1986) have found that socialist principles actually divide the working-class. Although approval for socialist principles increased somewhat among Labour voters (from 50 per cent to 61 per cent) from 1979 to 1983, as the party's vote has fallen, it is likely to decrease if and when the party's vote expands. There is no evidence that socialism will be a vote winner for the party. Indeed Goldthorpe's latest words on the subject acknowledge that 'social inequality has been effectively removed from the political agenda' and 'its restoration in the foreseeable future is highly uncertain' (1987, p. 31). Goldthorpe also allowed for such an eventuality in the final sentence of *The Affluent Worker in the Class Structure*. If the Labour leadership opted for consensus rather than radical policies, then this would help to deradicalise the working-class and 'it will to some degree be also attributable to the fact that the political leaders of the working-class *chose* this future for it' (1987, p. 346).

Goldthorpe's work correctly reminds us of the openness of many social trends for voting behaviour and the opportunities for political choice. Indeed during the 1960s and 1970s one may point to the increases in the numbers renting council houses, in the proportion of male employees in trade unions (from 53 per cent in 1961 to 66 per cent in 1979) and in public employment as a proportion of the workforce (from 24 per cent in 1961 to 31 per cent in 1981) (p. 33). In other words, social changes have not been uniformly disadvantageous for Labour. There have been such remarkable shifts in political allegiances in recent years that social change alone is an inadequate explanation of Labour's decline. In the 1979 Parliament, for example, all three political parties saw their support in the polls vary between 50 per cent and the low 20 per cents. Heath, Jowell and Curtice are surely correct in claiming that the abrupt decline of Labour owes more to political factors than to social changes.

Goldthorpe (and Heath, Jowell and Curtice) correctly observe that Labour is still overwhelmingly a working-class party; it draws four-fifths of its support from the working-class. It does not make much sense to seek new voters at the expense of alienating existing supporters. It is inconceivable for the present day Labour Party not to advocate better public services, to promote the interests of the disadvantaged, to seek a bigger role for the trade unions and so on. Moreover, a programmatic, let alone an ideological, party cannot adopt and then abandon policies willy-nilly. But there are two uncomfortable features in a Labour strategy continuing to rely on this class-based heartland. One is that even among the 'pure' working-class of Heath, Jowell and Curtice, only 49 per cent voted Labour in 1983 and the proportion would not be much higher in 1987. Labour's electoral performance as a class party is poor. Secondly, Heath, Jowell and Curtice also show that the working-class shrank from 47 per cent in 1964 to little more than a third in 1983. Even if Labour does better among the working-class, it still has to look elsewhere for electoral salvation.

Goldthorpe argues that the party should still follow a class strategy and seek support in classes proximate to the working-class, i.e. those in 'jobs' rather than in 'careers' (1987, p. 350). It should particularly seek support among class III (routine clerical and other service workers) and the lower level of class IV (lower level of technicians and supervisors), two groups which amount to a quarter of the electorate but of which only a quarter voted Labour in 1983. The recommendation sits oddly with the insistence of Goldthorpe (and of Heath, Jowell and Curtice) on regarding these as quite separate classes, with different interests, for the purposes of class analysis. Predictably, this will be done by a set of radical policies which appeal to the shared interests of these classes. Equally predictably, these policies are not spelled out. If they cover more

Table 7.4 Changes in trade-union membership

Year	Membership (millions)	Density (%)
1964	10.1	44.0
1966	10.2	44.0
1970	11.2	47.7
1974	11.8	49.6
1979	13.3	51.1
1983	11.3	41.6

Source: Department of Employment *Gazettes*.

progressive taxation, no incomes policies, restoring pre-1979 trade-
union rights, reducing mortgage tax relief and opposing the sale of
council houses, sceptics will note that such policies have been
remarkable for dividing the working-class and Labour supporters.

CONCLUSION

Four points are worth emphasising in this discussion of Goldthorpe's
work about social class and Labour partisanship.

First, social change has reduced the size of the working-class and
with it Labour's core constituency. There has been at least one form
of *embourgeoisement* since the 1960s in that society is more white-
collar and middle-class and that a substantial minority of white-
collar and 'service' class people come from working-class origins.
This social change has occurred at the same time as a steep decline
in support for the Labour Party.

Second, Goldthorpe's early suggestion about the instrumental
attachment of many workers to the trade unions and the Labour
Party has been confirmed. Many subsequent surveys have shown
that there has long been public support for the rôle of trade unions
in workplace bargaining and generally defending the rights of
workers against employees, but little for the unions playing a larger
political role. Tables 7.3, 7.4 and 7.5 make interesting reading.
Table 7.4 shows the steady increase in membership of trade unions
between 1964 and 1979, Table 7.3 shows the sharp decline in

Table 7.5 Proportion of trade unionists voting labour

Year	%	Labour lead over Conservatives
1974 (Oct)	55	32
1979	50	15
1983	39	8
1987	42	12

Source: D. Butler and D. Kavanagh, *British General Election* series, reporting MORI data.

Labour's post-war vote over the same period and Table 7.5 shows the declining proportion of trade unionists voting Labour in these years. Since 1979, Labour support among manual workers in trade unions has fallen by almost twice the rate of Labour's national decline. Increasingly, union members are found in middle-class jobs and are home-owners (Gallup, September 1987). Moreover, trade-union campaign activity as distinct from union leaders' public statements of support on behalf of Labour is feeble. The tables make explicit the implicit point of Goldthorpe and Lockwood about the disassociation between workplace behaviour and political attitudes.

In the light of these tables it is interesting that Heath and McDonald (1987) have recently argued that the British Labour Party should draw on one feature of the Scandinavian model. They suggest that Labour should promote trade-union membership as a means of gaining votes. In Scandinavian countries affluence co-exists with a much higher trade-union density and Social Democratic dominance of the political system. In fact Tables 7.4 and 7.5 show the opposite relationship, Labour's absolute vote and its proportion of the electorate were appreciably higher in the 1950s and the 1960s, when trade-union membership was lower (There is a good debunking piece to be written on the alleged 'lessons' which Sweden has for the British Labour Party). Trade unionists do not vote just as trade unionists; they are also consumers, parents and home-owners (Webb, 1987). Subsequent electoral research has confirmed the importance of the economy's performance – though the measures of performance (e.g. unemployment, inflation or prosperity) vary over time – and instrumental voting (Alt, 1978). There is little evidence, however, that the policy and strategy recommendations of Goldthorpe or Heath and co-authors will improve Labour's chances of electoral success. The recommendations derive more from ideology than sociology.

Third, it is perhaps unfortunate that Goldthorpe's studies of changes in social class have been so narrowly related to the electoral prospects of the Labour Party. Such a concern perpetuates a long-standing feature of much political sociology in Britain – the greater body of research and commentary on the Labour Party compared to that on the Conservative Party. Many of the early studies of the deferential working-class Conservatives took as their starting point that it was 'natural' for workers to vote Labour. One was therefore dealing with *deviant* political behaviour.

Fourth, a problem for political and sociological analysis is why Labour has been doing so much worse electorally than most other centre–left parties in Western Europe. Compared to its Continental counterparts Labour has had many advantages. Since 1919 it has competed in a predominantly two-party system; social class has overwhelmingly been the main cleavage (religion, language and nationalism were weak); and the electoral system has meant that even with 40 per cent of the vote it could form a government on its own. In addition, Labour (and the TUC) has not been shadowed by a substantial Communist party, splitting the left politically and industrially. Yet most Continental socialist parties have coped better than the British Labour Party with affluence and the decline of the manual working-class. Most of these parties live with proportional electoral systems and multi-party politics, and have to settle for a share of power in government. It may be that these parties have had to be more innovative than Labour in making alliances with other parties, modifying their ideological commitments, and appealing beyond the ranks of industrial workers. Peter Pulzer notes that all West European léft parties have had to adapt to social change: 'All have found this difficult but few have failed as spectacularly as the British Labour Party' (1987, p. 383). In this respect the warnings of Goldthorpe and of Heath and colleagues against social determinism are apt. It is the policy prescriptions for reversing the decline that are unconvincing.

References

Alt, J., *The Politics of Economic Decline* (Cambridge University Press, 1978).

Butler, D. and Stokes D., *Political Change in Britain* 2nd Edition (London: Macmillan, 1974).

Crewe, I., 'The Politics of "Affluent" and "Traditional" workers in Britain: An Aggregate Data Analysis', *British Journal of Political Science* Vol. 3, No. 1, 1973, pp. 29–52.

Crewe, I., 'On the Death and Resurrection of Class Voting: Some Comments on *How Britain Votes*', *Political Studies*, Vol. 34, No. 4, 1986, pp. 620–38.

Dunleavy, P., 'Class Dealignment in Britain Revisited; Why Odd Ratios Give Odd Results', *West European Politics*, Vol. 10, No. 3., 1987, pp. 400–19.

Gallie, D., *Social Inequality and Class Radicalism in France and Britain*, (Cambridge University Press, 1983).

Goldthorpe, J. H. *et al.*, *The Affluent Worker: Political Attitudes and Behaviour* (Cambridge University Press, 1968).

Goldthorpe, J. H. *et al.*, *The Affluent Worker in the Class Structure*, (Cambridge University Press, 1969).

Goldthorpe, J. H., *Social Mobility and Class Structure in Modern Britain*, 2nd Edition, (Oxford: Clarendon, 1987).

Harrop, M., 'Labour–Voting Conservatives: Policy Differences between the Labour Party and Labour voters', in R. Worcester and M. Harrop (eds), *Political Communications, the General Election Campaign of 1979*, (London: Allen & Unwin, 1982, pp. 152–63).

Heath, A., Jowell, R. & Curtice, J., *How Britain Votes*, (Oxford: Pergamon Press, 1985).

Heath, A., Jowell R. & Curtice J., 'Trendless Fluctuations: A Reply to Crewe', *Political Studies*, Vol. 35, No. 2, 1987, pp. 256–77; 'Class Dealignment and the Explanation of Political Change: A Reply to Dunleavy', *West European Politics*, Vol. 11, No. 1, 1987a, pp. 146–8.

Heath, A. and MacDonald S. K., 'The Social Change and the Future of the Left', *Political Quarterly*, Vol. 58, No. 4, 1987, pp. 382–95.

Kavanagh, D., 'How We Vote Now', *Electoral Studies*, Vol. 5, No. 1, 1986, pp. 19–28.

Minkin, L., 'Against the Tide; trade unions, political communications and the 1983 general election', in I. Crewe and M. Harrop (eds), *Political Communications: The 1983 Election Campaign*, (Cambridge University Press, 1986, pp. 190–206).

Parkin, F., 'Working Class Conservatives: A Theory of Political Deviance', *British Journal of Sociology*, Vol. 18, No. 2, 1967, pp. 280–90.

Pulzer, P., 'The Paralysis of the Centre–Left', *Political Quarterly*, Vol. 58, No. 4, 1987.

Rose, R. and McAllister, I., *Voters Begin to Choose*, (London: Sage, 1986).

Rose, R., *Class Does Not Equal Party: The Decline of a Model*, (University of Strathclyde: Centre for the Study of Public Policy, 1980).

Webb, R., 'Union, Party and Class in Britain: The Changing Electoral Relationship 1964–1983', *Politics*, Vol. 7, No. 2, 1987, pp. 15–21.

8 Do We Need a Centre Party?*

Mrs Thatcher's dominance of British politics has been the main story of the 1980s. But the upsurge of support for a new political formation, the Alliance, and the creation and extinction of centre political parties, have been other significant themes. For a brief period it looked as though the two-party system would be overthrown. By the end of the decade, however, the Alliance looked like the latest in a long line of failures. The fate of break-away parties has been dismal. Joseph Chamberlain and about 100 MPs seceded from the Liberal party when Gladstone adopted Home Rule for Ireland in 1885 – they were soon absorbed by the Conservative party. In 1931 Ramsay MacDonald led a small group of National Labour MPs, and Sir John Simon a small group of National Liberals, and both were soon effectively absorbed by the Conservatives. Sir Oswald Mosley's New Party failed to win a single seat in 1931, and was no more successful when it renamed itself the British Union of Fascists in 1932. Only the Labour Party between 1906 and 1918 managed to establish itself, helped in part by an electoral pact with the Liberals, and not until 1945 did it gain a majority of seats in the House of Commons.

The melancholy tale of third party politics is also a story of lost leaders – Joseph Chamberlain, Lloyd George (post-1922), Oswald Mosley, Roy Jenkins and now David Owen. Third parties have been significant pressure groups in Britain – the Irish Nationalists between 1880 and 1918 and the Scottish Nationalists between 1974 and 1979. In the 1980s the Social Democrats and Liberals helped to stimulate discussion about constitutional change and electoral reform in Britain. The Nationalists were helped by the simplicity of their demands – Home Rule or independence – but constitutional reform was too vague a rallying cry.

Everybody 'knows' that since 1918 Britain has had a system of two-party politics, with effective electoral choice for a party of government confined to Labour and Conservative. So many features

* This chapter was specially written for this volume.

of the British political system have rested on the assumption of there being two major political parties. The dualistic party system certainly clarifies electoral choice. It also simplifies life in Parliament, perhaps making it even more intelligible, as a united government faces a united opposition. The two-party system and the virtual certainty that one party will have an overall majority of seats in the House of Commons lies at the heart of the British system of responsible Parliamentary government. In the post-war period it may have limited the area of political disagreement; in a largely consensual society two evenly matched (in terms of electoral support) political parties tended to converge to the metaphorical middle ground.

Yet the weakening of support for the two main parties has been a significant trend in the past two decades. From gathering an average aggregate 90 per cent share of the popular vote in general elections to 1970, the two parties have only once exceeded 76 per cent since (1979). Results from by-elections, opinion polls and surveys of party identification have shown a waning attachment to the Labour and Conservative Parties. Although we often talk of third-party and centre-party voting as if they are the same thing, they cover very different parties. In the last two general elections third-party voting has amounted to about 30 per cent of the total vote. But it has covered nationalism and sectarianism, as well as liberalism and social democracy. The Liberal Party had seemed poised for a break-through in February 1974, when it gained a fifth of the vote in the first general election of that year. The Nationalists in Scotland in the October 1974 election gained nearly a third of the Scottish vote and eleven seats. In 1981–2 the new Alliance of the SDP and Liberals was, for a brief period, actually the most popular party in the country, and in the 1983 general election the Alliance almost overtook Labour in popular support. In 1987 it was disappointed but still gained 22 per cent of the votes. Three-party politics would probably force a revision of Westminster's political rules, and textbooks on coalitions and multi-party politics fell off the printing press. In every case, however, it has been a story of failing to build on or even confirm initial gains. On each occasion electoral boredom, misjudgement by centre party leaders, and the effects of the electoral system prevented a break-through.

By 1988 the historic Liberal Party and the short-lived Alliance had both disappeared. In their place were the newly merged Liberal and Social Democratic Party and the separate Owenite SDP rump. Roy Jenkins, Shirley.Williams and David Steel were no longer central figures, having failed to force the realignment of party politics. The 1980s demonstrated that there exists a considerable centre-party vote. Unfortunately there was never a single centre party. In trying to make sense of this turbulent period in British party politics it is worth asking if there was a real possibility of a realignment.

The Liberals were of course a party of government until 1918. The split in 1916 between the Liberal Prime Minister Asquith and Lloyd George, the man who ousted him, speeded the decline of the party. But many of the policies the party espoused, such as free trade, Irish Home Rule, suffrage extension, temperance and anti-Imperialism, were less salient after the end of the war. Historians still debate whether the speed of the decline was inevitable, and whether it was largely caused by broader social and economic forces or by political divisions at the top. Either way, as rival groups of Liberals contested seats, Labour displaced it as the second single party in seats in the House of Commons in the 1918 general election. But the Liberal decline was not obvious to contemporaries. In the elections of 1922, 1923, 1924 and 1929 the party gained 29.1 per cent (combining the Liberals and National Liberal votes), 29.6 per cent, 17.6 per cent and 23.4 per cent of the vote. Only in the last two general elections did Labour decisively emerge as the second party in votes. At the same time the Liberals suffered considerably from the working of the electoral system, gaining only 7 per cent and 10 per cent of the seats in 1924 and 1929. The party was virtually wiped out in 1931.

Yet even after 1945 the Liberal Party obstinately refused to die. Its lowest point was in the 1951 general election when the party put up only 109 candidates and gained a meagre 2.5 per cent of the total vote; only forty-three Liberal candidates saved their deposits. As Beveridge and Keynes were Liberals, the party could claim some paternity for the post-war programmes of welfare and demand management. But to some commentators and politicians the acceptance of such liberal policies meant that there was little need for a Liberal Party: 'We are all Liberals now'. Unencumbered by the responsibilities or the prospect of office, the party sparked many ideas. It was the first to promote the causes of Britain's membership of the European Community, political decentralisation and devolution, constitutional reform and co-partnership at work. Although the party attracted a growing protest vote at by-elections, its few

Parliamentary seats were in the Celtic fringes. The Liberal Party seemed to have no place in an era of class and producer group politics.

To stage a comeback as a party of the centre, or the centre-left, the Liberals had to choose between one of two strategies. One was to replace Labour on the radical or centre-left in a two-party system. This gained credence after 1979, when it could be plausibly argued that Labour was tied to a social class and economic interest that were declining. Yet in the context of a disproportional electoral system the logic of this position implied that, as the Liberals struggled to overtake Labour, the Conservatives would be entrenched as the normal party of government. Indeed this is what happened both in the inter-war years and the 1980s, as the non-Conservative majority in the electorate divided its vote.

The alternative strategy was to build up a substantial third party which would be able to deny a Commons majority to either of the other two parties. Out of such Parliamentary deadlocks the need for political bargaining, perhaps the formation of coalition governments, would be recognised, and support for proportional representation would grow. The Liberal Party would be one party among many. The model Liberals had in mind was the 'balancing' role played by the Free Democrats between the Social Democrats and Christian Democrats in West Germany. A small party had to co-operate with others. In his campaign for the party leadership in 1976, David Steel explicitly called for such co-operation as the best way to implement Liberal policies. Of course this all depended on no one party having a Parliamentary majority.

Talk of a 'progressive alliance' between 'new' or social reformist Liberals and Social Democratic Labour has been a recurring theme of British politics in the twentieth century. Some historians (notably Peter Clarke)[1] argued that the Liberal party had already become the party of social democracy and welfare before 1914. It had ditched Gladstonian liberalism and *laissez-faire* and its future seemed assured. Before 1914 Labour MPs looked to the Liberal Party as the senior party in the progressive alliance, and many 'New' Liberals joined Labour after 1918 when the Liberal Party split. The minority Labour government of 1929 was negotiating for a parliamentary pact (in return for electoral reform) with Lloyd George's Liberals before it fell in 1931. Talk of some form of alliance has recurred during periods of Conservative dominance or minority Labour government. Following Labour's third successive election defeat in

1959, the Labour MP Woodrow Wyatt floated the idea of a Lib/ Lab electoral pact. In 1965, a time of a wafer thin Labour majority government, the Liberal leader Joe Grimond called for a realignment between the Liberals and Labour's right wing. At the time Labour leaders made friendly noises about PR.

Another chance came in 1977 when the Callaghan Labour government found itself in a minority. At the time the opinion polls predicted that an election would result in the annihilation of both Labour and the Liberals. It was in the interests of the two parties to postpone an election. Mr Callaghan and Mr Steel therefore formed a pact under which the Liberals would support the Labour government on key issues in return for a say in policies. David Steel, like Grimond, believed in Lib–Lab co-operation. He hoped that the pact experience would be an education for his party; though born of expediency, it would familiarise his activists and the electorate with the Liberals as a party of power.

But beyond a glimpse of the corridors of power the party gained little from the pact. At one point Liberal MPs only narrowly decided to continue with it; had they decided otherwise, Steel knew that he would have had to resign. Mr Grimond calculated that the Labour government should not have been given a lifeline but been allowed to collapse, and that this would have advanced the prospects for realignment. For realignment to occur, Labour had to be discredited and/or split. In the 1979 election the Liberals, along with Labour, were punished and actually ended with 2 million fewer votes. Mr Steel had a second chance in 1980, when he persuaded Roy Jenkins, seeking to return to Parliament, not to join the Liberals but to try to entice disillusioned Labour MPs and voters to a new and separate Social Democratic Party. The Liberals and the new break-away party agreed to fight the next election as an Alliance. To the fury of his activists Steel also agreed in 1983 that Roy Jenkins would be the Prime Minister designate in a future Alliance government.

The Alliance profited from dissatisfaction with the two main parties. Mrs Thatcher was widely respected but not liked and Labour was regarded as unelectable. The Alliance also profited from the adverse critique of the two-party system mounted by the Oxford academic Sammy Finer. This argued that Britain suffered from adversary politics, in which a new party in government was able to use the dictatorial powers of a sovereign Parliament to reverse its predecessor's policies. The disproportional electoral system had long been attacked because of its injustice. But when popular support for the two parties declined, they were protected by the electoral system. By allowing parties to gain total power with less than 40 per cent of the vote, it allowed these electoral minorities to wield full power. This did not matter, it was claimed, in the 1950s and 1960s, when there was much agreement between the main parties. But the changes of government in 1970 and 1974, at a time of such policy dissensus between the two traditional parties, were bad for the economy. In effect, the electoral system was attacked on the grounds that it provided bad government. Essentially this was the argument which Roy Jenkins used in his Dimbleby lecture in November 1979, and which planted the seeds of the Social Democratic Party.

The surge in support for the Alliance was a major feature of British politics in the 1980s. Only once in general elections between 1945 and 1970 (in 1964) had the Liberal Party gained more than 10 per cent of the vote. It gained nearly a fifth in the two 1974 elections but fell back to 13.8 per cent in 1979. Yet in the 1983 and 1987 elections the new force averaged 24 per cent of the total vote. It is interesting to note that this rise seems to have been almost entirely at the expense of the Labour Party. While the Conservatives have dropped about 3 per cent from their average share of the vote in the 1950s and 1960s, Labour has dropped a full 10 per cent. The result showed itself in the lop-sided Parliaments, as Conservatives were able to gain landslide victories with only 42 per cent of the vote. Compared to the 1950s and 1960s, when the two major parties were closely matched in electoral support, the Conservatives in the 1983 and 1987 elections enjoyed a lead over Labour of 14 per cent and 11 per cent of the electorate respectively. The rise of the Alliance also made the British electoral system operate more disproportionately than ever, largely at the expense of the Alliance. For the first half of the post-war period the two parties usually gained 90 per cent of the vote and 95 per cent of the seats. In general elections since 1970 they have averaged just over 70 per cent of the vote but still gathered 93 per cent of the seats.

The 1983 general election was an outstanding result in that it saw the Alliance challenge Labour for second place in votes, and gain over 25 per cent of the total vote. Yet the Conservatives still won by a landslide and the Alliance, with only 23 seats, was irrelevant in the new Parliament. A paradox in the election was that many of the Alliance (particularly SDP) leaders spent much of their time attacking Labour. Yet of the 80 or so most likely Alliance gains, over two-thirds of them would come from Conservative-held seats, usually in the South. The story was much the same in the 1987 election. The Alliance failed to advance, gaining 22.6 per cent of the vote, while Labour managed to reverse its decline a little. Within a year the Alliance was no more and most of the SDP membership threw in its lot with the Liberals to create a new Social and Liberal Democratic Party. Having spoken so much in the 1987 campaign about the need for co-operation and reasonableness, friends of the two leaders subsequently stridently attacked each other. Centre-party politics had been tested, to the destruction of both the Liberals and the majority of the SDP.

Surveys suggested that SDP voters, like the Liberals, tended to be weak partisans. The British Election Study surveys found that in general elections between 1959 and 1979 only a half of Liberals at one election voted Liberal at the next. The figure for Conservative and Labour voters was nearly three-quarters. Supporters liked the Alliance parties for their leaders, moderation and, above all, because they were neither Labour nor Conservative. The supporters tended to be 'in-between' the other parties on most policy questions. Apart from a commitment to constitutional reform (PR, devolution, Bill of Rights, open government, etc.), the Alliance lacked distinctive policy positions. Electoral support was drawn fairly evenly over the nation and different social strata, strongly indicating that it was a protest vote.

For a decade David Steel and David Owen were at the centre of media politics, though not of government. As Liberal leader, David Steel was a bit player in many minor political dramas for 12 years. With his tiny band of MPs he had to practise the politics of co-operation, the unheroic politics of wheeling and dealing. He wanted to use his handful of MPs as a negotiating ploy, hopefully with a moderate Labour government and, after 1981, with the SDP. He might have thrived in French politics in the 1950s or contemporary Italy; in such multi-party systems the leader of the small centre party has great opportunities for acting as a power broker. However, the British political system, with two dominant parties in the House of Commons, downgraded him and his party. The system failed to provide the deadlocked Parliaments in which he could hold the balance.

Steel found the 'flat earth' calls from his activists for going it alone, aiming for a Liberal government and sticking to 'true Liberalism' unrealistic, tedious and frustrating. He also found the complicated Liberal machinery and activists' love of discussing resolutions in minute detail tiresome. The Liberal Party, so long out of power, attracted many single-issue activists, political innocents and those who preferred the politics of purity to the politics of responsibility. Who can forget the agonising at the Liberal assembly in September 1974 about the resolution spelling out the conditions which the handful of Liberal MPs would insist on for serving in a government of national unity? When Steel mentioned in a party broadcast in Summer 1974 that Liberals might serve in a coalition, party headquarters was inundated with protesting phone calls. But what was the logical consequences of proportional representation but multi-partism and co-operation? His memorable words to the 1981 Assembly, 'Go back to your constituencies and prepare for government', fell on many deaf or frightened ears.

The birth of the SDP owed something to ideas and ideals. Roy Jenkins had called for a 'radical centre party' in his BBC Television Dimbleby lecture in November 1979, and the 1981 defectors were disgusted with Labour's change on so many fronts after 1979. But the new party also owed much to sheer opportunism. Jenkins needed a new base on his return from Brussels and more than a dozen Labour MPs feared deselection by constituency activists before the next general election. Of the original Gang of Four, Jenkins and Shirley Williams (until her return at the Crosby by-election in November 1981) were out of Parliament. Dr Owen had the most to lose. He was the youngest of the four and had been Foreign Secretary at the age of 38. He was the last of the original four to be convinced of the need to create a new party but then pushed ahead vigorously. The original alliance between the SDP and Liberal Parties owed much to the personal chemistry between Roy Jenkins and David Steel, and Jenkins always envisaged some eventual merger between the two. Owen, however, considered that the SDP's independence from the Liberals was essential if the new party was to appeal to disaffected Labour voters. By being separate it could add support to the centre force. The Liberals had shown that they could not break through alone. An impressive upsurge of support in the opinion polls for the Alliance was cut short by the Conservative government's success in the Falklands war. War concentrates attention on the government of the day, relegating opposition parties to virtual irrelevance. Ministers represent the nation, take action and, day after day, the government dominates the media. Yet Owen came to prominence during the Falklands with well-honed speeches on the floor of the House of Commons, marginalising Labour's front bench.

Dr Owen has presented himself as a man of destiny. At a Labour Party conference held at Wembley in May 1980 he was roundly booed from the floor while defending the Callaghan government. This increased his sense of self-importance as well as isolation in the party. He was given to repeating the comments of a Labour regional organiser about himself, 'that man is a future leader of the party'. In the SDP he had no time for Jenkins as leader. He thought that too many members were part of what he termed the 'Jenkins' fan club'. Indeed he did not oppose David Steel's attempt to dump Jenkins as leader of the Alliance during the 1983 election campaign.

When he took over from Jenkins as SDP leader immediately after the 1983 election, it was clear that there would be no merger. In 1983, as in 1987, the dual leadership idea confused voters and betrayed Alliance doubts about its identity. As SDP leader, his relations with Steel were dreadful. He regarded Steel as a lightweight, an untrustworthy though shrewd political operator. In spite of Owen's high profile the Liberals had greater strength on the ground. At the 1983 general election the SDP contingent in the Commons fell from 28 to 6, the Liberals increased from 13 to 17. The Liberals were also stronger in membership, activists and councillors. Throughout the 1983 Parliament, Owen resisted until the last anything that smacked of closer co-operation, let alone a merger of the two parties. He held out against joint spokesmen, joint candidate selection and joint policy. His stern unbending stand on policies and strategy was the means of keeping the SDP independent. As Roy Jenkins, Shirley Williams and Bill Rodgers moved in favour of merger, so he became more entrenched in his sense of mission. On the eve of the 1987 election he called his efforts to preserve the independence of the SDP 'the great untold story of British politics'. He wanted only an electoral pact between the SDP and Liberals. Friends of Steel thought that the 'sheer psychological wear and tear of working with the Doctor' accelerated the Liberal leader's weariness with politics. The joint campaign in the 1987 election diminished both men. After their shared morning press conferences, they would go separately to different parts of the country, giving very different briefings to their accompanying press entourages and disparaging the other.

In many ways Owen's obstinacy and sense of personal destiny have parallels with Churchill in the 1930s or de Gaulle in the 1950s.

Both men waited for the call to save their countries, and in the end they were vindicated. But centre-party politics in Britain has been more about by-election media hype, rows, leaks and splits. David Owen's attempt to arbitrate the nation's fortunes, backed by a party of two MPs, became more ridiculous than heroic. By 1989 he resembled a young man with a brilliant past. Observers may continue to speculate about his intentions and ask themselves 'what if?', as they did about Joseph Chamberlain, Lloyd George and Mosley in the inter-war years, and Powell after 1968. It is likely that his will be another notable talent which has gone to waste because of the rigidity of British party politics, as well as his own misjudgements. In the short term the future of the SDP depended on there being deadlocked Parliaments. But in such an event what would his three seats be worth compared with, say, the Ulster Unionists? And what was distinctive about the SDP compared to the new Labour Party or the SLD, apart from having Dr Owen at its head? Of course the electoral system has been a major barrier. But there were also many choices which Owen made – leaving Labour in 1981, refusing to merge after the 1987 election, and refusing to join the new SLD in 1988. Like Powell and Heath, Owen can continue to be a much-quoted commentator on politics.

Speculation about realignment on the centre–left has been a regular theme of British politics in the last 30 years. It grew more insistent and credible after 1981, with the creation of the SDP and Alliance. For a moment it seemed to represent the politics of the post-industrial future (its appeal was particularly strong to the well-educated public sector salariat). Yet there was little popular positive identification with its specific policies: it lacked a central convincing message. It depended on Labour's decline as an electoral force and the widespread perception of being unattractively left-wing. In 1989, as Neil Kinnock took steps to close that window of opportunity, support fell away. Ironically, so many of the policies which led Owen and others to leave Labour have been changed–Europe, defence and nationalisation.

The Liberals, and their successor parties, have had an important role in the two-party system. In the idealised version of the two-party system the Conservative and Labour Parties, evenly matched in electoral support, were forced to converge on the middle ground. It was also assumed that 'floating' voters or those weakly attached to the two parties were in the metaphorical middle ground. The committed Labour and Conservative voters had nowhere else to go if they were dissatisfied. The great danger to a party's electoral prospects was whether it was perceived to be incompetent or departing from the central ground; in this case weak supporters would desert to another party or abstain. In fact such voters were able to vote for the Liberals and then the Alliance. Support for these parties at general elections and in opinion polls varied with the unpopularity of one or both of the main parties. This happened in the by-elections in 1972-3 and again for much of the 1980s. The Liberals and then the Alliance appropriated the politics of reasonableness and moderation. They were a receptacle for the dissatisfied and could act almost as a built-in stabiliser for the two-party system.

For the time being the best opportunity for realignment in British politics has passed. Mrs Thatcher may reflect that it has been given to few Prime Ministers to see one opposition party in disarray. None, until now, has seen both opposition parties split.

NOTE

1. In *Liberals and Social Democrats* (Cambridge University Press, 1979).

9 Crisis, Charisma and British Political Leadership: the Case of Winston Churchill*

INTRODUCTION

Winston Churchill's performance as Prime Minister during the Second World War seems to challenge many assumptions about the low salience of personal leadership in British politics. To write of him, particularly in 1940, has been an invitation to parade superlatives. He has become, in Isaiah Berlin's words, 'a public image who is no longer distinguishable from the inner essence . . . a mythical hero who belongs to legend as much as to reality, the largest human being of our time' (Berlin, 1949, p. 39). The purpose of this chapter is to review the leadership of Winston Churchill during the Second World War and to see whether it meets the criteria for charismatic political leadership. Was he, for instance, a charismatic figure at a time of acute crisis in 1940? If not, is one entitled to suggest that charisma has very little place in the British political system?

It is hardly original to observe that the several refinements and different empirical definitions of Max Weber's notion of charisma (Weber, 1947) have weakened the precision of the concept. Charisma has been so stretched between advertising copywriters and social scientists that it now results in a form of conceptual misformation, meaning different things to different researchers. Various authors have argued very differently that it should be applied only in a religious context (Weber specifically mentions Buddha, Mohammed and Moses); that it may be institutionalised as in support for a party; that it applies to inspirational leadership in general; or that it is always present in any leader–follower relationship.

* This chapter was especially written for this volume.

134

Weber's intention was to point to a residual base or category of authority or legitimacy, a category sanctioned neither by tradition nor legal–rational rules, which might serve to account for such phenomena as the warrior, prophet, and demagogue. Weber borrowed the concept of charisma from a religious context and defined it as 'devotion to the specific sanctity, heroism, or exemplary character of an individual person and of the normative pattern or order revealed by him' (1947, p. 328). Clearly, charismatic authority describes a relationship between leader and followers and specifically refers to the followers' perceptions of, or beliefs in, the leader's heroic or superhuman qualities. This meaning has been lost sight of as a result of the emphasis which later writers have given to charisma as a personal trait of the leader.

I have abstracted five propositions from Weber's discussion. These five suggested indicators of charisma focus on the crisis situation; the interaction of leader and followers; the personal attributes and political style of the leader; and the instability of the leader's support:

1 Weber emphasised the importance of the crisis situation. The charismatic response was 'devotion born of distress and enthusi- asm', which thrived in emergencies such as war or revolution or the collapse of established norms and institutions. The scope for charisma increased where the traditional or legal–rational bases of authority were weakened.
2 Charisma is also relational, for it depends on the followers' perceptions of the leader. 'It is recognition on the part of those subject to authority which is decisive for the validity of charisma' (Weber, p. 330). The leader is seen to possess 'specifically exceptional power or qualities' (p. 329) and his authority 'rests upon the belief in magical powers, revelations and hero-worship'.
3 It is probable that Weber wants to alert us to the outstanding personality of the leader who, at a time of distress, appears as a messianic, salvationist type of leader (Tucker, 1968).
4 According to Weber (p. 342), the style of the charismatic leader is revolutionary. He is a 'revolutionary force', spurning traditional methods and values and his authority is 'specifically irrational' in the sense of defying rules (p. 332).
5 Finally, Weber points to the instability of the charismatic appeal and its inadequacy as a permanent basis for legitimacy. Retention of the charismatic relationship depends on the maintenance of the

crisis atmosphere and on the leader's confirmation of his grace by performing outstanding feats or "miracles".

In this chapter Churchill's leadership is examined under three heads. First, I want to establish if there is any evidence of charisma in British politics at a time of crisis. Second, I want to point to certain salient features of British political leadership in the twentieth century and to show how the combination of institutional and cultural factors greatly restricts the charismatic elements in any leader—mass relationship in Britain. I suggest, however, that in a crisis these constraints are relaxed and the scope for more personal leadership is enhanced. In the final section I distinguish between the heroic or crisis and routine styles of leadership in Britain. The conclusion is that Churchill was not charismatic according to strict reading of Weber's criteria, but that, along with Lloyd George, he exemplifies a model of crisis leadership in British politics which underlines the importance of both situational and personality factors.

THE OUTSIDER: CHURCHILL'S CAREER UNTIL 1939

As 1939 began, the future seemed to hold little for the 64-year-old Churchill. Although his early career had been marked by many achievements, he had been out of office for 10 years, and absent from the leadership ranks of the Conservative Party since January 1930. Since 1932 he had made himself unpopular by frequently warning against the Nazi menace in Germany. In September 1938 Chamberlain had concluded the Munich agreement with Hitler and was given a rapturous welcome in the House of Commons and by most of the press. The agreement increased Churchill's isolation and seemed to confirm his exclusion from government circles.

For most of this period Churchill had been isolated in the Commons, spurned by his party, claiming no personal following in the country and only narrowly surviving a vote of no confidence by his local constituency party for his criticism of Chamberlain. His shortcomings, particularly his warlike nature, outweighed his considerable abilities, especially at a time when avoidance of war was the overriding goal of British foreign policy. As war approached, however, so demands for Churchill's appointment to office grew. In September 1939, when war was declared, he was invited to join the administration and in May 1940, following the resignation of a discredited Chamberlain after the Norwegian fiasco, he became Prime Minister of a nation facing its most serious threat of invasion since the wars with Napoleon. In this role he was soon to gain a reputation as a national saviour and statesman comparable to that of Chatham and of Wellington. His rise to power illustrates the importance of situational factors in transforming a leader's assumed deficiencies into political resources.

Throughout his career Churchill drew battle lines with relish; often this combativeness was so maladaptive that one must infer that he could not help himself. His pugnacity frequently surpassed what was regarded as acceptable in British party competition. Here it is worth recalling that Churchill had been a soldier before he entered politics. As a young man he had been a noted war correspondent, positively seeking out danger and battle. In addition, he had re-enlisted in the First World War, after being a Cabinet Minister. His bitter attacks on Labour ('unfit to govern'); his abuse of Gandhi and vehement opposition to progress towards autonomy for India; his willingness to provoke a constitutional crisis over the Abdication in 1936; his warmongering reputation gained by his demands for the pre-1914 coercion of Ulster; his enthusiastic support of the Gallipoli expedition in 1915, and the post-war intervention in Bolshevik Russia; and his conduct in the general strike; made his predispositions very apparent. He lacked judgement, he liked a war, and he was often on the losing side. That his almost single-handed warnings against Nazism fell on deaf ears was due in large part to the fact that he had cried 'wolf' too often before. Harold Macmillan, also a Tory rebel, saw Churchill as 'reactionary and unrealistic . . . Churchill's speeches and demands for rearmament, however effective in themselves, were injured because of the general doubt as to the soundness of his judgement' (1966, p. 291). In early 1939 Chamberlain defended his refusal to give him office because of fears that Churchill would 'rock the boat'.

Churchill's highly exploitative view of political parties also gained him a reputation for unreliability; colleagues saw his ostentatious independence of party as adventurism and opportunism. His career had consisted of meanderings across the party system. He started off as a rebellious Conservative, switched to the Liberals, supported the Lloyd George coalition immediately after the war, then flirted with a centre party, and finally returned to the Conservatives in 1924. From 1930 to 1939 he was a back-bench rebel, vigorously differing from his leaders over foreign and imperial questions and the handling of the Abdication crisis in 1936. Though always something of a Tory and invariably a partisan, he was not 'a good party man' but rather a troublesome colleague. Asquith early noted his predilection for 'strange coalitions and odd regroupings'.

It may be a mark of his lack of political skill that Churchill so often found himself politically isolated; this was particularly true of his prominent association with the disastrous Gallipoli campaign in 1915 and his attempts to campaign for Edward VIII during the Abdication crisis in 1936. His reactionary stance over India and other questions in this decade kept him apart from Eden and younger Conservative critics of appeasement. In addition, Churchill also seemed *passé*. His was a voice from the past, with the fine rhetoric about the destiny of the English people, the romantic views of the monarchy and Empire, and the shrill warnings of impending disaster, failing 'a supreme recovery of moral health and martial vigour'. He opposed the extension of votes to women in 1928, and expressed the view that universal suffrage had lowered the quality of public life (James, 1969, pp. 301ff). He had a quaint view of the relationship between the Crown and the People, in which the masses, conscious of their place, would follow the lead of a disinterested aristocracy. This view of an organic English society was wedded to a belief in a world order consisting of a hierarchy of great states and civilisations which throughout history had been locked in an unyielding struggle between good and evil (Berlin, 1949).

Yet in spite of the weakness of Churchill's political position in early 1939, the onset of war transformed his standing. In September 1939 he was in the government, as First Lord of the Admiralty, and in May 1940 he became Prime Minister. His entry into the government and later possession of the first office were direct consequences of the threat of war and the unfavourable military position in 1940. His belligerance, so long a handicap, now stood him in good stead.

THE CHARISMATIC CONDITION

We return in this section to our five criteria for charisma, abstracted from Weber, and apply them to Churchill's war leadership.

The Crisis Situation

There is little doubt that in May 1940, Churchill took over from
Chamberlain at what was widely seen as a time of dire crisis. Britain
faced the prospect of defeat and occupation by Germany. France
was on the verge of collapse, Italy was about to enter the war in
support of Germany, 300,000 British troops were trapped in Dunkirk,
Russia was hostile and America neutral. There was also some
defeatism in high places. The King was very anxious about the
general situation, as 'everything we do appears to be wrong and
gets us nowhere' (Wheeler-Bennett, 1958, p. 456). The *Economist*
(4 May 1940) complained of a 'lack of courage and of resolution in
the nation's leadership'. However, although Chamberlain's downfall
and Churchill's appointment involved a collapse of Conservative
Party discipline and agreement on the need for all-party government,
there was no collapse of institutions or procedures, and no social
disorganisation or mass anomie.

The Relationship Between Leader and Followers

It is clear that Churchill showed little ability to attract a following
before he came to power − as indeed did Lenin, de Gaulle before
1958, and Castro (Tucker, 1968). There was some increase in public
approval when he was in the Cabinet in 1939 and a spectacular gain
when he became Prime Minister. In other words office seems to
have been essential to attracting support. This institutionalisation of
support − according it to a man only when he is in office − is very
different from Weber's idea of charisma.

We also need to decide the extent to which Churchill's appointment
in 1940 demonstrates that the 'original basis of recruitment is
personal charisma' (Weber, p. 337). Again this does not seem to
have been important. If during the debate on the disaster in Norway
between 7 and 9 May there was, according to one survey, 'now
genuine, though perhaps a passing, mass pressure to change the
Prime Minister' (M-O Report No. 91, 10.5.40), then Churchill was
only one among other names being considered. Halifax had wide
support in the press and elite circles, not least from Chamberlain
and the King. The majority of the Conservative Party still distrusted
Churchill (James, 1969, p. 349; Dalton, 1957, p. 346), and Halifax
or indeed any alternative was acceptable to Labour leaders who
were not prepared to serve in an all-party government, except under

Table 9.1 Preferred successor to Chamberlain as Prime Minister (among supporters of the government)

	March 1939 %	January 1940 %	March 1940 %
Eden	38	34	28
Churchill	7	9	25
Halifax	7	7	na
Others/Don't Know	48	50	47

Source: Gallup Polls. Question: 'If Chamberlain were to resign who would you prefer to see as his successor?'

Chamberlain (Butler, 1971, pp. 83–4). It is also retrospective judgement to see Churchill's appointment as a mark of the nation's wisdom, an example of 'a mass instinct for what is right' (as asserted by Morrison, 1960, p. 210). In fact there was little evidence of a widespread public demand for Churchill. Though the polls suggest that he was gaining in public esteem as the war progressed, it was Eden, in a vague and inarticulate way, who remained the preferred successor (Table 9.1).

The most readily available testimony to Churchill's public appeal lies in the surveys conducted at the time. These cast fresh light on the relationship between Churchill and the people. The data from the opinion polls enable us to explore the comparative popularity or approval of Prime Ministers over the past 30 years. Since 1939 the Gallup Poll has used such questions as, 'On the whole, in general, do you approve or disapprove of x as Prime Minster?', or 'Are you satisfied or dissatisfied with x as Prime Minster?' The Mass Observation data consist of the written reports of observers who 'listened in' to what their neighbours and friends were saying during the war. Obviously this latter material is impressionistic and suggestive rather than conclusive. However, it does provide helpful insights about the subjective meanings underlying the responses to the fixed choice of questions in the Gallup polls, which, while useful in establishing the durability and extensiveness of popular approval, do not tell us of the intensity of support. This is unfortunate because the charismatic relationship is properly regarded as an intense and emotional one. In spite of these imperfections, the poll data are

Table 9.2 Average annual rates of approval-disapproval for wartime prime ministers

Dates and numbers of polls	Approve (%)	Disapprove (%)
	Chamberlain	
1938 (3)	50	40
September 1939 (7)	54	39
October 1939 to		
March 1940 (6)	63	30
May 1940 (1)	32	58

Dates and numbers of polls	Approve (%)	Disapprove (%)
	Churchill	
June 1940 to		
December 1940 (3)	88	17
1941 (5)	86	9
1942 (12)	94	10
1943 (5)	92	6
1944 (7)	89	8
1945 (5)	83	12

Source: Gallup Polls.

useful in establishing certain distinctive features of the public appraisals of Churchill.

It seems to be generally true that external threats to the nation initially produce some rallying behind a president or premier (Mueller, 1970; Charlot, 1971). But in the case of Churchill this occurred to a remarkable degree in British politics, and the approval measured by the polls was higher than that for Roosevelt in wartime or for de Gaulle during and after 1958 (Table 9.2). For example, approval for Chamberlain at the outbreak of war moved up from 55 per cent to 65 per cent. It was already declining in 1940, and by the time of the Norway fiasco in May it had fallen to 32 per cent. Approval for Churchill, on the other hand, was offered by nearly 90 per cent when he took over and remained near this level for most of the war period. In Chamberlain's case war did not make the Prime Minister the focus of an individual national loyalty; Churchill, in contrast, clearly did manage to command such a loyalty. Under the threat of invasion, the British responded positively to Churchill's explicit patriotism and calls for sacrifice.

Popular assessments of Churchill tended to concentrate on his 'bulldog courage', or that he was 'a fighter' – ironically, the very qualities which had hindered his progress in the past. Mass Observation interviews found that the vast majority of people welcomed his appointment because 'he's hard' and 'there'll be trouble', and they anticipated 'bloody fireworks'. Less than a year later Tom Harrison contrasted the high morale under Churchill with the disunity and pessimism prevalent under Chamberlain; 'Under Mr Churchill something like a real unity was attained' (M-O Report, No. 562, 4.2.41). Gallup Polls found that people frequently offered comments to the effect that he was 'the right man in the right place', 'for war and not peace' and 'a match for Hitler' (M-O Reports, 654, 749).

The data in Figures 9.1 and 9.2 show the staggeringly high rates of approval for Churchill, even when many people disapproved of his government and/or party, and even when the war was clearly won. His approval ratings far outrank those available for any other Prime Minister. He was clearly perceived as the leader in war. Such data lend some solid substance to the proposition that Churchill indeed symbolised or personalised the determination to resist Hitler.

Figure 9.3, however, underlines the fact that this support was very specific; it did not derive from or carry over to the government or party. Only towards the end of 1942 did the government gain a measure of approval in any way approaching that of Churchill. For the first 2½ years of Churchill's war leadership there was a clear contradistinction in the public mind between the Prime Minister and the government. This was not so under Chamberlain and has never occurred to the same extent since. It is worthwhile bearing in mind that Churchill, though a Conservative, was leading an all-party government. Yet throughout the first half of the war his approval rating was often 40 points or more ahead of the government; it reached 43 per cent in March 1942, when one-half of the poll expressed their dissatisfaction with the government. This contrasts with the poll ratings of succeeding Prime Ministers, which, though somewhat higher, are always tied to those of their governments (Figure 9.3). These high ratings for Churchill showed only minor

143

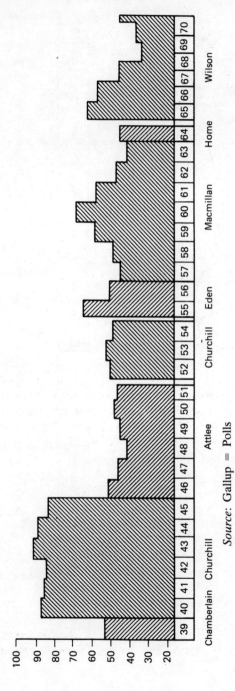

Source: Gallup = Polls

Note: These ratings are based on the average percentage of respondents who indicated satisfaction with or approval for the Prime Minister of the day.

Figure 9.1 Average annual approval ratings for Prime Minister, 1939–70

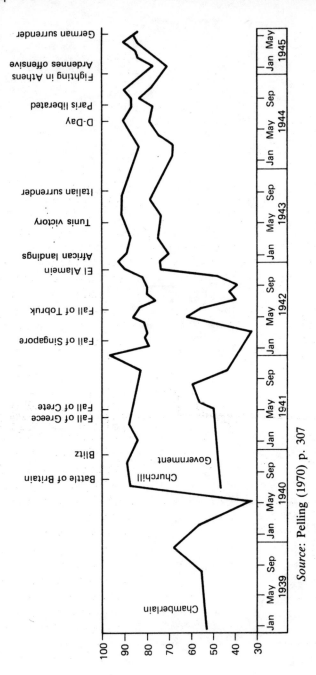

Source: Pelling (1970) p. 307

Figure 9.2 Approval ratings for Churchill and the government in the Second World War

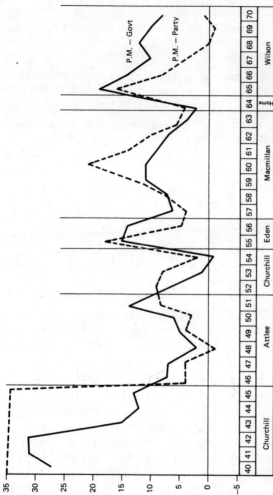

Source: Gallup = Polls

Note: Above the O line shows the amounts by which approval for the Prime Minister exceeded that for his party and government. Below the O line shows the amounts by which his approval fell below that for his party and government.

The annual and part-annual averages are based on the returns from Gallup polls which, since 1945, have usually been reported monthly. The figures for the Conservative Party between 1940 and 1945, however, are based upon fewer polls asking questions about party preferences.

Figure 9.3 Percentage differences between annual average approval for Prime Minister, party and government 1940–70

differences across age, sex and social class groupings. There was an impressively national distribution of support.

Support for Churchill was also independent of party preference. The outbreak of war coincided with some increase in support for the Conservative Party, as measured in the polls, and also for Chamberlain, although approval and disapproval for the latter ran largely along party lines. What is remarkable is that in spite of Churchill's appeal as a war leader and his leadership of the Conservative Party, there was a steady erosion of Conservative support and a swing to Labour from 1940 to 1945. Throughout 1942 and 1943 the Conservatives usually attracted the support of around 25 per cent of the respondents, Labour 45 per cent, the Liberals 6 to 10 per cent, and another 25 per cent were 'don't knows' or uncertain about voting. In April 1945, when 91 per cent approved of Churchill and 85 per cent of the government (the highest ratings ever measured by Gallup), only 24 per cent intended to vote Conservative. This split-ticket approach or marked discontinuity between choice of leader and party, with the latter decisively affecting the vote, also carried over to the hypothetical question of a successor if Churchill were removed from the leadership. The Conservative Eden was regularly the preferred choice; support for Attlee, the Labour leader, flickered between 1 and 3 per cent. But a personality or leadership-based orientation to party vote was significantly absent. Misunderstanding this point, and assuming that voters would vote along 'presidential' lines, many commentators and politicians were wildly amiss in their prognostications for the 1945 general election. The reverse side of this proposition is that support for Churchill as war leader transcended party loyalties.

Though there was some opposition and criticism in Parliament and the press of Churchill's leadership in 1941 and 1942, there is little evidence in the polls of a marked decline in public esteem from 1940, as suggested by Calder (1969) and Gardiner (1968, p. 173). Even after the loss of Tobruk and Singapore in 1942 nearly 80 per cent still approved of him. The polls found a hard core of 12 to 15 per cent expressing disapproval; these complained that he was too old, too dictatorial, 'all talk' and a Tory. In Parliament there was more open criticism of his conduct and of the war from such Tory malcontents as Winterton and Hore-Belisha, and Tribune Socialists; this stimulated Churchill to reconstruct his government in 1942.

The Outstanding Personality

On the question of personal qualities, there is little doubt that Churchill had a crisis temperament. He was energised and fulfilled by crisis; tranquillity was not soothing. As a young politician he confessed: 'I like things to happen, and if they don't happen I like to make them' (James, 1969, p. 186). In 1939 he wrote of his sense of relief and peace of mind at the declaration of war (Moran, 1966, p. 324). Another relevant aspect for the crisis leader is his sense of uniqueness, a belief in his own destiny. Churchill certainly believed that he had been preserved for a purpose (Cowles, 1953, p. 144; James, 1969, p. 34). In 1940, as Prime Minister, he claims to have felt:

> I was kept for this job . . . I felt as if I were walking with destiny and that all my past life had been but a preparation for this hour and this trial . . . power in a national crisis, when a man believes he knows what orders should be given, is a blessing (Churchill, 1948, pp. 526–7).

Such feelings may be contrasted with Halifax's reaction at the prospect of becoming Prime Minister – 'a feeling of physical sickness in the pit of his stomach' (Birkenhead, 1965, pp. 282–3). They are more usefully contrasted, however, with Churchill's depressions and lack of inner harmony when out of office or when remote from the scene of action.

Churchill's childhood experiences seem to be important in the context of understanding the sources of his personality, not least because of the explicitly political environment to which he was exposed. He was descended from the great Marlborough and was a son of Lord Randolph Churchill, the stormy petrel of late nineteenth-century politics. Explanations of the son's adult behaviour invariably focus on his strange relationship with an admired but remote and impersonal father, who seems to have met his son's craving for recognition and affection with 'calculating coldness' (Churchill, 1966). In his youth Churchill was often unhappy, frustrated and a disappointment to the father he idolised (James, 1969; Martin, 1970; Bonham-Carter, 1965).

Churchill's intense ambition, aggressiveness and search for action are so recurrent and interrelated that one is justified in referring to a political 'style'. Anthony Storr (1969) has suggested that Winston's desire for 'personal distinction' was so abnormal and the aggressiveness so marked that they should be traced to early deprivation of parental recognition and consequent acute lack of self-esteem, for both of which there is ample evidence. In this regard it is interesting to see that he seems to belong to a personality type. Lasswell and psycho-historical analysts have suggested that individuals concerned to transfer private ambitions on to a political stage are particularly drawn to a charismatic or crisis role (Erikson, 1958; Lasswell, 1948, 1960).

Storr has further hypothesised that Churchill's own depressive temperament and his personal struggle to combat despair helped his inspirational role in 1940. Inevitably one is encouraged to see Churchill in 1940, like Erik Erikson's 'great reformers', as a leader settling a 'personal account' on a grand scale, a case of 'an individual . . . called upon . . . to lift his individual patient-hood to the level of a universal one and try to solve for all what he could not solve for himself alone' (Erikson, 1958, p. 67). Churchill, in other words, was able to meet his own personal need to find a suitable adversary on whom his aggression might be displaced, by linking it to the solution of a major threat to his country. The obstinacy, aggressiveness, neurotic sense of mission and lack of 'balance', which had hindered him in the past, were successfully exploited for political purposes. Like other crisis-leaders in history he may have been enabled, because of the Nazi menace, to settle a personal account in a grand historical and political context.

In addition to this vivid and inspirational personality, one needs to acknowledge Churchill's other skills. (Indeed, the neglect of domestic issues may have contributed to public appraisal of his unsuitability for the task of post-war social reconstruction.) Alleged charismatic leaders are also invariably men of striking eloquence, and this ability is surely important in transmitting the qualities of leader to follower. Churchill's speeches to the House of Commons and his broadcasts are famous for their inspirational quality. One of the 1940 speeches was heard by as many as 70 per cent of the adult population (Calder, 1969, p. 97). Three elements recurred in these early speeches: first, a statement of the setbacks and the difficult times ahead; second, that this was a struggle between good and evil, made more heroic by the fact that Britain stood alone; third, the assertion that defeat was unthinkable, and, no matter what the cost, Britain would be victorious. Surveys suggest that people appreciated being told facts, no matter how unpleasant, and welcomed aggressive postures and statements. He probably was 'saying what (the people) would like to say for themselves if they knew how', (Moran, 1966, p. 12, see also pp. 13, 247). This ability to convince people of the inevitability of future victory, no matter what the present disasters, was the cause of Aneurin Bevan's later complaint that Churchill was a dreamer; for his 'greatest feat was to persuade people not to look at facts' (1965, p. 61). Though Churchill did not lack a sense of theatre and the dramatic gesture (particularly when compared with Chamberlain and Attlee), he achieved his popular approval without the use of television, press conferences, mass rallies or demonstrations; he placed an almost exclusive reliance on broadcasts and speeches to the House of Commons.

The Revolutionary Style of the Leader

In seeking the revolutionary or irrational aspects of Churchill's leadership, it is important to distinguish between his strong support for the institutions and régime, and his highly unorthodox working methods. Churchill's task was, as he saw it, a very 'simple' one: to defeat Hitler, and to preserve the *status quo* – the historical traditions and the political institutions. During the war there was a concentration of power in the hands of the government and of the Prime Minister. However, there was no permanent redefinition of the office as a result of Churchill's tenure. In his scrupulous regard for the forms of the constitution he was far less radical than Lloyd George, whose rise to the premiership involved a fatal split in the Liberal Party, and who ignored the House of Commons, altered the Cabinet and had little respect for most of the political conventions.

Again, in contrast to Weber's idea of the charismatic leader, Churchill did not dispense with organisation. His own institutional changes, although important for effective prosecution of the war, were modest. He introduced more of his personal friends into the executive, and with his appointment there was a greater source of urgency in the Civil Service. He set up a smaller War Cabinet but at first felt compelled to include many of the leaders associated with the appeasement policy, to placate the Conservative majority. After Chamberlain's death he took over the leadership of the Conservative Party, perceiving the potential weakness in the House of Commons of a Prime Minister who was not a party leader, and tried to maintain some all-party balance in his Cabinet. In other words, Churchill was prepared to operate as a political broker, and acknowledge the political expectations of other key political figures. Also, though he dismissed generals, he seems never to have over-ruled military advisers on defence matters. Notwithstanding his parliamentary skills, what was important for his domination of the House of Commons and Cabinet on war strategy was his combination of the office of Minister of Defence with that of Prime Minister. His chairmanship of the Chiefs of Staff, the military co-ordinating committees, and the Cabinet made him an indispensable link as well as keeping him in touch with various viewpoints and exposing him to the germinating stages of policies. By working through established institutions his performance runs counter to Weber's notion of the charismatic style.

On the other hand, his dislike of bureaucratic methods, the urge for action, the highly personal working habits (catnapping in the day and working through until the early morning hours), the imaginative appointments to office of men like Bevin, Beaverbrook and Lyttleton, and his restless personal interest in so many areas of the war effort were distinctly non-routine. Here his earlier exposure to and admiration for Lloyd George are instructive. In his history of the 1914–18 war, *The World Crisis*, Churchill wrote of the success of Lloyd George's dismissal of the expert advice of army generals: 'His intuition fitted the crisis better than the logical reasoning of more logical minds'. Halifax distrusted his emotionalism and lack of logic, finding his mind 'a most curious mixture of a child's emotion and a man's reason' (Birkenhead, p. 459). Some civil servants disliked his fixations and found his methods irritating (Liddell-Hart, 1969). He seems to have been a bad administrator, disliked routine matters and reserved himself for what he saw as the 'big' issues. Yet it is clear that associates were inspired and prepared to work disproportionately hard for him.

The Instability of the Charismatic Appeal

Given the uniformly high level of support for Churchill throughout the war there is little point in relating military reverses to the slight changes in approval. What the poll data show, and this is significant in understanding the electoral rebuff of Churchill and the Conservatives in 1945, is how the war situation created the judgement of the man. Even in mid-1941, Mass Observation found that opinions

Table 9.3 Would it be a good or a bad thing for Churchill to remain as prime minister after the war? (M–O, No. 2024)

	Good (%)	Bad (%)	Don't know (%)
19.11.42	38	45	17
8.2.44	28	62	10

were divided evenly on the desirability of Churchill's continuance as Prime Minister after the war. As the war progressed, so a radicalisation of public sentiment on domestic issues made Churchill's conservative outlook on social reform a disadvantage when people envisaged post-war society (cf. M-O, *What People Want From War*, 5.1.42). In October 1943, when the Gallup polls showed that over 90 per cent were pro-Churchill, only a small proportion considered him relevant to the tasks of post-war reconstruction; this is confirmed by Table 9.3. The general view was that he was too old and too much the man of war. This evidence has to be contrasted with the widely held view in the national press and among many Labour leaders, even as late as 1945 (Dalton, 1957, p.463; Williams, 1961, p. 119), that Churchill would win an election for the Conservatives. Such a view clearly failed to appreciate the goal-centred nature of the approval accorded to him; its specificity is evidence that it was not uncritical. The immense devotion given to Churchill in his capacity as war leader could not be converted into credit for any peace-time role. The scanty evidence of the polls was a guide to the overwhelming Labour triumph in the 1945 election.

How do we assess Churchill's leadership in the war according to the above criteria, bearing in mind that we are thinking of a charismatic condition as continuous and not as a sharply differentiated one? First, there certainly was a crisis, in a threat of military defeat and occupation. But it did not involve the breakdown of institutions or values, or even sharp institutional change, as emphasised by Weber. We have stressed the limited nature of the disturbance to British institutions and norms. The prospect of defeat in 1940 was sufficient to loosen the party system, and bring about the withdrawal of Chamberlain and the formation of an all-party government.

Churchill's support was distinctive in British politics over the past 50 years, not only for its abnormally high level but also because it was so clearly independent of his party and government. Although he met a demand for bold personal leadership, this support was neither unconditional nor uncritical. What people admired was his uncompromising and belligerent outlook. Indeed, from our examination of the relationship between Churchill and the public, we may be more impressed with an instrumental or 'rational' and not a charismatic interpretation of his authority. Many people seemed to adopt a highly calculating attitude towards him. Churchill's high rating, even at the times of poor governmental, military or even personal performance, reflected an assessment that nobody else would do the job as effectively.

Third, we have also seen that many of his personal and political qualities certainly fitted a crisis style of leadership. Fourth, though Churchill was unconventional in many of his working habits he was quite conservative in his orientation to the major political institutions. He did not permanently redefine the office of Prime Minister. He wanted to win the war, to defend the régime. Finally, his appeal was unstable in large part because it was so closely tied to evaluations of him as a war leader. His own leadership, which helped indirectly to preserve the institutional *status quo*, smoothed the path for a resumption of party government and his own exclusion from office by conventional electoral means.

CHURCHILL AND THE BRITISH POLITICAL TRADITION

Although he was a distinctive and extraordinarily popular leader, Churchill has hardly met established criteria of charisma. This is because of the institutional and cultural factors in Britain. In another beleaguered country a Churchill might have been more successful in attracting the awe, reverence and blind faith that mark the charismatic relationship (Willner, 1968, p. 6). The inference from this analysis is that if Churchill was not a charismatic leader in the war years, then it is very difficult to envisage such a leader in twentieth-century Britain. This in turn calls for an examination of the 'damping' influence of such factors as the structure of British government, the political culture, recruitment methods, and the expected styles of British leadership. These features depress the possibilities and scope for personal leadership in Britain.

Dual Executive

A British Prime Minister lacks the visible and dramatic trappings attached to the monarchy and 'fused' presidencies. The Queen manages to attract more positive affect than the party leader in office; she is widely if superficially seen as the symbol of a united nation, standing above political conflict. In contrast, as shown in Figures 9.1 and 9.2, the Prime Minister is invariably perceived by the electorate in a partisan perspective, even though usually more voters approve of him than of his party. Only for 5 years in the 25-year period 1946–70 has approval for a Prime Minister exceeded that for his party by more than 10 percentage points. This feature derives from stable party loyalties and a closer relationship between social class and party choice than is found in other Anglo-American societies. British Prime Ministers are hardly popular figures. In post-war years only Harold Macmillan and Harold Wilson have retained the approval of more than half of the electorate for 2 years or more. The absence of weak political parties and fluid pressure groups has prevented the leader building a personal coalition by making ad hoc appeals to build up coalitions à l'americaine or à la française. Where voters do find an inconsistency between leader and party preferences, it is invariably the latter which dominates.

Recruitment

There is a thorough sifting process for leaders in the British political system. Apart from the usual requirements for success, two obvious limitations in the British case are the conventions that the Prime Minister must be a member of the House of Commons and must lead the largest party in it (though Churchill was not leader of the Conservative Party for 5 months after his appointment in 1940). Political prowess and skill are proven at the parliamentary level; there tends to be little transferability of talent and prestige from the extra-parliamentary to the political sphere. As this feature is also true of most of the old Commonwealth states, it may be more related to the Cabinet system of government than it is a unique British phenomenon. Prime Ministers and Cabinet ministers undergo a very long parliamentary apprenticeship. The average length of membership of the House of Commons for an MP before becoming Prime Minister has been 26 years during this century – and Churchill waited nearly 40. This is an appreciably longer legislative

apprenticeship than that experienced by other Anglo-American
leaders. Such an enduring exercise in socialisation clearly provides
ample opportunity for learning skills appropriate to Parliament. It
is noteworthy that prominence outside this framework is a more
recognisable route to high office elsewhere, e.g. the soldier-statesman
(de Gaulle, Eisenhower), the administrator or banker (Pompidou),
the civil servant (Adenauer), or rank outsider (Hitler and Mussolini).
Notwithstanding the traditions of amateurism in British public life
there is an intense and constraining professionalism about the House
of Commons background from which the Prime Minister emerges.

Political Culture

A relatively weakly developed notion of the state and a self-reliant
citizenry have provided fertile ground for would-be great men;
politicians have rarely been 'history's commanding officers', able to
transform the life of the nation (Barker, 1945, p. 29). In the recent
past, fundamental issues in Britain have been resolved in Parliament
and in Whitehall by bargaining and along bipartisan lines; the
government has not been so paralysed that it had to invoke the
help of an outside *dramatis persona*. The emphasis on elite
accommodation to change and an incremental mode of development
is well illustrated in the gradual and relatively peaceful extensions
of the suffrage in the nineteenth-century. Even in such divisive times
as the General Strike of 1926 and the 1931 economic crisis, one is
impressed by the self-restraint of popular demands and the amount
of inter-elite agreement, particularly when viewed in comparison
with the manner in which other countries handled such issues. With
the significant exception of Ireland, it is a fair judgement that the
major issues have been muffled or solved at a low level of crisis,
before the system was brought into question. It seems clear that
neither the political culture nor the historical record provide the
kind of resources suitable for exercising heroic styles of leadership
in peacetime in Britain.

Elite Political Culture

More significant perhaps is the elite political culture – the conventions, nuances, understandings and 'codes' which govern the
behaviour of leading politicians and administrators. Given that ten
of the sixteen twentieth-century Prime Ministers first assumed that

office without the sanction of a general election, approval at this level is more decisive than a popular following. The 'code' of the small circle of a London-based, socially homogeneous and long-socialised elite is well-developed though often implicit. Acceptability to colleagues at the levels of party, Parliament and Cabinet have attracted and rewarded a personality and style in which such qualities as reliability, self-restraint, safety, trustworthiness – in short, 'character' – have figured prominently.

Dynamic and spectacular qualities have not been highly esteemed in a system of disciplined parties and collective leadership, despite the different emphases of the Labour and Conservative Parties. Objections to personality and style have been decisive, not least in the cases of Churchill and Lloyd George. Except in war, bold leaders have been treated harshly. The importance attached to party unity in the voting divisions and the collective responsibility of the Cabinet are interesting illustrations of the marked preference for consensual over individualist ideas. Until 1965, when the Conservative Party implemented a system of competitive elections, leaders 'emerged' by a consensus system in which acceptability to all significant groups in the party outweighed consideration of majority support. Perhaps Asquith, Baldwin, Attlee and Wilson, men skilled in the art of smoothing over party divisions, reconciling rather than mobilising, have come close to the notion of a leader most favoured by many voters.

It is easily seen how such an institutional–cultural matrix has depressed the opportunities for dramatic personal political leadership. A self-confident people, a relatively pluralistic and participant political culture, a lack of a tradition of 'the great man', durable and adaptable institutions, agreed procedures for transfers of authority and the resolution of crises at an early stage – often by accommodations between leaders of different parties – have not encouraged charismatic leadership. What has usually emerged has been what one may regard as a routine style which is, in a word, collegial not presidential. Whereas Americans may expect heroic leadership from the President, in Britain there is an aversion to dynamic leadership except in crisis times.

Clearly this study of Churchill shows that the British people are able to idealise and respond personally to an outstanding leader at a time of crisis. But the way in which the political agenda is usually met by the machinery of Parliament deprives them of the opportunity to make such a response. One risks a tautology by referring to the stability of the institutions and the intensity of demands on the political system. The more frequent a resort to the crisis leader and the abandonment of routine procedures, the more entrenched such a tradition becomes; ultimately it may even be institutionalised, as with de Gaulle's plebiscitarian amendment to the French constitution in 1962.

But institutions also require innovative responses from members if they are to survive pressing challenges and new or unexpected demands, and here the notion of 'outsider' is helpful. In France, under the Fourth Republic, Mendes-France and de Gaulle rebelled against the 'game' of politics, in which the leader was expected to settle for a modest broker role, choosing goals acceptable to the Assembly. In this sense both men were outsiders and were rejected. De Gaulle was able to return on his own terms when the Fourth Republic collapsed in 1958.

Churchill's strengths in 1940 lay in the fact that he was not compromised by the appeasement policies, and so clearly stood apart from the people and ideas associated with them. The most far-reaching innovations in the Cabinet and administration were effected by the readjustments of Lloyd George and, to a lesser extent, Churchill to the demands of large-scale war. New departments and ministries were created and non-career civil servants introduced in order to prosecute the war effort more vigorously and enable the leaders to impress himself more directly on that effort. Lloyd George established the Cabinet Secretariat, and both men had their own teams of unofficial advisers. Whereas the routine leader stepped into a pre-existing system, the two innovative leaders in British politics managed to redefine their offices along lines suitable for their own skill and ambitions.

If Lloyd George and Churchill illustrate the ability of the British political institutions and values to accommodate a style which does not conform to accepted ideas and even to respond positively in a crisis, then it is also the case that the careers of Sir Oswald Mosley and Sir Stafford Cripps (and, more recently, Enoch Powell) show its resistance to the outsider. The first two were examples of the upper-class recruitment to the Labour Party which so struck continental Socialists (Wertheimer, 1929); both held office in the second Labour government (1929–31); both assumed that they had large personal followings in the country and broke with the Labour Party in the 1930s; and the careers of both men, when detached from a major political party, were derisory.

Mosley's New Party, which offered an ambitious New Deal programme to combat the economic crisis, was swept away in the 1931 general election. Mosley then formed the British Union of Fascists in 1932 and called for a break with established institutions and values. With his open-air demonstrations and meetings, uniformed followers, the cult of his own absolute personal leadership, the call for national greatness and the emphasis on street politics, Mosley's personal behaviour has been the nearest approximation to that of a charismatic leader in Britain. However, he never attracted a serious political following. The party's performance at by-elections was feeble and he never sat in 'Parliament again after 1931. The limited popular support dwindled as the implication of Mosley's aims became clearer; even at a time when governments and institutions were demonstrably incapable of tackling the economic depression, the strength of the party system, parliamentary institutions and norms of the civic culture prevented Mosley's breakthrough. This 'non-event' is interesting when one considers that concurrently Germany and the United States responded to the economic crisis by installing bold leaders who, each in a different way, implemented sweeping reform programmes. In Britain, neither occurred.

The performance of Cripps in the 1930s and his breach with the party system also contain useful lessons. Cripps' disappointment with parliamentary and party politics after 1931 and his support for more left-wing causes and 'direct action' brought him into conflict with the Labour leaders. Yet he did not attract a substantial following and in 1939 he was expelled from the Labour Party for his insistence on campaigning for a Popular Front, in defiance of official Labour Party policy. Indeed the late career of Cripps supports the analysis. It was only after 1940, when he showed that he could work within the system, that he became an acceptable figure even to his Labour colleagues.

There are limits therefore to the extent to which the innovator can remain 'outside' and still be called to office in Britain. Consequences differ according to whether the politician rejects (a) the 'political formula' or widely held core values in a society; (b) the political institutions, including the parliamentary and party systems; and (c) the party leaders. Where a politician rejects the 'political formula' and/or the political institutions, it is difficult to imagine him coming to power other than by a breakdown of norms and/or institutions. Churchill and Lloyd George had limited their protests to the party (and government) leaders before they gained power. Only in the 1930s did Lloyd George, when he was no longer a serious contender for office, become impressed by the dictators in Germany and Italy and despair of Parliament. In the 1930s Churchill realised the importance of remaining tied to the Conservative Party and that without it he would be a spent force.

On the other hand, Sir Oswald Mosley broadened his attacks to encompass all three elements. The rise of Lloyd George and Churchill shows the force of the institutional constraints. Before becoming Prime Minister both were Members of Parliament, prominent members of the largest party, and ministers in the government. In other words, though outsiders they were still clearly 'in' the political system, and, in 1916 and 1940, they travelled short distances from the Cabinet to the Premiership.

What do these findings about crisis and routine styles of leadership in British politics imply for more general theories of leadership? The crisis situation may cause the collapse of (1) the incumbent leadership, (2) the institutions or (3) both the leader and institutions. In other words, crisis creates a potential for change and, more restrictively, a potential for charismatic leadership. The salience of the crisis may vary along such dimensions as intensity, durability and extensiveness, and its impact on the political system may vary according to the politicisation of the grievances, elite skills, and the effectiveness and legitimacy of the political institutions. In the British case the political culture and the widespread consensus about the institutions and procedures have helped the resolution of crises at an early stage and diminished the potential for charisma. The Third and Fourth French Republics, pre-Fascist Italy and the Weimar Republic, on the other hand, were characterised by low support for the institutions, fragmented and polarised party systems, and weak, unstable and irresponsible governments. In addition, these régimes were also unfortunate enough to be faced with severe demands. Not surprisingly, they rated poorly on both effectiveness and legitimacy.

These systemic features are important; different political systems have different 'boiling' points. To paraphrase Arthur Schlesinger, strong men flourish among weak institutions and weak peoples. In Britain the national crises in 1916 and 1940, which involved changes only in leadership personnel and style, illustrates one response, namely the change in leaders. This limited response may call for the rotation of familiar leaders and parties, as in non-crisis times, or it may necessitate the call for the outsider, the potential leader who had been scorned and rejected before the crisis, to sustain the established institutions against severe threat. Rousseau's ideal democracy even allowed for the dictator who would save the frequent resort to forms of 'constitutional dictatorship' or 'Man on Horseback' at time of crisis. Stanley Hoffmann has also written persuasively of heroic forms of leadership in France, exemplified by Mendès-France in 1956 and Clemenceau, called to office in 1917 at the age of 76, when France faced military defeat. Both men limited their innovations to those of personal style. Yet their personal styles and political methods earned the enmity of other politicians despite the fact that their actions helped to rescue the system. According to Hoffmann, 'When routine leaders can no longer preserve it (the system) or make change acceptable, heroic leadership serves the society by adapting it and perpetuates it by renewing it' (1967, p. 153).

Shortly after the crises were resolved, the two men were spurned and the 'game of politics' resumed. Churchill seems to resemble these two leaders: a leader who offers an inspiring, urgent and personal form of leadership within the existing institutional set-up. The effect is often to conserve the constitutional *status quo* by relieving it from potentially destabilising threats. This contrasts sharply with Weber's emphasis on the revolutionary change accomplished by the charismatic leader.

The third and more radical response involves change in both the leadership and the institutions. In contrast to the system-maintaining or conservative leadership in the first category, the emphasis here is on abrupt institutional change which may or may not be revolutionary and involves a leader who may or may not be charismatic. The crucial difference between the first and third courses lies in the weakness of the institution and the availability of the alternative leader. Where the leader helps to destroy the old order and create a new one, he clearly approximates Weber's idea of the charismatic leader as a revolutionary force. Leaders such as Nkrumah, Castro, Kemel Ataturk, Hitler, Lenin in October 1917, and perhaps de Gaulle in 1958 are charismatic. Such a leader seems to be inspired and heaven-sent for a crisis-ridden country – defeated in war, beset by economic depression, facing revolution, or newly independent. He repudiates and undermines the institutions and provides a new constitution. On the other hand, the formation of the Weimar Republic in 1918, or the Irish Free State in 1921, and of the Fourth Republic in 1946 would seem to provide examples of institutional-cum-leadership change being achieved without the charismatic figure.

The idea of charisma is not applicable to British politics. But an adaptation of Weber's emphasis on the crisis situation provides a useful vantage point for distinguishing routine from crisis forms of political leadership in Britain: by making research questions explicit, by alerting us to hypothesis and insights, and by emphasising the interaction of the leader's personality and situation. If Churchill was not charismatic *à la* Weber, he was also not like other British leaders with the exception of Lloyd George – which only underscores our emphasis on the crisis situation and the outsider. The importance of these factors is further emphasised by the pre and post-war careers and appraisals of both men, particularly Lloyd George.

Although the leaderships of Lloyd George and Churchill in wartime deviate from usual prime-ministerial rôles, it is also the case that their careers as a whole demonstrate the importance of the collegial style. Personality characteristics in both men were poorly suited for conventional rôles or expectations. Lloyd George – Welsh, a non-conformist, like Churchill non-university educated, and disrespectful of many of the political traditions and procedures – is the clearest example of the outsider as leader. His urge to get things done almost regardless of the means, and his redefinition of his office and rôle along frankly presidential lines after the First World War, proved to be major factors in his exclusion from power after 1922. The personal fund and the flagrant abuse of honours, his cavalier treatment of the Cabinet as a collective body and his independence from party commitments, the private secretariat and dictatorial treatment of departmental chiefs, were thought by many politicians to border on the unconstitutional. Lloyd George was opposed to the traditional influence of parties; he thought they should be instrumental to great causes and, as a coalition-monger, was prepared to smash the party system in 1910, 1922 and 1929. As Prime Minister he was a more disruptive force in British politics than Churchill. In the end his style, so useful in war and in a confused party situation, made him as mistrusted as Churchill and, given his destruction of the Liberal Party, he became a general without an army.

The careers of both men underline the importance of situational and cultural–structural factors. Lloyd George rose in large part with a crisis in the party system and fell in 1922, when many Conservatives were determined to restore 'normal' party politics. After his fall in

1922, Baldwin and MacDonald both reacted against his style; Lloyd George was a negative model. In a decisive speech which rallied Conservative backbenchers and brought about the collapse of the Coalition and Lloyd George in 1922, Baldwin claimed that Lloyd George was 'a dynamic force' and 'a dynamic force is a very terrible thing'. According to Baldwin, the Prime Minister should be 'plain, instead of brilliant; steady instead of ruthless; soberly truthful instead of romantic and imaginative.' (L.S. Amery, cited in Cowling, 1971, p. 168).

Such analysis only describes the probable or expected leadership styles. There is of course a large element of variety in the role performance of different Prime Ministers. Each incumbent has the opportunity to bring individual energies, skills and motives to the job. Again, it is the war records of Lloyd George and Churchill that stand out, and the vivid contrasts with their respective cultural and institutional confines. In both cases effective management of the war effort (the situational factor) increased the salience of a Prime Minister's personality and heightened expectations about his performance.

References

Barker, E., *Essays in Government*, (Oxford: Clarendon Press, 1945).

Berlin, I., 'Mr. Churchill in 1940', *Atlantic Monthly*, September 1949.

Bevan, A., in *Observer Tribute to Churchill*, (London: Hodder & Stoughton, 1965).

Birkenhead, Earl, *Halifax. The Life of Lord Halifax* (London: Hamilton 1965).

Bonham-Carter, V., *Winston Churchill as I Knew Him*, (London: Eyre and Spittiswoode, 1965).

Butler, Lord, *The Art of the Possible*, (London: Hamish Hamilton, 1971).

Calder, A., *The People's War*, (London: Panther, 1969).

Charlot, J., *The Gaullist Phenomenon*, (London: Allen & Unwin, 1971).

Churchill, R., *Winston S. Churchill*, Vol.1, (London: Heinemann, 1966).

Churchill, W., *Lord Randolph Churchill*, 2 vols, (London: Macmillan, 1906).

Churchill, W., *The Second World War*, Vol.1, (London: Cassell, 1948).

Cowles, V., *Winston Churchill: The Man and the Era*, (London: Hamish Hamilton, 1953).

Cowling, M., *The Impact of Labour*, (London: Cambridge University Press, 1971).

Dalton, H., *The Fateful Years: Memoirs 1931–1945*, (London: F. Muller, 1957).

Dalton, H., 'Churchill: A Memoir', *New Statesman*, 29 January 1965.

162   *Politics and Personalities*

Erikson, E., *Young Man Luther*, (New York: Norton, 1958).
Erikson, E., *Insight and Responsibility*, (New York: Norton, 1964).
Gardiner, B., *Churchill in His Time*, (London: Methuen, 1968).
Hargrove, E., 'Political Leadership in the Anglo-American Democracies' in Edinger, L. (ed), *Political Leadership in Industrial Societies*, (New York: Wiley, 1967).
Hoffmann, S., 'Heroic Leadership: The Case of Modern France', in Edinger, *op.cit*, 1967.
James, R., in Taylor, *op.cit*, 1969.
James, R., *Churchill: A Study in Failure*, (London: Weidenfeld & Nicolson, 1970).
Lasswell, H., *Power and Personality*, (New York: W.W. Norton, 1948).
Lasswell, H., in R. Christie & M. Jahoda (eds.), *Continuities in Social Research: Studies in Scope and Method of 'The Authoritarian Personality'*, (Glencoe, Ill: Free Press, 1954).
Lasswell, H., *Psycopathology and Politics*, (New York: Viking Press, 1960).
Liddell-Hart, B., in Taylor *op.cit.*, 1969.
Macmillan, H., *Winds of Change*, (London: Macmillan, 1966).
Macmillan, H., *The Blast of War*, (London: Macmillan, 1967).
Mass Observation (1940–4), Reports Numbers 91, 1940; 562, 654 and 749, 1941; 2024, 1944. Mass Observation Archives at University of Sussex.
Martin, R., *Lady Randolph Churchill*, (London: Prentice-Hall, 1970).
Moran, Lord, *Churchill*, (London: Constable, 1966).
Morrison, H., *Herbert Morrison: An Autobiography*, (London: Odhams, 1960).
Mueller, J.E., 'Presidential Popularity from Truman to Johnson', *American Political Science Review*, Vol. LXIV, 1970.
Observer Tribute to Churchill, (London: Hodder & Stoughton, 1965).
Pelling, H., *Britain in the Second World War*, (London: Fontana, 1970).
Storr, A., in Taylor, *op.cit.*, 1969.
Taylor, A.J.P. (ed), *Churchill: Four Faces and the Man*, (London: Allen Lane, 1969).
Tucker, R., 'The Theory of Charismatic Leadership', *Daedalus*, Summer, 1968.
Weber, M., *The Theory of Social and Economic Organisation*, (Glencoe, Ill: Free Press, 1947).
Wertheimer, Egon, *Portrait of the Labour Party* (London: Putney, 1929).
Wheeler-Bennett, J., *King George VI*, (London: Macmillan, 1958).
Wheeler-Bennett, J., *Action This Day*, (London: Heinemann, 1969).
Williams, F., *A Prime Minister Remembers*, (London: Heinemann, 1961).
Willner, A.R., *Charismatic Political Leadership: A Theory*, (Princeton: Princeton University Press, 1968).

10 Enoch Powell: Vision and Waste*

Enoch Powell is one of the few post-war politicians who has seized the public imagination. Remarkably he has done this without ever holding senior office. He was Financial Secretary to the Treasury (1957–8) and Minister of Health for 3 years, only one of which was in the Cabinet (1962–3). In an age which is not noted for oratory his fame came from his speeches, many of them made outside Parliament.

In the past two decades Richard Crossman, Barbara Castle, Tony Benn and of course Harold Macmillan kept themselves in the public eye, long after they had retired from Parliament or lost influence. How? By producing diaries and memoirs of yesterday's political events. But Enoch Powell is a non-diary, non-memoir-writing politician. There will be no memoirs or autobiography, even though a publisher would pay a huge sum for one. There are already about a dozen biographies, ranging from a German doctoral dissertation on his oratory to Patrick Cosgrave's *The Lives of Enoch Powell*.[1] He is always ready to read a piece about himself and to point out factual errors (as he has with this essay). The irony is that even in his 78th year the essays and reviews on foreign countries, history, literature and issues of the day, continue to pour from his pen. They are invariably self-revelatory but there is to be no autobiography. He claims to have a horror of dwelling on the past – his past. It would be like a dog returning to its vomit, even excrement.

He is also perhaps the only recent British politician of whom it is possible to write a serious study of his or her political thought. Indeed, there are at least four collections of his speeches; see three volumes by J. Wood (ed.), *A Nation Not Afraid: The Thinking of Enoch Powell*;[2] *Freedom and Reality*;[3] *Still to Decide*;[4] and R. Ritchie (ed.), *Enoch Powell, A Nation or No Nation*.[5] It is difficult to envisage a booklength study of the thought of, say, Macmillan, Wilson or Callaghan. Powell has always been concerned to derive

* This chapter was specially written for this volume.

his positions on issues from fundamentals and address the big questions of national identity, freedom, relationships between the individual and state, and the purpose of politics. This has given his political views both their consistency and rigidity.

Powell was born in Stechford, Birmingham, in 1912 to school-teacher parents. He was part of the stock of the improving middle-class, which made its way via scholarships to grammar schools and Oxbridge. Like Edward Heath and Margaret Thatcher after him, he sought political advancement through the Conservative Party. As a student he was singleminded, a swot. He was a classics scholar at Trinity College, Cambridge, gained a brilliant First, won most of that University's glittering prizes and was elected a Fellow of Trinity. He never lost this love and mastery of the classics or of German literature and Nietzsche. At the age of 25 he was made a Professor of Greek at Sydney University, Australia. On his arrival, he told a bemused Vice-Chancellor that he would resign on the day the United Kingdom went to war.

At the time he was the youngest professor in the Commonwealth (but was beaten by Nietzsche, who had been a Professor at the University of Basel at 24). Two years later, in 1939, he was appointed to the Chair of Greek and Classical Literature at the University of Durham, to take effect on 1 January 1940. Powell has always had a life outside politics, reflected in his writing and broadcasting on so many subjects in his retirement. His editions of Thucydides and Herodotus are still used by students. He has written books on the House of Lords, Joseph Chamberlain, biblical studies, poetry and a book in Welsh. Since 1972 he has been engaged in a study of the evolution of the Gospels and started to learn Hebrew for that purpose.

Before taking up the Durham chair, he had returned to offer himself for war service. After distinguished military service (he was one of a handful of soldiers to rise from private to brigadier in the war), he joined the Conservative Research Department in 1946, in part to secure the retention of India in the British Empire. At the time R.A. Butler was assembling a formidable research team, including Reginald Maudling and Iain Macleod. The well-told story, via R.A. Butler, is that Powell came to Churchill's attention by proposing a plan for the reconquest of India and that the great man wondered if Powell was of sound mind. The story is untrue and Powell still feels that 'R.A. Butler did me an injury'. He had written a long Research Department paper on the military and administrative consequences for Britain *if* it continued to rule in India. There was no discussion of conquest or reconquest. In 1948 Brigadier Powell was adopted as prospective candidate for the Labour-held marginal seat of South-West Wolverhampton. He won it in 1950 and held it until 1974.

In an age when political reputations are largely made in office, Powell's has been made with words. He is a highly intellectual man who speaks with great feeling, and with few notes. The combination of his uncompromising intellect (reflected above all in his precise, almost classical, rhetoric), military moustache, hypnotic eyes, flat Black Country accent, conviction and sheer intensity makes him a compelling speaker. Starting in 1964, he hit on the device of writing out his speeches and handing the entire speech (as opposed to a press release) to the media. In his own words, he felt 'the Egerian stream forcing itself up' within him. In his case 'the massive presentation' of what he had to say was best done by a combination of writing and speaking. His audiences were treated to a live platform speech and a treatise. He is lyrical when speaking of the English, Parliament and national identity.

Powellism was rooted in a coherent philosophy.[6] Powellism used to mean market economics until it suddenly was displaced by the issue of race (a word he never used – 'I have never discovered what it means'). But it was his fixation with single issues – race and immigration, defence, the economy, the Common Market and then Ulster – which commanded attention. He brought these issues to the forefront of politics: in his own words, he 'dislodged stones'. On all these issues he broke with the Conservative and Labour front-bench consensus and on the first two he spoke for a concerned public opinion. Yet surveys showed that of the many voters who supported Powell on immigration, few accepted his policies on the economy or on the European Community. He had a programme but it found few followers in the country.

In disowning his party over the issue of Europe he resembled another outstanding Midlands politician, Joseph Chamberlain, who had split the Liberals in 1886 over Home Rule for Ireland and then the Conservatives in 1903 over Tariff Reform. Indeed he made the comparison himself in 1977 in his biography of Chamberlain. Powell concluded that all political lives, unless terminated prematurely, end in failure, 'because that is the nature of politics and of human nature'.

First and foremost, Powell was a British nationalist. In 1955 he and Angus Maude wrote *Biography of a Nation. A Short History of Britain*. In the introduction he claimed that self-consciousness is the essence of nationhood and that it has two aspects – 'one looking inwards, the other outwards; one the sense of unity, the other a sense of difference'. Here are the seeds of his later rejection of black immigration as an 'invasion', and his opposition to British entry to the EEC and repudiation of any rôle for the Irish Republic in Ulster. Acceptance of any of the three steps would weaken national self-consciousness. Of course to die for the nation was the noblest sacrifice of all: in public he has said that he wished he had been killed in the war.

From the beginning Powell was one of the 'awkward squad', refusing offers of government office not once but thrice and resigning from office once. He was made Parliamentary Secretary at Housing and Local Government in December 1955, and became Financial Secretary to the Treasury. He was made Minister of Health in 1960 and then promoted to the Cabinet in that post in 1962. He was part of the Treasury team that resigned with the Chancellor, Peter Thorneycroft, in January 1958 over limits on greater public spending. Macmillan shrugged off the resignations as a 'little local difficulty' and the government was triumphantly re-elected in 1959. Powell looked back on the incident as a turning-point after which governments accepted higher levels of public spending and inflation. Macmillan later (1962) promoted him to a Cabinet appointment as Minister of Health but seated him out of his view because he was made uncomfortable by Powell's staring eyes.

When a number of Conservative ministers caballed in 1963 to promote R.A. Butler's claims to succeed the ailing Macmillan over those of Sir Alec Douglas-Home, they met at Powell's house in South Eaton Place. Sir Alec went on to persuade all the dissidents, except for Powell and Iain Macleod, to join his administration. Lord Home asked Powell hypothetically – assuming he was able to form a government – if Powell would accept office, and was given a negative. The next day, when it was clear that Sir Alec could form a government, he sent for Powell again, and was again turned down. 'If I gave a different answer I would go home and turn the mirrors to the wall.' To some, it was extraordinary that, once Butler had accepted, Powell refused to serve. He had earlier turned down offers of office in 1952 and 1959.

In these years Powell made his name for his eloquent defence of the free market. It was 'the subtlest and most efficient system mankind has yet devised for setting effort and resources to their best use'. The 'free economy' was essential for a 'free society', and when he saw a rich man 'he gave thanks to God'. He was the leading Tory exponent of economic liberalism, a hero of the Institute of Economic Affairs. In contrast to the consensual direction of post-war Conservatism, he favoured big cuts in public spending and direct taxation, sweeping denationalisation and floating exchange rates. He thought that trade unions indirectly worsened the living standards of their members, and opposed the corporate bias of the NEDC and economic planning. Macmillan thought he carried his logic too far: he thought Powell 'a fanatic'. Powell memorably dismissed incomes policies as 'A nonsense, a silly nonsense, a transparent nonsense. What is more, it is a dangerous nonsense'. The true cause of inflation was the printing of too much money, and responsibility for that was in the hands of government. Ministers were the guilty men. As an economic liberal he was surely ahead of his time. He was expounding many elements of Thatcherism two decades before Mrs Thatcher reached Downing Street. (But he opposed capital punishment, was suspicious of the United States, and rejected Britain's pretensions to a world rôle.)

Powell also had a distinctive outlook on the welfare state. He favoured the local and autonomous provision of services as far as possible; that way services could become more responsive and flexible. He opposed universal benefits, deplored the language of welfare 'rights' and thought the state should keep out of sectors where the private sector and charitable organisations could provide services. So far, so good for the idea of Powell as an economic liberal.

But Powell opposed education vouchers and dismissed as 'bunkum' claims for greater spending on education and health on the grounds of promoting economic growth. Such spending was the mark of 'a civilised nation', a 'corporate recognition' of the community's obligation to its members. This was pure One Nation Toryism. And in 1982 when the Education Minister, Sir Keith Joseph, was discouraging university studies which were not judged 'useful' or 'relevant' to the economy, Powell witheringly dismissed the policies as 'barbarism'. In contrast to Mrs Thatcher's rejection of the idea of society, Powell, echoing Edmund Burke, claimed: 'Society is much more than a collection of individuals . . . it has an existence of its own; it thinks and feels; it looks inwards as a community to its members'.[7] He was neither left nor right: he was an individualist, a Powellite.

In 1965 he ran for the leadership of the party but finished a poor third behind Mr Heath and Mr Maudling. Mr Heath made him shadow spokesman on defence. Relations between the two men were tense, ostensibly because Mr Powell insisted on speaking on so many issues beyond his defence brief. Mr Heath wanted his Shadow spokesmen to confine their speeches to their own policy area, whereas Mr Powell claimed the right to speak on all issues, and even to dissent from some of his colleagues' policies. Powell could capture the headlines and attract large audiences. Heath could not and, Powell thought, was jealous of his superior abilities as a communicator. It is easy to forget that Mr Powell in these years attracted large audiences (and growing media attention) for his speeches, particularly on the economy. There was dissatisfaction, particularly among party activists, with Mr Heath, and Powell was seen both as an alternative leader and as spokesman for an alternative direction.

The last straw for Heath, and the turning-point in Powell's career, was the Birmingham speech on 20 April 1968 to the West Midlands Conservative political centre. Few speeches have so dominated the media as that one did in the following weeks. Powell warned of the effects of immigration in the inner cities. 'Those whom the gods wish to destroy, they first make mad.' Like the old Roman he foresaw 'the River Tiber foaming with much blood' and called for repatriation. Mr Heath found his attitude 'inhumane', and with the unanimous support of the Shadow Cabinet sacked him. The speech was not cleared in advance with the Shadow Cabinet. Mr Heath and his colleagues saw the speech as a calculated threat to the leadership. Quintin Hogg, the party's spokesman on race and immigration, was furious, in part because Powell was speaking in his area of responsibility. Mr Heath objected to the tone, and called it racialist. The language was inflammatory. Thus Powell was undone by his gifts of eloquence. Mr Powell claimed to be flabbergasted by the reactions to his speech and felt he has been unjustly treated, for he did not go beyond party policy.

Until 1962 all Commonwealth citizens had the right to settle in the United Kingdom. In the 1950s immigration was modest; the 1961 census reported that there were 596,000 Commonwealth immigrants, including whites, in Britain. In 1961, however, the government introduced a bill to limit adult male immigrants while allowing entry for dependants and under-16s.

At the time of the 1962 Commonwealth Immigrants Act Powell thought that the problem had been largely solved. By 1964 the scale and age structure of past immigration (and its consequences in terms of bringing in spouses and dependents and having children) became apparent to him; and only in the process of studying the issue and speaking about it did he discover the full seriousness of the problem. The speech was occasioned by his (and his party's) opposition to the Labour government's Race Relations Bill (1968), which he likened to throwing 'a match to gunpowder'. He had support for the speech on the Conservative back-benches and there was certainly popular pressure in the West Midlands and in his Wolverhampton constituency to halt New Commonwealth immigration.

To charges that he was splitting the party and making a bid for the leadership, Mr Powell said that on immigration, 'to see and not to speak' would be the great betrayal. Like Martin Luther, he would say: 'God help me, I can do no other'. Politicians were like seeds and he could not control where the wind would take him. But here was a major figure lending credibility to what was often a squalid campaign.

In spite of unfavourable media treatment and being shunned in Parliament, even by many Conservatives, Mr Powell's mail was overwhelmingly behind him, the London dockers marched to Parliament in support, and he had a large following among the party activists. Henceforth, though only a back-bench MP, Powell's speeches attracted even larger audiences and more hecklers, and television cameras. A Powell speech was a grand media event. For some years, according to opinion polls, he rivalled Mr Heath as the most popular man to lead the Conservative party and was a major attraction at annual Tory conferences. Powell and race became synonymous. Most of the public were aware only of his position on this issue rather than on free-market economics. In fact he made only a half a dozen speeches on race and immigration in the next 3 years. Paradoxically, the greater his public support, the weaker his Parliamentary position. He regretted that on other topics, particularly the economy, his 'audibility' was reduced. His ministerial prospects were finished. For Mr Heath to recall him would be widely seen as an acceptance of racism. Twenty years after the speech universities still had to make massive security arrangements if Powell was speaking on the campus. He was reviled by Labour and the left, and many prominent Conservatives wanted nothing to do with him.

Mr Powell was humiliated by the abrupt dismissal and the knowledge that it was final. Although the party's policy on immigration moved to a more Powellite position, in January 1970 Mr Heath took the unusual step of announcing that if he formed a Conservative government after the next general election he would not include Mr Powell in it. Many senior Conservatives regarded his 1968 speech and his subsequent behaviour as a ruthless bid to topple Heath and seize the leadership. He hoped, it was alleged, to profit from a Conservative defeat in the 1970 election; after all he was 4 years older than Mr Heath. In fact, during the election, which the Conservatives looked certain to lose, Mr Powell was being blamed by the party leaders and much of the media for the party's poor showing. David Butler and Michael Pinto-Duschinsky in *The British General Election of 1970* (p. 210),[8] reported that 'Powell' (his views and the comments on them by others) accounted for a fifth of the mass media coverage of the election. In the press and on both BBC and ITV 'Powell' was the most covered topic. They note also (p. 208) that his appearances 'produced the most dramatic and compulsive viewing of an otherwise grey campaign'. Mr Heath and his colleagues, he complained, had pointedly refused him 'even the ordinary loyalties and courtesies that prevail generally between colleagues in the same cause'. They would never give him the benefit of the doubt, nor defend him from lies and insults in the House of Commons.

When, against the odds, the Conservatives won the 1970 general election, some commentators thought that Mr Powell's final speech on 15 June, 2 days before polling day, calling for a Conservative vote had been decisive. Certainly there were large pro-Tory swings in the Midlands and large anti-Tory swings there in February 1974, when he called for a Labour vote. Powell himself later claimed that 5 days before polling day a Central Office emissary had approached him and appealed 'only you can win this election for us'.

In the 1970 Parliament he was a frequent dissenter from the Conservative government's policies. When the government made its U-turn over incomes policy, he wondered if Mr Heath had 'taken leave of his senses', and he regularly voted against all stages of the prices and incomes policy legislation, the government rescue of bankrupt firms, as well as all stages of the Common Market legislation. He also opposed the government's policy on Ulster, regarding the attempts to seek agreement with the Irish government as a betrayal of the Unionists and the United Kingdom. The essential issue was not of religion, law and order, civil rights or participation but of national identity – who we are. Here was a fundamental issue, and the government gave the impression that it was negotiable. He continued his campaign for repatriation of New Commonwealth immigration, which after all was party policy. They were an 'alien wedge' (the expression was actually Lord Radcliffe's) in the community and would not identify with Britain.

But he knew that he was counter-productive to his causes; other Conservatives, although unhappy with the Heath government, were frightened to have his label put on them. When challenged or requested to stand as an independent, he would wave the party's 1970 election manifesto, saying that it was he and not the government who was faithful to the programme.

By 1973 he had already decided that, because of his disagreement over Europe, he could not stand at the next election as a Conservative. Although the decision to stand down came as a shock, his own view was that 'The trigger was pulled and I was there'. He made a decisive speech late in the election campaign of February 1974 calling on Tories to vote Labour, because the party was more likely to bring Britain out of the European Community. Here was a supreme national issue which he placed above party. Membership meant that the House of Commons, and therefore the British people, surrendered their exclusive rights over taxation and supremacy over legislation, in a word, its independence. His intervention may well have cost Heath victory in a close election, just as his speeches may have helped Heath to win in 1970.

At this time it was difficult to escape the impression that Powell saw himself speaking for the conscience and traditions of the Conservative Party and even as the saviour of the nation. Asquith was misleadingly called 'the last of the Romans'. His supporters would claim that the title is more appropriate for Powell; he placed his party above other parties, but the nation above all parties. They saw Powell as the man who spoke the truth, however inconvenient.

As we have seen, the refusals of office in 1952, 1959 and 1963 confirmed his strongly individualist stand. He refused to comply with the requirement to declare his interests for the new parliamentary register of interests, which came into effect in 1975. Here was a new qualification for being an MP which had been passed by a resolution of the House. He regarded it as illegal and alone ignored it. Such a step should only be accomplished by law. Mr Heath's colleagues in 1968 regarded his speeches as yet more 'impossibilism'.

'Not prepared to be part of the team' was the common view among prominent Tories. To reject so much of the conventional wisdom in so many policy areas, and so implacably and scornfully, made him feared. He was neither left nor right and organised no group. If his stands (and they were that) were dictated by opportunism, they were hardly calculated to gain the party leadership.

Contempt was not too strong a word to describe his feelings about the leadership of his party between 1965 and 1975. He would later dismiss Mr Heath and (what he called) 'the Heathmen' as people whose career was politics and to whom politics was a career. He claimed that Mr Heath had been chosen as a clone of the technocratic, managerial Harold Wilson. Mr Heath's liking for research groups, consulting experts and then applying their suggested 'solution' to problems was repugnant to Mr Powell. Where was the scope for the virtues of intuition, inspiration and instinct? The big issues of freedom, patriotism, nation and blood were not matters for experts.

He thought Mr Heath was second-rate. What could be a sillier slogan than Mr Heath's 'Action not Words' in 1970? Conservatism needed plenty of words, good words, and Mr Heath failed to provide them. Mr Powell could give the people a tune to whistle to. The choice in the 1970 election was, he claimed, between a man with a boat and a man with a pipe. The gulf between Heath and Powell was unbridgeable, and they helped to destroy each other. The former, speaking execrable French, was a passionate advocate of British entry to the European Community. Powell spoke against British entry in Italian in Turin, in French in Paris and in German in Bonn. On 8 January 1974, speaking in Derby, Powell scoffed at the rumours and counter-rumours about a snap general election on 'Who Governs?' The government, he claimed, had got itself into trouble because of its statutory policy for prices and incomes, which the miners were defying. He foresaw a tragedy 'of the Greek type, where the victim blindly brings disaster upon himself'. He was correct. It enveloped both Powell and Heath.

His hour might have come after Mr Heath's second general election defeat in October 1974. Mrs Thatcher, an admirer of Powell's (she has bestowed the term 'beloved' on him), assumed the leadership in February 1975. However, the previous October he had been elected as an Ulster Unionist for the Down South constituency, which was redrawn in 1983 as South Down (with a Catholic majority), a seat he was to hold until defeated in 1987. Mrs Thatcher and Mr Powell were the two major anti-Heath figures in the land. But when asked about the possibility of a reconciliation, he was brusque: the party would have to work its passage back to him. It was never on. In 1978 Mrs Thatcher alarmed colleagues when she said that people felt 'swamped' by immigrants. In spite of the positive response in the polls, however, she backed off. For Powell, she 'could not see a live wire until she has hit it. Only touch electric fuses when you understand them'.

Enoch Powell made many misjudgements. India was always 'lost' and with it the Empire. He never thought that Heath would call an election in February 1974 on the fraudulent prospectus of an incomes policy. But he still expected Mr Heath to win the election, notwithstanding his own efforts to prevent it (On the morning after polling day he was pleasantly surprised to collect *The Times* and see the headline, 'Heath's Gamble Fails'. He returned for his morning bath, singing the 'Te Deum'). He never believed that the House of Commons would pass the European Communities Bill (1972) or that the British people would actually agree to enter the European Community in the 1975 referendum. His undated forecasts of the racial conflagration in the cities have not come to pass on a large scale.

Powellism challenged the post-war front-bench consensus about immigration, membership of the European Community and Ulster. At times even friends thought he was paranoid about the mass media and about the country's leadership. He spoke of 'enemies within' in the media, civil service and universities. The Foreign Office and Home Office were the chief villains misleading the public.

In spite of having broken with the Conservative Party, he knew that the party system was crucial. He told his supporters in 1974 that they could not vote for a person but only for a party; party was the essence of British Parliamentary government. For him to stand as an Independent would be 'absurd'. The system broke him, like it broke such other powerful party renegades as Joseph Chamberlain, Lloyd George and Oswald Mosley.

The failure of Powell reinforces the lessons of the stabilising tendencies of the British political system. After 1968 his ministerial prospects were finished: he could not lead the party and was no longer acceptable to its leading figures. He was a 'bad team man', he went 'too far', 'brilliant but lacks judgement'. The more salient the issue of immigration, the more inflamed public opinion and the greater his popular appeal, so the weaker, paradoxically, was his position. Immigration was an issue which the leaders of all the parties wanted to keep off the agenda; the broad front-bench agreement until 1959 was for no controls. The Macmillan Cabinet decided in 1960 to bring in a bill to halt New Commonwealth immigration, introduced it the following year and it was on the statute book in 1962.[9] Thereafter the agreement between the Labour and Conservative front benches was for controls over entry and measures to limit racial discrimination.

British politics in the last century has known a number of mavericks: Joseph Chamberlain successively split the Liberals (1886) and then the Conservatives (1903). After helping to split the Liberals (1916) Lloyd George was regularly advocating special causes. He ended up leading a small group of personal followers in the 1930s. Both men regarded party as an instrument for advancing major causes. Oswald Mosley broke with Labour in 1930 and formed his own party. Churchill and Macmillan were in something of a political wilderness in the 1930s. Both were regarded as 'unreliable' and co-operated with supporters across the political spectrum. Ultimately, however, the last two had to make their peace with the party leadership. The Cabinet system with its emphasis on collective decision-making and compromise, the premium placed on party loyalty, and the electoral system which has protected the established parties, have all been discouraging for anti-system or dynamic personalities.

Yet Powell also made nonsense of the oft-repeated claims about the decline of the individual MP, crushed by the party machines. How silly to suggest that the proliferation of select committees and provision of more research facilities and assistants was the way for the MP to reassert himself. As Powell explained to a spellbound audience of students in Manchester in 1981, the rôle of an MP was to force the government to explain itself. All he needed was information from the mouth of government and then he could debate. Debates in the House of Commons gave the government the opportunity to persuade MPs about the merits of its policy. It ensured that government was carried on 'with the understanding and consent of the people through their respresentatives . . . in the House of Commons'.

Enoch Powell has lived and will die as a high Tory (though a liberal on the economy). After his apostasy in 1974 he was no longer a member of the party calling itself Conservative. He told the Kensington Young Conservatives in 1976 that, having surrendered an independent and self-governing United Kingdom, 'the Conservative

Party ceased to be the Conservative Party which I thought I knew and to whose cause my political life had been directed. It became an incomprehensible stranger to me . . .'

Preservation of national sovereignty was necessary for what he believed to be 'the instinctive self-expression of a national society'. In conversation in 1978 he said that, as a high Tory, he had an 'apostolic fervour' for setting the nation free, but the Conservative Party did not. His declared ambition was to lead the party, but after 1968 he knew it could never be. Paradoxically, he would say that only after he left the party (over the European Community) did he realise that he was a high Tory.

If there is no autobiography, he could still write his own epitaph. To a cry of 'Judas' from the galleries in 1974 he retorted 'Judas was paid. I made a sacrifice'. From the mid-1960s and particularly after 1968, many spoke of him as a prophet. But he ended in the wilderness. When praised for his 1981 lecture in Manchester he said that he was born to be a teacher, considering that both his parents were teachers, and added: 'But I had a higher mission, to save the nation'. He is a self-admitted didactic, 'an impulse not unconnected with my political recklessness'. Interrogated in a television programme in April 1988, he replied to the charge that his campaigns on repatriation, withdrawing from the EEC and integrating Ulster into the United Kingdom had all failed; 'I may have failed. That does not mean I was wrong'.

NOTES

1. Published by the Bodley Head, 1969.
2. Batsford, 1965.
3. Batsford, 1965.
4. Batsford, 1972.
5. Batsford, 1978.
6. See the fine study by K. Phillips, 'The Nature of Powellism', in N. Nugent and R. King (eds.), *The British Right*, (Farnborough: Saxon House, 1977).
7. *Ibid*.
8. Macmillan, 1971.
9. In May 1959 a right-wing Conservative back-bencher Sir Cyril Osborne had brought in a private member's bill to halt New Commonwealth

immigration. Powell opposed the measure on the grounds that (a) a
private member's bill was not appropriate, and (b) he was sure the
government could legislate after the next general election.

11 The Rise and Fall of Tony Benn: Nuisance or Conscience?*

By the end of the 1980s Anthony Benn was a diminished figure. Standing (at the age of 63) against Neil Kinnock for the Labour Party leadership in 1988 was surely his last hurrah. He still has his moments, particularly when addressing the adoring annual party Conference. In the evenings he darts across the fringe meetings saying pretty similar things and tape-recording each contribution. The recording will be both a contribution to history and a check on being misquoted by hostile journalists. The continuing publication of his diaries and revelations about the 1974 to 1979 Labour Cabinets will keep him in the public eye. Indeed he has gone the way of so many politicians: still in politics the publications of their memoirs of yesterday's events briefly makes them historical figures in their own lifetimes. It is as if, still alive, they are writing their own obituaries.

For some years he has been regarded as a pariah by many Labour MPs and dismissed as dotty or dangerous by others. Many Labour supporters hold him largely responsible for the party's steady electoral decline after 1979. But he also had a committed following among the activists. Like Mrs Thatcher, but unlike so many figures on the left, he has become more radical as he has grown older. Cripps, Bevan, Shinwell and Foot all ended up as respectable 'Establishment' figures. It is a remarkable evolution for the centrist Labour MP of the 1950s and the Minister of Technology (1967–70), who made deals with industrialists.

To the end, however disillusioned by Labour leaders, he remains enthusiastic, a missionary for his ideas, buoyed up, perhaps cocooned, by his supporters. It was Harold Wilson who unkindly observed in 1981 that Mr Benn immatured with age. His enthusiasm has stopped

* This chapter was specially written for this volume.

177

him becoming as embittered as R.A. Butler or even Ted Heath in the twilight of their careers.

Yet in the 1970s the fear of a possible Benn-led Labour government triggered schemes across the political spectrum to curb the executive. The ideas included a written constitution, proportional representation, or some grand coalition government which would stop Benn and the coming of a British version of East European socialism. Ironically, in recent years Benn has launched a campaign for constitutional reform – more open government, measures to make the executive more accountable to Parliament and more power for regional assemblies.

He has been one of the most significant figures in recent British politics. Almost single-handed, he has revised the British constitution. Having succeeded his father as Lord Stansgate in November 1960, he was disqualified from the House of Commons; however, he managed to renounce his peerage and returned to the House of Commons in 1963. Without his efforts to allow peers to renounce, Lord Home would not have become Prime Minister in 1963. After 1971 Benn upset other Labour leaders by successfully campaigning for a referendum in the hope of pulling Britain out of the European Community. This was adopted by the party and took place in 1975. He then spearheaded the movement which reformed Labour's constitution in 1979–81. One result was to help drive a score of Labour MPs into forming the Social Democratic Party.

At the age of 24 he was elected for Bristol South-East, a seat which he held until 1983, except for the period 1960–63, when he was debarred on the assumption of his father's peerage. He was returned to Parliament in the by-election at Chesterfield in 1984. He was Postmaster-General (1964–6), Minister of Technology (1966–70) under Wilson and then Secretary of State for Industry (1974–5) and Secretary of State for Energy (1975–9) under Wilson and Callaghan. In the 1987 Parliament only Denis Healey had a longer record of Labour government service.

Unlike so many British politicians, Mr Benn actually enjoys popular democracy. He loves elections. His campaign for the referendum on Britain's membership of the Common Market was, however, motivated as much by a desire to get Britain out as to consult the people. One benefit for him was that the party's adoption of it provoked the resignation in 1972 of Roy Jenkins as Deputy Leader of the Party. Mr Benn had already stood for the deputy leadership in 1971 and he stood for the leadership in 1976 when Mr

Wilson retired. At a bad time for Labour in 1981 he challenged the incumbent Denis Healey for the deputy leadership. There followed a long, bitter, divisive contest which he lost by a whisker. (He could fairly point out that if it had not been for the votes of some Labour MPs who later defected to the SDP, he would have won.) He stood for the leadership again in 1988.

Why did he seek the largely non-job of the deputy leadership in 1981? He might say: to test and safeguard the new machinery; to divert the energies of the right, while left-wing policies slipped through largely unchallenged; to carry out a campaign for socialism among the party membership; and, anyway, elections were a good thing. These were partly rationalisations and partly attempts to cloak his personal ambition. Although he denies it – 'it's the ideas that I represent' – he has been perhaps the most assiduous seeker of office in the party's history. His position in the PLP, however, has been much weaker than in the constituencies. His campaigns in 1981 and 1988 were explicit attacks on the Shadow Cabinet.

He lost his Bristol seat in the 1983 general election and so was not eligible to stand for the leadership when Michael Foot resigned. He quickly became disillusioned with Neil Kinnock and thought of challenging him in 1985. In 1988 he did so. As in 1981, the decision to stand had little to do with advancing Labour's case for forming a government but more to do with making the party safe for socialism. He had no hope of winning in 1988, did badly and probably weakened the left by his failure. Although there was dissatisfaction with Kinnock among MPs and front-benchers, the challenge of Benn only reinforced his leadership. In 1981 Benn had gained 80 per cent of the constituency votes against Denis Healey; in 1988 he gained less than 30 per cent. Neither he nor the Labour left gathered the fruits of the 1980–1 revolution in the party. In the country Mrs Thatcher, and for a time the Alliance, were the heirs, and in the party Mr Kinnock was the beneficiary.

Mr Benn was affected by the participatory explosion of the late 1960s, the glorification of youth, the counter-culture and the challenge to authority. He changed his name from Anthony Wedgwood Benn, son of Lord Stansgate, to plain Tony Benn. He dropped the references to his prestigious educational background at Westminster School and New College, Oxford. His recently published diaries reveal that in 1972 he also considered giving up his Privy Councillorship, his Oxford MA and various honorary doctorates. He attacked grammar schools, the House of Lords, the honours system, the BBC and the senior civil service. He became the voice of the anti-establishment. He became 'prolier' than the workers, took to wearing an anorak, and was famous for drinking tea from a tin mug. Before 1914 the German sociologist Robert Michels had warned that the process of *embourgeoisement* killed off the radicalism of socialist leaders. Benn's was a story of attempted downward social mobility and increased radicalism.

In opposition after 1970 he found new company. He rejected Mr Wilson's injunction that collective responsibility for the policies of the last Labour government carried over into opposition. He confessed to error, reasserted the sovereignty of the (left-wing) conference and repudiated the last government's policy on many fronts – incomes policy, industrial relations, the European Community and the US role in Vietnam. He stole the honours at conference. Just as Mr Heath and his supporters were furious at the way Sir Keith Joseph and Margaret Thatcher managed to dissociate themselves from the activities of the 1970–4 government, so Tony Benn enraged his former Cabinet colleagues by seeming to disclaim responsibility for its work. No picket line and no anti-establishment cause went without his support. Striking workers, feminists, gays, a variety of minority causes and left-wing Labour local authorities all attracted his uncritical support. As a key figure on the NEC, he allowed, even encouraged, the 'entryism' of far-left groups into the Young Socialists and the party. Mr Benn had no enemies on the left.

It is a measure of his influence in the party that when Labour returned to office in 1974 he was given the crucial Cabinet position of Secretary of State for Trade and Industry, with a remit to overhaul faltering capitalism. The crisis of profitability called for the state to step in and fill the investment gap, *via* the National Enterprise Board. Labour would do this, but only in return for firms making planning agreements with the National Enterprise Board. Benn made needlessly provocative speeches, which alienated industrial management. He managed to help workers set up co-operatives at Kirkby, Meriden and Glasgow. But behind his back Wilson redrafted his White Paper on industrial regeneration, reassured the captains of industry and told the civil servants to ignore him. He found himself blocked in Whitehall and Mr Wilson moved him to Energy once the referendum on the EEC was safely out of the way.

It is remarkable that all recent Labour leaders – Gaitskell, Wilson, Callaghan, Foot and Kinnock – distrusted him. Gaitskell and Wilson (before 1970) found him a schemer, too unpredictable, and somehow not quite 'grown up'. After 1974 Wilson thought Benn was being used by others and tried to provoke him to resign. Ultimately, neither Callaghan nor Foot had the energy or political resources (because of obvious failures in government and in the country) to outface him. Kinnock simply regarded him as dangerous, a personification of so much of what had gone wrong in the party.

During the crucial negotiations for an IMF loan to save the pound in 1976, Mr Benn circulated to ministers minutes of the fateful 1931 minority Labour government Cabinet meeting on the economic crisis. Then Ramsay MacDonald and Philip Snowden had sought to cut unemployment benefits to secure a loan from American bankers. The TUC said no, the Cabinet split and resigned and MacDonald went off to form a National Government. This was the great 'betrayal' that still sears the party's memory. The Prime Minister, James Callaghan, resented the analogy with MacDonald. He supported Chancellor Healey's spending cuts, accepted IMF terms and kept the party together. Benn was given the chance to argue in Cabinet for his alternative economic strategy of a siege economy, and failed to convince anybody. Unabashed, he regarded the IMF negotiations as a demonstration of international capital dictating to an elected Labour government, and spoke of the public spending cuts as the 'death of Croslandism'.

In these years he showed himself a consummate machine politician. Outside the Cabinet he played another game, securing his base in the National Executive Committee. He was one of the most dominating figures in the NEC's history and used it systematically against the Parliamentary leadership. As Chairman of the Home Policy Committee (1974–81) he played a crucial role in developing policies, often contradicting those of the Labour government. In Cabinet he was like an independent extra-Parliamentary force. At this time there was a growing gap between conference and the PLP. The party faced a constitutional dilemma when he and some other left-wing ministers on NEC committees supported conference policy even when this conflicted with the Cabinet. Wilson and Callaghan both restated the doctrine of collective responsibility and on the surface Benn complied. Harold Wilson let it be known that he was 'pissed off' with the predictable sniping from left-wing critics on the NEC. Mr Callaghan found the monthly meetings of the NEC the most dispiriting part of his premiership. As the resolutions of conference and NEC veered to the left and further from the government, so there were hints of Benn calling it a day, and he consulted his Bristol constituency party over a resignation. It told him to remain and fight for his left-wing policies. In opposition after 1979, as he had done in 1970, he disowned the work of the Labour government; he was 'unmuzzled'. Other left-wingers, including Michael Foot, watched in amazement as he attacked root and branch the policies of the previous Labour government for which he had been collectively responsible.

So many of the causes he took up happened to coincide with his career interests. This was true of his renunciation of his peerage, opposition to the European Community via the referendum (which dished the party's right-wing) and reforms in the Labour party structure. He could never win a leadership election among Labour MPs, or among Labour voters – were one held. But he might win if the election of leader were given to the extra-Parliamentary party. Increasingly, he used the extra-Parliamentary wing against the Parliamentary party. Support for him correlated with distrust of the Parliamentary leadership. At conference he was received rapturously, though analogies with Nuremberg were silly. Nothing was more telling than to see Benn bring the conference to its feet while the ranks of sullen MPs remained seated.

How could he have led the party in Parliament? In December 1980 he failed to be elected by MPs to any of twelve places in the Shadow Cabinet. After 1979 he called for a 'constitutional' premiership in which the PLP would effectively decide the composition of the Cabinet and the date of dissolution, leaving the NEC control over the contents of the manifesto. Just as conference and the NEC would control the PLP, so the PLP would control the Prime Minister.

After 1974 he learned very little. The party's subsequent history only confirmed his warnings. Thus the 1974 Labour government ended in conflict with the unions, because it defied conference and the TUC in insisting on a 5 per cent limit for wage increases; Labour had tried to save capitalism and failed. By 1979 a disastrous trade balance between Britain and the European Community had developed, as he had forecast; many conference policies appeared unpopular because the leader did not believe in them or campaign for them; Reg Prentice did leave the party and became a Conservative, and other right-wingers left in 1981. Nobody ever believed that Benn would resign or ever desert Labour – though in 1987 and 1988 he talked of the possibility that he might be expelled under Kinnock's 'authoritarian' regime.

The years 1945–51 were for a long while his model of what a Labour government could do, if it fought on a radical socialist programme. In fact much of the Attlee government's programme grew out of the wartime coalition government and built on many assumptions shared across the parties. Beveridge's welfare reform, the commitment to full employment, Keynesianism, and plans for public ownership had all originated then. As the historian Paul Addison noted: 'the new consensus fell like a bunch of ripe plums into the lap of Mr Attlee'. Yet Benn always believed there was a silent majority for socialism, waiting to be mobilised. The 1983 general election provided such an opportunity, when Labour fought on a left-wing programme. If others were shocked by the result, the disaster in that election consoled Benn; it showed that there were 8 million votes for socialism which could be built on. There was now a clear choice, and Labour would never go back to the centre. Opinion polls were useless; they dispirited and minoritised the left. If Labour would fight on conference policies, people would come over. He knew from his personal contacts what the people wanted. His view was that 'at the end of the day, you have got to believe'. In many ways he resembled Eric Hoffer's *The True Believer*[1], who had an ability to 'shut his eyes and stop his ears' to facts that do not deserve to be either seen or heard, and which is the source of his unequalled fortitude and consistency.

After 1979 he forecast that the establishment would drop Mrs Thatcher and put David Owen in. There would be a cross-party coalition to keep Labour out. Elections would not make a difference; SDP consensus policies would prevail. There was a hidden elite, represented by the bureaucracy in Brussels, the BBC, press barons, city, business, multi-national corporations, IMF, the USA and civil service. After years of serving in government he had learned that the old consensus did not work. He and Mrs Thatcher were the immediate beneficiaries of the end of consensus in the 1970s. But in his detection of all-encompassing conspiracies he resembled Enoch Powell. Unlike Mr Benn, however, Powell had a popular and populist following, outside his own party. Indeed ultimately Powell was prepared to break with his party. Benn was a party man, with little or no following outside Labour.

Cabinet colleagues could be amused at his schemes for wrong-footing the opposition. But few of his policies commanded the confidence of colleagues. The diaries of Richard Crossman and

Barbara Castle express admiration for his presentational skills. But in May 1968 Crossman thought that what Benn actually said was 'second rate and sometimes disastrously stupid'[2] and, by October, Benn was 'philosophically not second rate, but non-existent'.[3] Historians may judge that the Wilson governments of 1964–1970 were remarkable more for their diaries than for their legislative accomplishments. That a government of such meagre achievements has been so heavily documented from the inside can only be explained by the fact that it contained so many dons and journalists.

Volume I of the Benn diaries evokes the spirit of the 1960s: the tired ending of the Macmillan – Home era, the optimism surrounding the grammar school boy Wilson and the 'new look' Labour Party, the creation of the Open University, the problems over Rhodesia, the excitement about the new technology, and the Prices and Incomes Board. Above all, like the Castle and Crossman diaries, Benn is concerned about who is in and who is out of Harold Wilson's political court. Like Mr Wilson's memories, Benn's diaries often refer to various 'sensations', 'important announcements' and 'significant' policies; most were ephemeral.

Like other diaries of the period, it also portrays the author as rushing to departmental meetings, dashing to party gatherings, travelling to his Bristol constituency, and generally bustling about. Not surprisingly Benn makes frequent though uncomplaining references to having had only 3 or 4 hours sleep. At the end of the first volume Benn wonders whether he has organised his time properly in his first year as a Cabinet minister. Although he has worked prodigiously hard, he knows what the answer to that question is. These are less the diaries of a Socialist in the making than of a man tilting at the familiar targets of radicals.

'Bennism' became a catch-all term, referring to observance of conference divisions, conference distrust of the PLP, greater party democracy, a vague form of syndicalism, and a suspicion of all elites. At times between 1979 and 1983 the movement for party democracy and the left seemed to be little more than a vehicle for the promotion of his career. In fact he came late to the left, only joining Tribune in 1981. Even well-disposed Labour members pointed to basic flaws in his thinking. How could he reconcile central economic planning with industrial democracy, decentralisation and greater participation? How could government control of the media be reconciled with greater freedom? He lumped socialism with the

Sermon on the Mount, the Levellers, Tolpuddle Martyrs, Chartists, Suffragettes and Marxism, even the Militant Tendency. What they had in common was their hostility to the establishment: he knew his friends by their enemy.

How deep was his democracy when it conflicted with the advance of socialism? He quickly dropped the referendum when it came up with the wrong result on the European Community in 1975. He did not want Militant, despite its contempt for Parliamentary democracy, to be expelled from the party. On such matters as the first-past-the-post electoral system, the conference block vote of the trade unions, and the failure of the unions and constituency parties to consult their members in the 1981 deputy leadership election, he was silent. In fact he was an elitist, campaigning for a democracy of the activists.

His base was in the constituencies. As the membership of constituency parties shrank, particularly in the inner cities, so they were sometimes captured by the extreme left. These, he presumed, spoke for the party. The 1918 party constitution gave the constituency parties a limited role, reflecting Sidney Webb's belief that they were unrepresentative, 'dominated by fanatics, cranks and extremists'. From 1962 Benn was always elected to the constituency section of the NEC, and in the 1970s regularly topped a list which was dominated by left-wing MPs.

In many ways the recent history of the Labour left has been shaped by the growing mutual disenchantment of Kinnock and Benn. Benn cynically watched the young upwardly mobile left-wingers, Robin Cook, Jack Straw, David Blunkett, Michael Meacher and Kinnock move to the right, all, as he judged, corrupted by the Parliamentary embrace. Benn's long-standing friendships with Michael Foot and Peter Shore were destroyed. In the 1974 government he regarded Foot as the Morrison of the left – willing to concoct deals with Ulster Unionists and Nationalists so long as Labour stayed in office. Kinnock came to prominence as an oppositionist, making common cause with left-wing groups who accused the Wilson and Callaghan governments of betrayal. But when Benn stood against Foot, Kinnock broke with him. He supported Foot in the NEC and the PLP and crucially refused to support Benn for the deputy leadership against Healey. The abstention of Kinnock and a handful of other soft-left MPs made all the difference. Benn and his supporters never forgave Kinnock. The left was henceforth divided into hard and soft groups, the former assembling around Benn, the latter around Kinnock. The young Kinnock, never having held office, followed Max Weber's ethic of responsibility. The veteran Benn, a minister for 9 years, offered utopianism, waiting for the inevitable crisis of capitalism. The two were travelling in different directions. Kinnock attacked Benn for offering 'fantasies' and 'impossibilism', and as leader promised to make markets work more efficiently. Kinnock, for Benn, followed Aneurin Bevan and Michael Foot in compromising with power.

Yet Benn did not rise in a vacuum, and it would be unjust to conclude without noting the correctness of some of his claims about British society and British labour. He and the left were shamefully treated by most of the press. Frequently he was reported only when he appeared to be attacking the Labour leaders. Like so many left-wingers, he was an inviting target for the right-wing press and party leadership. Moreover, the Labour governments of Wilson and Callaghan *were* failures. Conference was treated contemptuously, in particular by Wilson. Those who argued for a change of direction had a case. Throughout its history Labour has been something of a living lie. Front-bench spokesmen paid tribute to the idea of intra-party democracy in opposition but ignored it when in office. This was blatantly the case under the Wilson and Callaghan governments. The campaign for greater democracy in the party was fuelled by events such as Harold Wilson's threat in 1973 to veto conference's nationalisation proposals in the next Labour manifesto and Mr Callaghan's actual veto of left-wing policies in the 1979 manifesto. The poor record of Labour governments in the 1960s and 1970s, and the consequent disappointment and disillusion, were stimuli to radicalism.

The 1970s and 1980s were a disaster for Labour, and Benn is one of the most significant actors in the story. He was the voice of the activists at a time when they were increasingly less representative of Labour voters. As the party gave a greater role to the activists, so it was pulled away from the people they incorrectly claimed to represent. The party activists increasingly talked to themselves and forgot the electorate. Mr Benn wanted to save the party for Socialism. But by the end of the 1980s, as the East European states abandoned economic planning, Socialism appeared a highly conservative ideology. At the turn of the century the ideology and its promises mattered to Labour activists; the party, after all, had no patronage and no record in government. Is it because it is one of the few Socialist parties in Western Europe not to have a revolutionary past that the British Labour Party has made such a fetish of nationalisation, the union connection and support for the have-nots? It has been almost the last of Western Socialist parties to dump the old baggage. Mr Benn has been a formidable advocate of Socialist traditionalism yet an embarrassment to his colleagues as he speaks of a mythical left-wing past. His tragedy is that his analysis – like his Utopia – is so firmly rooted in the past, whereas Socialism essentially is a future-oriented ideology.

NOTES

1. New York: The New American Library, 1951, p. 78.
2. *Diaries*, 1951, Vol. III, p. 80.
3. *Ibid*, p. 234.

12 The Deferential English: a Comparative Critique*

All political cultures are mixed and changing. What is interesting in the English case, however, is the way in which a veritable army of scholars has seized on the deferential component. Other features in the overall cultural pattern have been neglected. This chapter is devoted to an examination of the concept of deference as it is applied to English politics. In particular it will focus on the different meanings that the concept has assumed in the literature describing and analysing the popular political attitudes, and those aspects of the political system, including stability, which it has been used to explain.[1] My concluding argument is that deference, as the concept is frequently applied to English political culture, has attained the status of a stereotype and that it is applied to such variegated and sometimes conflicting data that it has outlived its usefulness as a term in academic currency.

BAGEHOT AND DEFERENCE

We might, however, first take note of the academic derivation of the term and familiar starting-point of most of the studies which are referred to below. Writers on English political culture have rediscovered Walter Bagehot with a vengeance; no discussion of the subject gets under way without a ritual bow in Bagehot's direction and an invocation of his thoughts, penned more than a century ago, on the subject. There is no little irony in this predilection of more empirically minded writers on politics to cite the impressions of the intuitive if distinguished author of *The English Constitution* in order to lend historical depth to their findings.

Now Bagehot is not responsible for the borrowings and elaborations of his notion of deference by latter-day social scientists. Bagehot

* *Government and Opposition*, 1971.

188

talked about deference almost as an aside; for proof of its existence he invited his readers to witness the behaviour of domestic servants and rustics.[2] Because deference was paid to the dignified or theatrical element in British government – 'to something else than the (actual political) rulers' – the effective or real government was hidden from popular gaze and scrutiny. In other words, the respect accorded to the monarchy and the House of Lords allowed the more prosaic members of the Cabinet to rule almost by deception; the bulk of the population was largely unaware of the seat of effective government. According to Bagehot there was a differential level of political realism between the classes: the middle class saw through the façade but the 'poorer and more ignorant classes' did not; the latter actually 'believed that the Queen governs'. But there was another aspect to this deference. The mass, according to Bagehot, also deferred to the middle class, to the £10 borough renters and the £50 county renters who dominated the suffrage, and who were entrusted with the choosing of the political rulers. The meritocratic Bagehot was relieved that the mass 'has a kind of loyalty to some superior persons who are fit to choose a good government'. He was bold in relating these two tiers of deference and their effects to the success of British political institutions. Deference was 'more suited to political excellence' and Cabinet government was thought possible only in 'deferential nations'.

But a fair assessment of the English political culture needs to take account of two other neglected themes that Bagehot raised. First, he observed that passivity and social deference were not confined to the lower classes; the distribution of social status was pyramidal and the middle class was quite willing to defer to the aristocracy. Thus, deference was not a property unique to the working class.[3] In addition, Bagehot was more careful than his latter day emulators to avoid confusing political with social deference. An important and neglected strand in the thesis of *The English Constitution* concerns Bagehot's analysis of *the lack of political deference* among the population.[4] He suggested that the natural impulse of the 'English people is to resist authority' and that state legislation was widely seen as 'alien action' and government as 'an extrinsic agency'. These attributes, which to Bagehot were 'a peculiarity of the English', are very close to the present academic and popular characterisation of the *incivisme* of the French and Italians and to traditional republican virtues.

What is interesting is that Bagehot's discernment of deference in

1867 was in opposition to equally broad generalisations about English society being offered by Marx, Disraeli, John Stuart Mill and de Tocqueville. Sociological use of the term deference prior to *The English Constitution* had been most frequent in description and analysis of traditional authority relationships. According to these writers, traditional (or pre-industrial) relationships between master and servant, superior and subordinate were based on the notion of mutual dependence: and deference was a key element in the reciprocal pattern of the obedience and respect accorded by the employee to the employer, who in turn assumed a sense of responsibility and obligation for the welfare of his workforce.[5] According to Mill:

> The relation between rich and poor should be only partially authoritative: it should be amiable, moral and sentimental; affectionate tutelage on the one side, respectful and grateful deference on the other. The rich should be *in loco parentis* to the poor, guiding and restraining them like children.[6]

However, deference, though opposed to the idea of equality, was not inimical to the worker's sense of self-esteem. Because of the dependant's subjective identification with his master, the deference accorded in exchange for material and moral protection could actually bolster the deferer's sense of his own worth. Moreover, gradations in society were widely recognised as being part of the natural order.

It was the breakdown of this social contract and deference that Marx, Mill, Bonald, de Maistre and de Tocqueville saw as the consequence of industrialism. In place of the reciprocal and benign pattern of relationships between ranks, the new entrepreneurial ideology rejected the idea of a social bargain and aimed to regulate workplace relations on the basis of an impersonal cash nexus. While these observers of industrialism agreed with Bagehot that the end of deference was fatal to social and political cohesion, they differed from him in that they proclaimed the death of deference.

So much for the famous analysis expressed in elegant aphorisms. What is of interest to this chapter is the effort of contemporary political scientists to assert the continuity of these features discerned long ago by Bagehot, in the face of political changes, such as the rise of universal suffrage and mass political parties, and the decline of social leaders in politics, that, according to Bagehot, would totally destroy the deference he cherished. However, before doing this it is necessary to place this formulation of deference in a broader perspective on two counts. First, the notion that British government is *strong* and the electorate politically docile, has, till recently, imposed a stranglehold on interpretations of English politics. It has conveniently suited the purposes of conservatives like Leo Amery, the Labour Left in their more disillusioned moments, and anglophile political scientists, to interpret Bagehot's highly elitist view as the approved model of English politics.[7] Second, it is clear that conservative social and political thought, with which we should associate Bagehot, has traditionally attached great significance to deference as a means of safeguarding the principles of hierarchy and order in mass society. Alienation, loss of identity, social disintegration and dictatorship have been seen by conservative sociologists (Bonald, de Maistre, Ortega y Gasset, etc.) as the inevitable chain reaction to the collapse of the hierarchic and solidary *Gemeinschaft*.[8] Ortega y Gasset's *The Revolt of the Masses*, and Walter Lippmann's *The Public Philosophy* are sombre warnings of the destruction of a politics of civility which will follow from the death of deference to the elite.

ONE WORD: MANY MEANINGS

A reasonable test of the utility of a concept is to ask how precise it is: what do people mean when they use it? Survey researchers are not usually reluctant to define their terms, for the nature of survey investigation demands a facility in empirically defining and rendering effective relatively abstract ideas. Deference, as a brief combing of the literature will confirm, is a frequently and variously used word. It will not be without significance if we find that researchers into British politics are measuring and talking about differing phenomena yet continue to maintain that they are locating a property they call deference.

Power of the Monarchy

Appreciation of the monarchy and attribution to it of effective political power were central to Bagehot's use of deference. A review of available empirical evidence suggests that while there is strong support for the institution of the monarchy, this is combined with a realistic appraisal of the monarch's limited political powers. The vast majority of people now seem able to appreciate the distinction

between a ruling government and a reigning monarch, or between
the dignified and the efficient. A recent sample of British voters
was asked to evaluate the influence of nine groups on government.
Of these the Queen was decisively thought to be the least influential:
nearly half of the sample thought that she wielded no influence at
all and only 13 per cent thought she had a lot of influence.[9]

Strong Leadership

Other commentators find that deference is reflected in the popular
desire for strong and explicit political leadership, even to the point
of the leader taking unpopular actions. Nordlinger, Rose and Birch[10]
all quote in support of their thesis of English political deference the
survey finding that voters most highly esteem the quality of strength
in a political leader.[11] Now both the survey and the item relating
to political leadership qualities have been subjected to some telling
criticisms which should make us wary of placing too much credence
in the finding.[12] But there is ample alternative evidence to suggest
that this quality of strength (which may, of course, be valued by
voters for instrumental and not deferential reasons) is no more
highly appraised than the qualities of trustworthiness and honesty
in a leader.[13] Efforts to explain the British voter's preference for
strong leadership by means of survey data are as yet inconclusive
and are available for other and often conflicting lines of conjecture.

Political Leadership Based on Ascriptive Criteria

Other observers have discussed deference in the context of favourable
orientations to political leaders of differing social status. The studies
by Eric Nordlinger[14] and Robert McKenzie and Allan Silver[15] tied
the deferential outlook to a preference among the working class for
political leaders of aristocratic birth and a public school education
over leaders of comparable political qualifications, but lacking these
social origins. In Nordlinger's case the item is a measure of social
deference: for McKenzie and Silver the item was combined with
other indicators which purported to measure working-class support
for traditional institutions and conservative values.[16]

In fact these indicators proved to be poor predictors of (a)
working-class support for the Conservative Party, and of (b) political
passivity or docility. A possible explanation for this might be that
the assumed indicators of deference were rather weak. It is not at

all clear why preference for an aristocrat over a non-aristocrat *per se* is a proof of deference. Respondents may choose the former for a number of quite pragmatic or instrumental reasons which have little to do with the ascriptive criteria these writers are concerned to locate. Indeed, Nordlinger's data show that some 'deferential' respondents prefer an Eton-educated man as a political leader for the (achievement-oriented) reason of his superior education; moreover, such a judgement is also expressed by some of the classified 'pragmatists'. It is plausible to argue that it is the reasons which lead voters to their preferences which are the more valid indicator of the underlying orientations, and that this might profitably have been the subject of more rigorous research in both studies. As noted, the other indicators of political deference employed in *Angels in Marble* would seem to be more directed to traditionalism and conservatism.

In addition, the emphasis of both studies on an aristocratic background would seem to be misplaced. Social class hardly seems to figure in popular evaluations of a political leader. Aristocratic background accounted for only 6 per cent of all favourable references to Harold Macmillan in 1963, and a mere 9 per cent for Sir Alec Douglas-Home in 1964.[17]

Political Passivity

The authors of the imaginative *The Civil Culture* also employ the term deference to describe British political orientations. However, Almond and Verba never define it directly but prefer to interchange it with a number of other terms. At one point they see it displayed in working-class conservatism;[18] at another they suggest that it is reflected in the greater sense of administrative competence displayed by the British compared to their other national samples.[19] We shall later see that working-class conservatism is not an impressive correlator with either social or political deference and it is not immediately clear why the confidence of British voters that they would receive serious consideration from the police and the civil service is an indicator of deference. More helpful and more acceptable perhaps is their exchange of the concept of deference with that of *subject political outlook*. Though the outlook allows for a limited degree of political competence, confidence and activity, it is 'essentially passive',[20] and to be contrasted with the participant orientation. Britain, the authors conclude, is 'A Deferential Civic

Culture'.[21] This formulation of the subject of deferential political orientation has been quoted with approval by other observers of British politics.[22] In fact a close reading of the data reported in *The Civic Culture* lends very little support to the authors' interpretation of the British political culture. The participatory outlook and sense of civic competence are only slightly less widespread in Britain than in the United States. Moreover attempts to isolate political subjects in England suggest that only 7 per cent of voters belong in this category.[23]

A similar notion of deference was central to Arend Lijphart's study of Dutch political culture. According to Lijphart such an attitude involved respect for and submission to the political elite, or the citizen's 'acceptance of his position both in the social hierarchy and on the scale of political hierarchy, accompanied by a low level of . . . interest in politics'.[24] To apply this complex concept of deference among Netherlanders he borrowed one terse item from *The Civic Culture* interview scale, which asked respondents across five nations to indicate the most admirable quality in a person. Those Dutch respondents who chose 'Respectful, does not overstep his place' were classified as deferentials.[25] It is doubtful if such a shorthand measure adequately taps the battery of qualities and orientations to the political and social system which Lijphart wishes to associate with the concept. The selection of this response could well have come from an interviewee who himself expected to receive respect and obedience.

Finally, W.G. Runciman suggests that political deference is the expression of an acquiescence in, or acceptance of, the existing pattern of inequalities.[26] Aspects of Runciman's later practical application of deference seem to have little in common with this formulation for he classified as deferentials those manual workers who explained their support for the Conservative Party in terms of the party's greater political competence.[27]

In this section we have examined some of the more empirically oriented definitions of deference, as the term is usually applied to English political attitudes. Researchers have employed different, though perhaps related, indicators and all claim to be measuring the same phenomenon. The most popular use of deference is as a relational property: e.g. *a* defers to *b* because *b* has certain qualities such as rank or wealth. We have also suggested that some of the indicators are rather weak; there is no clear reason why, for instance, idealised support for the monarchy, or preference for a strong Prime

Minister measures deference. The varying indicators and measures
of deference are set out summarily in Table 12.1.

ONE WORD: MANY CONSEQUENCES

If the idea of deference has been traced to several phenomena or
defined in differing terms, then it is not surprising that it should
have a wide range of explanatory power. We now turn our attention
to those features of British politics which writers have tried to
explain as deriving from social and political deference.

High Status Political Leaders

It is frequently alleged that social deference leads to a process of
leadership recruitment which places a high premium on the possession
of high social status.[28] Two caveats might be entered on this assumed
connection between deference and recruitment. One is that high
status political leadership is not unique to Britain; it is a feature of
many other political systems.[29] The other is that the working-class
is better represented in the British House of Commons than it is in
Germany, in Italy, and in other Anglo-American legislatures; since
1945 about one fifth of the membership of the House of Commons
has been working-class in origin.[30] A more substantive query,
however, concerns the validity of making inferences about the
political culture on the basis of the social backgrounds of the elite.
This is especially questionable in Britain where the selection of
candidates is closed to all but a small handful of party activists and
where, in general elections, the party label is overwhelmingly
more salient for voters than a candidate's personality and social
background.[31] Study of recruits to positions of political leadership
may tell us something of the values of the tiny fraction of
predominantly middle-class conservative activists but it is doubtful
if it can tell us much about the social deference of the general
population.

Strong and Effective Governments

Efforts have also been made to link deference with outstanding
features of British political institutions and the quality of political
performance. For example, Harry Eckstein has recently argued that

Table 12.1 Social and political deference

Author	Area	Sample	Indicator	% Deferential
Almond and Verba	Great Britain	Adults	Most esteemed quality in a person†	11
Rose and Mossawir	Community (Stockport)	Adults	Subject political outlook (not very interested in politics, no sense of political efficacy, awareness of government's effect on life)†	7
Rose and Mossawir	Community (Stockport)	Adults	Monarch has a significant political power	13
Gallup– March 1963	Great Britain	Adults	ditto	19
Gallup– June 1968	Great Britain	Adults	ditto	12
Goldthorpe et al.*	Community (Luton)	Affluent workers	Mention of superior quality of Conservative leaders as reason for voting for the party†	4
Runciman*	England and Wales	Manual workers	Image of the Conservative Party as more competent to rule†	10
McKenzie and Silver*	English Towns	Manual workers	Preference for social elite as political leaders†	22
Nordlinger*	English Towns	Male Manual workers	ditto†	10
Butler and Stokes	Great Britain	Adults	Monarch is very important	63
Wolfinger et al.‡	Community (Grantham)	Adults	MPs should be middle or upper class	13

*Calculated by present writer for entire samples in the survey.
†Authors explicitly related the indicator to deference.
‡Popular Support for the British Party System', a paper delivered to the American Political Science Association, 1970.

the British political performance is of a high quality because of the correspondence between the leadership's confidence that the public will defer to its wishes and the willingness of the latter to accord the deference.[32] Eckstein elsewhere has made clear that by high quality he means not only the appropriateness of the leaders' expectations to the mass outlook but also the strength and effectiveness of the government.[33] Thus '. . . the British conception of authority . . . attributes to leadership a far larger scope of legitimate independent action than that of any other democratic country . . .' and '. . . the British expect their rulers to *govern* more than to represent them'. According to Gabriel Almond there is 'a strong deference to the independent authority of the government'.[34] In addition, several aspects of the political system have been related to the strain of deference. These include the dominance of the Prime Minister over his Cabinet colleagues, of the Cabinet over Parliament, of the party leaders over their followers – 'the meek submissiveness to leadership by ordinary MPs itself reflects the habit of deference in British society'[35] – the relative independence of MPs from constituency pressures, and the hierarchical authority patterns of pressure groups.[36]

As descriptions of the British political system, as it has performed throughout most of the century, the propositions about its strength and its effectiveness are questionable. Let us examine them separately.

The judgement that British politics is hierarchical in spirit is the subject of a continuing polemic among observers. Detailed and impressive studies of policy-making have tended to conclude that post-war Britain is characterised not by strong political leadership but more by 'a directionless consensus'.[37] Samuel Beer has traced the emergence of a 'stalemate state' where large groups are able to veto or frustrate government policies, and emphasised the immobilism which results from the government's inability or unwillingness to impose its policies on major groups like business, the City, and the trade unions.[38] The alleged 'lawlessness' of the trade unions, so topical at present, is not only a continuation of the traditional working-class fear of the courts but also an expression of the very anti-deferential belief that unions should be allowed to make rules for themselves and that the process of collective bargaining should be insulated from government influence. The handling of the economic depression of the late 1920s did anything but support notions of strong government. The leaders of the Conservative and

Labour parties were, in varying degrees, paralysed by their fear of how the unions, business, or the financial community would react to radical policy change.[39] Similar analyses, suggestive of weak government, could also be plausibly made for the government's handling of Irish affairs in 1914, foreign policy in the 1930s, and the repeated abandonment of economic restraints in the face of electoral unpopularity.

In terms of the distribution of influence between the party leader and his party followers the evidence suggests that Eckstein's portrait is one-sided. A recent study of party discipline had questioned the elitist formulation and shown how an agreed party line is not so much imposed by the leaders as produced by the leaders' self-restraint and anticipation of back-bench demands and objections: the flow of influence is more reciprocal than one way.[40] As for the strength and security of tenure of the party leader, one has only to think of the circumstances which led to the resignations of Balfour, the two Chamberlains, Lansbury and Douglas-Home, and the troubled leaderships of Baldwin and Gaitskell to appreciate the strength of anti-leadership trends in both British parties. Finally, the ease with which most legislation is passed through the House of Commons is a misleading index of government strength. As S.E. Finer has observed, most legislation is specialised and of little general interest. But on controversial legislation, where the government may face a mobilised sectional or general public opinion, an easy passage is far from assured.[41]

But even if, for the sake of argument, one grants the case of the theorists of 'strong' British government, one is entitled to ask how far this has enabled Britain to meet her problems: i.e. how 'effective' is the political system? In many fields of policy-making, British political institutions have come under scathing attack.[42] Indeed, many criticisms have directly pointed to the domination of elite positions by an hereditary 'establishment', and to the elite's preference for diffuse gentlemanly qualities at the cost of expertise. British economic policy since the end of the First World War, in particular the outstanding and longstanding failure to sustain a satisfactory rate of economic growth, has signified anything but high quality political management.[43] The same is true of the history of Anglo-Irish relations from 1800 down to the present. On criteria of the provision of social welfare and rising living standards, many countries with less 'strong' governments are manifestly performing better than Britain. Evaluation of political performance or effectiveness is obviously fraught with difficulties but if one moves beyond criteria of political stability and turns to the problem-solving capacities of political institutions in the face of demands from the international and internal environments then one is tempted to take a much less rosy view of the effectiveness of British political institutions. *The strength and effectiveness of the British political system, then, are not facts, but debatable assumptions.*

Related to this description and evaluation of the system is the significance attached by deference theorists to Leo Amery's interpretations of the British constitution.[44] I have already suggested that for many this interpretation is authoritative.[45] According to Amery, there is an unidirectional flow of influence from the Crown (or the executive) to the people: the political role of the latter is 'essentially passive', and this subject status is accepted by them.

In one way this thesis, though exaggerated, is unexceptionable. After all it seems to be a feature of most large industrialised societies.[46] But such an unabashed Tory conception of the British political tradition is highly partial. A.H. Birch has painstakingly reconstructed the strands which have contributed to a political tradition which is highly complex and variegated.[47] A realistic interpretation of the style of British politics needs to acknowledge the strength of the liberal (or popular influence) model as well as the Whitehall one (Amery). The latter interpretation accords too little importance to general elections which decide the composition of the House of Commons, and the Commons itself which determines the party in government and where the political leaders emerge. Looked at in an historical and comparative perspective it is probable, contrary to Amery's almost legal formulation, that the English have a peculiar lack of any concept of 'the state'. The notion of the freeborn Englishman has long been entrenched, and assumed rights of resistance and the refusal to be the objects of a state will have, as Bagehot and Halevy noted,[48] been tantamount to rights of rebellion. The pretensions of absolute monarchy were checked earlier in England than in other European states. In consequence popular perceptions of the monarch as a protector faded earlier in England than was the case in Prussia, France or Russia.[49] Study of early cases of state and nation-building, including France, Britain and Prussia, emphasises the comparatively slight role played by a centralised, authoritarian government in Britain. Again, although fashionable, it is not strictly accurate to see something un-English about revolutionary activity. In reality one is impressed by two aspects of the attitudes of the English working-class throughout modern history.[50] One is the high degree of self-confidence and consciousness of their rights which workers often possessed. The other is their traditional suspicion of and hostility to the state apparatus, especially the police, the courts, and the bureaucracy.[51] Viewed in such a perspective one is not so much impressed by the image of a strong government and a deferent population as by the early limitations on government and the development of a pluralistic political culture.

But are Amery and those who approvingly cite him correct in asserting that the British public accepts the passive status attributed to it? There is ample evidence in *The Civic Culture* which shows the contrary: a large section of the British public not only feels that it has the right to try to influence government policy but also that its efforts stand a good chance of being successful. This normative aspect of political deference, so emphasised by Amery, Eckstein and others, does not seem to be widely held.

Working-class Conservatism

A number of writers, while not disputing that there is general political and social deference among the English or British, have emphasised its concentration among the working-class. In particular, frequent efforts have been made to link deference with (a) support for the Conservative Party among a third of the working-class,[52] and (b) the electoral successes of the Conservative Party. According to Robert McKenzie these amount to '. . . one of the most striking political achievements in modern history'.[53] Fortunately, recent research into working-class political attitudes enables us to measure the extent of social deference among the working-class conservatives. On the McKenzie and Silver and Nordlinger definitions it appears that about a quarter of the conservative English urban workers are deferentials: Goldthorpe's small sample of affluent workers found that a sixth shared deferential attitudes.[54] Bearing in mind that the Goldthorpe sample was confined to the South of England, that half of the McKenzie and Silver sample was drawn from Greater London, and that Nordlinger's sample was confined to England, it is clear that these samples are heavily skewed in favour of working-class Conservatives. Samples which included non-English regions and gave representative weight to the north of England would locate much smaller proportions of Tory workers and, arguably, a smaller percentage of deferentials.[55] But establishing a chain of causation between social deference and Conservative voting among the workers is rendered difficult by two inconvenient pieces of data. One is that some Labour voters are also 'deferential' – between a fifth (McKenzie) and a sixth (Nordlinger); the other is that many middle-class conservatives share socially deferent attitudes.[56] The failure of studies of deference to include middle-class respondents and thus permit cross-class comparisons has meant that working-class support for the Conservative Party and for elite and traditional symbols like the House of Lords and the monarchy has been sweepingly attributed to its social deference. To date then, social deference has not performed impressively as a predictor of party choice by workers.

But it can be argued that the whole debate on working-class support for the Conservative Party has been based on three questionable assumptions, which, if disproved, place the phenomenon in a new light. The first is the vulgar Marxist assumption that what is called cross-class voting (Conservative workers and middle-class socialists) is anomalous, a case of false consciousness almost. Why should one start with this assumption? Both Nordlinger and McKenzie show that working-class Conservatives see little that is anomalous in their behaviour. It is also clear from the massive Butler and Stokes survey that British voters have other loyalties and identities than those of social class, and that when they vote with the correct (sic) class, many do so for reasons which have little or no connection with class interest. Moreover, cross-class voting is not unique to Britain. In the United States and Germany, workers vote in large numbers for ostensibly non-working-class parties.[57] Even the Swedish and Norwegian Socialist Parties, which have enjoyed great electoral success, only garner the same two-thirds of the working-class vote that British Labour does. The electoral success of Scandinavian socialism rests on the party's ability to attract substantial middle-class support.[58] More than hair-splitting is involved here. Comparative perspective highlights the generality of cross-class voting; it emphasises that British workers are no less class-oriented in voting than workers elsewhere; and it indicates that the British middle-class is remarkably homogeneous in its voting. It is this last factor that separates the electoral record of British Labour from that of the Scandinavian Socialists. What is significant about party and class in Britain, compared with other states, is not Labour's

Table 12.2 Party support by class self-images, 1963 (%)

	Middle class	Working class
Partisan Cons.	79%	28%
Self-image Lab.	21%	72%

inability to hold the working-class but its failure to attract significant middle-class support.

A second questionable assumption is that social class in Britain can simply be discussed in terms of manual and non-manual occupations and that these are identical with working and middle-class respectively. Such a fashionable dichotomy grossly inflates the number of working-class Conservatives and gives that party a great advantage among cross-class voters. If, on the other hand, we re-allocate the lower grade of non-manuals who, for the most part think of themselves as working-class anyway, then this advantage is reduced. Clearly the size and significance of the working-class Conservative vote varies according to where the line is drawn between the classes. In terms of subjective class perceptions and life-styles the more natural break seems to be one that casts the lower non-manuals with the working-class (Table 12.2).[59]

This absence of control groups in much of the empirical research is a serious omission in view of the fact that a major thrust of the research has been designed to prove that:

(a) the English workers are particularly deferential; presumably in comparison with the middle class or with other national working classes.
(b) the English as a whole are characterised by deferential attitudes; again presumably in comparison with other nations.

The third point concerns the late arrival of the Labour Party as a national contender for political power. The question of the timing of the entry of Labour on to the political stage is important for an understanding of working-class Conservatism and the electoral record of the Conservative Party. In 1966 there was still a third of British electors who had reached adolescence before the early 1920s, the period when Labour first became a serious national contender. This meant that they were socialised into a party system which excluded Labour and, given the importance of the family in the transmission of party loyalties, Labour was still relatively at a disadvantage as the next generation of voters developed their attachments to a party.[60] Again, no major study of working-class Conservatism and deference has reckoned with the vital extraneous variable of parental party loyalties. If we do reckon with it we see that much of working-class support for the Conservative Party is inherited.[61] Here, it appears, is the much more mundane and plausible explanation of the Conservative working man (and, perhaps, of the deferential Tory worker). Since 1945, when inter-generational patterns of socialisation are more equal and comparison between Conservative and Labour Parties becomes more meaningful, the electoral record of the party pales somewhat when compared to McKenzie's eulogy: over the past 25 years the two parties have shared office for an equal number of years.

Socialisation

There are also those who link the deference phenomenon with the process of political socialisation. Great importance is attached to the homogeneity of experiences with parents, teachers and employers and, it is argued, these experiences are significant in instilling the modest expectations and low influence into the vast majority which are appropriate to a deferential or subject political culture. On the other hand, the experiences of a small minority who will form the political elite amount to a form of anticipatory socialisation for positions of political dominance.[62] More broadly Harry Eckstein has seen in the 'congruence' between authority patterns in the political institutions and the other associations such as schools, trade unions, families and the workplace, the secret of Britain's stability and effectiveness as a democracy.[63]

Again, however, the available data lend little support to those inferences. The only empirical study of the role of the public schools as a political socialising agent questions the readily accepted belief of their efficacy in inculcating elitist values and expectations of a political career among students.[64] The high levels of participation, particularly in the family and at place of work, viewed both absolutely and in comparison with data for other nations, reported in *The Civic Culture*, would tend to throw doubt on the hypothesis of political deference as cause and effect of the kind of the socialisation practised in Britain.[65] More disconcerting perhaps for the hypothesis are the findings of a recent study of the attitudes of 1500 adolescents drawn from a variety of schools. The author, Ted Tapper, found that most students saw society as undemocratic and unfair, the educational system as inequitable, the political system as oligarchic, class relations as rigid and unfair, and occupational opportunities as unjust. The pattern of responses, across school and social class, was summarised by Tapper as 'dissatisfied'.[66] Certainly these young people, the majority of whom were shortly to take up full-time and permanent employment, had failed, as yet, to acquire the 'appropriate' deferential responses to the dominant political and social institutions. Moreover, though secondary modern schoolchildren invariably had appreciably lower occupational aspirations than grammar school pupils, there was only an insignificant difference when it came to aspiring to a career in politics; for many working-class and secondary modern adolescents politics seemed to be perceived as a more open and effective channel of social mobility than other occupations.

Stable Democracy

Finally, many students of English political culture have been inspired by a search for the attitudinal and social bases of stable democracy. For many, a reading of English political development enables them to trace the emergence of an ideal or civic culture: ideal because it is the culture most appropriate to the development and maintenance of a stable democracy. These writers have felt that political and/or social deference not only renders contemporary English political culture distinctive but it has been useful in bringing about a desirable balance between directive and passive attitudes, in underpinning the regime's ability to withstand threats and change, and in preventing the emergence of alienation or *incivisme* among the working class. However, efforts to trace a connection between the cultural factor and English political institutions and performance have also been invested with a more general significance.[67] Eckstein and Almond and Verba agree that deference is an essential component in the dualistic orientation to authority thought to be a precondition or facilitator of stable democracy. Runciman's work on reference groups and their importance as a traditional means of diverting working-class discontent can also be linked with this theory.

According to Runciman it is the modest expectation of workers and the fact that much deprivation has been felt *relatively* and not *absolutely*, because of their narrow frames of comparison, that explain their political acquiescence and English political stability.[68]

These attempts to relate the political culture to democratic stability are open to a number of important objections. Often the interpretation goes a long way beyond the data base. In addition, key elements in the theories are poorly applied, measured and tested.[69] For example Almond and Verba are imprecise about what constitutes an appropriate or balanced fusion of directive and acquiescent attitudes. The ingenious analytical framework outlined in the opening chapters of the book is hardly integrated with the rest of the book at all.[70] Again, the measures of degrees of democracy or democratic stability are inadequately dealt with. Ideally, as Brian Barry points out, empirical theorists of democracy would like to know the consequences for democratic stability which would follow from, say, a given increment in the diffusion of participatory orientations. Finally, the direction of the causal relationships is not clearly specified. Do the deferent-cum-participatory values cause the stability and effectiveness, or vice-versa, or are both produced by something else? Much of the theory of stable democracy, found in the empirical restatements of democratic theory, seems to involve a good deal of rationalisation of the data on British and American political orientations.[71]

It is certainly plausible to argue that the popular orientations are a by-product of the working of the political system; that in Britain, for instance, it is the responsiveness of the political elites which encourages a sense of political competence among voters. Almond and Verba found that more than half of their British sample think that the civil service will give serious attention to their problems and three-quarters feel the same way about the police. In addition large majorities feel able to influence the national and local political systems.[72] In other words, support for British political institutions does not co-exist with widespread political passivity or deference but with comparatively high levels of political participation and widespread sense of political competence. Thus, the allegiance or support (or deference) is based on the perceived responsiveness of the system and the elites.

Although deference has been central to theories or hypotheses of why the political system in England has been more successful in acquiring legitimacy and allegiance than that in France and Italy, such a view seems to involve putting the cart before the horse. What seems to require emphasis in comparing the English with the continental political cultures is not merely the greater allegiance of the former but rather where it came from. The often mentioned *incivisme* of the Italian and French voters seems to derive from a sense of frustration with the non-responsiveness of the political institutions and from the relative absence of a sense of sharing in the determination of the political outputs. *What such political societies seem to lack is not deference but rather a perception on the part of more citizens that they are meaningful participants in the political process.*[73] When this is achieved, the trust or deference may follow. To explain this difference between the English and the continental political cultures one has to explore the distinctive paths of these countries' political development. In England the authority of the central government developed gradually and did not obliterate local and regional centres of authority. Such a mode of development was conducive to the growth of a political culture which blended participant with allegiant values.

Again, we could more explicitly recognise the possibility of mutual reinforcement over time of the two variables, 'stable English democracy' and 'the political culture'. Instead of assuming that the relationship between them is linear, one acting as the dependent and the other as independent variable, we might entertain the likelihood that the two factors are mutually interactive. Given that the political culture is something of an analytical abstraction anyway, its role in empirical research is more likely to be that of an intervening variable. Values, attitudes and beliefs are clearly relevant to an explanation of some forms of political behaviour and to the performance of political systems, but eventually we have to explain how a nation's political culture came to be formed and expressed in the way it is.

In this section we have examined some of the assumed political consequences normally traced to deference. Some of these assumed effects or correlations, e.g. 'strong English governments', were far from being conclusive, while others, e.g. the strength of the Conservative Party in the working class, seemed to be better explained without resort to the deference hypothesis.

The dilemma facing the present body of theory and research on stable democracy and the nature of the English political culture is twofold. One is that if other national populations and working classes are more deferential than the English, then efforts to attribute certain aspects of English politics to this cultural component will remain unpersuasive. The other is that the slender evidence available suggests that the spread of political deference in England is not impressive when compared with that of other states.

DISCUSSION

The large number of pitfalls surrounding the work on English political culture would seem to derive from a certain stereotyped way of thinking about English politics and this, in turn, for a number of reasons. The attractiveness of the deference theory lies in its plausibility; it seems to tie together so many established ideas in a relatively coherent form. Here is the lynchpin which seems to explain the absence of a revolutionary tradition in Britain, the continued existence of the monarchy and the House of Lords, the ability of the Tory Party to gather a large minority of the working-class vote and other features to which foreign observers, particularly those from across the Atlantic, seem to be most sensitive. Deference is an example of what Maurice Farber warned was the potentially beguiling '. . . single concept (which) appears successfully to subsume a number of discrete phenomena, or at least to relate them'.[74] Undue satisfaction with the theory, it seems clear, has weakened the researchers' sensitivity to the unexpected and inconvenient in their data and the term often seems to redescribe what requires to be explained.

A poignant example of how this *déjà vu* condition can mislead even the most sensitive of researchers is available in Fred Greenstein's extremely original work on the socialisation patterns of English schoolchildren.[75] Greenstein found that working-class children were slower to shed idealised and unrealistic images of the monarchy than were middle-class children. He then proceeded, cautiously, to claim that these sharp class differences in childhood political realism might constitute a major explanation for the well-known political docility and passivity of the adult English workers, often summed up by the term deference. Maybe; but first we need to establish that large sections of the British working class are indeed deferential, or at least appreciably more so than the middle class. So far we know neither.

Political culture itself is a peculiarly slippery abstraction which we use to summarise salient aspects of a nation's affective, cognitive and evaluative patterns: and emphasis on the deferential strain (among, say, Tory workers) represents a further abridgement of these complex patterns. Trouble seems to emerge from the frequent utilisation of deference in (a) the historical context, e.g. English state and nation-building, and the political integration of the working class; and (b) impressionistic appraisals of the 'style' or 'ethos' of the English political system. However, the survey instrument is both a-historical in that it provides a snap-shot of the system at a particular time, and only measures the frequency with which attitudes are held rather than weighing them. But the quality of these orientations, their intensity, the motives behind them, and their distribution according to region, class, party and level of political activity pose an acute macro–micro problem. How valid is it to make inference from individuals to the whole, by simply aggregating individual responses as if they were all of equal weight? As yet the data supplied by surveys hardly supports the notion of deference discerned from the impressionistic and historical perspectives. This may mean, of course, that the research tools of social science are being exploited at a time when the British deference is waning.

A final cause centres on the question of comparison. It is difficult to overemphasise the importance of the reference point in any study of political culture. Patterns of a nation's political orientations only become distinctive when they differ from those in another nation. Traditionally, England has most frequently been compared with France and the United States, and, arguably, *these perspectives have coloured many interpretations of English politics and led to the deference stereotype.* Comparison with France has seemed to provide a ready contrast in values; highlighted for England are the allegiant working class, the absence of a revolutionary tradition, the homogeneous political culture and the stable political system. From the early nineteenth-century the two political systems have been placed at opposite poles, England exemplifying the incremental mode of political development backed by a largely loyal population, and France the revolutionary model only partly accepted by a people deeply divided over French political institutions and the values they expressed. Anglo-American comparison invariably emphasises the greater elitism and deference of the English political value system.[76] Thus, Almond and Verba describe Britain as a deferential political culture, but this only emerges from their explicit comparison of it with America; comparison with Italians, Mexicans and Germans, who exhibited markedly more signs of political docility than the

British, would demand a different assessment. Such an abridged and selective basis of comparison has also led Lipset to exaggerate political and social deference in England.[77] It seems that some of this exaggeration results from the conceptual polarisation of deference and equality. In American society, ostensibly committed to achievement norms and egalitarianism, deference is a frequent compensation or rationalisation for low status or low achievement.[78] The conclusion of this argument is not that the Anglo-American comparison should be abandoned; rather that its monopoly of much of the writing about British politics provides a convenient take-off point for the application of the ready-made label of the 'deferential' English, and that an alternative comparative framework might cast English political culture in a new light.

If characterisation of popular English political attitudes would seem to be more complex than the conventional resort to the deference syndrome would have us believe, then this applies *a fortiori* to the bulk of the working class. Indeed, the willingness of several writers to focus solely on the workers for purposes of empirical research and, at the same time, offer assessments about the general political culture has led to some confusion. For example, the Nordlinger, McKenzie and Silver, and Runciman surveys all confined their studies of deference to the working class: though the implication of this research focus is that there is something both distinctive and significant about the concentration of deferential political attitudes among workers. Nordlinger and McKenzie characterise the culture as a whole as deferential.[79] However, regardless of the research focus it is important to distinguish between properties of the general population and those of a sub-culture.

An argument of this conceptual critique of deference is that any reappraisal of popular, and particularly working-class, orientations to the political system should reverse the traditional emphasis on deference. Certainly there is ample evidence provided in the *Civic Culture* data to cast doubt on ideas of the political passivity of British workers, in relation to workers in other nations. On a number of tests, including subjective competence, sense of obligation to take part in political activities, and perceived freedom to protest at work, the British workers show a more participant outlook than those of other nations, including the United States. Moreover, the difference in political competence tends to be quite marked in favour of the British worker. Similar findings emerge from a sophisticated secondary analysis of this data; regardless of the level of voluntary organisational involvement, low-status Britons perform better on elaborate tests of political participation than those from other nations.[80]

In other words, the available evidence – and one must be cautious at this point, for no empirical research has been specifically addressed to the study of cross-class political passivity – suggests that this aspect of deference is not a singular feature of the English working class.

Certain historical and institutional factors would lead one to expect a high degree of activism among English workers compared with those in many other countries. The fact that class interest has been the most salient aspect of British politics since the end of the First World War has mobilised the working class into politics. The workers also have readily identifiable class institutions like trade unions, co-operative societies and the Labour Party which, in turn, promote working-class political participation and the entry of workers into the House of Commons.[81] However, the other commonly emphasised aspect of deference, namely the workers' benign and uncritical outlook on the political elites and the political system, is also in need of revision. An impressive feature of the surveys is the decline of deference, as empirically measured, among the younger generation. Equally notable is the assumption of new and often 'bourgeois' reference groups by the more affluent workers, and, withal, the adoption of outlooks which have little in common with the traditional working-class images of society and politics.[82] The evaluation of political instrumentalities such as trade unions, political parties and Eton-educated sons of peers has become more detached and pragmatic; at times this can carry over to quite cynical assessments of the political elite.[83] The lack of deference among workers becomes even more marked if one moves from the political to the industrial realm. Here, the widening of the traditionally restricted frames of social comparisons seems, since 1945, to have heightened the aspirations of many workers and to have increased their resentment of the pattern of social as well as income inequalities and, it can be argued, these attitudes have threatened the realisation of a stable regulation of economic life. One has only to think of successive government failures to impose wage restraint, the unpredictable and 'unofficial' interruptions to the process of production, the comparatively low increase in output per man, and the almost anomic pattern of industrial relations to recognise the plausibility of such an interpretation.[84]

CONCLUSION: WHITHER A STEREOTYPE?

The argument of this paper can be briefly summarised. We have criticised the term deference as it is applied to English politics on the grounds that it is used in various ways and often with insufficient precision: (a) as an ill-defined and sometimes undefined concept; (b) as a poorly operationalised and sometimes non-operationalised measure; and (c) as a variable which is only imperfectly linked in a causal sense to factors which it purports to be associated with. Also, there seems little basis in the existing empirical work to warrant the strength with which the stereotype of the deferential English political culture or the deferential working class is held in academic literature; such characterisations are generally beyond (and at times contradicted by) the data base.

The failure of empirical research to demonstrate the existence of large-scale deference should provoke a reassessment of this aspect of English political culture. At present there is a theory of deference in search of data. It may also be that the abandonment of this concept might result in more fruitful research. The contemporary secularisation of English political attitudes – and the growth of a more critical outlook – would seem to deviate from the model suggested by Bagehot and perhaps too readily accpted by his successors.

NOTES

1. Accordingly, I ignore Harold Lasswell's use of the term; for him deference, which entailed properties like prestige, status and respect, was a basic value sought by politicians. I also ignore Edward Shils's highly persuasive refinement of the concept for sociological purposes. See 'Deference', in J. A. Jackson (ed.), *Social Stratification* (Cambridge, 1968).
2. The quotations in this paragraph are drawn from Ch. 8 of *The English Constitution*.
3. Engels made a similar observation. See *Socialism, Utopian and Scientific* (New York, 1938), p. 26).
4. Bagehot, Ch. 9.
5. The argument in this section is heavily indebted to Reinhard Bendix, *Nation Building and Citizenship*, Ch. 2, and his *Work and Authority in Industry*, (New York, 1956), Ch. 2. Also see Asa Briggs, 'The Language of "Class" in Early 19th Century England', in A. Briggs and John

Saville (eds.), *Essays in Labour History* (London, 1960).

6. Cited in Bendix, *Work and Authority in Industry*, *op.cit.*, p. 47.
7. W. J. M. Mackenzie has suggested that Bagehot offered an *esoteric* model of English politics; it asserts the primacy of social power over political institutions and forms. Mackenzie, however, suggests that there are other models. See his 'Models of English Politics', in Richard Rose (ed.), *Studies in British Politics* (London, 1976). See above, pp. 5–15.
8. On the conservative effects of the French Revolution on many sociologists in the nineteenth-century, see Leon Bramson, *The Political Context of Sociology* (Princeton, 1961), Chs. 1 and 2.
9. Richard Rose and Harve Mossawir, 'Ordinary Individuals in Electoral Situations', in Richard Rose (ed.), *Policy Making in Britain* (London, 1969), p. 75.
10. Richard Rose, *Politics in England* (London, 1965), p. 41; Nordlinger, *The Working Class Tories* (London, 1967), pp. 17–18; and A.H. Birch, *Representative and Responsible Government* (London, 1964), p. 245; and *The British System of Government* (London 1967), pp. 27–8; also see Harry Eckstein, 'The British Political System', in Samuel H. Beer and Adam Ulam (eds.), *Patterns of Government* (New York, 1965), pp. 75–7.
11. The citation is from Mark Abrams and Richard Rose, *Must Labour Lose?* (Harmondsworth, 1960), p. 25.
12. See Robert Alford, *Party and Society* (Chicago, 1963), pp. 164 ff., and Ralph Samuel, 'Dr. Abrams and the End of Politics', *New Left Review*, 1960, pp. 2–9.
13. See the evidence in the very thorough analysis of Jay Blumier and Denis McQuail, *Televisioh and Politics* (London, 1969), pp. 115–17. Also see National Opinion Polls for February 1968 and May 1969 and Butler and Stokes, *Political Change in Britain* (London, 1969), pp. 378–80.
14. *The Working Class Tories.*
15. *Angels in Marble* (London, 1968).
16. It should be noted that McKenzie and Silver employed a composite index for the major part of their work. McKenzie and Silver, however, at one stage, had to employ a single item, namely the leadership one; they report that they found that this item was an excellent predictor of deference according to the more inclusive scale (Appendix B).
17. Butler and Stokes, *op.cit.*, pp. 378–80. Moreover, only 3 per cent of Nordlinger's working class Tories mentioned the leaders' social status as a reason for liking the party, *op.cit.*, p. 155.
18. Gabriel Almond and Sidney Verba, *The Civic Culture* (Princeton, 1963), p. 456.
19. *Ibid*, ch. 8.
20. *Ibid*, p. 19.
21. *Ibid*, p. 455.
22. 'The political culture of democratic Britain assigns to ordinary people the role, not of citizens but of subjects', McKenzie and Silver, *op.cit.*, p. 251.

23. Harvé Mossawir, *The Significance of an Election* (MA Thesis, University of Manchester, 1965).
24. *The Politics of Accommodation: Pluralism and Democracy in the Netherlands* (Berkeley, 1968), p. 208.
25. *Ibid*, p. 145.
26. *Relative Deprivation and Social Justice* (London, 1966), pp. 146 and 180–1.
27. Ibid, pp. 180—1.
28. Rose, *Politics in England op.cit.*, pp. 100–1 and Nordlinger, *op.cit.*, p. 63.
29. See the data reported in Ralph Miliband, *The State in Capitalist Society* (London, 1969), ch. 3, pp. 66–7; V. Subramanian, 'Representative Bureaucracy: A Reassessment', *American Political Science Review*, LXI, 1967, pp. 1010–19; and *Men Who Govern* (Brookings Institute, 1968).
30. Allen Kornberg and N. Thomas, 'Representative Democracy and Political Elites in Canada and the United States', *Parliamentary Affairs*, 19, 1965–6, pp. 91–102. On the gradual withdrawal of the social elite from politics, see W.L. Guttsman, *The British Political Elite* (London, 1963), ch. 3.
31. On this see D.A. Kavanagh, *Constituency Electioneering in Britain* (London, 1970). Japanese voters appear to be highly aware of and deferent to the candidates. See Scott C. Flanagan, 'Voting Behaviour in Japan', *Comparative Political Studies*, 1, 1968.
32. 'Authority Relations and Governmental Performance: A Theoretical Framework', *Comparative Political Studies*, Vol. 2, 1969, pp. 269–326, particularly p. 304.
33. *The British Political System* (London, 1965), p. 77.
34. *The Civic Culture, op.cit*, p. 455.
35. Eckstein, *The British System of Government* (New York, 1958), p. 90.
36. See Nordlinger, op.cit., Ch. 1, for a summary of the literature.
37. E.g. Brian Chapman, *British Government Observed* (London, 1963), and Richard Rose, 'The Variability of Party Government', *Political Studies*, 17, 1969.
38. *Modern British Politics* (London 1965).
39. Robert Skidelsky, *Politicians and the Slump* (London, 1967).
40. Robert Jackson, *Rebels and Whips* (London, 1968). For a sample of similar arguments see George Jones, 'The Prime Minister's Power', *Parliamentary Affairs*, 18, 1965, pp. 167–85; and Richard Rose, 'The Variability of Party Government', *Political Studies*, 17, 1969, pp. 413–45; and 'Complexities of Party Leadership', *Parliamentary Affairs*, 16, 1963, pp. 257–73.
41. *Comparative Government* (London, 1970), pp. 170, 183–5.
42. Brian Chapman, *op.cit*; Thomas Balogh, 'The Apotheosis of the Dilettante', in Hugh Thomas (ed.), *The Establishment* (London, 1962); Samuel Brittan, *Steering the Economy* (London, 1969); and the contributions in W. J. Stankiewicz (ed.), *Crisis in British Government* (London, 1967).

43. See Samuel Brittan, *Steering the Economy, op.cit.*
44. *Thoughts on the Constitution* (London, 1947).
45. See Nordlinger, *op.cit.*, Ch.1; Eckstein, *The British System of Government*, pp. 76 ff; McKenzie and Silver, *op.cit.*, p. 251.
46. See Joseph Schumpeter, *Capitalism, Socialism and Democracy* (New York, 1943), and Giovanni Sartori, *Democratic Theory* (Detroit, 1962).
47. *Representative and Responsible Government.*
48. *A History of the English Speaking People*, Vol. 1 (London, 1937), pp. 193–8.
49. G. Rudé, *The Crowd in History, 1730–1848* (London, 1964), p. 228.
50. E.P. Thomson, *The Making of the English Working Class* (London, 1963).
51. Henry Pelling, *Popular Politics and Society in Late Victorian England* (London, 1968), pp. 5, 71. For a similar argument but from a different perspective see Richard Hoggart, *The Uses of Literacy* (London, 1957), Ch. 3.
52 For particularly sweeping statements of this thesis, see S.M. Lipset, 'Must the Tories always Triumph?', *Socialist Commentary*, November, 1960; and Peter Pulzer, *Political Representatives and Elections* (London, 1968), p. 20.
53. *Angels in Marble, op.cit.*, p. 12.
54. David Goldthorpe *et al*, *The Affluent Worker* (Cambridge, 1969), p. 20.
55. Butler and Stokes, *op.cit.*, Ch. 6.
56. *Ibid*, pp. 87 and 113.
57. Robert Alford, *Party and Society* (Chicago, 1963), and Juan J. Linz, 'Cleavage and Consensus in West German Politics', in Seymour M. Lipset and Stein Rokkan (eds.), *Party Systems and Voter Alignments* (New York, 1967).
58. See Nils Sternquist in Robert A. Dahl (ed.), *Political Oppositions in Western Democracies* (New Haven, Conn, 1965), p. 371.
59. Butler and Stokes, *op.cit.*, pp. 70, 77.
60. *Ibid*, Chs. 3 and 5.
61. *Ibid*, pp. 104–9.
62. Nordlinger, *op.cit.*, pp. 27–8 and 131; Ralph H. Turner, 'Sponsored and Contested Mobility in the School System', *American Sociological Review*, 1966; Richard Rose, op.cit., *Politics in England*, pp. 69–71 and Ch. 3, and Rupert Wilkinson, *The Prefects* (London, 1966).
63. 'A Theory of Stable Democracy', in *Division and Cohesion in Democracy* (Princeton, 1966).
64. Denis McQuail *et al*, 'Elite Education and Political Values', *Political Studies*, 16, 1968, pp. 257–66.
65. Ch. 12.
66. E.R. Tapper, *Secondary School Adolescents* (Manchester PhD, 1967), Ch. 6. For data supporting this position see also Richard Rose, *Students in Society* (Manchester, 1963) and Jack Dennis *et al* 'Support for Nation and Government Among English Children', *British Journal of Political Science*, Vol. 1, 1971, pp. 25–48.

67. See Almond and Verba, *op.cit.*, Ch. 8 and Ch. 15; and Nordlinger, *op.cit.*, Ch. 9.·

68. Runciman, *op.cit.*

69. The problems involved in applying these hypotheses and the short-comings in the theories themselves are brilliantly explored in Brian Barry, *Sociologists, Economists and Democracy* (London, 1970), Chs. 3 and 4. I have relied heavily on Barry in this paragraph.

70. Actual attempts to isolate such types as parochials, participants and subjects are likely to be unrewarding given that the qualities of such types are often mixed in most individuals. See Harvé Mossawir, *The Significance of an Election*, (MA Thesis, University of Manchester, 1965).

71. Heinz Eulau has noted that much of this analysis has led to the establishment of functional rather than causal relationships between variables. *The Behavioural Persuasion in Politics* (New York, 1963), p. 128.

72. Data from Almond and Verba, op.cit. Also see Butler and Stokes, *op.cit.*, p. 32.

73. To argue, as does Martin Needler, that a larger dose of 'English deference' is what Latin-American states need if they are to achieve greater political stability seems to me quite naive. It is a view which is too deterministic and involves a misperception of English political culture. See his *Political Development in Latin America* (New York, 1968), p. 91.

74. 'The Problem of National Character', in N. J. and W. T. Smelser, *Personality and Social Systems* (New York, 1963), p. 86.

75. 'Queen and Prime Minister: The Child's View', *New Society*, 23 October, 1970.

76. Many early nineteenth-century observers of English and American life were interested, for a variety of motives, in exaggerating the differences between the old world and the new. On this see Edward Pesson, *Jacksonian America: Society, Personality and Politics* (Illinois, 1969), p. 44.

77. *The First New Nation*, Part III, and 'Anglo-American Society', *International Encyclopedia of Social Science* (New York, 1967).

78. For evidence of American deference, see Robert Lane, *Political Ideology* (New Haven, 1962), Ch. 2.

79. It is fair to add, however, that Nordlinger admits his expectation that the middle class is also likely to possess politically acquiescent attitudes, see pp. 235–5. This admission is hardly reconcilable with the emphasis he places on hierarchy and working-class submissiveness to classes above them in status.

80. Norman Nie *et al*, 'Social Structure and Political Participation: Developmental Relationships', *American Political Science Review*, Vol. LXIII, 1969.

81. For a similar line of argument relating to Norwegian workers, see Stein Rokkan and Angus Campbell, 'Citizen Participation in Political Life: Norway and the United States of America', *International Social Science Journal*, Vol. 12, 1960, pp. 66–99.

82. Butler and Stokes, *op.cit.*, pp. 104–7; John H. Goldthorpe *et al*, *The Affluent Worker: Political Attitudes and Behaviour* (Cambridge, 1968); David Lockwood, 'Sources of Variations in Working Class Images of Society', *The Sociological Review*', Vol. 14, 1966, pp. 249–67.

83. Pollsters have found that members of the working class are more likely than members of the middle class to agree with such cynical views as: 'Most politicians will promise anything to get votes'; 'Most politicians are more about their party than about their country'; 'Politicians are all talk and no action'; 'Most politicans are in it for what they can get out of it'; 'Once they become MPs they forget all about the people who elected them'. The average agreement per social class with these judgements was AB–55 per cent, C1–62 per cent, C2–65 per cent, DE–68 per cent. Calculated by the author from *National Opinion Polls* (February, 1968).

84. For more sustained argument along these lines, see John H. Goldthorpe, 'Social Inequality and Social Integration in Modern Britain', *Advancement of Science*, December 1969, pp. 190–202, and Alan Fox and Allan Flanders, 'The Reforms of Collective Bargaining: from Durkheim to Donovan', *British Journal of Industrial Relations*, Vol. 7, 1969.

13 An American Science of British Politics*

This chapter attempts to review certain salient themes in the substantive literature on British politics by American political scientists. More diffidently, it also suggests some reasons for these American perceptions. It is as well to be clear that the paper does not cover certain areas. It does not compare American and British politics or discuss the extent to which one system has tried to learn or copy from the other. I have also left aside the interesting exercise of regarding the American writings on British politics as part of a larger American literature on British history, society and *mores*.

The American literature on Britain commands attention for a number of reasons, apart from the sheer interest involved in observing the way in which foreigners describe and evaluate our politics. First, it is large; second, there is much that is of high quality; and, third, Americans have been influential in colouring the assessments in other countries of our political system. From Woodrow Wilson and A. L. Lowell to Almond, Eckstein and Beer, a legion of respected American political scientists has analysed and enriched the study of British politics. It is open to speculation as to why the ties of language, sentiment and history have apparently led many American political scientists to view Britain as a second intellectual home and why the British have hardly reciprocated. There are exceptions but the flow of major research between the two countries to date has been almost wholly one way – by Americans on Britain.[1]

It is foolhardy to attempt to generalise about this vast literature. My own sampling of the major studies suggests, however, that a number of features stand out. These include the following.

First, British politics is worth studying because it is interesting in itself, contains practical lessons for Americans and is useful for building theories of political change.

* The paper was originally presented at the annual conference of the Political Studies Association in Lancaster, Marsh 1974. I am grateful for the comments of Fred Greenstein, Erwin Hargrove, Richard Rose and Richard Pear on an earlier version.

Second, for the most part, American political scientists have admired the British political system, or at least certain features of it. Not all American political scientists have been approving but those who actually wrote about Britain seem to have done so partly because they found it attractive. The system is frequently presented as a model of stable democracy and of an incremental and reconciliatory style of political change. According to one well-known textbook, 'Just as Alexis de Tocqueville travelled to America in 1831 to seek the secrets of democracy, so today we might travel to England in search of the secrets of stable representative government.'[2]

Third, a certain limited vocabulary on the political institutions, history and culture recurs throughout much of the literature. The overriding theme is that there is a *balance* between a government which is confident and effective and yet which is also responsible, in the forms of its executive accountability to Parliament, responsiveness to the public interest, and general sense of self-restraint. There is also a balanced political culture which blends the participatory outlook with popular trust in the government, and a historical development which has allowed a balanced achievement of liberty and order. The system facilitates leadership *by* the government while providing for the control *of* government and satisfies the twin claims of hierarchy and collegium. Other regular themes in this formula of responsible leadership are gradualism, stability, consensus, deference and *elitism*. A later generation of American political scientists has, however, reacted against this view. From the 1950s to 1960s the metaphor changed from *balance* to *stalemate*.

Fourth, there is, not surprisingly, an Anglo-American framework of comparison. The many similarities between the two systems may be noted, but more frequently the two systems have been presented as opposed ideal-types. In contrast to the features of responsibility, popular trust in the government, and co-ordination attributed to the British system, most American writers on Britain have been concerned to criticise the Madisonian model of their own system. This model stresses the several restrictions on majoritarianism, the checks and balance between groups and institutions, and the suspicion of collectivist government, and emphasises the values of representation and egalitarianism over leadership and hierarchy. It is fair comment that in much of this literature the British model has taunted the American. From the 1880s to the mid-1950s many writers were precursors and legatees of a progressive mood, and ambivalent about mass democracy. On the one hand, they favoured more direct democracy as a check on party bosses and 'malefactors of great wealth'; at the same time they were concerned about the illiberal attitudes of mass democracy. The British system seemed to blend liberal and conservative values in its institutions and provide safeguards against populism by virtue of the culture and the character of its *elites*.

Fifth, it is possible but not, I hope, contrived, to link these features in the person of the ubiquitous Mr Bagehot, the patron saint of the American science of British politics. I suspect that the benevolent view of British politics entertained by many American (and British, let me acknowledge) political scientists is in some measure a consequence of Bagehot's status as their Baedeker. It is interesting that Bagehot's elegant aphorisms are still so readily invoked, almost as a conditioned reflex, in spite of the great political and social changes over the last 100 years. Foreign observers may see interesting and important features of our society that we miss; Bagehot's appeal even now is that he was an insider who perceived what the outsider would notice. But present-day Americans may have been inclined to inherit Bagehot's views too uncritically. As Richard Neustadt has noted caustically, 'Americans have been brought up on Bagehot, read at first- or second-hand, which is a pity'.[3]

It is easy to forget that Bagehot's famous essay, *The English Constitution*, was the occasion of an unfavourable comparison of American with British institutions.[4] It was one of the few articles on American politics written in England in the half-century between de Tocqueville's volume and Bryce's classic study in 1889, and is also a precursor of many American academics' belief that the grass is greener on the other side of the Atlantic. What several Americans, starting with Wilson and A. L. Lowell, have taken from Bagehot is his praise of the elitist-deference strain in the British culture, the role he attributed to the Cabinet in providing the centralisation and co-ordination of political power, and his claim that the fusion of the executive and legislature provided for accountability and a *balanced* relationship between Cabinet and Parliament.[5] And each of these features was distinguished by Bagehot and the Americans from the situation in the United States. Britain's fortune, according to Bagehot, was that it possessed an admirable governing class which was a model for a 'deferential nation'. In contrast, America was badly served both because of the absence of a natural governing class and the influence of the notion of popular sovereignty; it lacked the British attribute of a 'dignified and overawing government getting its subjects to obey'. Again, the British Cabinet, described in the famous passage as the buckle and hyphen which fused the executive and legislature, was explicitly contrasted with an immobilism alleged to be inherent in the American separation of powers.

There are some signs that Bagehot is presently suffering from a revisionist climate of opinion. Though his account of British politics was inaccurate in many respects even at the time of writing, he (along with L. S. Amery) has influenced many later Americans to see British parliamentary government as a superb device for 'harmonising' the competing functions of leadership by government and popular control of government, without a formal separation of powers.[6]

It is worth reminding ourselves that a historian of pre-Revolutionary America would hardly be surprised by the frequently favourable assessment and the emphasis on balance. In the years after 1688 the British Constitution was admired by Americans as 'the most perfect combination of human powers in society'.[7] In particular, as Bernard Bailyn has documented at length, it was the 'mixed' or 'balanced' character of the British Constitution which was approved; there was a balance between the socio-political elements of royalty, nobility and commons, in which the powers and functions of government were so allocated as to prevent domination by any one institution or interest. Indeed, it was what Americans regarded as the abrogation of this balanced constitution that alienated them from Britain. It is possible to trace here the British origins of many ideas of the Founding Fathers. It is also possible to link Almond's pluralist celebration of sub-system autonomy and structural differentiation with this old separation of powers paradigm; there is a new vocabulary but there is also a shared approval of the British system and of an equilibrium attained *via* the separation of functions among different institutions.[8]

In the remaining sections of the paper the sampling of the distinguished American political science writings on the *general character* of British politics over the past century is organised under four headings. First, there is the study of specific institutions such as the Cabinet, the civil service, and the political parties; second, the study of the political culture; third, the study of the process of political change and development; and finally, a contemporary literature which is more general, policy-based, and critical. In the conclusion I shall consider the intellectual, social and political contexts of the American assessments.

THE BALANCED INSTITUTIONS

Any explanation of American perceptions of British politics must note that the American constitution was the product of a revolt by people of British stock against the perversions of a once admired 'true and balanced British constitution'. The American Founding Fathers produced an ideal of what they thought the British constitution *ought* to be. The intellectual origins of the American constitution, so important for an understanding of the selective transplantation of approved British features and the attempts to marry a distinctive American political identity to an adherence to certain Anglo-American values, have been well told elsewhere. It seems clear that for much of the nineteenth century many Americans, having fashioned a 'new world', were convinced of the superiority of their way of life and political institutions over the British and the European. British radicals, impressed by the wide suffrage and available land, readily concurred.[9] There was a marked change, however, in the universality of these assessments towards the close of the nineteenth century. A medley of political idealists, progressives and professional people offered a wide-ranging critique of American political institutions. They focused on the unsavoury features of the dominant party caucus, corruption, plutocracy and the 'spoils' system. At a time when the Presidency seemed impotent in the face of an ambitious Congress and the growth of the caucus system, the paradigm of a separation and balance of institutions and functions no longer seemed an accurate description. Moreover, the neglect of urgent social and economic issues also appeared to justify a new system.

This critique coincided with the growth of an academic political science in America and the study and more favourable appraisal of other systems, in particular that of Britain. It is true that some populist critics, who demanded fundamental and egalitarian changes in the political structure, looked elsewhere for the devices of direct democracy and were neutral about the British system. But other writers, more concerned to raise the moral tone of politics, were prepared to derive lessons from British political institutions and practices, and especially from the role of the Cabinet, the nature of the party system and the methods of recruitment to the civil service. *In an important sense then, the American study (and approval) of British politics originated in a reformist climate of American opinion and academic study of government.*

The young Woodrow Wilson shared much of this concern, and his influential *Cabinet Government in the United States* (1879) and *Congressional Government* (1885) looked to Britain as an inspiration. He perceived in Britain a high moral tone of public life and a balance between the institutions, qualities which he admired and found signally lacking in the United States. The principle of Cabinet government, based on the fusion of the Executive and Leglislature, provided for the *responsible* exercise of leadership, for *'Power and strict accountability for its use* are essential constituents of good government'. Wilson attributed the secret of the British combination of leadership with responsibility to its Cabinet system. The presence of Cabinet members in the legislature enabled the government to initiate legislation in Parliament, and dependence on its Parliamentary majority made the executive accountable to Parliament. Drawing on Bagehot's portrait of 'government by discussion', Wilson also enthused over the role of debate and oratory in the Commons; debate was so decisive in the chamber that the life of the government depended on its ability to *persuade* its back-benchers to vote for it. Moreover, in such a system, 'None but the ablest can become leaders and masters in this keen tournament in which arguments are the weapons and the people the judges'.[10]

In America, however, Wilson charged that the dispersal of powers both precluded the possible leadership of the President and rendered him practically immune to the attempts of Congress to topple him or hold him accountable. Instead of a healthy balance there was a stalemate; committee rule in Congress and caucus control of the electoral process and bureaucracy denied leadership which would be intelligible and responsible. Wilson therefore recommended 'responsible Cabinet government' for the United States as a means of producing the qualities of coherence. Such a reform would involve Cabinet officers sitting in Congress, initiating bills and answering to Congress for the work of their departments. Wilson argued that such a system would ensure the recruitment of the class of honourable and able politicians and administrators found in Britain, would encourage a more intelligent public opinion and would provide for 'the renewal of the now perishing growth of statesmanlike qualities'.[11]

The young Wilson was infatuated with the British system (and never lost this admiration in later years) not least, we may presume, because it seemed to provide more scope for his own political skills and highly moralistic, intellectual approach to politics. Later critics have rightly fastened on Wilson's belief in the efficacy of institutional change, his neglect of the reciprocal relationships between the institutions and the wider aspects of British society and culture, and also on the largely unexamined status of his basic premises that it was concentration of power in the formally accountable British institutions which clarified responsibility and the fragmentation in America which bred irresponsibility and confused electors.[12] A more serious complaint was that Wilson, drawing on Bagehot, portrayed a 'balance' between Parliament and the executive which was already being eroded. This notion of balance emphasised the effectiveness of such instruments as Question Time, ministerial responsibility, and the willingness of Parliament to dismiss governments. However, as A. L. Lowell was to recognise in his superb *The Government of England* (1908), such features as the growth of the executive, the development of disciplined party voting and the greater government control of the Parliamentary timetable had already undermined Parliament's control of the Cabinet. Such a 'liberal' view of the British constitution was of course purveyed long after Wilson's essay.[13]Lowell is to be distinguished from Wilson in another context. Though he agreed that British governments and parties were more accountable than those in America, he did not believe in the possibility or desirability of the introduction into America of the Cabinet system.

Wilson has been treated at some length here because he was the first in a long line of Americans who have contrasted the Presidential and Cabinet systems around the theme of balance and responsibility. Indeed, subsequent American proposals for improving co-ordination between the executive and Congress and for making the former more responsible to the latter have invariably involved attempts to incorporate parts of the Parliamentary system, particularly a more invigorated Cabinet. This has also been the case when proposals have been made for reducing the dependence of the executive on the health and ability of the President, and for promoting a more collective form of leadership. Attempts to strengthen and reform the Cabinet on British lines have a long history, from 1864, when the first Pendleton bill proposed that Cabinet officers sit in the

House. Woodrow Wilson employed his Presidential press conferences in large part as a substitute for the Parliamentary Question Time, and his revival of the practice of Presidential addresses to Congress was in keeping with his view of the President as a leader of the legislature. In 1945–6 the Joint Committee on the Organization of Congress again found wide support for the direct questioning of members of Cabinet by Congress. Dwight Eisenhower was impressed by his experience of the British Parliamentary system; in 1955 he established a Cabinet Secretariat and, as President, attempted to transform the Cabinet into a collective decision-making body, meeting regularly and formally.[14] It is beyond my brief here to retail the dissimilarities between the two Cabinet systems but there is much justice in Fenno's complaint against the several Americans, starting with Wilson, who have assumed that the function and form of the American Cabinet should follow the British, not least because of the similarity in terminology.[15]

Following the Northcote-Trevelyan reforms the British civil service also attracted the admiration of American reformers. The reformers of the American civil service in the late nineteenth century invariably adopted the British civil service as a reference point. Interestingly, this outlook was a reversal of the older desire by British radicals to emulate the economy and efficiency of the American federal civil service, prior to the introduction there of a more sweeping spoils system in 1829.[16] What the American reformers admired in Britain were such features as the apparent separation of the administration of government from party politics, the appointment of civil servants by competitive examination, and the officials' security of tenure in spite of changes in party control of government. Reformers also noted how these appointments in Britain were regarded as a public trust and as a career; the explicit contrast was with the spoils system in America. A very useful study cum panegyric of the reformed British civil service was the influential *Civil Service in Great Britain: A History of Abuses and Reforms and their Bearing upon American Politics* (1880) by Dorman B. Eaton.[17] This study was requested by the President for the Commission for the Reform of the United States Civil Service and traces the impact of the mid-century reforms in loving detail, identifies the merit system with a wide range of virtues in British society and politics, and eloquently states the case for a similar reform in America. Eaton wrote to the President of his astonishment 'at the immense length the English have outdistanced us, in the great cause of honest and efficient administration;

and I assure you our partisan and venal ways will show a sad
contrast with their regular and upright methods'.[18] Eaton was later
to become Chairman of the United States Civil Service Commission
and the demands for appointment by merit met with some reward
in the Pendleton Act of 1883.

In this century American perceptions of the British civil service
have been more ambivalent. There is general admiration for such
features of the Administrative Class of the civil service as its
permanent and highly educated elite, its generalist orientation and
ability to co-operate with the changing governments. The admiration
has been reflected in some measure in the long-standing demands
for a similar career service for top administrators in America, the
equivalents of the class of permanent Secretaries in Britain. Leonard
White and Herman Finer were weighty proponents of this change
in the inter-war years and the Hoover Commission of 1955 eventually
recommended a class of non-specialist and politically neutral top
civil servants.[19] But the goal of a permanent elite administrative
class has competed with concerns for a 'representative bureaucracy'
(reflected, for example, in the provision for balanced geographical
representation of recruits), for flexibility in the system of bureaucratic
appointments, for the recruitment of advisers who will be committed
to the President's policies. In the light of these countervailing values
it is not surprising that the proposal has made little progress.
These features contrast with the recruitment process of British
administrators. What is striking in a comparison of the alternation
of governments in the two countries, is the much greater change-
over of key administrative and management personnel which occurs
in America; the in-coming President and Cabinet members make
several political and semi-political appointments to posts that would
be held in Britain by permanent civil servants. The private staffs of
the British Prime Minister and ministers are puny in comparison
and, arguably, the scope for the incoming party to impress its
policies on the bureaucracy is thereby limited.

Another contrast between the two systems lies in the nature of
the two-party system. Before 1914, Wilson, Lowell, Henry Jones
Ford and Frank J. Goodnow contributed to a large body of literature
on the functions of American political parties.[20] All were impressed
by the greater concern with policy of British parties by their
disciplined voting in Parliament; all agreed that these features made
British parties more responsible than the American. Again, each
writer favoured greater American party responsibility, defined as

226   *Politics and Personalities*

'more popular choice between and control over alternate sets of accountable rulers'.[21] They differed, however, on the best methods of reforming the parties and the extent to which Britain was a useful exemplar. But scholarly Anglophilia perhaps reached its height in the 1950s with the debate over the functioning of the American parties when the American Political Science Association's Committee on Responsible Political Parties carried on the pre-1914 debate on the need for reform of the parties.[22] Some of the Committee's evaluations of the American parties and their recommendations were clearly influenced by their perceptions of the British parties. Discussion focused on four salient features of the British system. First, that the two major British parties provided voters with clear choices between policies and comprehensive programmes at elections. Second, that candidates were nominated and elected primarily for their loyalty to the party and its programme; the parties therefore were able to make national appeals. Third, that the government was able to implement the programme it was elected on because of the disciplined party voting in the Commons. Governments, in other words, were 'mandated' by the electorate. Finally, because of these features, the British parties were effectively representative of and responsible to their memberships and the electorate, and better able to resist the pressure of interest groups and facilitate the co-ordination of the executive and legislature. The Committee's general view was that such a responsible party system ensured the coherence and consistency of governmental policies and promoted a more 'rational' or issue-based style of politics.

The report, though sincere and honourable in intention, is now acknowledged to be something of an embarrassment as a contribution to the study of Anglo-American parties and to policy science. It is of some interest, however, as a codification of a certain type of conventional American wisdom on the nature of the British political system and of the parties in particular. The Report presumed two opposed ideal-types, the highly disciplined, programmatic and responsible British parties versus the fragmented, sectional and irresponsible American parties. The two respective political systems were counterpoised in similar terms. It goes without saying that both party systems were more complex than the models allowed. In the case of Britain, the several assumptions that the parties provided voters with clear policy choices, that the voters provided 'mandates' of programmatic support for policies at elections, that the parties were more successful than the American in resisting the claims of special interest groups,[23] and that party leaders were effectively in control of nominations or of the back-benchers were all questionable. Indeed the bolder statements of these features were soon to be controverted or substantially qualified by research. Of course British parties are more cohesive than the American. But the Committee's view exaggerated the amount of control exercised by the parliamentary leaders and party headquarters and laid too much stress on the role of ideology and the power of the whips in ensuring the cohesion of the parties.[24]

In this literature on the parties one is often reminded of Wilson. There is the same admiration of an energetic British executive, able to act in the name of a popular mandate, the same assumption that it is the centralisation of power which makes it more easily comprehensible and subject to control, and the same reformative application of this perspective to American politics. But the belief (and hope) that the importation of features of the British parties would produce the desired coherence and responsibility in the American system betrayed a naive view of political causation. Both Wilson and the Committee were aware of the interconnections of the party and Cabinet systems; where they differed was in their assessment of whether the Cabinet or responsible parties would most effectively further the co-ordination and responsibility. The simplified view of the causes of the approved features of British politics (and the anticipated consequences of more responsible American parties) marked a reversion to the primitivism of Wilson. The more important question, hardly confronted by the Committee's Report was: if British politics was marked by responsibility then how important were the parties, as compared to such features as the society, the culture or the parliamentary Cabinet structure, in bringing this about? It is worth adding that more recent American studies of the principles and practices of the parties have been more sensitive to the pluralism of British parties and to their limitations as policy-oriented or programmatic bodies. In large part this more realistic assessment stems from a greater willingness to see the British party system as the outcome of a complex matrix of historical, cultural and structural features and, correspondingly, to view the American party system also as the response to the very different context of a pluralistic society and a fragmented system of decision-making. This larger perspective is most notable in Eckstein's work on the pressure-group politics of the BMA, Beer's appreciation of the historical and institutional setting of the groups and parties, and Almond's placement of the functions of groups and parties in a broad cultural setting.

What emerges in these assessments is a general impression of the *efficiency* of the British institutions, in the sense of relatively friction-free procedures, and of their *effectiveness* in the sense of getting things done. Three features in particular, the collective responsibility of the Cabinet, the disciplined parties, and the dependence of the life of the government on its Parliamentary majority, have usually been thought to increase the scope for leadership and accountability *via* the centralised government and cohesive parties and to contrast with the American system. The Founding Fathers separated powers and functions because they feared tyranny; the British, on the other hand, have appeared to centralise decision-making and still achieve responsible government without these formal restraints. We shall see that more recent American writings, however, have reacted against this long-standing benign view.

THE BALANCED POLITICAL CULTURE

The absence of a written British constitution has challenged foreign commentators to try and elicit the norms, informal rules and usages. Indeed the late nineteenth-century American commentators on British institutions were impressed by such qualities as the high moral tone of British political life, the moderate and pragmatic style and the public respect for the leaders.[25] These themes have continued with the distinct shift of emphasis by a later generation of American writers away from the institutions to the culture in which the institutions are embedded. A substantial body of American political science literature which regards Britain as a prototype stable and effective democracy has emphasised the significance of the underlying culture. The writings of Lipset, Almond, Eckstein, Nordlinger, Beer, McKenzie and Silver are invariably impressed with the British synthesis of traditional and modern values, and this dualistic culture is advanced as a major explanation of 'the unique effectiveness' and 'truly distinctive character' of British politics.[26] The culture is thought to balance the competing requisites of consensus and cleavage, commitment to principle and willingness to compromise, popular trust in the government and self-confidence by voters that they can influence decision-makers. For Almond and Verba such a balance is best achieved by a 'civic culture' and indeed they suggest that 'the making of the civic culture is told in English history'. It is worth noting that this balance is biased more to the deferential, acquiescent side and that writers are impressed by the considerable respect for hierarchy.

Implicit in this literature and in the earlier work of Eaton, Wilson and Lowell, is a contrast, firstly, between the consensus and balance in the British approach to politics and the divisive spirit of continental politics. This is most apparent in Almond's cultural-structural mapping of an Anglo-American style of politics, in which it was suggested that the cross-cutting ties of society and the party system facilitates a process of bargaining and compromise, in contrast to the pattern in France and Italy where cumulative cleavages and the multi-party system have made politics more ideological and the governments unstable.[27] But there is also a second and implicit contrast with the greater egalitarianism of the United States. The different writers are fascinated by the symbolic and ritualistic aspects of the British constitution,[28] they parade survey evidence of the lower-class preference for aristocratic political leadership and support for the Conservative party,[29] and emphasise the unrepresentative social and educational backgrounds of MPs, and the relatively low proportion of young people in higher education, as illustrations of the deferential and elitist nature of the society and culture.[30] Both countries are democratic insofar as they have a near universal suffrage. But, as S. M. Lipset has argued, almost *ad nauseam*, in spite of the non-democratic social relationships in Britain, political democracy is perhaps more assured here than in America. Such a 'relationship' has encouraged some American writers to explain the stable British democracy partly in terms of these elitist values.

In the 1950s a number of American sociologists, concerned at the support for Senator McCarthy's campaign against Communism and implied threats to the liberal values of dissent, minority rights and the spirit of free intellectual inquiry, also found much to admire in the British culture. Writers such as Parsons, Shils, Bell, Lipset, Hyman and Hofstadter, criticised a style of 'mass politics' in general, and populism, egalitarianism, super-patriotism, status anxieties and radical right-wing politics in America in particular.[31] The general assessment was that American egalitarianism diminished respect for civil liberties and minority rights. The politics of civility and tolerance, it was argued, is the concern of an educated and enlightened minority, and its preservation requires the relative autonomy of political leaders. Such features are facilitated by the discretion and privacy of British government and the greater deference of the culture and the homogeneity of British society. The sociologists, like the political scientists, were also impressed with how the respect traditionally paid to the monarchy and the aristocracy has been transferred to the political leaders and the civil servants. According to Shils, the government '...enjoys the deference which is aroused in the breast of Englishmen by the symbols of hierarchy which find their highest expression in the monarchy'.[32] They admired the public acceptance of government by a small circle of decision-makers, the absence of vigorous Parliamentary investigating committees and the low-key treatment of politics by the mass media. The reward for the closed, *elite*-managed British political system, according to these writers, has been the absence of emotional campaigns against suspected dissenters and subversives and the greater security of civil liberties.

It is possible to criticise much of this literature on culture at several points. The survey evidence is open to many objections, both conceptual and empirical, and it is remarkable how research into so small a proportion of the British electorate (i.e., the 10 per cent who are working-class, Conservative deferentials) has been generalised to the whole culture. But the major point is that the *elitist*-deference model of the political culture is very selective. Like most such national character stereotypes it is not so much inaccurate as one-sided. What emerges is a regurgitation, albeit in fashionable social-science prose, of Bagehot's elitism and L. S. Amery's Tory view of the Constitution. Of course there is tolerance and much consensus on the political institution and procedures. But in its concern to stress the popular submission to and respect for leaders, the deference model underestimates both the frequent cussedness of the population and the caution of the government *vis-a-vis* influential groups. Although very recent American comment has questioned whether this British culture with its class consciousness and low achievement orientation is able to adjust to the needs of a rapidly changing world and casts doubt on the level of toleration in the field of race relations, it seems fair comment that there has been a stereotyped American view of the deferential British culture.[33] The attractiveness of the deference theory lies in its plausibility; it seems to tie together so many established ideas in a relatively coherent form. Here is the lynchpin which seems to explain conveniently and parsimoniously the absence of a revolutionary tradition in Britain, the continued existence of the monarchy and the House of Lords, the ability of the Tory party to gather a large minority of the working-class vote and other features to which foreign observers, particularly those on the other side of the Atlantic, seem to be most sensitive (See Chapter 12).

BALANCED POLITICAL CHANGE

American students of political development are currently showing a more explicit concern with the historical experiences of the long-established states. A problem with the behavioural approaches to development is that it has only been possible to establish correlations. Explanations have been offered more in functional than causal terms; hence the retreat to history, as a form of more genetic inquiry. In the case of Britain the historical dimension is obviously important, given the gradual evolution of the constitution over eight centuries and the legacy of the past reflected in so many of our present institutions and practices. Attempts are now under way to examine historical political change in Britain and other states in order to test and improve our stock of largely implicit propositions about the importance of historical experiences, about the manner and order in which stages in the developmental process are confronted, and even to elicit lessons which might be applied to the newer states.[34]

Britain is important not only because she introduced the world to 'modernity' (Rothman) but also because she has seemed to many to provide a model of a high-yield, low-cost path to modernisation. In large part this has derived from her island position, which lowered the level of geo-political threat and from the sequential confrontation of the major aspects or 'crises' of state and nation-building and participation and welfare. Such a process, it is claimed, has allowed a 'balanced' progress on several fronts. Under the Tudors a moderate centralisation of power, the separation of the English church from Rome and more established national boundaries were achieved. Yet this centralisation did not exclude a culture that was comparatively participant and pluralist for the time–as reflected in the vigorous Parliamentary institutions. Much royal power was exercised indirectly *via* the authority of the local gentry and not by a standing royal army. By 1688 a balance was struck between the competing claims of Parliament and monarch and, most important, the claims of an absolute monarch were checked more effectively and at an earlier stage than on the Continent. Reforms of the suffrage and welfare were gradually achieved after 1832; indeed, the passage of the first major Reform Bill of that year is regarded as a classic case of elite accommodation.[35] Further expansion and centralisation of the bureaucracy in the nineteenth and twentieth centuries occurred after the democratisation of the suffrage and the emergence of political parties, thus safeguarding the representative institutions.

I have summarised this particular pattern of historical change too abruptly. But the main themes are clear. The emphasis is on the incremental and conciliatory nature of the development; change has been evolutionary, cumulative, and, by permitting the adaptation of such elements as the monarchy and the House of Lords, it has enabled the fusion of traditional and modern institutions and values. Such a pattern is to be contrasted with the experiences of Prussia and France, where centralisation was achieved earlier and proved to be more thorough, the elites were less accommodating to demands for modern reform, and the prospects for a gradual democratisation and 'balanced' development were therefore reduced. In these states social and political change has veered between revolutionary and counter-revolutionary cycles. The pattern is also to be contrasted with the cumulative demands and the demonstration effects from the long-established states which beset newly independent states. Where historical enquiries into modernisation and political development have proceeded by study of the major industrial states, then Britain has been seized upon almost by default. For obvious reasons the histories of Russia, France, Italy and Germany have not appeared attractive.

CRISIS IN BRITISH POLITICS?

These generally laudatory accounts of British politics, society and culture were punctuated by occasional critical comments, as in Don Price's analysis of the decline of the Parliamentary model in Britain and its irrelevance to the American experience, J. D. Kingsley's critique of the civil service, John F. Kennedy's *Why England Slept* in 1940, and the contrast of Britain with the greater vigour of the New Deal administration during the 1930s. But we were quite unprepared for the current slashing critiques by a more critical revisionist school of Americans, intent on dissecting our politics, and charging us with amateurism, inefficiency and the general need for political modernisation and innovation. This mood goes beyond the general critiques of the shortcomings of Anglo-American pluralist and liberal-democratic politics; in the case of Britain, the criticism has coincided with a shift of the academic attention from 'mere' regime-maintenance to the problem-solving capacities of elites and institutions in the face of domestic and international demands. The institutions may still be efficient but are they effective? There is now more awareness of persistent policy failures and the startling gap between the aims and actual achievements of British governments, not least in the sphere of economic management.

I am tempted to paraphrase Kuhn's notion of paradigms here; persistent anomalies and inconvenient data have so challenged and eventually undermined the traditional American model of the efficient, effective, responsive British system that a new model is demanded. Sustained poor performance in several policy fields has been linked with a more general malaise, affecting even the much-vaunted political institutions and political culture. The elite culture, with its emphasis on make-do and mend, attachment to the empirical and pragmatic approach, and the disavowal of coherent and overall thinking, is frequently indicted.[36] The poor performance has also been related to structural failures, particularly to the archaic procedures and institutions, the lack of expertise and general amateurism of decision-makers and the decline of the famed balance between an effective leadership and its accountability to the legislature. Parliament is seen to be weak in the face of the Executive (without the last-named being able to provide 'strong' government) and has surrendered its educative function. Yet Beer (like Crick), has eloquently argued that this task—the mobilisation of consent— is more than ever necessary for the collectivist politics of the late-industrial society in which government plays an increasing rôle in the extraction and allocation of resources.[37]

Instead of the vision of a smoothly efficient yet responsible government, the contemporary writings of Neustadt, Beer, Waltz, Putnam, Rose, Hargrove and the Brookings Institution are more impressed by an immobilism or 'pluralist stagnation'.[38] Kenneth Waltz, as a result of his comparative study of foreign policy decision-making and institutions in Britain and America, was convinced of British inferiority 'in the quick identification of problems, the pragmatic quest for solutions, the ready confrontation of dangers, the willing expenditure of energies, and the open criticism of policies'.[39] Recent studies of policy-making and party discipline go beyond the surface phenomena of law-abiding citizens, monolithic parties, united Cabinet, subservient back-benchers, and the assured passage of government legislation through an acquiescent Parliament. Instead, the emphasis is more on the pluralism within the parties, on the constraints on the government and Prime Minister and the need for elaborate and lengthy negotiations with interested parties within and outside Whitehall. The emphasis is on the extent of compromise, negotiation and anticipation of demands by government, and on the government's preparedness to move only where wide agreement has been reached with large producer and consumer groups. What emerges, for example, in such studies of the frequent changes in defence and policy since 1945, the manifest failure to keep pace with the economic growth rates of other countries, and the protracted negotiations preceding British application to join the Common Market, is a picture of an irresolute government moving by a 'directionless consensus'.[40]

To some degree, the different view of Britain is the consequence of a younger generation of Americans asking different questions. But other texts have had to be hastily rewritten. Perhaps nowhere is the change of mood better reflected than in the contrast between Beer's glowing portraits of British politics in the early 1960s and the diffident Epilogue to the second edition of his *Modern British Politics* in 1969. In the former, the coherence of government and the capacity for decisive action by responsible parties are praised; in the latter, the governmental system appears almost fossilised and the speculation is about the end of party government and the development of a corporate state. There is an indecent haste about the transition from the admiration for the British political system to the mood of 'what's wrong with British politics' in the scope of a decade. Indeed, there are recommendations that American practices, such as congressional investigating committees, legal provision for civil liberties, a larger personal staff for the Prime Minister, and the recruitment of outsiders into the top ranks of the civil service, would help to restore the qualities of effective political leadership and accountability.

There is a new vogue word to describe these features of the late industrial societies; they are said to suffer from an *over-institutionalisation*.[41] New states may suffer from a lack of effective institutions, but in Britain and other industrial societies the Parliamentary institutions, bureaucracy, parties and groups may be too well entrenched to collapse, yet frozen in defensive postures and too rigid to respond creatively to rapid socioeconomic change. Their own stake in the *status quo* makes them resist forces for reform, and innovative response actually requires their thorough dissolution. The current impression, therefore, is more of the burdens than the benefits to Britain of her institutions, culture and history.

DISCUSSION

In this paper it is impossible to provide any sustained explanation of the context and origin of these themes. This would require a separate and elaborate essay on the sociology of American knowledge about Britain. I cannot, however, resist the temptation to speculate on the possible reasons for the suggested American perspectives. In the first place, surely, the context of American political and intellectual life has been important. One needs to take account of such factors as when the Americans were writing, the contemporary image of Britain, and what the writers actually favoured for America. Because the writers often compose morality tales about their own society, we not only see ourselves as others see us, but we also see them in the process and they may tell us almost as much about the contemporary aspects of politics in America as in Britain. Admiration for the way in which the British have reconciled the claims of the twin functions of 'governing' and 'control of government' usually coincided with dissatisfaction with these aspects of the American political system. Obviously this stance has not been shared by all Americans; but if fits much of the literature till very recently. In the late nineteenth century, for example, proponents of reform of the civil service and parties and critics of the consequences of separation of powers were alienated by the prevalence of graft, boss-rule, scandals and by the assassination of President Garfield. The sociologists in the 1950s admired the apparent security of civil liberties in Britain, the general discretion in public life and the citizens' self-restraint *vis-à-vis* government; the McCarthy campaign endowed these writings with the character of tracts for the times. The American Political Science Association's proposals for responsible party government in 1950 took place against the background of a deadlocked Congress and President, a party system that appeared confusing and irresponsible, and a fragmented political system. In other words, there is a prescriptive as well as a descriptive

side to these writings; they are often written by advocates of stronger
Presidential rule and a greater role for the Federal government, by
elitist theorists of democracy, and by proponents of liberal policies
in such fields as civil rights and welfare reform and by admirers of
a more stable, orderly society. Americans, when dissatisfied with
their system, have looked abroad for the components that would
trigger off improvements in the system and, for understandable
reasons, they have usually looked first to Britain. Britain therefore
has been admired for reasons extraneous as well as intrinsic to her
policy. Currently, however, we have noted the greater criticism of
the hierarchy and centralisation of British government and the
deferential culture. It is suggested that the American decentralisation
and respect for expertise may provide more scope for adaptability
and innovation.

Yet it is remarkable how very little borrowing there has been of
British procedures. Moreover, where British-style reforms have been
implemented to improve co-ordination, responsibility, or the 'tone'
of government (as in civil service recruitment, Cabinet procedures
and the reorganisation of the Treasury), they have been adapted to
American purposes and circumstances. The great differences between
the two countries have hindered the cross-cultural transplantation
of institutions and procedures. For example, the civil service
examinations placed more emphasis on the practical abilities of the
entrant and were never so closely aligned to the curriculum of the
universities as in England. The greater scope given the American
Treasury by the establishment of the Bureau of the Budget in 1921
followed favourable appraisal of the role of the British Treasury in
administrative control and co-ordination. But the American Treasury
has never acquired the system of prior financial control of its British
counterpart, and approval of the federal budget by Congress is a
much more hazardous enterprise than in Britain. Moves to permit
Congressional questioning of the Cabinet members have always
foundered on the assumed constitutional separation of powers and
personnel.[42] One is left to wonder to what extent this reform mood
has stemmed from a desire to bring the American institutions into
line with like-named British institutions. In 1942 Don Price, impatient
of the Anglophile perspective of would-be reformers of Congress,
understandably complained that it needed 'a psychoanalyst to explain
America's peculiar nostalgia for the obsolete political institutions of
the mother country'.[43]

The American concern that knowledge and research produce payoffs also explains some of the urge to draw lessons from the British experience. The tensions between (a) the normative and practical concern to promote 'better' government and 'good' citizenship and (b) the precept to be value-free and scientific, are long-standing in American political science. The contradictions are perhaps easily exposed in the case of Wilson and in that of the responsible parties' literature. These works were patently normative both in the sense of trying to influence and advise decision-makers and in their unconcealed admiration of the British system. The preferred *civic culture* model and structural–functional style of politics were also heavily influenced by perceptions of Britain. More recently, Almond, an exponent of the British style in his work on political development, has admitted that he is 'now traumatized by the arrogance of pre-World War II theory, which viewed Anglo-American political institutions as the ultimate in man's capacity for creativity and as the evolutionary end-state of all politics'.[44]

Finally, there is the question of the Anglo-American framework of comparison in which so much discussion of British politics has taken place. Some writers are impressed by the many similarities between the two countries. We have noted Almond's commentary on an Anglo-American style of politics, contrasted to that of France and Italy. In this case, Almond's mapping of a broad range of different systems sensitised him to the similarities between Britain and America in culture and rôle structure. But much of the literature, written from a narrower comparative perspective, seems to be impressed with the contrast between a simple, elitist, concentrated and unitary British system versus a complex, egalitarian, fragmented and pluralist American one. I have elsewhere argued that such an abridged and selective basis of comparison has led writers such as Lipset and Almond and Verba to exaggerate differences between the countries and place too much stress on political and social deferences in Britain. Again, however, this emphasis on *comparison as contrast* has a long tradition. Writers see virtues in the opposite system which compensate for shortcomings in their own or they do the reverse and see their own virtues but not the shortcomings. In the nineteenth century British commentators on America were invariably interested, for differing motives, in exaggerating differences between the old and new worlds; conservatives pointed to the defects or excesses of American democracy, while the radicals lauded the equality, social mobility and democratic suffrage. Both sides, however, emphasised the contrast to Britain.[45] Similarly, both the American political left and right have found solace in looking across the Atlantic. In the twentieth century, American conservatives, lacking such conservative perquisites as a feudal tradition, an established church, a traditional ruling-class and the sense of belonging to an organic community, were inclined to turn wistfully to Britain; American socialists, who mourned the lack of a class-conscious proletariat and an explicitly working-class political party and the dominance of a free enterprise, anti-welfare state ideology, could also look to Britain.

In sum, the Anglo-American perspective has for long derived from and confirmed a critique of the Madisonian model and egalitarianism of American politics. The critics have charged that the American institutions, particularly the parties, have represented the divisions in society too well and that the checks and balances have immobilised the leadership in the face of urgent tasks at home and abroad. Sceptical accounts of American pluralism have argued that such a cumbersome system fails to provide leverage for disadvantaged groups, enables entrenched minorities to defend their interests and makes it difficult for potential majorities to implement their programmes. It is a system which seems only to respond to crisis and skilful crisis leadership. In contrast, the British system has long been viewed as providing greater scope for majorities, the Cabinet as facilitating more co-ordination and accountability, the party system as encouraging a more national, rational, policy-based and intelligible style of politics, and the culture as offering greater resources for leadership. On the other hand, we have seen that recent writers such as Kenneth Waltz perceive virtues in America which are not found in the British system and use the comparison to point them up.

What is one's assessment to be of this vast and diverse literature? My major complaint would be about the generalising quality of the more ambitious work. Much of the comment by Lipset, Eckstein and Almond, insightful though it often is, is by writers who are interested in Britain as a *type* or *class* of politics or for applying Parsonian or structural-functional categories, rather than in Britain *per se*. These writers have also invariably been concerned with the 'grand' questions of stable democracy and with drawing on the British experience in that quest. But it is the ambitious exercises which require a formidable amount of contextual and historical knowledge if the case study is to be married successfully with the general theory. This is undoubtedly true of the more theoretical American writings on other states as well. Although Americans are well-served in terms of the available historical and contemporary information about Britain (though with the exception of Beer the writers' knowledge of British history is hardly above sixth-form level), there still seems much point to La Palombara's general castigation of whole-system theorists who generalise on the basis of very slim evidence. His charge is that American 'political scientists are loath to make high-flown generalizations about the American political system (the one about which we have the greatest amount of information) while they will, at the slightest stimulation, generalize about large-scale societies in Africa, Asia and Latin America' (about which we lack this information).[46]

Much of the writing on the themes of strong government and the deferential society has been from an excessively Londonised and English perspective. Like a paradigm the perspective has for long confined research, constricted interpretations of British politics, and blinded observers to *anomalies*, even to the point of misreading facts.[47] One suspects that the present bout of 'crisis' of British politics literature will similarly be a form of overkill. Much of the literature on the culture, which is concerned with hypothesis-testing and making assertions about the government being strong, effective, responsible and so on, often lacks good empirical evidence. Given the status of such a perspective on Britain as a model for purposes of theory-building and political engineering, these are no small complaints. Part of the problem here resides in the primitive state of such key concepts as stable or effective democracy. (Once we move to harder indicators of economic growth, the economists have reversed the question and usually asked 'what's wrong with Britain?')

Again, we have seen that some of the commentary on the balanced, or, alternatively, *elitist* character of the British institutions, and on the Cabinet and the party system was inaccurate at many points. Assessments of the 'big stick' of dissolution, the dominance of party in policy formation, the equilibrium between Cabinet and Parliament, the consequences of ministerial responsibility and the forces for party discipline were misperceived. Different theories of the constitution, whether Liberal, Tory, or Party Government, were taken too literally as a guide to practice. Finally, the frequent urge to describe and evaluate aspects of British politics with reference to America, allied of course to a reformist stance *vis-a-vis* American institutions, has undermined the work.

Are we to conclude then that Americans or outsiders are debarred from understanding our politics? The question echoes Bagehot's unfair charge that the Founding Fathers imagined themselves to be copying the British Constitution but simply misunderstood it. It also links with the more general claim that one can only know one's own society, that behaviour is a rule-governed activity whose meaning is only dimly perceived by the non-members. A classic recent example in support of the charge is an American 'one-off' study of the values of British schoolchildren which appears to have been composed by the infamous visitor from Mars. In the survey, the comparatively low proportion of affirmative responses by British children to American-based concepts of pride in the political system (e.g., perception of the benevolence or infallibility of the government) provided the data-base for a wildly speculative discussion about a future crisis of legitimacy in Britain.[48] (The interpretation ignored the greater emphasis on civics courses and 'Americanism' in the American schools, and dichotomised criticism and support. Detachment and non-idealisation towards government by British children was conflated to a lack of support.)

But it would be foolish to dismiss the American work, not least because Americans have provided the impetus for theoretical innovation, for mastery of a broad range of social science techniques and perspectives, and for more rigorous study in the discipline. Many British political scientists have also described the political process in an outdated 'liberal' language or in unwarranted favourable terms. Again, much of the solid corrective knowledge about British parties and electoral behaviour, for example, has been provided by such Americans as Beer, Epstein, Janosek, Ranney, Rose and Stokes. The wide appreciation of Beer's *Modern British Politics* and Lowell's work earlier this century, which do have a 'feel' for British history and behaviour, suggests that our politics is not an occult mystery, demanding the talents of the anthropologist or the frames of reference of the native political scientist. Even where we would dissent we are forced to be specific in demonstrating 'how this is not us at all'. The ability to convey a 'feel' for British politics differs with the empathic qualities of the writer and these in turn are likely to be conditioned by the variables of skill, sensitivity, knowledge and, of course, personal familiarity with the terrain. And if the library shelves on British politics are impressive, then American political science has played no small part in producing this healthy condition.

At the end of the day, much of the best political science is written by Americans and they dominate the literature on British voting behaviour, political culture, parties and pressure groups and policy-making.[49] Perhaps the danger is that even the more self-critical British political scientists are left to assume the role of the armchair critic, leaving the Americans to ask the interesting questions and conduct the original empirical work, while we condescendingly mutter about the American failure to appreciate the nuances and understandings of our political practice. It may be a form of American intellectual imperialism but we can hardly complain if they reap where we scarcely even sow.

A theme of this essay is that comparison is difficult to do well, since it is rare for one person to know more than one society well and because the comparisons are time and culture-bound. To my mind the more persuasive American writings tend to come from those who select narrow subjects which are, *ipso facto*, more easily mastered rather than the more synoptic essays on the political culture and political development. The limited and explicitly comparative studies of such segments of British and American politics as race relations (Katznelson), agricultural lobbies (Pennock), city government (Sharpe) and decision-making (Waltz and Neustadt) justify the comparative focus and blow away a larger number of myths about both countries. These are the gains from the narrower focus of the 'strong' telescope. Gains also tend to come from those who do not regard Britain as fertile territory for the rapid extraction of 'lessons' for America. This is not to denigrate the more general or theoretical studies which apply the 'weak' telescope. One may still read them with profit without getting a 'feel' for British politics; presumably, one can get that elsewhere.

CONCLUSION

We have sampled nearly a century of American writings on British politics. The starting-point for many of the studies has not been how Britain differs from America or how things work in Britain but rather with attempting to explain how Britain acquired the approved qualities of stability, legitimacy and the successful blending of 'strong' government with popular accountability. In other words, there is a strong vein of causal analysis in the literature and sometimes an explicit search for the factors which might 'improve' the American or other political systems. The academic emphasis has shifted over time (as it has in the discipline) from the institutions to the political culture and to the rôle of history in fashioning the balance in the culture and between the institutions.

Finally let me suggest one gap that a science of Anglo-American politics might help to close. Richard Neustadt's study of the series of Anglo-American misunderstandings in defence policy is a damning catalogue of how decision-makers in the two countries were often either innocent or wrong about the 'rules of the game' in the other system; cues, roles, pressures and messages between London and Washington were persistently misperceived with disastrous effects on the formation and implementation of policies.[50] We surely have a wider duty as citizens and scholars *not least to the policy-makers* to improve our mutual knowledge of the operating procedures of the two political systems.

NOTES

1. See N. Polsby, 'The British Science of American Politics', *British Journal of Political Science*, 1972, pp. 491–501.
2. R. Rose, *Politics in England* (London, 1965), p. 1.
3. *Alliance Politics* (New York,1970), p. 82.
4. Bagehot's essay is an important landmark in the comparative study of Presidential and Parliamentary systems.He claimed that 'The practical choice of first-rate nations is between the presidential government and the parliamentary ... and nothing, therefore, can be more important than to compare the two, and to decide which of them is the better'. *The English Constitution* (Fontana edition, London, 1963), p. 310.
5. Both Wilson and Lowell quoted extensively from Bagehot. For Wilson's admiration see 'A Literary Politician', in *Mere Literature and Other Essays* (New York, 1914).
6. For a useful critique of Bagehot's views, see M. J. C. Vile, *Constitutionalism and the Separation of Powers* (London, 1967).
7. B. Bailyn, *The Origins of American Politics* (New York, 1968), and *Origins of the American Revolution* (New York, 1967).
8. Vile, *op.cit.*, p. 317.
9. The change of mood is traced in H. Pelling, *America and the British Left* (London, 1956). Also see Vile, *op.cit.*, Chap. 10.
10. *Cabinet Government in the United States* (Stamford, Connecticut, 1947), p. 23.

11. *Ibid.*, p. 25. By 1885, however, in *Congressional Government* (New York), Wilson was less explicit about the centrality of the Cabinet and placed more emphasis on responsible political parties, and in later years he became more optimistic about the prospects for Presidential leadership. In 1908 he argued that the President should be elected on a programme and supported by a Presidential party in Congress.

12. This belief in narrow institutional causation was a feature of the discipline of the time and affected even A. L. Lowell. For example, the early Lowell argued that the Cabinet system was the major cause of the two-party system in Britain. See *Government and Politics in Contential Europe* (New York, 1896), pp. 71–2. Later, in *The Government of England* (1921 edition) he argued that the strength of the Cabinet system was a consequence of the parties. See *Ibid.*, Vol. 1, p. 457.

13. See A. H. Birch, *Representative and Responsible Government* (London, 1964).

14. H. Finer, *The Presidency: Crisis and Regeneration* (New York, 1960).

15. See R. Fenno, *The President's Cabinet* (Cambridge, Mass., 1959).

16. S. E. Finer, 'Patronage and the Public Service; Jeffersonian Bureaucracy and the British Tradition', *Public Administration*, Vol. XXX, 1952; and P. P. van Riper, *History of the United States Civil Service* (Evanston, Illinois, 1958), chap. 2.

17. New York, 1880. Also see R. S. Spann, 'Civil Servants in Washington', *Political Studies*, 1953, pp. 143–61.

18. Ari Hoogensboom, *Outlawing the Spoils* (Illinois,1961), p. 176.

19. For the comparison with Britain, see L. D. White, *Government Career Service* (Washington, 1935); C. E. Merriam, *On the Agenda of Democracy* (Chicago, 1935); *Report on Better Government* (Washington, 1935), and Report of the *President's Committee on Administrative Management* (Washington, 1937). Also there were two influential essays by H. Finer, 'The Hoover Commission Report', Parts I and II, *Political Science Quarterly*, Vol. 64.

20. For a convenient summary of the debate, see A. Ranney, *The Doctrine of Responsible Party Government* (Illinois, 1962).

21. *Ibid.*, p. 154.

22. See the Report in the *American Political Science Review* (Supplement, Vol.44, 1950). For similar Anglophile statements, see J. MacGregor Burns, *Deadlock of Democracy* (New York, 1963), and S. H. Beer, 'New Structures of Democracy in Britain and America', in W. N. Chambers and R. Salisbury, *Democracy in Mid-Twentieth Century*.

23. For an interesting comparative study of the agricultural lobby in the two countries, see J. R. Pennock, 'Responsible Government, Separated Powers and Special Interests', *American Political Science Review*, 1962.

24. For a thorough reappraisal, see E. M. Kirkpatrick, 'Towards a More Responsible Two-Party System, Political Science, Policy Science or Pseudo-Science', *American Political Science Review*, 1971, pp. 965–90.

25. See Lowell's comments on the moderation of the political culture. For example, 'the nation is ruled mainly by the centre rather than by the extremes of right and left' and 'a healthy political condition ... does

not obstruct progress, but prevents the movement from being too rapid, and avoids violent change', *The Government of England*, Vol. II, p. 539.
26. H. Eckstein, 'The British Political System', in S. H. Beer and A. Ulam (eds) *Patterns of Government* (New York, 1962).
27. 'Comparative Political Systems', *The Journal of Politics*, 1956, pp. 391–409.
28. E. Shils and M. Young, 'The Meaning of the Coronation', *Sociological Review*, 1953.
29. E. Nordlinger, *The Working Class Tories* (London, 1967), and R. T. McKenzie and A. Silver, *Angels in Marble* (London, 1968).
30. *The First New Nation* (New York, 1967).
31. See the essays in D. Bell (ed.), *The New American Right* (New York, 1955), and E. A. Shils, *The Torment of Secrecy* (Glencoe, Illinois, 1956).
32. *The Torment of Secrecy, op. cit.*, p. 48.
33. For fuller argument, see D. Kavanagh, 'The Deferential English: A Comparative Critique', *Government and Opposition*, 1972, particularly pp. 354–55. See above, Chapter 12.
34. For example, see G. A. Almond and C. Tilly (eds) *The Formation of Nation-States*, Princeton, 1974; G. A. Almond *et al.*, *Crisis, Choice and Change: Historical Studies of Political Development* (Boston, 1973); B. Moore, *Social Origins of Dictatorship and Democracy* (Boston, 1966); and S. Rothman, 'Modernity and Tradition in Britain', *Social Research*, 1961.
35. See G. B. Powell, 'Incremental Democratization: The British Reform Act of 1832', in Almond *et al.*, *op. cit.*
36. For example, see R. Putnam, *The Beliefs of Politicians* (New Haven, 1973).
37. Beer, 'The British Legislature and the Problem of Mobilizing Consent', in B. Crick (ed.), *Essays on Reform* (London, 1967).
38. R. Caves *et al.*, *Britain's Economic Prospects*, Washington; Brookings, 1968); K. Waltz, *Foreign Policy and Democratic Politics* (Boston, 1967); S. H. Beer, *Modern British Politics*, 2nd edition (London, 1970); E. Hargrove, *Professional Roles in Society and Government: The English Case* (London 1972) and R. Neustadt, 'White House and Whitehall', *The Public Interest*, 1966, pp. 55–69.
39. Waltz, *op.cit.*; pp. 311–12.
40. On this see Pennock, *op.cit.*, Beer, *op.cit.*, and Rose, The Variability of Party Government, *Political Studies* (1970).
41. M. Kesselman, 'Overinstitutionalization and Political Constraint', *Comparative Politics*, 1970, pp.21–44. For a critical study of the response of British and American political institutions to the demands of non-white groups, see I. Katznelson, *Black Men, White Societies* (London, 1973).
42. Strictly speaking there is no constitutional barrier to Cabinet ministers being questioned in Congress. They did appear on the floor of Congress in the early nineteenth century, and Acheson, as Secretary of State under Truman, answered questions in the auditorium of the Library of

Congress. But the belief about the barrier has the status of convention.

43. D. K. Price, 'The Parliamentary and Presidential Systems', *Public Administration Review*, 1943. But see also M. Needler's warnings on the British influence on constitution-making in several countries in 'On the Dangers of Copying From the British', *Political Science Quarterly*, 1966.
44. G. A. Almond, *Political Development* (Boston, 1970), p. 26.
45. E. Pesson, *Jacksonian America: Society, Personality and Politics* (Illinois, 1969), Chap. 3.
46. 'Macrotheories and Micropolitics in Comparative Politics', *Comparative Politics*, 1968, p. 63.
47. For a forceful statement on this point, see L. J. Sharpe, 'American Democracy Reconsidered'; *British Journal of Political Science*, 1973.
48. For example, J. Dennis, *et al.*, 'Support for Nation and Government Among English Schoolchildren', *British Journal of Political Science*, 1971, pp. 25–48. See also the critical comments of A. H. Birch and D. Kavanagh in later issues of the journal.
49. Such a view emerged very strongly in the conference discussion.
50. Neustadt, *Alliance Politics, op. cit.*

14 From Gentlemen to Players: Changes in Political Leadership*

It is a very difficult country to move, Mr Hyndman, a very difficult country indeed, and one in which there is more disappointment to be looked for than success. Disraeli (1881)

Only a generation ago Britain's political institutions were the object of widespread admiration. Churchill's wartime leadership, the successful mobilisation of people and resources against Hitler, and the Attlee government's achievements in social welfare and economic reconstruction all provided evidence of the ability of the institutions and leaders to cope with problems and maintain consent.

This admired political leadership emerged from the interplay of a number of features. These included:

1 the *political institutions*: the existence of disciplined, programmatic parties facilitated one-party majority government, and the concentration of formal political power in the Cabinet provided coherent, stable government;
2 a *governing class*: this was drawn largely from the upper and upper middle classes, which had a long tradition of exercising political authority;
3 the *political culture*: this included a consensus about political procedures, an incremental approach to bringing about change and trust in government and leaders.

Amid growing criticism of the British political system there have been significant alterations in each of the three features mentioned above. First, the declining support for the two main parties and a fragmentation of the party system have already produced two periods of minority government since February 1974, and limited the Cabinet's ability to dominate the legislature. Membership of the

* *Britain, Progress and Decline* (Macmillan, 1980).

EEC and referenda pose further challenges to established forms of political leadership. Second, there has been a trend towards the recruitment of *meritocrats*, or well-educated, self-made professional politicians, away from the *patricians*, who moved almost as a matter of course into public life, and from the *proletarians*. The new generation of top political leaders is drawn from people whose social backgrounds are more modest than those of Attlee, Gaitskell, Churchill, Butler and Macmillan, and yet more elevated than those of Morrison, Bevin or Bevan. Finally, there are signs of a less *deferential culture*. The authority of government is less secure. A Parliamentary majority securing the passage of legislation says little about a government's ability to gain compliance from society.

This paper focuses on two aspects of change among the post-war British political leaders. In *composition* there has been a marked *embourgeoisement* of the new generation of leaders. In *political style* there occurred a move in the 1960s to one which was oriented to change. Study of the composition is relatively straightforward and the subject is well-documented. The notion of political style, however, is more elusive and less easy to measure. By a style of leadership, I am referring to the leader's purpose or objects in politics and how he tries to achieve them. One broad distinction is between routine and crisis styles of leadership, in which there is a conjunction of the leader's style and circumstances. For example, the political crises associated with the two great wars this century opened the way for Lloyd George in 1916 and Churchill in 1940.[1] The dynamism of both men had previously made them widely distrusted and, except for the war years, they spent long periods in the political wilderness. But a more useful distinction for our immediate purpose is between styles which are *mobilising* (emphasising decisions and task-performance, particularly a change in the *status quo*) and *expressive* (emphasising the maintenance of consensus and cohesion). The distinction is not dissimilar from David Apter's mobilising and conciliatory leader.[2] The former is mainly concerned to achieve his goals, and not overly concerned about opposition and the costs of disturbance; the latter is more concerned to represent and respond to diverse interests and arrive at compromises, if necessary sacrificing policy goals, as long as group unity is maintained.

Effective leaders have to take account of both rôle demands. It is possible, however, to classify most British Prime Ministers according to the relative importance they attached to being either mobilising or expressive leaders. For example, Stanley Baldwin and Ramsay MacDonald, both by temperament and political conviction belong in the latter category. They saw themselves as reconcilers, within and between parties, were weak partisans, and limited changes to those which would least disturb the social fabric. Churchill, as a peacetime Prime Minister, was concerned to live down the memories of his record in the 1920s and to promote social peace and placate organised labour. Joseph Chamberlain and Lloyd George are classic cases of mobilisers. Chamberlain campaigned for social reform and then tariff reform. Lloyd George, before 1914, was a powerful advocate of social reforms and then rearmament and, after 1928, measures to combat unemployment. Neither man was a respecter of party lines and both were widely distrusted among Parliamentary colleagues. Hugh Gaitskell's commitment to new goals provoked intense opposition, inside and outside the Labour party. Attlee and Macmillan are difficult to cast in one or other group. Attlee's government took many important decisions but, as leader, he did not himself initiate a policy that would create divisions and was careful to align himself with the majority on divisive issues. Mr Macmillan straddles both groups. He was a skilled party manager, attentive to the needs of party unity, but one who also managed to set in train a number of new policies.

The mobilising or instrumental style has a greater appeal when there is dissatisfaction with the *status quo*, a sense that new directions and policies are required. This has been cyclical in Britain. Such a mood developed in Britain in the early 1960s. The election of Harold Wilson as leader of the Labour party in 1963 and Edward Heath as leader of the Conservatives in 1965 introduced younger men who self-consciously distinguished themselves from their predecessors. Changes in political generations coincided with new types and styles of leadership from the era of Attlee and Churchill. It is tempting to perceive a relationship between the two themes of social background and styles, a transition from political leadership as a *status* (a position occupied by someone of high social status, and whose style is primarily expressive) to leadership as an *activity* (the leader as a person who is concerned with mobilising resources and doing things). However, I shall argue that there is little relationship between the two: in part the new men simply invoked new rhetoric and in part they accommodated themselves to a cyclical demand for change.

COMPOSITION

Historically, political leadership in Britain has been exercised by men of high birth and breeding. The effects of universal suffrage, organised mass political parties, increasing professionalisation of political life, and decline of the landed interest, have combined to erode the political influence of the aristocracy. But men from an upper class background have stubbornly retained a large hold in Parliament and Cabinet.[3] Of the members of Cabinets from 1884 to 1924 (the year of the first Labour government), 43 per cent were aristocrats (born or married into titled families); between 1933 and 1964 the figure was still an impressive 26 per cent. For the same two periods the proportion of ministers educated at expensive public schools actually increased from half to three-quarters. Yet there have been some interesting changes in recent years.

Labour

Before the war there were stark differences in the social backgrounds of Conservative and Labour MPs. Conservative MPs were drawn largely from the upper middle and middle classes and usually attended public school followed by Oxbridge. Many Labour MPs, on the other hand, came from the ranks of manual workers or trade union officials and, before 1922, few had attended a university. The party, indeed, had been formed in 1900 explicitly to increase representation of the working class in the House of Commons, when the Conservative and Liberal parties refused to adopt working-class men as candidates. In terms of Parliamentary representation the party system at that time institutionalised class differences.

Since 1922 and, *a fortiori*, since 1945, embourgeoisement of the Labour party has produced a remarkable narrowing of this social 'gap'. Both parties now draw their MPs mainly from the ranks of the professions and the graduate middle class, though Labour still has a (shrinking) minority from the working class. Between 1906 and 1918, 89 per cent of Labour MPs were working class and between 1922 and 1935 the figure was still 71 per cent.[4] Since 1945, however, an average of 34 per cent have been former manual workers; the figure dropped to 29 per cent in the 1974 Parliament and the proportion is even smaller if we consider newly recruited MPs. Even trade-union sponsorship, originally a device for recruiting

Table 14.1 Prestige and merit in the education of politicians

Type of education	1945 (%)	1959 (%)	1979 (%)
Conservative:			
Pure prestige	29	24	20
Pure merit	3	12	16
Prestige and merit	56	48	52
Neither	12	16	12
Numbers	213	365	339
Labour:			
Pure prestige	4	2	2
Pure merit	18	23	37
Prestige and merit	15	15	16
Neither	61	58	45
Numbers	400	258	269

Note: See text for details. Data for 1945 extracted from Colin Mellors, *The British MP* (Farnborough,Hants: Saxon House, 1978). For subsequent elections data drawn from Nuffield election studies.

workers to Parliament, is increasingly offered to university graduates and people with no background in industry.[5]

The main 'switchboard' for entry to politics now is attendance at a university, usually by way of public school and then Oxbridge for a Conservative, or by grammar school and then non-Oxbridge for a Labour MP (though Oxbridge for Labour ministers). Emphasis on academic achievement for political recruitment and promotion has particularly affected the type of Labour MP. The 1944 Education Act enabled more children from the working and lower middle classes to enter grammar schools and universities and thereby achieve social mobility. Constituency selection committees increasingly see ability as requiring a university degree and professional qualifications.[6]

The shift to recruitment by educational merit is shown in Table 14.1, which presents figures on the education of MPs after the general elections of 1945, 1959 and 1979. This shows the proportion of MPs whose education has been purely prestigious (public school only), purely meritocratic (non-public school and university), prestigious and meritocratic (both public school and university) and lacking both prestige and merit.[7] The most striking change has occurred on the Labour side, with the median MP changing from one whose education lacks both merit and prestige in 1945 and 1959 to one who now has merit, i.e. a university degree. Between 1945 and 1979, while the proportion of graduates grew on the Conservative side from 59 per cent to 68 per cent, on the Labour side it grew from 33 per cent to 53 per cent.

There are, however, two distinct types of middle class members on the Labour and Conservative benches. First, although we lack authoritative data, many Labour MPs appear to be first-generation middle class, having come from working or lower-middle class homes, making their way *via* grammar schools and university into the professions and thereby acquiring skills useful for politics. Another contrast is that middle class Labour MPs are usually employed in the public sector, often in the service sphere, being teachers, lecturers, welfare and social workers. Conservative middle-class MPs, on the other hand, usually come from comfortable middle-class families, have been to public schools and are drawn from the private sector, being lawyers, accountants and business executives. As Johnson notes, insofar as the Labour MPs now send their own children to independent schools and universities, then they are a generation behind most Conservative MPs.[8]

If we turn to Cabinet appointments, the more interesting change is also on the Labour side. A feature of political recruitment in Britain, as in other societies, is that the higher one ascends the political hierarchy, the more socially and educationally exclusive it becomes. Cabinet ministers are usually of higher social and educational status than those ministers outside the Cabinet, who, in turn, stand above back-benchers.

In terms of social background, most Labour ministers have fallen into one of three broad groups. Labour has always found a place for the *patricians* (MPs who come from established upper middle class families, attended the prestigious public schools and Oxbridge and entered one of the professions). Attlee, Dalton, Cripps and Gaitskell represented this *genre* and, more recently, Crossman, Gordon-Walker, Jay and Benn. In the inter-war years the party's willingness to find a place for men and women of high social standing, who often had previously been associated with other political parties, contrasted sharply with the practice of Socialist parties on the Continent.[9]

Table 14.2 Social and educational composition of Labour Cabinets, 1924–76

Date	Size	Aristo-crat	Middle Class	Working Class	University (All Oxbridge)	
1924	19	3	5	11	6	6
1929	20	2	4	12	6	3
1945	20	—	8	12	10	5
1964	23	1	14	8	13	11
1974 (Mar)	21	1	16	4	16	11
1976 (Apr)	22	1	13	7	15	10
Average	20	1.5	10	8.5	11.5	7.5

Source: D. E. Butler and Anne Sloman, *British Political Facts*, 5th edn (London: Macmillan, 1979).

This group supplemented the *proletarians* (MPs from working-class families, who left school at an early age and then became manual workers, trade-union organisers, or lowly clerical workers). Many of the pre-war leaders came from this second background. Herbert Morrison and Aneurin Bevan, who contested the 1955 leadership election with Hugh Gaitskell, and George Brown, who was runner-up to Wilson in 1963, were in this group. Table 14.2 shows that the Labour Cabinets of MacDonald, Attlee and Wilson in 1964 drew about half of their members from this group. During Mr Wilson's leadership, however, there was a steady exodus of proletarians from the Cabinet and they were replaced by the graduate middle-class ministers. By 1970 only three Cabinet ministers were drawn from this group. Although Mr Callaghan restored the social balance somewhat (the 1979 Cabinet contained Eric Varley and Roy Mason, both former miners,[10] Stan Orme, an ex-engineer and Albert Booth, an ex-draughtsman), the erosion of the working class element is clear.

The third group, now numerically and politically the most significant, are the *meritocrats*. These come from working or lower middle-class backgrounds, attend state schools (usually winning scholarships to grammar schools) and go on to university. (In recent Labour Cabinets the group has been represented by such people as Wilson, Healey, Mrs Castle, Crosland, Dell, Hattersley, Shore, Rodgers, Rees and Jenkins.) These are scholarship boys and girls whose parents are from the working class or the lower ranks of the

Table 14.3 Percentage of 'talking' professions among
Labour MPs

	1951	October 1974	1979
Among Labour MPs	26	38	30
Among Labour candidates	27	43	43

Source: Dennis Kavanagh, 'Still the Workers Party?', in
D. Kavanagh (ed.), *The Politics of the Labour Party*
(Allen & Unwin, 1982, p. 99).

professions or white-collar occupations. After university they usually
enter the professions, becoming academics, journalists and consultants.
In contrast to the proletarians, their social mobility has been achieved
prior to a political career by dint of going to university. The contrast
is seen in the reflections of Clynes, waiting to be sworn in by the
monarch as Labour's first Lord Privy Seal in 1924:

I could not help marvelling at the strange turn of Fortune's wheel,
which had brought MacDonald, the starveling clerk, Thomas the
engine-driver, Henderson the foundry labourer and Clynes the
mill-hand, to this pinnacle . . .[11]

These changes have coincided with a steady increase in the
proportion of Labour MPs who come from the 'talking' professions
(such as lecturing, teaching, journalism and political and group
organisers). The 'talkers' rose from a quarter of Labour MPs in
1951 to two-fifths in 1974 and fell back again to 30 per cent in 1979.
The fall is largely a consequence of most safe Labour seats being
held by union-sponsored MPs, who were more often manual workers
than non-sponsored. The loss of seats at an election normally entails
a fall in the proportion of middle-class Labour MPs. By 1987 the
rise in the number of Labour MPs increased the number of 'talkers'
to 38 per cent. More significant is the bottom line of Table 14.3,
which shows the occupational backgrounds of Labour candidates.
This shows that nearly a half of Labour candidates are 'talkers'.
Indeed the growth of the middle class among Labour MPs is almost
solely a function of the recruitment of more teachers. Other studies
have shown that well-educated children from working class and

lower middle class families are more likely to aspire to becoming teachers rather than becoming members of more prestigious and exclusive professions.

Any discussion of the changing social backgrounds of Labour MPs and ministers invites the question 'so what?' It also has to take account of subtle differences in the political socialisation of members of the same objective social class. The gradual decline of working-class members on the Labour benches is clear. The main source of supply of workers now is the trade unions and these are usually former officials, with desk-bound jobs. It is extremely difficult for a working-class activist, a self-starter like MacDonald, Snowden or Morrison, to enter politics unless it is through a trade union. 'The political class' is now probably more homogeneous in occupational and educational terms than at any time since 1922, when Labour MPs were first returned in large numbers. It is already possible to discern the emergence of a Labour 'establishment', based on dynastic and kinship ties. In the 1974 Parliament children of former Labour MPs included Jenkins, Marquand, Foot, Benn, Janner, the Silkins, Mrs Summerskill and Mrs Dunwoody. They followed in the steps of Noel-Baker, Henderson, Cripps and others. And if we also took account of MPs who were the sons and daughters of trade-union officials (e.g. Barbara Castle) or local Labour politicians (e.g. Roy Hattersley), then membership of a 'political family' would emerge as an important factor cutting across social class.[12]

Conservatives

On the Conservative side the change has been more modest. Compared to the inter-war years, the party has shed the aristocrats, landowners, big businessmen and idle rich. Hence, following the Maxwell-Fyfe reform (1949), which prohibited constituencies from accepting large donations from candidates and members – thereby helping the less affluent candidates – the type of Conservative MP has within limits broadened. Since the war only two Conservative MPs have been from the working class; the party stubbornly remains the preserve of upper middle-class professional and business occupations. The proportion of MPs coming from public schools has remained steady at around 75 per cent and, though more MPs have a university education, the Oxbridge dominance is unchallenged. The middle-class MPs who have gradually replaced the aristocrats on the Conservative benches tend to share the same educational

Table 14.4 Conservative MPs, 1923 and 1974

Date	No.	Etonian (%)	Public school (%)	Oxbridge (%)	All uni-versity (%)	Pro-fessional (%)	Manual (%)	Women (%)
1923	258	25	79	40	50	52	4	1
1974 (Oct)	277	17	75	56	69	46	1	3

Source: David Butler and Michael Pinto-Duschinsky, 'The Conservative Elite, 1918–78: Does Unrepresentativeness Matter?', in Z. Layton-Henry, *Conservative Party Politics* (London: Macmillan, 1980).

background. The continuity in the educational and occupational background of Conservatives is illustrated in Table 14.4, which compares Conservative MPs in 1923 and October 1974. The former year is chosen because it comes nearest to matching the 277 Conservative MPs of 1974.

The Conservative party has sometimes been led by men who, though wealthy, lacked blue blood and estates; Disraeli, Bonar Law, Baldwin and Neville Chamberlain are examples. But throughout the twentieth century the party has been suffused with upper-class values, an 'establishment' of wealth, exclusive London clubs and major public schools. Until 1964 more than half of Conservative Cabinet ministers in this century had been old Etonians, and a large minority belonged to or were related to the aristocracy. Churchill, for example, was the grandson of a duke, Eden owned vast estates and was related to Lord Grey of the 1832 Reform Act, and Sir Alec Douglas-Home was related by marriage to the same Lord Grey and was the first hereditary peer to become Prime Minister since Lord Salisbury. Macmillan, though himself a wealthy publisher, the product of Eton, Balliol and the Guards, and married into the Cavendishes, one of England's oldest political families, counts as a *parvenu* in this gallery. Reading the biographies and memoirs of Churchill, Eden, Macmillan, Sir Alec Douglas-Home and others, one is reminded of the life-style of the eighteenth- and nineteenth-century aristocracy. There is the same friendship and kinship with other 'notables', the same early entry to politics, and the same anticipation of political success that so impressed W. L. Guttsman in his study of the nineteenth-century political elite. He commented:

'One is struck again and again by the extent and intimacy of their personal contacts. They are inevitably related to the greater freedom and ease of intercourse which stems from a considerable degree of independence'.[13]

Not surprisingly, ministers from different backgrounds felt uneasy. Even Bonar Law regretted 'his wanting of birth . . . afraid that the Party might follow unwillingly because he had no blue blood in his veins'.[14] In the 1960s outwardly confident ministers such as Reginald Bevins and Charles Hill felt isolated among colleagues whose privileged family background and education seemed to give them an assured social status and cohesion.[15]

In little more than a decade that apparently secure Establishment, which confidently managed the emergence of 'the leader', has almost disappeared. The watershed was the election of Edward Heath as Conservative leader in 1965. Before the war Heath and Mrs Thatcher would have been unlikely choices as Conservative MPs, let alone as leaders.[16] Heath's mother was a housemaid and his father had started his working life as a carpenter, and Mrs Thatcher's father was a grocer. Winning scholarships to local grammar schools and Oxford established their claims for advancement.

Many of Heath's close Cabinet colleagues in 1970 were also from non-upper class backgrounds and were soon dubbed 'Heathmen' by the mass media. The number of old Etonians in Heath's Cabinet dropped sharply to four from eleven under Sir Alec Douglas-Home. The *'products of opportunity'* (Mr Heath's phrase), self-made professional politicians from the city and suburbs, took over from the products of political families and possessors of landed estates.[17] They were the equivalent of Labour's 'meritocrats'. However, we need to repeat the limited nature of the social revolution, Mr Heath and Mrs Thatcher were not typical of their front-bench or even back-bench colleagues. Both were and are surrounded by public school, Oxbridge MPs. The 1979 Conservative Cabinet, for example, includes, in addition to Mrs Thatcher, only John Biffen who did not attend a select Headmasters' Conference school, and only four non-Oxbridge ministers.

We have noted that knowledge of the social origins of politicians does not on its own permit one to make confident predictions about their behaviour or attitudes. But the general shift from *patricians* and *proletarians* to *meritocrats* does provide a link with other changes in the context of British politics. There is, for example, the decline of social deference among the working class as a basis for voting

Conservative in the 1950s and 1960s, though one may doubt whether it was ever so important. According to McKenzie and Silver, the deferential voter believes that these patricians are 'uniquely qualified to govern by birth, experience and outlook',[18] as Bagehot noted, high social status was an outward sign of political talent.[19] This view commanded acceptance outside Britain. Schumpter, for example, in stressing the importance of well-born politicians, suggested, 'experience seems to suggest that the only effective guarantee (of quality) is in the existence of a social stratum, itself a product of a severely selective process, that takes to politics as a matter of course'.[20] He regarded Britain as the only country which possessed a political society, endowing its members with traditions, experience and a professional code.

That social and cultural context has almost vanished. The increasing demands on politicians and governments mean that both are expected to justify themselves by performance. The shift has been to a more instrumental evaluation by voters. In the rural areas the influence and participation of local aristocrats and landowners in Conservative politics has declined. In urban areas the leadership of substantial business men has also largely disappeared.[21] Contemporary local leaders are more 'ordinary' professional and business men, solicitors, executives and accountants. There is now less agreement about the bases of deference to leaders, and probably less social and cultural distance between leaders and voters.

There is now less hierarchy in the Conservative Party. Traditionally, a Conservative leader's self-confidence rested both on his high social status and ideas about the independent authority of government; government was, in L. S. Amery's words, an 'independent body' which derived its authority from the Crown. The sense of hierarchy was also reflected in the way the leader 'emerged' before 1965. There was little pretence to democratic selection. Senior party figures, after sounding out opinions, designated one man, and the appointee was then universally acclaimed by the party. But neither Mr Heath nor Mrs Thatcher was able to exploit a superior social status. The adoption of formal election procedures for the leadership in 1965 meant that they owed their elevation (and, since 1975, possible dismissal) to competitive election by backbenchers, further weakening the sense of hierarchy.

The changes in the social background of the two front benches have also affected the image of the parties. The diminution in ostensible class difference, particularly with regard to university education, between the two front benches in the 1960s coincided with a decline in the number of voters perceiving 'a good deal' of difference between the parties and with a weakening of the class voting. Obviously, the convergence in policies in the 1960s was important here, as was the growth of television as a source of political information. But the idea that one party represented the poor and the other the privileged hardly fitted the homogeneous middle-class graduate character of the two front benches that viewers could see for themselves on the television.

More speculatively, we might expect a different attitude to political activity. Patricians, after all, learned a tradition of politics that arose from practice and relied on hunch and instinct; they usually had a sceptical view of what could or even should be achieved by government. Many Conservatives enjoyed private incomes, saw politics as a part-time activity and came into politics to enjoy the amenities and companionship of a fine club. Aristocrats in high office have usually been easy-going (though the judgement is equally applicable to such non-aristocratic Prime Ministers as Campbell-Bannerman, Asquith, Bonar Law and Baldwin), attracted to public affairs by family traditions and '*noblesse oblige*'.[22] Politics was not a 'vocation' which excluded other activities, for 'The man who puts politics first is not fit to be called a civilised being, let alone a Christian'.[23] In contrast the socially mobile meritocrats, lacking this background, might be expected to be more motivated to bring about change and to see their task as 'making' instead of 'attending to' the arrangements of society.[24]

STYLE

Change is a convenient rallying cry of the political 'outs' of the day. British politicians are ambiguous about change *per se*, however. Historians usually emphásise the gradual nature of change in British politics and the preference for an adaptation of existing forms, combining the values of tradition and modernity. At times, however, dissatisfaction with the *status quo* and demand for change have decisively affected the political agenda, in terms of what politicians propose as policy, how they justify their preferences on the issues of the day, and the image they present to voters. At the beginning of the twentieth century, for example, it was the demand for National Efficiency, and in the 1960s it was Modernisation or

Remodernisation.[25] The thematic similarities between demands made by opinion-formers in these two cases is remarkable and in both cases transcended party lines. For example, the main complaints of both were addressed to Britain's economic weakness, international decline, and the amateurism and lack of expertise among administrative and economic elites.

Many of the prescribed remedies were also similar; new men who would be 'experts', possessing scientific or technical skills; reforms of government institutions which would permit more 'rational' policies; and the integration of Britain within a larger unit (the Empire in 1900, the EEC later). In 1900 the target was the set of assumptions represented by Gladstonian Liberalism, in the 1960s it was tradition and rule by an 'old boy' network. Both would agree with Sidney Low's claim in 1904 that 'Government in England is government by amateurs' and that the complexity of government required new skills beyond those of 'good intentions and a respectable character'.[26] Finally, in the 1960s, as at the beginning of the twentieth century, there was optimism that the importation of new men and new techniques would arrest the British decline.

During the first half of the post-war period the two main parties had been largely satisfied with the state of Britain. There was room for improvement, but in the 1945 Parliament Labour had achieved much of its long-standing programme, consolidating the welfare state and bringing the basic industries under public ownership. The succeeding Conservative governments accepted most of these changes. There was some common ground between the parties on maintaining full employment, the mixed economy, the welfare state and granting independence to the colonies. Winston Churchill observed to his doctor, Lord Moran, 'I have come to know the nation and what needs to be done to stay in power'. The Conservative's third successive election victory in 1959 showed that the party was adjusting successfully to the prosperous electorate. The government's use of Keynesian techniques of economic management banished the twin evils of unemployment and economic stagnation.

The satisfaction of the 1950s, however, was soon followed by a sense of failure – political, economic and international – that led to the 'great reappraisal' of policy in 1961. In that year the Macmillan government made the first overtures for membership of the Common Market and turned to economic planning to find a way out of the stop-go cycles of the economy. The sense of decline was fuelled by a number of events: the Suez failure in 1956, the abandonment of the Blue Streak and with it any credible claims to possess an independent nuclear deterrent, sterling crises and growing awareness of the low rate of economic growth compared to other countries.

Both parties responded to the sense of decline by looking for new policies, a process accentuated by the election of new and younger leaders. Both the new leaders were grammar-school boys, had entered Parliament after the war and spoke of the challenge of change. Mr Wilson became leader of the Labour party in February 1963. Making an issue out of Britain's low rate of industrial growth, he emphasised the importance of science and technology and held out the prospect of a new Britain 'that is going to be forged in the white heat of this revolution'.[27] His promise was that Labour's plans would get the economy moving and society modernised. In retrospect it is remarkable that so many communicators (having led the cry for change and modernisation) saw Wilson as the British version of Kennedy's 'New Frontier'; here was a youthful technocratic leader promising modernisation and transcending the old divisions in the Labour party. According to Anthony Sampson, Harold Wilson was 'a man of determined isolation and professionalism, different from any previous incumbent in Downing St'. In his company, 'pretensions and passion dissolve in the dry atmosphere of technical discussion'.[28]

Mr Heath became the Conservative leader in 1965, after the party's first open competitive election. He was chosen for qualities which were thought to match those of Mr Wilson and which Sir Alec Douglas-Home lacked – toughness, industry and expertise on the economy. Though a 'new man' in terms of his social background, he had established his credentials by rising through the ministerial hierarchy. Mr Heath's determination had already been demonstrated as Chief Whip at the time of Suez, in his handling of the EEC negotiations, and the abolition of resale price maintenance in 1964 in face of bitter opposition within his own party.

Mr Heath expressed impatience with the flabby consensus of the post-war era, years of British decline. He was committed to more personal responsibility, incentives, taking decisions which would adjust to an increasingly competitive world, and avoiding 'the easy way of subsidy, and still more subsidy, of Government intervention, and still more Government intervention'. The party had to find new ground from that occupied in the 1950s. The new policies, foreshadowed in *Putting Britain Right Ahead* (1965) and the Conservative manifesto in 1970, aimed at changing the structure within which government and the economy worked. It was anticipated that cutting direct taxation, reducing government intervention in industry and wage bargaining, reorganising central government, relating welfare benefits to need, requiring trade unions to operate within a tighter legal framework, and gaining entry to the EEC would create the climate for greater enterprise, competition, efficiency and economic growth. This package was accompanied by a more abrasive style. The new, middle-class Conservatives were less guilty about the 1930s than their Conservative predecessors and adopted a tougher approach to the trade unions.

If one tries to capture the central themes which the leaders projected in the 1960s the *leitmotif* is competence and efficiency, with little reference to the traditions or ideologies of the parties. In common with President Kennedy's call, 'Let's get America moving again', the parties moved from a stationary to a dynamic view of society. At the same time voters appeared to be more interested in the performance of the parties, judging them instrumentally, according to the benefits they were likely to deliver.

An important theme was 'the scientific revolution' (first referred to in Labour's policy document, *Signposts for the Sixties*) and its implications for modernisation and economic planning and growth. There were demands for more economists to be taken into government and more physicists and chemists recruited to the civil service. There was a shift from the patrician's Parliamentary skills to the technocrat's expertise; the amateur and dilettante were out, the professional and specialist were in. Witness Mr Wilson addressing the Labour Conference in 1963: 'in the Cabinet room and the boardroom alike, those charged with the central direction of our affairs must be ready to think and to speak in the language of our scientific age'.

A good illustration of the change in mood was seen in 1964 in the resigned acceptance by many Conservatives that Sir Alec Douglas-Home was an electoral liability and in his replacement by Mr Heath. Sir Alec's aristocratic background and grouse-moor image (though not dissimilar from his immediate predecessor's), and his lack of authority on questions of industry and the economy, were thought to disqualify him from the top job.

There was, appropriately enough, a belief that problems would be solved by a new technique, a reorganisation of institutions and the managerial approach. In 1964 Labour established the Department of Economic Affairs to formulate a national plan for the economy,

Politics and Personalities

and a Ministry of Technology to explore advanced technology. There were also new techniques of central resource allocation (e.g. PESC, for public expenditure, and PAR, the Programme Analysis Review); the creation of new ministries and then the amalgamation of ministries into super-departments in 1970; aids for policy analysis (e.g. the Central Policy Review Staff in 1970 to look at the broader strategic aspects of policy, the importation of business consultants in 1970, and then the Prime Minister's Policy Unit in 1974). The motive was a 'managerialist' search for a greater central capability and more coherent policy-making at the centre.[29]

It was also a period of institutional reform. The decade saw an orgy of Royal Commissions and committees of inquiry into Parliament, the civil service, the Constitution, local government and trade unions. The chief reforms affected the civil service and local and central government. The emphasis again was on greater efficiency. The Report of the Fulton Committee on the Civil Service indicted the tradition of the arts graduate, 'generalist' administrator. The report called for the recruitment of civil servants with more relevant specialist knowledge of the work of government departments, though, as critics observed, it failed to present criteria of relevance.

Finally, government became larger and more interventionist, though this was contrary to Heath's original intentions. Government tried to reform the trade unions, and took sweeping powers to control prices and incomes and intervene in industry. The growth in the size of departments, proliferation of new ministries and responsibilities (e.g. Arts, Sport, Disabled, Prices and Consumer Protection, Energy), and the increasing share of the national income passing through the government's hands are measurable if crude indicators. Mr Wilson frequently complained that during his last spell as Prime Minister the burdens had greatly increased since 1964 in the shape of papers to read, people to see and international gatherings to attend. The need for more co-ordination was a measure of the growing complexity of government. Party manifestos and policy-making by the parties became more wide-ranging and detailed. For example, R. A. Butler's policy exercise after 1945 relied on three broad committees and sketched themes; in contrast Mr Heath had thirty committees, many of which went into detail on specific points.

The fashion for economic growth, modernisation and efficiency said little about the direction of change or the nature of the desired society. The party slogans 'Let's go with Labour' (1964), 'You Know Labour Government Works' (1970) and the Conservative 'Action Not Words' (1966) and the habit of Wilson and Heath to claim they were 'getting on with the job', suggested a restless concern with activity or movement for its own sake. In common with trends in Western Europe and the United States, there was a convergence of policies and a sense that many major social problems had been or could be solved, producing the depoliticisation of the 1960s. The politicians' technocratic approach involved a preference for

> minimising the apparent relevance of rival ideologies, while maximising that of non-ideological, pragmatic, techno-administrative solutions (and the reduction of politics) . . . haggling over the respective merits of those 'solutions' which the experts deemed to be possible.[30]

In 1964 Mr Wilson defined Socialism as 'applying a sense of purpose to our national life' and 'purpose means technical skill'. He went on to praise skill in various occupations and complained that in government and business people too often considered social qualifications rather than technical ability as desirable. In introducing the policy document *Putting Britain Right Ahead* in 1965, Heath defended its concentration on details and neglect of philosophy by claiming that people were more interested in '*how* we do things rather than in what needs to be done'. And the 1966 manifesto stated, 'Our first aim is this: to run this country's affairs efficiently and realistically, so that we achieve steadier prices in the shops, high wages, and a really decent standard of social security'.

ASSESSMENT: PROGRESS AND DECLINE

We now know that the Wilson – Heath era coincided with a continued relative decline in Britain's position in the world. The country's relative economic performance, however measured, declined even more sharply in the decade 1965–75, and this when the parties had based their appeals explicitly on an ability to 'get Britain moving'.

With Mr Wilson the break-through was to come about through 'purposive' intervention and economic planning. This ambition was finally abandoned with the forced devaluation of the pound in 1967.

Mr Heath was committed in 1970 to a smaller scale of government and allowing the market a greater influence in the economy. Yet within 2 years his government was armed with a full-blooded set of controls over prices and incomes and far-reaching powers to intervene in industry. The sense of failure and the diminishing correspondence between what the parties said they would do and what they actually accomplished contributed to the general lack of confidence in the party leaders and the political institutions. The governments of Mr Wilson and Mr Heath inherited many common problems and often turned to similar policies. But there was one important difference between the two men, when it came to inducing change and modernisation.

For Mr Wilson, modernisation was effective rhetoric; to be for change was fashionable in the early 1960s, just as the rhetoric of conciliation became fashionable a decade later. Ministerial colleagues suggested that Mr Wilson was more interested in the image than in the substance of government. Crossman's diaries reinforce claims that the government lacked a coherent policy or firm direction, frequently treating major issues in a perfunctory manner. As early as 1965, Crossman reports Wilson saying: 'my strategy (!) is to put the Tories on the defensive and always give them awkward choices'.[31]

Talk of the scientific revolution enabled the Labour Party to paper over its cracks on public ownership and defence. By temperament, Wilson proved a conciliator, in marked contrast to his predecessor, Hugh Gaitskell. Gaitskell was impatient of equivocations and formulae which compromised fundamental policy differences. His habit, as a self-confessed rationalist, was to bring differences into the open, articulate disagreements, take a vote on an issue and then declare the majority view as party policy. He was not sympathetic to traditional symbols and myths, such as Clause IV, when they interfered with his task of reforming the party's policies and image.[32] For much of his leadership, the party was bitterly divided and Gaitskell himself was regarded as a factional leader.

Wilson thought that this directive style was no way to lead the Labour Party; the party was a 'broad church', its different factions had to be coaxed to a common course of action. His primary objective was to keep the Labour Party together. This is the not dishonourable explanation of the way he held himself apart from factions, his refusal to take an early firm stand on several issues (the outstanding exceptions were on devaluation and trade-union reform), his apparent changes of mind, in line with majority party opinion, and his careful balancing of different factions in the Cabinet. The critics inveighed against the fudging, the soothing formulae, the trimming, and the unheroic style. But it kept the party together and Mr Wilson safely in the saddle.

Mr Heath was a more determined character, and radical rhetoric was backed by appropriate actions. Many of the party's specific policies were enacted after 1970, often in face of bitter opposition in and out of Parliament. In speaking of 'the challenge of change' he told the 1970 party conference that 'If we are to achieve this task we will have to embark on a change so radical, a revolution so quiet and yet so total, that it will go far beyond the programme . . . far beyond this decade and into the 1980s'. Perhaps a mark of the radical nature of the Heath government's legislation is that much of it was withdrawn from the statute book soon after it left office and its policies reversed by the succeeding Labour government. The Housing Finance Act was scrapped, the statutory controls on incomes and the Industrial Relations Act were repealed, and the terms of membership of the EEC were renegotiated. By tradition major reforms in Britain usually undergo a gestation period, in which they germinate, gather support and gradually come to be regarded as inevitable.[33] Mr Heath felt that vested interests had been accommodated for too long and that action was necessary if the country's decline was to be arrested. But his forthright appeal to the electorate in 1974 for support was rebuffed.

It is worth noting how the two 'disturbers' of the mid-1960s were chastened by experience. By 1970 Harold Wilson was already being compared with Baldwin as a safe, easy-going leader. In the 1974 elections he presented himself as a healing, unifying figure. In a revealing interview he compared himself with a family doctor helping people 'to achieve . . . peace and quiet', rather than wanting to 'sit on people's doorsteps'.[34] By October 1974 Mr Heath had also lost his cutting edge; he then espoused the cause of conciliation and national unity, arguing that the problems facing the country and the necessary mobilisation of consent required a coalition. Bold leadership in the style of a British Gaullist had been frustrated.

Two interesting questions arise: first, why the failure and second, what might be done to improve the performance of leadership? If we ask why things did not turn out better, only a small part of the answer lies in the shortcomings of the parties and the leaders. The optimist may point to a few crucial decisions which, from hindsight, might be judged poor – e.g. not entering the Common Market in the 1950s, not devaluing the pound before 1967, trying to play a world rôle with inadequate resources, maintaining the pound as a reserve currency and so on. The difficulty with this type of analysis is not only the simple assumption of causality – if *x*-policy were followed then *y* and *z* would happen – but also that any system has to allow for errors. Moreover, if there are several poor policy decisions, then one has to look deeper. The monolithic and adversary style of party politics is at present a favoured candidate for blame. But the problem with this as a comprehensive explanation is that excessive partisanship and abrupt discontinuities of policy between the parties is only apparent in the years 1970–4, whereas the shortcomings pre-date this short period.

It may be that Britain has become a more difficult country to govern during the post-war years. Governments are beset by more intractable problems.[35] The effectiveness of public policies is now more dependent on the co-operation of other groups and the actions of other governments, interests are better organised to refuse compliance, and resource constraints limit the possibility of increasing both take-home pay and public benefits. Complexity and resource constraints are universals of the policy process, yet we have to acknowledge that they affect other countries too.

This is not to deny that formal power is still concentrated in the Whitehall machine, that a determined minister can get his way, or that Cabinet domination of Parliament speeds the passage of legislation. It is still the case that, in spite of a more populist tone, demands for more open and accountable government, the broadcasting of Parliament, and the light shed by the Crossman diaries, British government remains closed. Ministers are still comparatively free from scrutiny and the public detached from politics. In this sense one may agree with Lord Hailsham that political power in Britain is concentrated in the executive and that the Cabinet resembles an 'elective dictatorship'.

But today this formal power matters less in its impact on society. Here is the major paradox about British politics, which a latter-day Bagehot would surely spot. While the political institutions are strong or *mobilising*, the political culture is constraining or *conciliatory*. The surface strength and stability of British government appear to help the mobiliser. Government derives its authority from the ancient prerogatives of the Crown, a Cabinet with a majority in the Commons exercises full sovereignty. The attitude is exemplified in L. S. Amery's statement that British democracy is 'government of the people, for the people, with, but not by the people',[36] or, more prosaically, that 'the government's job is to govern'.

But at the same time, the policies of other centres – producer groups, international corporations, trading partners – have crowded the rôle of Parliament and Cabinet in the last 30 years. The need to take these groups into account seems to produce immobilism. The cultural factors are also important in depressing the scope for the mobilising style. British government has traditionally been exercised within certain parameters; it is limited in its remit, leadership is parliamentary and liberty is negative, i.e. the people are left alone. The other side of this relationship is that only in wartime have the British been responsive to energetic or mobilising leaders. British Prime Ministers are hardly popular figures; they are regarded as partisan leaders. Since 1945, only Macmillan and Wilson have maintained the support of more than half of the electorate for 2 years or more, according to Gallup polls.

Political skill is shown within the Parliamentary arena. Approval among this Parliamentary elite is more decisive than a popular following in reaching the top in British politics. Thirteen of the eighteen Prime Ministers of the twentieth century first assumed office without the sanction of a general election. The average times spent in the House of Commons for an MP prior to becoming a party leader and Prime Minister have been 24 and 26 years, respectively. This lengthy apprenticeship provides ample opportunity for learning the skills appropriate to managing the party and Parliament and usually ensures that leaders have those qualities.[37] Acceptability to colleagues at the levels of party, Parliament and Cabinet have attracted and rewarded a personality and style in which qualities of reliability, self-restraint, and trustworthiness have figured prominently. Managing the party and Cabinet, or advancing in the civil service all place a premium on the avoidance of conflict. Foreign observers are struck by the emphasis on *community* over performance among the Whitehall elite.[38] Objections to dynamic personalities who posed threats to the consensus system have usually been decisive. It also suggests why – apart from exceptional circumstances like wars – those leaders who enter as mobilisers, like Wilson in 1964 and Heath in 1970, gradually find it necessary to conciliate.

Assertions of a national destiny by Joseph Chamberlain or Oswald Mosley, a national identity by Enoch Powell, and the Dunkirk spirit by Wilson in 1967 or Heath in 1974, all fall on deaf ears in peacetime.

The 'State of England' literature, with its call for directive leadership implicitly, though mistakenly, suggests that things were different in the past. In view of this disjunction between the institutions and the culture it is more understandable why the diaries and autobiographies of recent ministers convey a sense of governments being hemmed in, of trying to cope, rather than adhering to an overall strategy. Harold Macmillan thought that over the years authority had increasingly been concentrated in the hands of Prime Ministers. But he also felt that power seemed 'like a dead sea fruit, when you achieve it, there's nothing there'. Another Cabinet Minister entitled the first chapter of a book on British politics, 'Where Has All the Power Gone?'[39]

There have been two broad reactions to awareness of interdependence, diffusion of power and sense of decline. One is to call for 'strong' leadership, a strengthening of the authority of political leaders and government institutions in Western states. The purpose of such a leadership is to roll back demands by groups and lower expectations of what government can do. Both Mr Wilson and Mr Heath tried to tame the trade unions by legislation and appeals to public opinion. The former retreated when he found he could not carry his Cabinet or party, and Mr Heath's Gaullist use of a general election in 1974 failed. In 1979 Margaret Thatcher has come to office acting much as Mr Heath did in 1970. It remains to be seen how she will cope with the great interests of the realm.

An alternative is that maintaining consent and coping with complexity require more power-sharing. The greater the number of decision-points and decision-makers the greater the need for agreement. Effective leadership may now depend on a modern version of John Calhoun's doctrine of concurrent majorities among big groups, giving 'to each division or interest . . . either a concurrent voice in making and executing the laws, or a veto on their execution'. The two emphases fall respectively on the mobiliser and the conciliator.

To be more effective the conciliator requires different institutions. It is here that the adversary nature of the two-party system, combined with the effects of the winner-take-all Parliamentary battle and electoral system, and more interventionist government which does require consent if it is to be effective, is important. Electoral reform (and its probable offshoot, coalition), corporatism, devolution, membership of the Common Market, and resort to referenda, have been canvassed as devices for promoting more consensual or co-operative policies. There have been moves in all directions in recent years, and each represents a turning away from the one-party, centralised, hierarchical form of government we have known since 1945.

This article has discussed the post-war changes in composition and style of British leaders. While the move away from the patricians and the proletarians is probably irreversible, the consequences of trends to the meritocratic leaders are complex. There seems to be little relationship between social background and the adoption of mobilising or conciliatory styles. Wilson and Callaghan are examples of the conciliator, Lloyd George, Heath and Mrs Thatcher are examples of the mobiliser; but all are self-made. Mobilisation is not a function of being in or out of government nor is it the exclusive property of a party. If anything, movement between the two styles of leadership appears to be cyclical, with one eventually breeding a reaction in favour of the other. The leaderships of both Wilson and Heath show how one may end with a style radically different from that assumed at the outset. The task of British leaders is, as ever, to speak the two languages, conciliatory and mobilising. The one seeks consensus as a necessary basis of policy effectiveness. The other is 'hard', concerned with earning Britain's place in a competitive world, rooting out economic inefficiencies at home and winning markets abroad. There seems little doubt that, borne down by the inertia of institutions and values, leaders have failed to achieve a happy combination of the two voices.

NOTES

1. The distinction is often applied to France and the United States. For Britain, see Dennis Kavanagh, *Crisis, Charisma and British Political Leadership* (London: Sage, 1974).
2. David Apter, *The Politics of Modernization* (Chicago: Chicago University Press, 1945).
3. W. L. Guttsman, *The British Political Elite* (London: MacGibbon & Kee, 1963).
4. R. Rose, 'Class and Party Divisions: Britain as a Test Case', *Sociology*, II (1968) 129-62.
5. W. D. Muller, *The Kept Men?* (London: Harvester Press, 1977).
6. On this trend, see Michael Young, *The Rise of the Meritocracy* (Harmondsworth: Penguin, 1961).
7. See R. Rose, *Politics in England Today* (London: Faber, 1974), p. 159.

8. R. W. Johnson, 'The British Political Elite, 1955-1972', *European Journal of Sociology*, XIV (1973) 35–77.
9. Egon Wertheimer, *Portrait of the Labour Party* (London: Putnam, 1929).
10. Both these former ministers had received further education. However, two other Labour ministers, Roy Jenkins and Merlyn Rees, were sons of miners.
11. Quoted in C. L. Mowat, *Britain Between the Wars* (London,: Methuen, 1955), p. 173.
12. Johnson, in *European Journal of Sociology*, XIV, p. 51.
13. *Ibid*, p. 181.
14. Quoted in Eric Nordlinger, *The Working Class Tories* (London: MacGibbon & Kee, 1967) p. 42.
15. Reginald Bevins, *The Greasy Pole* (London: Hodder & Stoughton, 1965); Sir Charles Hill, *Both Sides of the Hill* (London: Heinemann, 1964).
16. Nigel Fisher, *The Tory Leaders* (London: Weidenfeld & Nicolson, 1977).
17. On the decline of landed estates among Conservative MPs, see Andrew Roth, *The Business Backgrounds of MPs* (London: Parliamentary Profiles, 1972), p. 94.
18. R. T. McKenzie and A. Silver, *Angels in Marble* (London: Heinemann, 1968), p. 242.
19. W. Bagehot, *The English Constitution* (London: World's Classics, 1955).
20. J. Schumpeter, *Capitalism, Socialism and Democracy* (London: Allen & Unwin, 1943), p. 291.
21. D. Butler and M. Pinto-Duschinsky, 'The Conservative Elite 1918–78: Does Unrepresentativeness Matter?', in Zig Layton-Henry, *Conservative Party Politics* (London: Macmillan, 1980).
22. Guttsman, *op. cit.*
23. Lord Hailsham, *The Case for Conservatism* (Harmondsworth: Penguin, 1959), p. 13.
24. Cf. Guttsman, *op. cit.*, p. 310.
25. B. Semmel, *Imperialism and Social Reform: Social and Imperialist Thought 1895–1914* (London: Allen & Unwin, 1960); G. R. Searle, *The Quest for National Efficiency* (London: Blackwell, 1971).
26. Sidney Low, *The Governance of England* (London: Ernest Benn, 1914), pp. 197 and 304.
27. Harold Wilson, Speech to Labour Party Conference, Scarborough, 1963.
28. Anthony Sampson, *Anatomy of Britain Today* (London: Hodder & Stoughton, 1965), pp. 172–3.
29. See Peter Self, 'Are We Worse Governed?', *New Society*, 19 May 1977.
30. John Goldthorpe, 'Theories of Industrial Society', *European Journal of Sociology*, 12, 1971, p. 284.
31. R. H. S. Crossman, *The Diaries of a Cabinet Minister*, Vol. I (London: Hamish Hamilton and Jonathan Cape, 1976), p. 50.
32. Wilson compared Gaitskell's reform to 'Taking Genesis out of the Bible'.

33. Anthony King, 'The Election that Everyone Lost', in Howard Penniman (ed.), *Britain at the Polls* (Washington: American Enterprise Institute, 1974), p. 7.
34. See D. Butler and D. Kavanagh, *The British General Election of October 1974* (London: Macmillan, 1975), pp. 256-7.
35. Anthony King, 'Overload: Problems of Governing in the 1970s', *Political Studies,* XXXIII, 1975, pp. 483-505.
36. L. S. Amery, *Thoughts on the Constitution* (London: Oxford University Press, 1947), p. 22.
37. For a further development of this argument, see Kavanagh, *op. cit.*
38. On this feature, see Robert Putnam, *The Beliefs of Politicians* (New Haven: Yale University Press, 1975); and Hugh Heclo and Aaron Wildavsky, *The Private Government of Public Money* (London: Macmillan, 1974).
39. Ian Gilmour, *The Body Politic* (London: Hutchinson, 1960).

15 The Timing of Elections: Fair Play or Fiddle?*

The dissolution of a legislature raises several interesting political and constitutional issues. Traditional studies of the subject have largely concentrated on the legal and institutional aspects of dissolution. More recently, constitutional experts have regarded the power of calling an election as a device which can shape the conduct of parties and politicians and produce more effective government. The contrast usually drawn was between the stable British governments, which possessed the power of dissolution, and the unstable governments in many West European states (notably France), which usually lacked such an effective power. Interestingly, in recent years in Britain, a growing number of critics have argued that vesting the control of dissolution in the hands of the government actually produces an imbalance in the constitution, allows the government unfair advantage over the opposition in manipulating the economy for its own gain, and opens the way for executive dominance.

This paper examines the political and economic circumstances surrounding a British government's decision to call an election. It proceeds in five parts. First, it presents a brief list of the conditions in which elections have been held this century. Second, it studies the extent to which prime ministers alone decide to dissolve. Third, it considers whether the government's control over timing, and its ability to manipulate the economy, virtually guarantee electoral success. Fourth, it discusses the relationship between a government's popularity in the opinion polls and its economic performance. Finally, it discusses Mrs Thatcher's decisions about dissolution in 1983 and 1987.

---

* First presented a conference on the media and the 1987 British General Election (University of Essex, October 1987).

272

DISSOLUTIONS

Dissolutions in the British parliament in the twentieth century have fallen into one of five categories.

The first consists of elections called because the parliament is at or near the end of its life. In this case the element of choice for the prime minister is virtually non-existent. The elections of 1906, 1918, 1929, 1945, 1950 and 1964 fall into this category.

The second is where the government lacks an assured parliamentary majority or has such a small one that it can no longer be confident of conducting business. The elections of 1951, 1966 and October 1974 were examples of appeals to the voter to produce a party majority sufficient to allow for losses in by-elections, absence of members from key votes, and possible defections. In many West European states coalition or minority government is frequent and the lack of a majority for one party is not regarded as furnishing an adequate pretext for a dissolution. In the twentieth century, however, the view has grown that a British government must have a majority sufficient to 'run' parliament.

The concept of a 'working' majority, however, has altered in recent years. In 1951 Mr Attlee regarded a majority of six as inadequate and in 1964 Mr Wilson's majority of four (later whittled down to two) was similarly regarded. But in October 1974 Mr Wilson's initial majority of three (which had disappeared by 1976) allowed the government to continue for nearly 5 years. The major change between 1950 and October 1974 was the fragmentation of the opposition, so that the Labour government's lead over the Conservative Party was a comfortable forty-two compared with seventeen in 1950.

The third category is the defeat of the government on a vote of confidence or on a major measure in the House of Commons. Although a frequent occurrence in the nineteenth century, such defeats are now regarded as abnormal, because of the governing party's control of the House of Commons. The only occasions in the twentieth century when the government has lost such a vote and then dissolved have been in 1924 and 1979 – and both were minority Labour governments. Such an occasion is the classic justification of the dissolution power – to end parliamentary deadlock, clarify electoral choice, and produce a working majority. But, as in the first category, the prime minister of the day has little effective choice over timing.

The fourth category occurs when a changed political situation, perhaps the emergence of a salient new issue or a change of prime minister, prompts a government to seek a fresh mandate. In 1910 Asquith dissolved Parliament, seeking a mandate to reform the House of Lords; in 1923 Baldwin did so because he wanted to introduce a protective tariff, contrary to the policy promised by his party in the 1922 election. In 1931 the leaders of the newly formed National Government also called an election to seek 'a doctor's mandate' to tackle the economic crisis. In 1955 Eden wasted little time after his appointment in calling an election. One might also want to add Mr Heath's dissolution of parliament in February 1974. The oil crisis and miners' strike made it essential, in his view, for the government to make a fresh start backed by a clear expression of public support. But, as Asquith, Baldwin and Heath found, there are dangers in calling single-issue elections.

The fifth and final category is where a prime minister calls an election because he judges that this is the most opportune moment to maximise an already comfortable parliamentary majority. It is important to note, however, that a prime minister will want to time a dissolution well into the second half of the parliament for fear of being accused of 'scuttling'. In the dissolutions of 1959, 1970, 1983, and 1987 the parliaments still had about a year or a little more to run, there was no significant change in the political situation requiring a fresh mandate, and the government had a comfortable parliamentary majority. The 'political' aspects of such a decision are discussed further below.

PRIME MINISTERIAL CHOICE?

The right of the prime minister to recommend a dissolution of parliament to the monarch is frequently advanced as an illustration of, among other things, his or her power. Acknowledgement that the decision is exclusively the prime minister's prerogative is a recent constitutional development. In the nineteenth century the cabinet usually made a collective decision to approach the monarch. Lloyd George was an innovator in this as in other respects, with his unilateral request for dissolution in 1918. Baldwin's request for a dissolution in 1923 was much criticised but it was already recognised that it was the prime minister's decision.[1]

In a general election a prime minister always has the most to lose – office itself. It is one of the loneliest decisions he can make. He can lose all or his government may simply be returned. The responsibility cannot be shared. If the party loses, his position will be damaged, while that of his rivals for the leadership may improve. The loss of office by Sir Alec Douglas-Home in 1964, Mr Heath in 1974 and Mr Callaghan in 1979 effectively terminated their leaderships of their respective political parties, and Mr Wilson's defeat in 1970 severely undermined his authority in the party.

Not surprisingly, prime ministers frequently seek the advice of heavyweight colleagues – particularly Chancellors about the likely state of the economy – and have generally sought to dilute their own personal responsibility.[2] In 1945 an election was already 5 years overdue and after Labour withdrew from the wartime coalition a speedy dissolution was almost inevitable. Churchill invited ministers to write to him with suggestions for a suitable date and conducted a semi-public debate on the matter. In 1950 and 1951 Mr Attlee consulted most of his senior cabinet ministers. However, Eden's decision in 1955 was largely his own, and in 1959 Mr Macmillan shared his thoughts with very few ministers. In April 1964 Sir Alec Douglas-Home sought the advice of party officials and ministers over timing. The cabinet was split between June and October, but officials were overwhelmingly in favour of the later date. As a result Sir Alec publicly stated that there would be no election before October 1964. By then he had no option. In 1970 Mr Wilson invited the cabinet to Chequers in April to discuss his idea of a summer election.

In December 1973 and January 1974 Mr Heath listened to the views of ministers, Central Office directors, regional officials, and back-benchers. Most of the advice suggested an early election, timed for 7 February. In early January the party's private opinion pollster, Opinion Research Centre, suggested that a late January or early February election would offer a good chance of victory but that a later one would be more risky, as the issue of the miners' challenge to the government might be overtaken by other issues. Mr Heath listened to the advice, ignored it, dissolved later, and lost.

In the summer recess of 1978 there was general expectation of an autumn election. Mr Callaghan expressed his willingness to listen to the views of colleagues on the matter. Some of the input, notably about the bad state of Labour's organisation (hardly unusual) and private opinion poll reports about Labour's position in the marginals, were discouraging. At the end of August Mr Callaghan sought the views of the cabinet about election timing: a majority favoured

October. When the cabinet met again on 17 September it expected Mr Callaghan to name the date. Instead, he declared that there would be no election. The decision to delay was clearly his own but he had already discussed his views with two prominent ministers, Mr Foot and Mr Healey, neither of whom dissented from his view that Labour was unlikely to improve its position in an October poll.[3] When the election was announced on 29 March 1979, after a defeat in the Commons, Mr Callaghan had little control over the date.

In 1983 and 1987 Mrs Thatcher consulted widely with key party officials and senior ministers. From May 1982, in the wake of the Falklands victory, the government enjoyed a handsome lead in the opinion polls. In March 1983 the party chairman Cecil Parkinson effectively persuaded Mrs Thatcher of the case for June 1983, when inflation was likely to be at its lowest and the unemployment figures not yet boosted by the summer school-leavers. In late March 1987 Mrs Thatcher and the Cabinet discussed possible election dates and the choice was effectively between June and October (see below).

The record seems clear. Although the decision is ultimately the Prime Minister's, most prime ministers are concerned to consult and to be seen to consult senior colleagues. As far as possible a prime minister wants to arrive at a consensus. The decision about timing is tied up with problems of party management and cabinet management.

Prime ministers are also increasingly concerned to prepare public opinion for an election. In 1983 and 1987 speculation among the media was allowed to develop to such an extent that the outcome was widely expected for a month or so in advance of the actual decision. On both occasions Mrs Thatcher was able to announce her request for a dissolution by mentioning the need to curb the speculation and uncertainty, features which she and her office had done a good deal to encourage, and little to dampen.

INCUMBENCY ADVANTAGES

The main resource a British government possesses is control of election timing. In theory this allows it to adopt a more efficient scheduling of pre-campaign efforts, such as purchasing poster sites and press advertisements. In 1959 the Conservative government had a massive advertising campaign 6 weeks ahead of the dissolution. In opposition, the Labour Party machine wrongly anticipated an election in 1963 and spent heavily on advertising for this. But even in office a party may throw away the advantage of timing. In 1970 the Labour machine mistakenly planned its publicity (and spending) for an October, not a June, election. In 1978 the Labour Party confidently expected Mr Callaghan (on the grounds that he had not said anything to the contrary) to call an election in the autumn, and spent £200,000 in advertising over the summer.

A second political advantage of incumbency is the ability to make news. In the run-up to the 1987 election the government's position was strengthened by a tax-cutting budget in March, increased spending on health and education and buoyant economic statistics. In 1983 and 1987 Mrs Thatcher made eve-of-election overseas tours which gained extensive publicity. In January 1983 she visited the Falklands, evoking memories of the successful war 9 months earlier. Between March 28 and 2 April 1987 she was given a triumphant reception by Mr Gorbachev in the Soviet Union, confirming her position as a successful international stateswoman. Both visits created numerous photo opportunities. This is something of an old trick. In 1959 Harold Macmillan, wearing the mantle of international statesman, also made a well-covered visit to the USSR. Mr Gaitskell tried to follow suit in 1959 but he had to cut the tour short when Mr Macmillan called an election. During the summer recess of 1974 the minority Labour government constantly made headlines – and conveyed an impression of activity of a sort – by publishing a series of White Papers outlining its plans for industry, land, pensions and devolution. In the first 4 months of 1983 Mrs Thatcher gave sixteen interviews, compared to the usual four for such a period.

A British government can also time an election to take advantage of events and announcements that are bound to occur in the campaign. Ever since the 'bad' news of the balance of payments deficit 2 days before polling day in June 1970, and the series of unfavourable official statistics released during the February 1974 campaign, government election advisers have been careful to make a prior assessment of the dates of routine monthly statistics on prices, unemployment and trade, and of their possible electoral impact. Party headquarters are now expected to have calendar charts for different target election dates, covering the dates of key events and publication of key statistics. Election planning means 'no surprises'. A notorious attempt to 'manage' these statistics was made in September 1974 by the Labour Chancellor of the Exchequer, Denis Healey. He used the 2.2 per cent increase in retail prices within the May/August quarter to claim that the annualised inflation figure was only 8.4 per cent. This took account of one-off factors such as the government's July reductions in VAT, rate relief for householders and the seasonal fall in foodstuffs. In 1982 and 1983 the Conservative government reduced the official unemployment figures by omitting those looking for work but not claiming benefit and then removing from the register those aged 60 or more.

Government ministers time their economic measures to have maximum electoral impact and, where they are able, choose the date of the election to coinicide with economic 'good times'. The effects of the electoral–economic cycle are seen in the general tendency for rates of unemployment and inflation to level off or fall in election years and for real wages to increase sharply in the 6 months before general elections. Compared to previous years in the parliament, inflation was falling in the election years 1959, 1966, 1979 and 1983. It was rising gently in 1964, 1979 and 1987 and rising steeply in 1970 and February 1974. In Britain there have been sharp increases in real disposable incomes in most election years; usually followed by a sharp slowdown or even decline in mid-parliament. This was the pattern in 1954–55, 1958–59, 1970, 1983 and 1987. Only in February 1974, an unexpected election, was the run-up accompanied by a fall in real disposable incomes.[4] There was also a sharp increase in 1978, a good launch for an October 1978 election, but not for the May 1979 one. Richard Crossman, a minister in the 1964–70 Labour governments, confessed in 1971: 'The main fact is that we won the 1966 election by choosing the moment of wage inflation before the prices had really been felt to rise and obviously we were seeking to do it again in 1970'.

The record of post-war general elections hardly supports the thesis that incumbents are overwhelmingly favoured or the contrary claim that there is a swing of the pendulum against the government. Of the twelve cases of dissolution since 1945 the government has won seven and lost five. Sir Alec Douglas-Home, Mr Heath and Mr Callaghan each dissolved once and lost. Sir Anthony Eden, Mr Macmillan, and Mrs Thatcher (twice) were successful. Mr Attlee won one and lost one, and Mr Wilson lost one and won two. But of the seven successes, Attlee's 1950 victory was indecisive and he dissolved again after 19 months, and Wilson's two election successes in government were consolidations of earlier knife-edge results. Mrs Thatcher's clear victories were in large measure due to the divisions in the opposition parties. The record hardly bears out the claims

Table 15.1 Fate of incumbents in British general elections, 1950–87

Election year	Incumbent Party	Change in per cent vote
1950	Labour	−2.2
1951	Labour	+2.7
1955	Conservative	+1.7
1959	Conservative	−0.3
1964	Conservative	−6.0
1966	Labour	+3.8
1970	Labour	−4.9
1974 (Feb)	Conservative	−8.6
1974 (Oct)	Labour	+2.1
1979	Labour	−5.3
1983	Conservative	−1.5
1987	Conservative	−0.1

that the dice are very heavily loaded in the government's favour.

In the seven cases of a successful post-war dissolution, governments saw their share of the popular vote increase in only four elections – 1951 (+ 2.7 per cent), which Labour lost, 1955 (+ 1.7 per cent), 1966 (+ 3.8 per cent) and October 1974 (+2.1 per cent). The average change in share of the vote for incumbents has been a decline of 1.5 per cent, with the biggest falls being in February 1974 (8.5 per cent), 1964 (6 per cent) and 1979 (5.3 per cent) (see Table 15.1).

During the 1960s and 1970s the trend clearly worsened for the government. In part this was a consequence of the decline in support for each of the two main parties and the country's relatively declining economic performance. Of the four dissolutions in the 1970s the government of the day lost three and suffered an average fall of 4.5 per cent in its share of the vote compared with the previous election. Holding office was a disadvantage and between 1959 and 1983 no government was able to gain re-election after a near full-term of office. Of course, without the control of timing the losing governments might have done even worse. This probably applies to the Conservative dissolution in 1964 – so nearly a victory. But in February 1974 and 1979, the prime minister of the day simply got it wrong. Mr Heath's personal view after the election was that his mistake had been less in not going earlier than in calling an election at all.

An international comparison shows a mixed pattern. In the 1970s and early 1980s the dismissal of long-established government parties in Sweden, Norway and France encouraged speculation that governments everywhere were finding it more difficult, with the slow-down of economic growth, to get re-elected. Keynesian techniques of producing pre-election booms no longer worked. In fact, examination of the elections across Western states before and since 1968 show that governments were still as likely to be re-elected, although with a fall in their share of the vote. In the coalition governments of many West European states the election is usually more significant as a verdict on the relative standing of the parties in the governing coalition.[5]

Systems of proportional representation often have the effect of stabilising the legislature; they produce smaller changes in the parties' relative share of seats and governing parties have a better record of holding on to office.[6] By contrast, a swing of the pendulum against the government is more often found in Westminster systems which have the first-past-the-post electoral system. Note also that it is only in Westminster-type models that the prime minister effectively has the right to dissolve parliament.

CYCLES IN POPULARITY

Before deciding to call an election, governments have traditionally taken soundings about the public mood. Until recently they relied largely on by-elections, local elections and information from party organisers. Disraeli misread two successful by-elections in 1880 and Winston Churchill wrongly assumed that Lord Beaverbrook, as a press proprietor, would have expert knowledge of the public mood in 1945.

Since 1959 the major new factor has been the development of public and private opinion polls, although the party leaders are careful to consider them along with other sources of information. The gloomy opinion polls in 1963 were certainly important in convincing Sir Alec Douglas-Home to delay going to the country. When the polls turned around in favour of the government of the day in early 1970 and January 1974, they had some effect in convincing Mr Wilson's and Mr Heath's associates to call an election.

In both cases, however, the government enjoyed only a short-lived (and therefore perhaps fragile) lead in the polls. Private polls in the marginals by MORI in the summer of 1978 persuaded Mr Callaghan to soldier on and the pro-election advice (in spite of qualifications) from ORC failed to persuade Mr Heath to go earlier in January 1974. In both these cases the opinion polls were acting to reinforce the inclinations of the prime minister of the day.

Study of the opinion polls in the past two decades shows that there is something of a cyclical pattern in the popularity of a government.[7] Between 1947 and 1956 the electorate was fairly steady in its allegiance to the two main parties and the coming of a general election did little to disturb this pattern. Since then, however, governments have usually experienced a significant loss of support with corresponding huge leads for the opposition – regardless of how the economy performs – followed by a recovery as the election approaches. There were spectacular collapses in support for the government between 1957 and mid-1958, between late 1962 and mid-1964, and between December 1967 and December 1969. The Labour government trailed by double figures for most months between October 1976 and August 1977, recovered, and then fell away again in the first 4 months of 1979. The same happened to the Thatcher government between the end of 1980 and April 1982. In each of these cases there was a swing-back of support to the government of the day as the election approached. The one exception to this trend was Mr Callaghan's forced dissolution in 1979. The regular swing-back had occurred in 1978 but support fell away again at the turn of the year with the onset of the industrial disruption in the winter of discontent. The Falklands success in April 1982 helped to accelerate the recovery of support for the government of the day.

A good lead in the opinion polls may still not be sufficient to reassure a prime minister. An increasingly volatile electorate and the ability of election campaigns to switch votes can quickly change the poll readings. In 1970 the poll predictions were confounded and in every subsequent election until 1987 the party that started the campaign with a handsome lead saw it significantly reduced by election day; 1987 is an exception in that the government preserved its big lead to polling day.

But one may make too much of the influence of the electoral–economic cycle on the governing party's popularity. Other influences disturb a pure one-to-one relationship between changes in economic conditions and changes in the levels of party support.

Voters' expectations of economic benefits may be scaled down, a foreign crisis or another issue may become important, or the public's tolerance of levels of inflation or unemployment may change over time. The small changes in economic conditions in the 1960s and 1970s were accompanied by big changes in the parties' standing in the polls.

What seems more significant for the standing of the government than absolute levels of employment or inflation is the direction of the trends and how these affect the mood of the electorate. Robert Worcester of MORI reported an impressive positive correlation between Labour's lead over the SNP and Scottish voters' feeling of optimism about the future of the economy in the late 1970s. In the run-up to the election in 1983 the Conservative government gained from such optimism. During the 48 months of the 1983 parliament (between June 1983 and May 1987) there was a positive correlation of .450 between the government's popularity (MORI) and economic optimism, and between August 1986 and May 1987 it reached .938. In January 1987 a net 27 per cent expected economic conditions to improve over the next 12 months, rising to 38 per cent in April and 44 per cent in June.

THE 1987 DISSOLUTION

The background to Mrs Thatcher's timing of the 1987 election was remarkably similar to that in 1983. There was the same popular March budget, a successful overseas trip, good local election results, a big lead in the opinion polls, a favourable set of economic indicators, and a general expectation that June was the 'right time' to call an election. The encouragement of media speculation about an election was again important both in preparing public opinion for the event and testing (*via* opinion polls) the likely public mood. There was the same meeting of Mrs Thatcher and senior ministers at Chequers on the Sunday after the local elections, to confirm the decision.

The Alliance gain at Greenwich in February had certainly caused some Conservatives to think in terms of an election no earlier than October 1987. But when the Alliance bandwagon was not maintained, June became a popular option again. Although the favourable news in the opinion polls and on the economy encouraged party pressure for June, Mrs Thatcher refused to commit herself without the evidence of 'the biggest poll of all' – the local elections. Some ministers, including Lord Whitelaw, John Moore and Nigel Lawson, were believed to favour October, but by the time local results were out, they switched.

Mr Tebbit was widely credited with advocating an early (May or June) election. He was, however, more concerned with the party regularly scoring 40 per cent or above in the polls and having a lead of 6 or 7 per cent over the second party, and with gaining reassurance that an Alliance upsurge would not threaten too many Conservative seats. A consequence of the arrival of the Alliance as a significant third electoral party is that parties, particularly the Conservatives, have to make more complex calculations about electoral trends.

When senior ministers met Mrs Thatcher at Chequers on May 10 they were presented with a Central Office computer prediction – based on an analysis of local elections and private polls – for a ninety-four seat Conservative majority. Even allowing for an Alliance upsurge and some Conservative defections, it seemed impossible to lose. June it was to be. There was little discussion among ministers over the exact date; 4 June was excluded because of problems of clearing essential legislation through parliament and because it was a Jewish holiday; 18 June was also ruled out because the campaign would be too long and might allow an Alliance momentum. The natural date seemed to be 11 June; it would complete 4 years in the administration, the benefits of the budget tax cuts would be in voters' pockets, house mortgage cuts would be in effect, and the impression of the Moscow triumph would still be present.

As in 1983 the government called an election against a background of a remarkably favourable set of economic and political indicators. The five national polls (NOP, Gallup, Marplan, Harris for *Weekend World* and Harris for TV-AM) reporting in May before the election date was announced, averaged Conservatives 42 per cent, Labour 30.5 per cent and the Alliance 25.5 per cent. On Friday 10 May the bank rate was reduced to 9 per cent, the fourth cut in 2 months, and there were much publicised and optimistic reports about the economy from the CBI and Institute of Directors. Wage settlements were running at an annualised average 7.5 per cent compared to inflation at 4 per cent – representing a substantial increase in living standards for those in work. Interest rates were coming down and the unemployment figures fell for the eighth month in succession.

The prime minister's control of the dissolution is central to the claim that Britain has prime ministerial government. Lord Hailsham portrays the prime minister 'with his hand on the lever of dissolution, which he is free to operate at any moment of his choice'. The lever, combined with the opinion polls and manipulation of the economic electoral cycle, allegedly loads the electoral dice too heavily in favour of the government of the day.[8]

I am sceptical. The post-war record, with the exception of the Thatcher victories in 1983 and 1987, hardly bears it out. It is worth adding that the government was well placed for most of the 1983 parliament and its successes in 1983 and 1987 were in part a consequence of the divided opposition parties. Timing was not as crucial as participants have made out.[9] Even with fixed calendar elections there would still be scope for economic pump-priming and news management. There would still be electioneering in the last year of the parliament, the government tempted to postpone unpopular measures, and investors and others would hold off making decisions until the election was decided.

What calendar elections might prevent is the increasing tendency for government to tease the electorate with the prospect of an election. Ministers then plead that they call the election to put an end to the 'intolerable' uncertainty which holds up investment and other decisions. Anthony Bevins protested in *The Independent* in February 1987 that Mrs Thatcher was 'neutering' the Parliament: 'This Parliament is wasting away, dying before our eyes. The prime minister should be ashamed of herself'. Speculation about timing makes for good journalistic copy. Apart from that I am not sure that the absence of calendar elections makes much difference.

In a world of uncertainty, and with a lot to lose, prime ministers might follow certain guidelines in deciding when to seek a dissolution:

1 Prepare public opinion: the expectation of an election seems to produce a recovery in government popularity before an election.
2 If more than a year of the parliament remains and you have a good majority, justify your decision in terms of the national interest, e.g., the need to end uncertainty or to cope with changed circumstances.
3 Consult colleagues, so that they are implicated in the final decision. If you lose, the blame will be yours but the appearance or reality of consultation may help to deflect some of the criticism.
4 Ensure that the economic indicators are moving in a positive direction, but above all rely on the electorate's optimism that the economy will improve over the next 6 to 12 months.

5 Have a substantial lead in the opinion polls, over the opposition, for 6 months or more, so that the lead is not a flash in the pan.

According to the above guidelines the dissolutions of 1983 and 1987 were timed to perfection.

NOTES

1. J. Mackintosh, *The British Cabinet* (London: Stevens, 1962), p. 449.
2. See R. K. Alderman and J. A. Cross, 'The prime minister and the decision to dissolve', *Parliamentary Affairs*, 28, 1975, pp. 386–404.
3. See B. Donoughue, *Prime Minister* (London: Cape, 1987); and 'The winter of discontent', *Contemporary Record*, 1, 1987, pp. 34–44.
4. J. Alt, *The Politics of Economic Decline* (Cambridge University Press, 1978), p. 136.
5. See S. M. Lipset, 'No room for the ins: elections around the world', *Public Opinion* 5 October/November 1982, pp. 41–3.
6. See R. Rose and T. Mackie, *Incumbency in Government: Asset or Liability?* Studies in Public Policy, No. 54 (Glasgow: University of Strathclyde, 1980).
7. W. L. Miller and M. Mackie, 'The electoral cycle and the asymmetry of government and opposition popularity', *Political Studies*, 21, 1973, pp. 263–79.
8. 'The elective dictatorship', *The Listener*, 21 October 1976, p. 497.
9. At the Essex Conference Mr Tebbit claimed: 'The timing of an election is as important as the final campaign'. For Labour, Peter Mandelson stated: 'We could not overcome the problem of timing, enjoyed exclusively by the Conservatives'.

16 The Monarchy in Contemporary Political Culture*

POPULAR ATTITUDES TOWARDS THE MONARCHY

In view of the interest and emotion that the monarchy excites among social scientists as well as journalists, one might expect that the varied and sometimes contradictory hypotheses and speculations about the topic would have stimulated careful empirical examinations.[1] Such is not the case. There have been few attempts to specify the dimensions of attitudes to the monarchy,[2] or to test the relationships between these attitudes and other political orientations.[3] In an area as little documented and as charged with emotion as the monarchy, social scientists should move warily – but some move deferentially, and others aggressively. With unintended irony Edward Shils and Michael Young comment, 'Even the most eminent scholars lose their sureness of touch when they enter the presence of royalty'.[4]

The pre-eminence of the British Crown, both in antiquity and in social scientific discussions of the monarchy, makes it eminently reasonable to use British survey data here. The absence of questions about the monarchy in comparative survey studies which focus upon elections,[5] makes it necessary to rely upon survey data from a single country for intensive analysis. The data analysed here come from a specially designed survey of attitudes toward the monarchy among a random sample of the adult population of the city of Glasgow. This particular survey has three limitations. The first is that the data came from a single city, rather than from a nation-wide sample. This need not detract from validity; e.g. both the McKenzie and Silver and the Nordlinger studies of working-class deference,[6] were

* *Comparative Politics*, July 1976.

based upon community surveys. Secondly, the total size of the sample was limited by resources; the response rate was 60 per cent, yielding a total of 416 interviews.[7] Although this limits the analysis of sub-groups of the population, the questions of first importance in an uncharted field concern the overall distribution of attitudes. Thirdly, the fact that the survey was conducted in February–March 1968 is a limitation only if there have been substantial changes in attitudes toward the monarchy in the intervening period.[8] It is reasonable to assume that no change has occurred in popular attitudes toward the monarchy, because the chief royal events since the survey have been favourable; the investiture of Prince Charles as Prince of Wales and the wedding of Princess Anne.[9]

Any measure of popular opinion toward the monarchy immediately raises questions about the relative importance of attitudes toward a particular reigning incumbent and the persisting office. The institutional significance of the monarchy, like that of any leadership role in politics, is independent of the attitudes inspired by an individual incumbent, whether male or female, young or old, extrovert or withdrawn, moral or libertine. For example, Walter Bagehot's classic statement of the significance of the British Crown was not stimulated by a popular or venerated personality but prompted by 'the actions of a retired widow' (Queen Victoria in the least popular part of her reign) and 'an unemployed youth' (the loose-living Prince of Wales, later Edward VII).[10] The hereditary nature of the monarchy can make everyone involved in the actions of the royal family particularly sensitive to the importance of maintaining 'brand loyalty' to the family business, the Crown.

Attachment to the office of the monarch, rather than to the individual, was unambiguously demonstrated during the abdication crisis of Edward VIII. For 26 years prior to his accession in January 1936, Edward was the immediate heir to the throne. As Prince of Wales, he had received a generally favourable press, and was considered suited to the 'modern' requirements of the monarchy. Yet in spite of his personal popularity *and* his status as King, Edward VIII was unable to convince the government of the day that he should be allowed to make a morganatic marriage with Wallis Warfield Simpson, an American divorcee. The Conservative government of Stanley Baldwin wished to protect the institution of the monarchy from associations with 'disreputable' (or, one would now say, permissive) ways of life. Edward VIII was forced to abdicate as King to make the marriage of his choice. His younger brother, the scarcely known and shy Duke of York, immediately stepped into his elder brother's role, becoming King George VI. No royalist movement arose proclaiming loyalty to Edward VIII as the 'true' King. *The Times* noted that the abdication strengthened the principle of constitutional monarchy, for it made clear that the Crown was to be viewed 'not in terms of personal affection for an individual but in the prosaic terms of a working institution'.[11]

To emphasise the importance of the institution rather than the personality of the monarchy, questions in the Glasgow survey consistently referred to the Queen, rather than to Elizabeth II. Even if some respondents thought of other incumbents when asked about the Queen, they would have almost inevitably been thinking about the same type of person, the 'good, dutiful monarch', for a question asking who was the first King or Queen that respondents remembered found that only 10 per cent first named a 'free-living' King (Edward VIII, 3 per cent: Edward VII, 7 per cent). By contrast, 81 per cent recalled a dutiful monarch: Queen Victoria, 11 per cent; George V, 43 per cent; George VI, 25 per cent; and Elizabeth II, 2 per cent.

By the standards of political opinion surveys, the monarchy study found that respondents had a relatively high level of knowledge of the subject. For example, only 9 per cent could not remember who was the monarch when they were a child, compared to 24 per cent who could not recall either parent's party identification. In answers to questions asking for the names of the Queen's four children, 34 per cent of Glasgow respondents named all four, and another 39 per cent could name three. By comparison, 56 per cent of a national British sample could name three or more party leaders, 17 per cent less than could name at least three royal children. Similarly, 20 per cent of a national sample could not think offhand of the name of any party leader, as against 8 per cent of Glasgow respondents unable to name any of the royal children.[12]

Whatever the question taken as an indicator, most people frequently express a positive evaluation of the Queen. For example, when asked if there is there is anything they particularly like about the Queen, 71 per cent can find at least one favourable attribute to mention. The most frequently approved characteristics of the Queen are her agreeable personality, 46 per cent; the conscientious way she performs her work, 27 per cent; and her rôle as a mother and moral example, 21 per cent. By comparison, only 16 per cent voiced criticisms when asked what they disliked about the Queen. Among criticisms, the most frequently cited are: dislike of the cost and

Table 16.1 The evaluation of political rôles

Rôle	Importance Very important %	Important %	T %	Performs role Very well %	Well %	T %
Prime minister	59	32	91	24	38	61*
MPs	34	56	90	12	54	66
Top civil servants	32	48	80	17	52	70
The Queen	22	32	54	—	88 —	88†

*The question asked for an evaluation of 'whoever is Prime Minister', rather than naming the incumbent, Harold Wilson.
†The two positive replies were merged in coding; the percentage refers to all identifying some royal rôle.

status, mentioned by 7 per cent, and dislike of the Queen's aloof personality, 6 per cent.

When questions are directed to the explicitly political rôle of the Queen, positive replies are again usual, but less frequently so than to questions about personality. This is because a larger proportion express no opinion about the Queen's political role. When people were asked whether the Queen did her job well or badly, 66 per cent said she did it well, as against 3 per cent saying she did her job badly; the remainder could not ascribe any specific political duties to the Queen. The rôle assigned to the Queen in government is seen as of limited significance. When asked what part the Queen plays in the government of the country, 86 per cent with views said she was a figurehead, signing laws and doing what the government directs her to do; 14 per cent with opinions saw the Queen as a generally steadying influence upon government.

The popular assessment of the Queen's political importance is best seen by comparing popular evaluation of the monarch's political duties with popular evaluations of other major figures in government. The Queen is seen as much less important than the Prime Minister, MPs or top civil servants (Table 1). The finding is confirmed by a contemporaneous nationwide Gallup Poll survey, which found that the royal family was ranked tenth out of twelve in influence upon the country, with 38 per cent giving it great or some influence. More influential institutions included business, trade unions, the press and the Church, as well as politicians; the respondents are only the leaders of the armed services and the voter's own role was seen as less influential than that of the royal family.[13] But by comparison with other political figures, the Queen is more often seen as doing well the ceremonial tasks assigned her. In other words, the Queen is a good actor of a minor part in a play. This is better than playing a major role badly. One cannot, however, judge the whole of government by the performance of a single minor actor.

Because so few people voice criticisms of the monarchy as an individual or as a political figure, any attempt to analyse differences in attitudes toward the Queen risks creating a pro/con dichotomy where there tends to be consensus. The Queen is a figure who unites rather than divides the British people. A study of those who reject monarchy would either be a deviant case analysis of a small group of republicans, or result from the confusion of criticisms of particular features of the monarchy, e.g. its cost, with something very different, rejection of the institution as a whole. The measures of differentiation that follow distinguish between those who show a positive attitude and those who show apathy but not antagonism to the monarchy.

To obtain a meaningful assessment of the positive value that each individual assigns the monarchy, respondents were asked: 'Some people say we really don't need a Queen; others disagree. What do you think?' A total of 69 per cent said that Britain did need a Queen, and 27 per cent that the country did not; only 4 per cent were 'don't knows'.[14] In this paper, those who say the country needs a Queen will be regarded as positively valuing the Queen, and those saying the country doesn't need a Queen as not valuing the monarchy highly.

The fact that the reigning monarch is a woman, rather than an ex-sailor like her two predecessors and her husband, might be considered to enhance the emotional appeal of the Queen. To measure emotional orientations, respondents were asked: 'Do you feel proud or not proud because we have a Queen?' The replies showed that 16 per cent felt very proud, 49 per cent proud, and 21 per cent not proud; 14 per cent were 'don't knows'. The great majority of respondents thus feel some pride in the monarchy, but it is not especially strong. Having a Queen is a source of emotional satisfaction, but the same could be said for many other things, e.g. a favoured team's victory in a European football competition, or an election result contrary to what opinion polls had forecast. Unlike

Table 16.2 Political and emotional evaluations of the Queen

	Proud	Not proud	Don't know	Total
Queen needed	80	9	11	69
Not needed	28	48	24	27
Don't know	55	40	5	5
Total	65	21	24	

persons who occasionally gain headlines by criticising the Queen or by assaulting the critics of the Queen,[15] ordinary people are relatively unemotional in the face of criticism of the royal family. While four-fifths say that they sometimes hear such criticism, only 30 per cent say they dislike such statements: the majority reflect indifference. Respect for traditional values of free speech is at least as important as respect for the monarch.

Political and emotional attitudes toward the Queen are related in expected ways. Those who think that Britain needs a Queen are overwhelmingly proud of their monarch. Among the minority thinking a Queen is not needed, less than one-third show pride in the monarch (Table 2). Taken together, the answers emphasise that confirmed monarchists, proud of the Queen and believing royalty necessary, outnumber the strict utilitarians, feeling no pride or need for a Queen, by a margin of more than four to one.

SOCIAL INFLUENCES UPON POPULAR ATTITUDES

Because popular attitudes toward the monarchy are not unanimous, one can investigate the extent to which differences in the felt need for a Queen or pride in the Queen are related to differences in an individual's position in society. One might hypothesise that positive attitudes toward the monarchy vary with the age, sex, or party loyalty of an individual. Insofar as positive attitudes toward the monarchy are distributed equally in all parts of society, one can say that there is a common regard for the Queen among all classes and conditions of people.

Bagehot provides the classic statement of the reason why sections of the population should differ in their attitudes toward monarchy, and toward the political system of which it is a part.[16] At a time when there was a great gulf between the education of the governing class and the four years of schooling of the mass of the populace, the monarchy represented government to the masses in its dignified, theatrical form: only a traditional form of government was assumed to be comprehensible to the masses. Members of the governing class would understand that the monarchy was not part of the efficient machinery of government – but they risked the loss of popular allegiance if they disabused the masses of traditional beliefs. While the balance of tradition and modernity has clearly shifted in Britain, both elements can still be found in the political culture.[17] It is appropriate to test the following hypothesis.

1 Positive reaction to the Queen is Most Often Found Among the More Traditional Groups Within Society

The operational indicators of membership in a more traditional group are by no means easy to specify. Therefore, a variety of social conditions that are often cited as part of a traditional attachment will be examined for potential influence.

The survey provides limited evidence to support Hypothesis 1. Younger persons (i.e. those below 40) are less likely by 15 per cent than their elders to see a need for a Queen and, by 16 per cent, to feel pride in their Queen. In both instances, however, a majority of younger people show positive responses to the monarch. Women are more likely than men to favour the monarchy, but the differences are again limited: 9 per cent more see a need and 14 per cent more feel pride in a Queen. Education discriminates even less. When respondents are divided into two groups, the minority who have passed a school-leaving examination and the majority with only the minimum of state education, the less educated and, potentially, the more traditionally oriented, are 6 per cent more likely to think a monarchy needed, and 9 per cent more likely to feel pride in a Queen.

Because the religious animosities of Ireland can also be found in Glasgow, findings about religiosity and attitudes toward the monarchy cannot be automatically generalised. The Catholic quarter of the city's population would be expected to be less in favour of the British Crown, because of historic links with Republican Ireland.

Similarly, Protestants would be expected to be more pro-monarchy, as their Ulster kin have been. The survey confirms expectations. Among Protestants, 9 per cent more see a need for a Queen than do Catholics, and 17 per cent more have pride in the Queen. The different rate of church-going among Protestants and Catholics requires a control for religion before analysing the effect of church-going. Within each religious denomination, church-goers are more likely to see a need for a Queen; the difference is 10 per cent among Catholics and 8 per cent among Protestants. Church-going Protestants are more likely to feel pride in the Queen than non-church-goers, by a margin of 8 per cent, but church-going Catholics are less likely to feel pride in the Queen than non-church-goers, by 14 per cent. Those who say they have no religion (13 per cent of all respondents) are least likely to regard a Queen as necessary, or have pride in a monarch. But a majority of secular respondents none the less gives a positive response to each question.

Critics of the monarchy in Britain and elsewhere have emphasised the association of royalty with more 'right-wing' (i.e. conservative) social, economic and political groups. Glaswegians see the Queen as a political Conservative. When asked what party the Queen would vote for if she had a vote, only 15 per cent were 'don't knows'; 70 per cent saw her voting Conservative, as against 4 per cent Labour. Both general argument and specific circumstances therefore suggest the following hypothesis.

2 Individuals Identifying With Groups Associated With the Monarchy will be more Ready to React Positively to the Monarchy

In Frank Parkin's words, the monarchy embodies 'values which are in close accord with the ideology of Conservatism and which, conversely, are out of harmony with the value system of Socialism'.[18]

Political party preferences and attitudes toward the monarchy are correlated. Among Conservative supporters, 87 per cent said a Queen was needed; among Labour, 70 per cent, and among Scottish Nationalists, the proportion was 57 per cent. Similarly, 91 per cent of Conservatives, 76 per cent of Labour voters and 63 per cent of SNP voters said they felt pride in having a Queen. The lesser readiness of SNP supporters to respond positively to the monarchy is consistent with the 'protest' nature of the party's appeal. The SNP is not a Republican party; it wishes an independent Scotland to give allegiance to the Queen as head of the Commonwealth, a position like that of Australia or New Zealand.

Social class is less linked with attitudes toward the monarchy than is party. Manual workers are only 3 per cent less likely to see a need for a Queen than the middle class; they are 3 per cent more likely to take pride in the Queen. Among members of trade unions, 3 per cent fewer thought a Queen was needed, and 9 per cent less felt particular pride in a Queen. The plurality of respondents who said that classes could get along with each other are more inclined, by 14 per cent, to see a need for a Queen than are the 29 per cent who saw the classes in conflict. A similar tendency is found regarding pride in the monarchy. But even among those who see classes in conflict on what was once 'red' Clydeside a majority (59 per cent) think a Queen necessary, and 53 per cent feel pride in their monarch.

The differences identified in the preceding paragraphs are differences of degree, not kind. In all of the social categories mentioned, *an absolute majority* of respondents felt a need for a Queen, and also showed pride in having a Queen. The relatively limited influence of standard socio–economic attributes suggests a *Common Regard* hypothesis.

3 Among all Social Groups There is a Positive Reaction to the Monarchy

The proposition does not assume unanimous endorsement for everything that the monarchy symbolises. It asserts that those who deviate from support for the monarchy are not clustered within any particular social or economic group within society.

The hypothesis can be tested in a precise manner by the use of AID (Automatic Interaction Detector) multivariate statistical analysis. AID divides a population initially into two groups, according to the social characterisitic that maximises the proportion of persons favouring the Queen in one category, and minimises this proportion in the other. Each of the two dichotomised groups is, in turn, subdivided into two groups, according to the attribute that most differentiates the respondents in their view of the monarchy. The process is repeated in a successive series of branching operations until no significant amount of variation can be explained.[19] In so far as social determinants are important in shaping attitudes toward the monarchy, the AID analysis should explain a relatively high proportion of the variance in attitudes. In so far as the Common

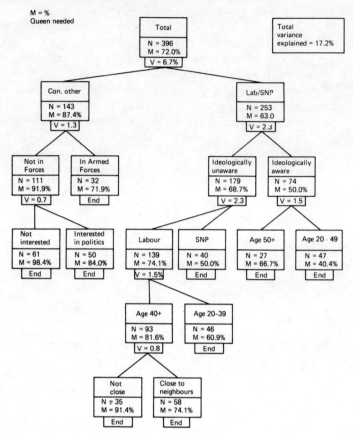

Figure 16.1 An AID analysis of social structure and need for a Queen

Regard hypothesis holds, then social characteristics will explain a small proportion of variance.

Figures 16.1 and 16.2 show the limited extent to which social characteristics influence attitudes toward the Queen, thus confirming the Common Regard hypothesis. Of the variance in the perceived need for a Queen, 82.8 per cent is unexplained by social characteristics; 80.6 per cent of the variance in emotional pride in the Queen is unexplained by social characteristics. Of the 21 social characteristics[20] included in the AID analysis, only one – party choice – explains as much as 5 per cent of the total variance in need for a Queen. Among Conservatives in the tree in Figure 16.1 the only other noteworthy influence is service in the armed forces; those

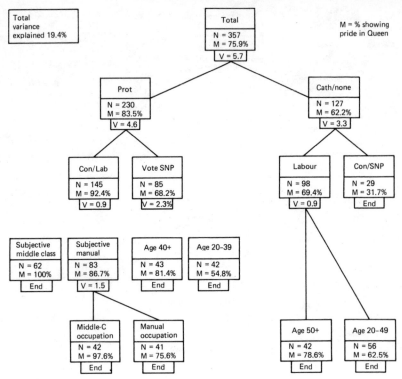

Figure 16.2 An AID analysis of social structure and pride in the Queen

who have done military service are less likely to see a need for a Queen. The patriotic risk of dying for Queen and country appears to have a slightly negative effect upon those experiencing risk. Among those favouring Labour or the SNP, less favourable attitudes toward the monarchy are found among those with a minimum ideological awareness, that is, an inability to think of politics in terms of left and right. The remaining divisions refer to distinctions already identified above.

Religion is of first importance in determining whether or not a person feels pride in the Queen, explaining 5.7 per cent of the initial variance in Figure 16.2. Party choice was almost as important initially, and emerges as significant in subsequent branches of the tree analysis. Since Labour- and Conservative-voting Protestants differ from their SNP co-religionists in pride in the Queen, it is reasonable to find the former group subsequently subdivided by class differences. Age differences also appear of some consequence, with younger sub-groups less likely to show positive pride in the Queen.

In order to reject the Common Regard hypothesis, one must show that there are groups within society where a negative view of the monarchy is the norm. The data in Figures 16.1 and 16.2 permit a precise test of this condition, for the end groups in the branches of the tree consist of individuals who combine all the social attributes signified at each of their preceding branches. A total of eight end groups are identified by the AID analysis of the perceived need for a Queen (Figure 16.1). In seven of these eight end groups, at least half the respondents state that a Queen is necessary. At one extreme, 98 per cent of Conservatives without military service and not interested in politics say that a Queen is needed. At the other extreme, among ideologically-aware Labour or SNP voters age 20 to 49, 40 per cent say that a Queen is needed. The most extreme pro-monarchy group is more nearly homogeneous than the least pro-monarchy group. It is also larger. The one group in which the majority think the Queen is not necessary constitutes but 12 per cent of the total sample.

The AID analysis of pride in the Queen (Figure 16.2) also produces eight end groups. Once again, in seven of these groupings, at least half the respondents express pride in a Queen. In the second largest end group, consisting of Conservative or Labour Protestants who see themselves as middle class, 100 per cent (N = 62) express pride in the Queen. In only one end group – Catholics who favoured the SNP or the Conservative parties – did less than half (32 per cent) show a positive pride in the Queen. The category almost certainly includes some Glaswegians whose Irish Republican sympathies would be triggered by a survey about England's Queen. It constitutes but 8 per cent of all respondents.

While the analysis confirms the commonplace assumption of social scientists that social groups differ in their attitudes toward the monarchy, what is consistently most important is the small size of these differences. Moreover, the most important influences – Irish Catholicism and support for the Scottish National Party – are peculiar to Scotland, and unlikely to be replicated in England. The relative unimportance of social determinants or conventional political influences is not surprising, however, for all social groups within Britain, including Labour voters, have been socialised to favour the monarchy, thus producing a Common Regard for the Queen.

THE POLITICAL CONSEQUENCES OF POPULAR ATTITUDES

A major reason for political scientists, as well as biographers of Freud[21], to write about the monarchy is that attitudes toward a monarch are significant for the political culture as well as significant in individual or social psychology. Bagehot provides the classic argument for the political importance of the dignified and theatrical appeal of the monarchy to win 'loyalty and confidence' for a regime, a necessary precondition for efficient governors to 'employ that homage in the work of government'.[22] Writing in a different historical context, Max Weber similarly argued the importance of a monarch to sustain political authority: 'Despite his lack of parliamentary power, the constitutional monarch is preserved, and above all, his mere existence and his charisma guarantee the legitimacy of the existing social and property order, since decisions are carried out in his name'.[23]

Contemporary social scientists have been equally ready to argue the political importance of monarchy, whether writing specifically about Britain or more generally.[24] The reasons advanced vary with the context. In the words of Almond and Verba, it is assumed that political allegiance requires an individual to have 'a balance between instrumental and affective orientations to politics'.[25] In a celebration of the Queen's Coronation in 1953, Edward Shils and Michael Young portray the monarch as playing 'a part in the creation and maintenance of moral consensus' upon which political authority rests, helping 'to weld the Labour Party and its following firmly into the moral framework of the national life'.[26] S. M. Lipset endorses a similar view concerning another stratum of society: 'The preservation of the monarchy has apparently retained for these nations the loyalty of the aristocratic, traditionalist and clerical sectors of the population which resented increased democratization and equalitarianism'.[27] The influence of monarchy upon political authority is also accepted by those who react against royalty.[28] Thus, many different theorists subscribe to the following statement.

4 Those who React Positively to the Monarchy are Also Most Likely to Endorse the Authority of Their Regime

Nowhere in the Anglo-American literature is there a statement of the royalist hypothesis, that is, that support for a monarchy shows disaffection from contemporary forms of representative government. Because political authority has two components – diffuse support for the institutions of a regime, and compliance with its basic political laws[29] – hypothesis 4 must be tested with several sets of questions.

Diffuse support for political authority is an abstract concept, hardly ever discussed in colloquial language in a society with a history of fully legitimate government, such as Britain. It is thus difficult to measure by questionnaire techniques. In one attempt to elucidate a general attitude, respondents were asked: 'Regardless of the party in power, what do you think of our system of government by Parliament and Cabinet?' The replies could be classified into four groups: exclusively favourable, 50 per cent; mixed, 9 per cent; exclusively unfavourable, 31 per cent; and no opinion, 10 per cent. The positive comments about the system of government were usually clear, e.g. fairness, justness, the best form of government, etc. The negative responses tended to be vague, e.g. don't think much of it. Among those who saw a need for the Queen, 9 per cent more expressed unqualified approval of the system by comparison with those who felt no need. Among those proud of having a Queen, 15 per cent more expressed unqualified approval of the political system. These two tests indicate a tendency for pro-monarchy views to correlate with general approval of the system of government. But the overall effect is limited, for 47 per cent of those considering a Queen necessary do not give unqualified approval to the system, and the same is true of 46 per cent expressing pride in the Queen.

As a second measure of support, each person was asked: 'Can you think of any country that has a better system of government?' This question avoids the problem of asking ordinary individuals to grapple with theoretical abstractions. A total of 70 per cent responded with a clear-cut 'No', and 23 per cent named another country of a Western democratic character, e.g. America, Scandinavia, Switzerland or Australia. The answers did not reflect a desire for a completely different type of government, but rather for a government better in a limited number of respects. Among the minority who regarded another country as better than Britain, 55 per cent thought a Queen necessary, and 44 per cent were proud of the Queen. These figures were, respectively, 18 per cent and 28 per cent less than the pro-monarchy sentiments of those regarding Britain as the best government in the world.

Positive attitudes toward the monarchy can correlate with support for the régime for two very different reasons. In some theories of the monarchy, support for the Queen is expected to supplement other justifications for endorsing authority, adding an emotional appeal. Another formulation regards the monarchy as a substitute for other justifications of authority, influencing those who respond to emotional rather than legal or national appeals. Each respondent was asked whether he agreed or disagreed with six different statements sometimes advanced to justify support for the system of government: 'It's the best form of government the people want. It's good because it's traditional. We've got to accept it whatever we think. It's the best kind of government we know. It usually provided the right things for people. It's the best kind of government in the world. It's the kind of government the people want'. An average of 54 per cent endorsed each of these statements. The replies support the supplementation hypothesis. Those who feel a Queen is needed endorsed an average of 3.5 additional reasons for supporting the British system of government: those who did not, 2.5 additional reasons. Persons with pride in the Queen averaged 3.0 reasons for supporting the system, as against 2.5 reasons favoured by those without pride in their monarch.

Political authority requires citizens to comply with basic political laws. In Britain, law enforcement is ceremonially linked to symbols of monarchy. The courts are the Queen's courts, crimes are crimes against the Queen's peace rather than against the state, and laws are not cited by anything as prosaic as calendar years, but by the year of the monarch's reign in which they were adopted. Yet, in extreme circumstances, loyalty to the Queen is cited by those who defy political authority. The Rhodesian government of Ian Smith saw itself as 'ultra-loyal', upholding the British Constitution even when unilaterally declaring independence of Westminster because the British government of the day ignored its wishes. Two days before its defiance of Westminster, the members of the government wrote to assure the Queen: 'We, your Ministers, wish respectfully to convey to your Majesty, both on behalf of all the peoples in our country and on our own behalf, our constant loyalty to your Majesty'.[30] The proclamation of independence similarly pledged loyalty and ended, 'God Save the Queen'. The history of Protestant politics in Ireland is replete with examples of the activities of 'ultra-Loyalists' defying elected governments while asserting allegiance to the Crown.[31]

To test popular predispositions to comply with basic political laws, the monarchy survey asked whether there are any laws that a self-respecting person would not have to obey. A total of 35 per cent said that in certain circumstances it was all right to break a law. The violations of the law most frequently endorsed by this group – stealing food if out of money and work, 'fiddling' the income tax, or breaking traffic laws – do not constitute political crimes. Only 8 per cent of the respondents agreed that individual conscience can justify breaking a law. Among those seeing a need for a monarch, 13 per cent less said laws could be broken. There is thus a weak relationship between positive reactions to the monarchy and general readiness to comply with laws.

It is often overlooked by social scientists today that those who favour a monarch might favour a challenge to political authority if the Queen herself, in violation of the conventions of constitutional monarchy, vetoed an Act of Parliament. When respondents were asked whether they thought the Queen could refuse to sign an Act of Parliament that she did not like, 65 per cent said that she could do so. Among those who think the country needs a Queen, 12 per cent more say that she could act unconstitutionally; among those with pride in the Queen, 21 per cent more accept a royal veto. The readiness to say that the Queen could veto an Act of Parliament does not necessarily indicate that a substantial proportion of the British people wish a return to the days of the Stuarts, when the monarch sought to command Parliament. Instead it probably reflects a felt need for some residual restraint upon the government, for there is in the British constitution no judicial restraint upon the executive's will.

Indirectly, the monarchy may increase political authority by encouraging a generally deferential attitude among the masses of society toward authority in a variety of social manifestations.

5 Those who React Positively to the Monarchy are Also Most Likely to Defer to Politicians of High Status

Bagehot argued that deference to the monarchy could substitute for, rather than supplement deference to the English aristocracy of his day, which provided, through the House of Lords and family connections in the House of Commons, a very substantial proportion of the nation's governors.[32] The monarch's rôle, Bagehot argued, was to keep aristocrats and plutocrats from competing with each other through conspicuous consumption for first rank in society. Today, the decline of the aristocracy has left the monarch in an unchallenged position of eminence.

Table 16.3 Attitudes to the Queen and deferential attitudes

Bases of authority (% endorsing)	Queen needed %	Differ- ence %	Proud %	Differ- ence %
(a) Some people are born to rule				
Agree (61%)	76	+23	75	+29
Disagree (31%)	53		46	
(b) Gentlemen are best to govern				
Agree (15%)	78	+13	78	+16
Disagree (75%)	65		62	
(c) Most educated are best to govern				
Agree (60%)	68	+3	68	+12
Disagree (25%)	65		56	

While many contemporary social scientists have cited Bagehot in discussions of deference, they have ignored the sharp distinction that Bagehot drew between monarchy and aristocracy, assuming that the two groups can be made interchangeable – and that they are the only elites to which deference may be shown.[33] In fact, there are many values to which a citizenry can defer. The presence or absence of a monarchy is not, of itself, a guarantee of deferential attitudes within a culture. Norway can be cited as an example of a monarchy without an aristocracy claiming deference,[34] and David Halberstamm has argued, in his study of America in the Vietnam war, that *The Best and the Brightest* expect deference to their views about foreign policy under a form of government that explicitly prohibits titles of nobility. The short-lived 'Camelot' period of John F. Kennedy illustrates that those who govern under republican institutions may none the less wish deference because of their social graces. Presidents Johnson and Nixon differed only in that they expected deference because they were crowned by popular election.[35]

To test the relationship between attitudes toward the monarchy and deferential outlooks, respondents were asked whether or not they agreed with statements describing as best suited to govern a country: those who speak like gentlemen, those with the most education, and those born to rule. A majority agreed that those with the most education and those who are born to it make the best

rulers. The data in Table 16.3 show that those who endorse the
monarchy are, not surprisingly, much more inclined to believe that
some people are born to rule. There is a lesser but consistent link
with the belief that gentlemen or educated men are best suited to
govern. There is, however, no generalisation of the specific
relationship between respect for birth and the monarchy to more
central attitudes in the political culture. Confidence in some people
being born to rule explains less than 1 per cent of the variance in
respondents' views of the system of government, or of British
government in comparison with régimes of other countries.[36]

Another way in which monarchy may influence political authority
indirectly arises from the monarch's presumed rôle as the symbol
of the organic unity of a nation. Durkheim as well as Bagehot
emphasised the importance of totems around which members of
society can gather to affirm their unity. He wrote, 'There can be
no society which does not feel the need of upholding and reaffirming
at regular intervals the collective sentiments and the collective ideas
which make its unity and its personality'.[37] For Shils and Young,
'The monarch is the one pervasive institution, standing above all
others, which plays a part in a vital way comparable to the function
of the medieval Church'.[38] The authorised study of *The Work of
the Queen* shows how royal visits are carefully organised to
incorporate contact with different groups in a community, consistent
with the Queen's rôle as 'the embodiment of the whole life of the
people'.[39] Such theorising implies the following:

**6 Those who React Positively to the Monarchy are Also Most
Likely to Feel a Sense of Organic National Unity**

In contemporary political systems, the unity that a monarch can
stimulate is considered particularly valuable as a counterpoise to the
divisiveness generated by electoral politics and party competition.
A British monarch is thus contrasted, both by Englishmen and
Americans, with a popularly elected president, who must be both
partisan figure and head of state.[40] In a constitutional monarchy,
the prime minister attracts controversy and negative emotions, while
the monarch remains above the political battle, Dr Ernest Jones,
the psychoanalyst biographer of Sigmund Freud, argued that the
dignified and efficient tasks of government must be divided among
two persons:

One untouchable, irremovable and sacrosanct, above even criticism, let alone attack, the other vulnerable in such a degree that sooner or later he will surely be destroyed, i.e., expelled from his position of power. The first of these, the king, is the symbolic ruler, one not directly responsible to the people, the second, the Prime Minister, is the functional ruler, exquisitely responsible.[41]

The division is justified as necessary 'to prevent the murderous potentialities in the son–father (i.e. governed–governing) relation from ever becoming too grim and fierce an expression'.

First of all, it is necessary to ascertain to what extent individuals do feel some sense of community with their fellow citizens. In the monarchy survey, 59 per cent said that they had 'a lot' in common with the people who live around them, 22 per cent some things in common and 17 per cent nothing in common with those around them. But the survey found no relationship between positive feelings toward the Queen and social solidarity. Among those who had 'a lot' in common with their neighbours, 69 per cent felt a Queen needed and 68 per cent felt pride; these proportions are, respectively, 7 per cent lower and 4 per cent higher than among those with nothing in common with their neighbours.

Any community exists by virtue of those it excludes, as well as those it includes. The Queen's role as head of an Empire and latterly, the Commonwealth, makes the monarchy a national symbol in world affairs. The greater the positive orientation to the monarchy, the greater the belief in a collective national purpose, that Britain does (and ought to) play a major role in international affairs. Only 19 per cent believe that other countries follow Britain's lead in world affairs, and 27 per cent that other countries ought to follow Britain. Those with favourable attitudes toward the monarchy are slightly readier to see Britain playing a leading rôle in the world. Among those with pride in the Queen, 18 per cent more believed other countries should follow Britain. This tendency does not make those favouring the monarchy jingoistic Imperialists, for there is still a plurality who think that there is no need for other nations to follow Britain's lead. The retention of a monarch does not maintain a sense of Imperial mission in a post-Imperial era.

It is sometimes argued that monarchy can strengthen organic unity by symbolising common moral standards. According to Shils and Young, the monarchy in Britain represents 'fundamental moral standards' such as 'loyalty, love, generosity'. Bagehot advanced the opposite view. He contrasted the virtues of Queen Victoria with the character of her predecessor George IV, 'a model of family demerit'. Moreover, he considered that the very institution of monarchy, and even more, of a Crown Prince, placed 'greater temptations than almost any other' in the way of an individual, and left 'fewer suitable occupations than almost any other'.[42] Events since have justified his view. If George V and George VI were models of family virtues, Edward VII and Edward VIII erred in the opposite direction. Moreover, Fascist and Communist governments have provided examples of the use of government powers to impose common standards of morality that were anything but benign. Today, the rise of permissiveness in every Western society presumes that no one – priest, landlord or monarch – can define standards of conduct that must be accepted by everyone. If anything, it appears that a reigning monarch is expected to be a symbol of a morality that is being abandoned, setting a standard for admiration because such behaviour is rarely found in the workaday world.

Hence, one must first establish whether there is today a felt need for a single standard of morality that can be prescribed or symbolised by a royal figure. In an effort to assess this, respondents were asked whether everyone should obey the same standards of right and wrong, or decide for himself what is and isn't right to do. Individual liberty is pre-eminently valued; 66 per cent said that each person should decide things for himself, as against 32 per cent wishing to apply the same standards for all. There is a slight relationship between attitudes toward conventional standards of morality and the monarchy – but in the opposite direction from that hypothesised. Those who felt no need for a Queen were 4 per cent more likely to uphold conventional standards, and those who felt no pride in the monarchy were 5 per cent more likely to believe in conventional standards.

Religion is often mingled with monarchy in social science theory and in ceremonial evocations of national unity. In England, the relationship between throne and altar is evident upon many occasions, from the Coronation to daily proceedings in Parliament. The monarchy is not only Queen 'by Grace of God', but also 'Defender of the Faith'. Sanctions of religion and sanctions of royalty are meant to reinforce one another in a mystical union of symbols of authority.

As a test of this argument, respondents were asked to say whether they agreed or disagreed with the statement that 'God guides this

Table 16.4 Belief in divine protection and attitude to the monarchy

	Believe %	Do not believe %	DK/ Other %
(a) *Need*			
Need a Queen	63	28	9
Do not need a Queen	32	57	11
Don't know	35	30	35
(b) *Pride*			
Proud of Queen	67	26	9
Not proud	33	56	11
Don't know	35	50	15
Total	53	36	11

country in times of trouble'. Notwithstanding the low level of church attendance in Britain today, 53 per cent agreed with the statement. Of those with positive views of the monarchy, about two-thirds expressed a belief in divine protection for the country, as against one-third without favourable opinions. The margin of difference is 34 per cent among those with pride in the Queen and 31 per cent for those who think a Queen needed. These differences are greater than for any of the other hypotheses tested heretofore. Support for the monarchy thus appears to encourage irrational and mystical confidence in political authority. This may be considered a handicap instead of an asset. For example, Bismarck's saying that 'God looks after drunkards, fools and the United States of America' was not meant as a compliment. In so far as people believe they are protected by Providence, they may be less inclined to make efforts to provide for the future. Neither governors nor social scientists would today wish to put their faith in God's guidance as the sole source of policy-making. Since Oliver Cromwell's time, the dominant norm of British government has been secular. It is summed up, not in terms of a royalist faith, but rather in the Cromwellian charge: 'Trust in God and keep your powder dry'.

'FAREWELL, A LONG FAREWELL, TO ALL MY GREATNESS!'[43]

The most important general finding in the monarchy survey is the shallowness of the British response to their Queen. The Queen's dignified rôle as head of state is clearly recognised but of little political import. In the words of one Englishwoman interviewed in *The Civic Culture* survey, 'You've got to have somebody at the head. It might as well be her'. The Queen is held in common regard in every section of society, with respect to class, education or other social or political characteristics. Those who do not express positive views about the monarchy are either apathetic don't knows, or show a neutral reaction. Neither pre-coded nor open-end questions found any indication of antagonism or republican sentiments. Theories of the political potency of a monarch in a democratic era are interesting but not true.

Any general theory of the political significance of the monarchy must account for the observable fact that some countries are monarchies, whereas others have republican forms of government. Two related hypotheses can be advanced.

7 The Survival of a Monarchy Depends Upon the Readiness of the Reigning Family to Withdraw From a Politically Active Rôle

8 The Repudiation of a Monarchy Results From the Continuation or Adoption by the Monarchy of an Active Political Rôle

In short, the less politically significant a monarchy is, the better its chances of survival; the more politically active a monarchy is, the less the chance that the throne will survive. The propositions can be tested by reviewing the evolution of European states from the middle of the nineteenth century.

A main feature of European political history since 1850 has been the downfall of monarchies (Table 16.5). Royalty has survived continuously in only seven European states. There has been no successful restoration of a monarchy in a one-time republic. Among contemporary European states, fourteen are republics that have supplanted monarchs. In the case of Italy and Germany, a republic

Table 16.5 The career of monarchy in European regimes since 1850

(a) *Continued/commenced as monarchy* (7)
Belgium (but Leopold II abdicated 1951)
Denmark
Luxembourg
Netherlands
Norway (Haakon VII, son of Danish King, established royal
house in 1905, when Norway became independent of Swedish
Crown)
Sweden
United Kingdom

(b) *Continued/commenced as republic* (8)
Switzerland (old-established republic)
Czechoslovakia (ex-Habsburg domain)
Estonia, Latvia, Lithuania, Finland (ex-Russian Czar's domain)
Poland (from domains of ex-Russian Czar, German Emperor and
Habsburgs)
Ireland (seceded from British Crown)

(c) *Monarch deposed* (14, plus monarchs deposed in predecessor states
and principalities)
Albania
Austria–Hungary (the successor state of Austria commenced as a
republic in 1918; Hungary became a kingdom without a king in
1920, under Admiral Horthy as regent)
Bulgaria
France (governed by Orleanist dynasty, 1830–48; Second Empire
of Napoleon III, 1852–70)
Germany (formed by an amalgamation of 38 German states under
the Prussian Kaiser, whose Empire included four kingdoms,
five grand duchies and 13 duchies, all of which disappeared by
the end of the First World War)
Greece (intermittently monarchy and republic: of six most recent
sovereigns, one assassinated, and three exiled one or more
times)
Iceland (sovereign state under Danish Crown from 1918;
proclaimed a Republic in 1944)
Italy (formed by an amalgamation of territories under several
royal houses and the Pope; monarch deposed by plebiscite,
1946)
Portugal
Roumania
Russia
Spain (House of Savoy, then Carlists overthrown. In 1947 Spain
proclaimed a monarchy with General Franco as regent. In 1969
the Carlist claimant to the throne sworn in as successor to
Franco as Head of State)
Turkey (abolition of the Sultanate of the Ottoman Empire in
1922, followed by proclamation of the Turkish Republic)
Yugoslavia (established as Kingdom of Serbs, Croats and
Slovenes in 1918, under Serbian King; created republic at the
end of the Second World War)

has supplanted a monarch that previously had engrossed lands from a number of lesser or weaker royal houses. There is nothing in the presence of a monarch to ensure the persistence of a regime's authority or, for that matter, the persistence of a state. The survival of monarchies in Europe today is not a cause of a regime being fully legitimate; the persistence of monarchy is, instead, a consequence of a fully legitimate régime. Monarchs have remained in power where the reigning family has been willing to withdraw from a politically active rôle. Reciprocally, monarchies have fallen when the monarch has sought to continue to assert.

The surrendering of power to survive is clearly illustrated by the history of the British Crown. The foundations of constitutional monarchy were established in the seventeenth century when Charles I's assertion of royal supremacy was followed by parliamentary rebellion and the beheading of the King. Following the death of Oliver Cromwell, the Lord Protector, the leaders of the Commonwealth faced a classic revolutionary problem: how to institutionalise government beyond the lifetime of a single leader. The immediate outcome was the restoration of the exiled Stuart monarch, Charles II. He accepted the limits of royal power, saying, it is claimed, 'Brother, I am too old to go again to my travels'. The attempt of his successor, James II, to reassert royal power in order to re-establish the Catholic religion led to the Glorious (i.e. bloodless) Revolution of 1688, with the new King, William III, holding office by authority of Parliament, rather than by divine right. In the eighteenth century the Prime Minister and Cabinet gradually assumed the powers of the Crown, while nominally acting as servants of the Crown. During the nineteenth and twentieth centuries, in the major crises of the Constitution, such as Catholic Emancipation in 1829, the Reform Act of 1832 or the House of Lords controversy of 1911, the monarch followed the advice of 'his' ministers. By withdrawing from, rather than intervening in, constitutional crises, the Crown preserved itself from the inevitable bitterness of these controversies.

The epiphenomenal character of monarchy today by comparison with a century ago need be no occasion for surprise. It is even explicable within Bagehot's terms of reference. The reason he gave for valuing monarchy was not the heroic or awesome character of successive English monarchs, but rather, the infirmities of understanding among the masses of the population. To remind his rationalist readers of the limits of popular understanding, he suggested that they go into the kitchen to talk to their cook. The world of today is vastly changed from that of Bagehot, Queen Victoria, the Emperor Franz Josef and President Andrew Johnson. Few social scientists employ cooks. The disappearance of a servant, servile class has happened concurrently with the rise of mass education and popular demands for representative government throughout the Western world.

As the level of understanding of the population has changed, so too has the behaviour of monarchs. Contemporary European monarchs are not the remote or awesome figures of a nineteenth-century court, to whom every form of obeisance was owed. The characteristic European monarch of today is a 'bicycling' monarch.[44] Members of a royal family no longer expect to be treated as if they are different in kind from other mortals. One might even argue that Edward VIII, by claiming to marry a woman whom he could lawfully have espoused had he been a commoner, was doing no more than asserting the rights of man for monarchs as well as subjects.

Where the populace lacks education, as in most of the non-Western world today, then the 'theatrical' role of political leaders remains important, whether asserted in the style of a European Man on Horseback, e.g. Colonel Nasser; a charismatic leader modelled on Weberian prototypes, e.g. Kwame Nkrumah in Ghana; an indigenous leader, e.g. Gandhi in India; or a figure cast in the style of one of the later Roman Emperors, e.g. General Amin in Uganda.[45]

Given a government which, by its efficient actions, is deemed to merit support and compliance, citizens will accept as part of the package a symbolic leader in any of several forms: a monarch, a President or even a Man on Horseback. A non-political monarch may add something to the life of a nation by stimulating popular emotions. What is added is superficial. The Queen is like a colour photograph covering a large box of chocolates. The photograph gives pleasure to some, while others hardly think about it. Only a deviant few would refuse a box of chocolates because they were emotionally upset by such a photograph. The proof of its value will not be in its packaging, but in the eating. The same is true of government in the contemporary world. A good monarch cannot save an unpopular regime, and a bad monarch is an argument for the establishment of a republic. If a monarch is to survive, he requires the creation of a constitutional order in which he becomes a figurehead. The job of maintaining authority is the task of politicians whose careers are transitory. If a monarch also becomes engaged in this work, his career is likely to be transitory too.

NOTES

1. Cf. the discussion of the monarch's rôle in the 1931 British crisis. R. Bassett, *Nineteen Thirty-One; Political Crisis* (London, 1958), Appendix I, with problems arising in the Netherlands, see Jan Kooiman and J. Vis, 'Parliament in a System in Flux: Netherlands' (Luxembourg: European Parliament Symposium on European Integration, EP 35.656, May 1974, duplicated), p. 6 Austria, see Kurt Steiner, *Politics in Austria* (Boston, 1972), pp. 111–13: and Finland, see J. Nousiainen, *The Finnish Political System* (Cambridge, Mass, 1971), p. 240.
2. Except for the study analysed herein, the only full-length academic survey of attitudes toward the monarchy known to the authors is that by J. G. Blumler, J. R. Brown, A. J. Ewbank and T. J. Nossiter, 'Attitudes to the Monarchy: their Structure and Development during a Ceremonial Occasion'. *Political Studies*. XIX, June 1971. The study is concerned with the investiture of the Prince of Wales in 1969. Socialisation studies sometimes contain a question or two about attitudes toward the monarchy, but even where there is an attempt to explore these attitudes in detail there remain major objections to extrapolating adult attitudes from these findings. Cf. Fred Greenstein, V. M. Herman, R. N. Stradling and Elia Zurick, 'The Child's Conception of the Queen and the Prime Minister: Bagehot Revisited; *British Journal of Political Science*, IV, July 1974, pp. 260ff; and David Marsh, 'Political Socialization: the Implicit Assumptions Questioned', *British Journal of Political Science*, I, Oct. 1971.
3. But for a caution against the misuse of survey data to describe properties of institutions and systems, see Erwin Scheuch, 'Cross-National Comparisons Using Aggregate Data', in Richard L. Merritt and Stein Rokkan, (eds.), *Comparing Nations* (New Haven, Conn., 1966).
4. Edward Shils and Michael Young, 'The Meaning of the Coronation', *Sociological Review*, I, 2, 1953; cf. Norman Birnbaum, 'Monarchs and Sociologists: a Reply to Professor Shils and Mr Young'. *Sociological Review* III, 1, 1953, p. 13; Raymond Williams, *The Long Revolution* (Harmondsworth, 1965), pp. 101–2; and for an orthodox Communist view, James Harvey and Katherine Hood, *The British State* (London, 1958), p. 5–67.
5. For a minor exception, see David Butler and Donald Stokes. *Political Change in Britain*, 2nd ed. (London, 1974) pp. 190ff.
6. See Eric Nordlinger, *The Working-Class Tories* (London, 1967), p. 242; and R. T. McKenzie and Allan Silver, *Angels in Marble* (London, 1968).
7. The number of respondents remains one-third greater than that in the Leeds survey of Blumler *et al.*, *op. cit.*, and the response rate is higher

than that in the British section of The Civic Culture survey, 59 per
cent. See Gabriel Almond and Sidney Verba. *The Civic Culture*
(Princeton, 1963), p. 518.

8. This does not appear to have happened. See David Butler and Donald
Stokes, *op. cit.* p. 466.

9. On the limited but measurable short-term increase in public endorsement
for the monarchy arising from well-publicised media events involving
members of the royal family see J. G. Blumler *et al., op. cit.*

10. Walter Bagehot, *The English Constitution* (London: World's Classics
edition, reprinted in 1955).

11. *The Times* (London), 12 Dec 1936.

12. See Richard Rose, *Politics in England Today* (London, 1974), p. 147;
and Mark Abrams, 'Social Trends and Electoral Behaviour'. *British
Journal of Sociology*, XIII, 3, 1962, Table 7.

13. Gallup *Political Index*, Report no. 98 (London, 1968), p. 67.

14. A nation-wide survey in October 1969 by National Opinion Polls
reported that 84 per cent said that Britain needs a Queen, and 16 per
cent said it did not. This indicates that, if anything, the extent of pro-
monarchical attitudes is slightly underestimated by the Glasgow survey
rather that overestimated. Cf. NOP, *Political Bulletin*, supplement II
(London: Oct. 1969), p. 2.

15. Lord Altrincham *et al., Is the Monarchy Perfect?* (London, 1958).

16. See Walter Bagehot, *op. cit.*, Chs. I-II.

17. See Richard Rose, 'England: a Traditionally Modern Culture', in Lucien
Pye and Sidney Verba (eds.), *Political Culture and Political Development*
(Princeton, 1963); and, for a community study, Margaret Stacy,
Tradition and Change: a Study of Banbury (London, 1960).

18. Frank Parkin, 'Working-class Conservatives', *British Journal of Sociology*, XVIII, 3, 1967, p. 280.

19. On AID generally, see J. A. Sonquist and J. N. Morgan, *The Detection
of Inter-Action Effects* (Ann Arbor: Survey Research Center, Monograph
no. 35, 1965).

20. The twenty-one variables included in the AID analysis were: age,
sex, years of education, educational qualifications, religion, church
attendance, national identity, membership in organisations, trade-union
membership, occupational class, party preference, vote at next election,
subjective class identification, interest in politics, common sympathies
with neighbours, recognition of left-right differences between parties,
inter-generational social mobility, class links of parties, place of birth,
discussion of politics, and military service. Absence of reference to any
of these influences in the test signifies that they were of less importance
statistically, than the influences that are discussed in the prose and
tables herein.

21. See Ernest Jones, 'The Psychology of Constitutional Monarchy'. *New
Statesman*, 1 Feb 1936, pp. 141–2.

22. See Walter Bagehot, *op. cit.*, p. 4.

23. *From Max Weber*, ed. H. H. Gerth and C. Wright Mills (London, 1948
ed.), p. 264.

24. It is noteworthy that the arguments in favour of monarchy have invariably been advanced by authors who are citizens of a Republic (i.e. the United States) and of much more explicit 'liberal' and 'democratic' sentiments than Bagehot, who had a Whig's distrust of the masses as well as a Whig's dislike of an hereditary monarch playing an active part in politics.
25. Gabriel Almond and Sidney Verba, *op. cit.*, p. 488.
26. Edward Shils and Michael Young, *op. cit.*, p. 77.
27. S. M. Lipset, *Political Man* (New York, 1960), p. 79.
28. Kingsley Martin, *The Crown and the Establishment* (Harmondsworth, 1963), p. 18–72.
29. For a definition of allegiance to authority, see Richard Rose, 'Dynamic Tendencies in the Authority of Régimes', *World Politics*, XXI, July 1969.
30. Quoted in *African Research Bulletin*, II, 1965, p. 404.
31. See e.g., Sir James Fergusson, *The Curragh Incident* (London, 1964); Richard Rose, *Governing without Consensus* (London, 1971), especially Ch. 5.
32. See Walter Bagehot, *op. cit.*, Ch. 2, and W. L. Guttsman, *The British Political Elite* (London, 1963).
33. For a detailed discussion of deference, see Dennis Kavanagh, 'The Deferential English: A Comparative Critique', *Government and Opposition*, VI, 3, Summer 1971.
34. Harry Eckstein, *Division and Cohesion in Democracy: a Study of Norway* (Princeton, 1966).
35. See e.g., George Reedy, *The Twilight of the Presidency* (New York, 1970).
36. The Best Sum of Squares/Total Sum of Squares ratios are 0.8 per cent and 0.6 per cent respectively. Cf. Figures 16.1 and 16.2.
37. Emile Durkheim, *The Elementary Forms of Religious Life* (New York, 1961).
38. Edward Shils and Michael Young, *op. cit.*, p. 79.
39. Dermot Morrah, Arundel Herald Extraordinary, *The Work of The Queen* (London, 1958), Ch. 2.
40. Cf. Dermot Morrah, *op. cit.*, p. 45; Richard Crossman, *Inside View*(London, 1972), p. 53; and Fred Greenstein, 'What the President Means to Americans', in James David Barber (ed.), *Choosing the President* (Englewood Cliffs, NJ, 1974).
41. Ernest Jones, *op. cit.*, pp. 141–2.
42. Edward Shils and Michael Young, *op. cit.*, Walter Bagehot, *op. cit.*, p. 47.
43. From a speech by Cardinal Wolsey in Shakespeare's *Henry VIII*, Act III, ii, 351.
44. In view of the tendency of some Americans to regard the President as a regal figure, it is noteworthy that Richard Nixon's tenure of office, which bears perhaps some comparison with that of England's Richard III, was not followed by a strong, centralising monarch in the tradition of Henry VII, but by a man who has been anxious to establish his *bona fides* as a 'bicycling' Head of State in the Scandinavian manner.

45. For a general discussion of the rôle and risks of monarchy in non-Western nations, see Samuel P. Huntington, *Political Order in Changing Societies* (New Haven, Conn., 1969) pp. 177 ff.

17 Public Opinion Polls*

Election campaigning has of late become increasingly professional. Candidates and party organisers have devised more elaborate strategies; they have spent more money; and they have relied on new mass media techniques. The emergence of public opinion polling on a regular and systematic basis has coincided with all three of these developments.

Parties and candidates have long relied on intuition and impressions for interpreting the mood of voters and explaining election outcomes. But opinion polls, based on the questioning of a representative, systematically drawn sample of the electorate, date from the 1930s. A key date is 1936, when the Gallup poll and the Elmo Roper polls correctly predicted the outcome of the Roosevelt–Landon presidential election in the United States. In 1937 and 1938 Gallup affiliates were established in Great Britain (the British Institute of Public Opinion) and France (the Institut Francais d'Opinion Publique, generally known as IFOP) to use similar methods for assessing public opinion. But it was only in the 1960s that polls were widely used by the mass media and parties for election purposes. Since then the use of polls has grown almost exponentially. There are more polls and competition among them has stiffened. 30 years ago Gallup and its affiliates were dominant in Britain, Australia, and the United States. Now there are at least half a dozen large and specialised firms in these and most other countries.

An easily overlooked condition for the activity of market and opinion research is the freedom to interview people and publish the findings of polls on political views and voting intentions. This freedom is found mainly in the Western European and Anglo-American societies. In a number of third world states in Africa, the Middle East, and Southeast Asia there are opinion polls, but they usually avoid questions on national politics. In Spain the liberalisation since Franco's death has seen a growth of polling activity, and the

* D. Butler, H. Penniman and A. Ranney, *British Democracy at the Polls* (Washington, DC: American Enterprise Institute, 1981). For comments on an earlier version of this paper I would like to thank Hugh Berrington of Newcastle University, Seymour M. Lipset of Stanford University, Humphrey Taylor of Louis Harris and Associates, Inc., and Robert Worcester of MORI, London.

315

polls now report voting intentions. Some political and media authorities remain uneasy about the influence which the findings of opinion polls may have on the actual vote. In France, West Germany, Brazil, and South Africa opinion polls freely report between election campaigns, but for the duration of the offical campaign, or in its later stages, these countries ban reports of the polls' findings or, as in West Germany, their forecasts.

This overview of public opinion polling in a dozen Western countries concentrates on the following five areas: the background to the polls' development; their uses during elections; the role of the private polls; objections to the polls; and, finally, an assessment of their significance for modern democratic elections.

BACKGROUND

There are broadly three categories of polling in Western countries. First there are the *public polls*, conducted by national public opinion firms or research institutes. Their findings on the standing of parties and personalities and on attitudes to issues are presented for public consumption. A handful of these organisations, like the George Gallup, Louis Harris, and Daniel Yankelovich firms in the United States, the Swedish Institute of Public Opinion Research (SIFO) in Sweden, and IFOP or the Societe Francaise d'Enquetes par Sondages (SOFRES) in France, dominate. Their main clients are the press and major television networks, although some of these companies also do private work for parties and candidates. Notwithstanding the publicity which attends their voting surveys, these major market research companies derive only a small fraction of their incomes from political surveys.

Second, there are *private polls*, conducted by commercial firms. For example, in the United States the Opinion Research Center was associated with the Republicans between 1960 and 1972; Market & Opinion Research International (MORI) has worked with the British Labour party since 1969; and the Institut fur Demoskopie (IFD) has worked with the German Christian Democrats off and on over 30 years. Some of this material eventually finds its way into the public domain. There are also polling organisations which are formally linked to or founded by political parties. For example, in West Germany, Intermartel is linked to the Free Democrats, and the Social Democratic party has a share in the Infratest organisation.

In Britain, the Opinion Research Centre was established with the encouragement of the Conservatives, and the firm has conducted surveys for the party in every election since 1966. In France it is usual for the commercial polling firms to hive off the sections that deal with private polls for political parties. It is also interesting to note the ways in which some opinion polls become 'reserved' for a particular political party simply by tradition: for example, the Louis Harris, Oliver Quayle, and Pat Caddell firms work for the US Democratic party, IFD for the West German Christian Democrats. In France SOFRES and IFOP are remarkable in working for all political parties. Parties in West Germany, Austria, and the Netherlands also have their own well-funded research institutes which provide a polling capability. The Konrad Adenauer Stiftung regularly conducts independent survey research for the Christian Democrats.

Third, there are polls conducted for what might be termed *scientific purposes*. These differ from the commercial polls in three respects. Their primary purpose is to promote understanding of electoral behaviour rather than to provide an up-to-the-moment reading of current opinion or to predict the winner of a particular election. In France, for example, important surveys have been conducted by the Fondation Nationale des Sciences Politiques. The second difference is that they are usually financed by the government or by academic agencies. In the United States, for example, the National Science Foundation funds studies of presidential and congressional elections by the University of Michigan's Center for Political Studies. In Britain funds for academic surveys are provided by the Social Science Research Council (SSRC). In Sweden the government sponsors two kinds of academic surveys: annual omnibus surveys conducted by the National Bureau of Statistics; and national election studies, begun in 1956 and now jointly conducted by the National Bureau of Statistics and academic political scientists. The final difference is the fact that, whereas the media polls and private polls are analysed and reported in a matter of days after the interviews are conducted, academic research is usually reported several months or even years after the interviews. Scholarly testing of hypotheses imposes costs in terms of elaborate statistical analysis and careful presentation, as well as delays in publication in learned journals. The content of academic surveys is, understandably, more detailed than that of the faster and cheaper commercial polls.

There are different clients for opinion polls. All, presumably, have a common interest in understanding public opinion, but their purposes differ. A newspaper editor, for example, is interested in a good story; polls appear to be a growing source of journalistic copy during elections. A pressure group wants to get its issue position on the agenda or to change public opinion. Political parties are mainly interested in affecting electoral behaviour. Some voters may use poll information about other voters' electoral preferences to make their own decisions.

Polls appear to be used as frequently by parties of the right as of the left. But to what extent is it easier for pollsters to work with right-wing parties than with the left-wing ones? Arguably, the former will be more sympathetic to free enterprise and commercial considerations. But in Sweden and Germany, at least, this does not hold; there, the Social Democrats are avid users of polls. More important than a left/right division may be the extent to which a party's orientation is determined by ideology or pragmatism. Some leaders on the right as well as the left may believe that the polls simply 'take the poetry out of politics', as Aneurin Bevan once complained. Insofar as public opinion on issues is clustered in the ideological middle, then poll findings are likely to disillusion politicians on the extreme left and right and reinforce centrists. The findings of polls therefore have consequences for factional fights in parties. The spokesman for a minority viewpoint can either disbelieve or ignore inconvenient information; alternatively, he may also regard it as an indicator of how much ground he has to make up in overturning the dominant views.

WHAT OPINION POLLS DO

In a short chapter such as this, one can only generalise about the polls' activities across a range of countries. Their electoral rôle varies in part according to the nature of the particular political and electoral system. In two-ballot electoral systems, such as that in France, knowledge of the second preferences of voters is important. In presidential systems key questions will focus on the personalities and the strengths and weaknesses of the candidates. By contrast, parliamentary elections in Britain and West Germany have shown that the popularity of a leader may be relatively poorly correlated with support for his party. In federations or decentralised party systems there are more local polls. This obviously applies in the

United States, where candidates are the main users of polls and a single congressional district may contain as many as a half-million voters. Mayors in France are also major users of polls. Where there are sharp regional differences in party lineups or the strengths of the parties, a national poll has to be used cautiously for understanding the mood of voters or predicting the outcome. This is the case with opinion polls in Canada where, according to one authority, 'regional climates of opinion are frequently at variance with national patterns'.[1]

The American example might be distinguished from the others. Parties in most parliamentary countries are largely national, have large central offices, and do not hold direct primary elections. In the decentralised American system, on the other hand, the national committees of two main parties do relatively little polling. Pollsters work directly for candidates in the primary elections and then in the general election. There are a myriad of pollsters working for state, congressional, and local candidates. Since the organisations and the data do not belong to parties *per se*, there is little cumulation of knowledge. In Germany, Sweden, Britain, and other countries where the same pollsters work regularly and systematically for the central party office, they can do research, relate current results to past ones, and advise on strategies to improve the party situation over a five- or ten-year period.

Prediction

Most public attention is paid to public polls as tools for prediction. 'Getting it right', in the polls, however, may variously refer to predicting the winner or predicting the gap between the main parties or, most difficult of all, predicting the main parties' shares of the votes. Collating the findings of the *At the Polls* series shows variations in the polls' success in predicting election outcomes. In Australia the Morgan Gallup poll's average error in forecasting the gap between the two main parties in eight House elections between 1958 and 1975 was 3.6 percentage points. Only in 1972 and 1975 was the margin of error less than 4 points, when it was 1 and 0.4 points respectively.[2] In British elections between 1964 and 1979, the mean error of the public polls' final forecasts of the gap between the two leading parties was 3.5 points. Only in 1964 and 1979 was it less than 2 points, and in 1970 it was as high as 6.7 points.[3] In France, in both presidential and parliamentary elections, and in the United States, the public polls have been remarkably close to the final gap, even in such close elections as 1960, 1968, and 1976 in the United States and 1974 and 1978 in France. Lancelot has referred to the French polls' 'incontestable accuracy'.[4] The predictions of SIFO in Sweden, which are made three days before election day, proved remarkably accurate in the 1970s.[5] The average deviation between the polls' forecast and each party's share of the vote was 0.62 percentage points in 1970 (for seven parties), 0.68 points in 1973 (for eight parties), 0.78 points in 1976 (for seven parties), and 0.65 points in 1979 (for five parties). Doing better than predicted may confer a moral victory on the loser. In American primary elections this interpretation has sometimes been important in giving 'momentum' to a candidate.

Prediction is a hazardous occupation for pollsters. In view of the difficulties, it is surprising that they do as well as they do. The normal sampling-error margin of about 3 percentage points (at the 95 percent confidence level) may be too wide for predicting a closely contested election correctly. Another problem lies in the translation of votes (which are what the polls measure) into seats (which usually decide elections in parliamentary systems). Electoral systems do not always work proportionately or predictably. In Britain there have been two occasions since 1950 (1951 and February 1974) when the party with the most votes 'lost' the election in that it had only the second-largest number of seats. In 1979 the Canadian Liberals suffered the same fate, and in 1979 the Japanese Liberals increased their share of votes but lost seats. In Ireland in 1973 the ruling party, Fianna Fail, gained first-preference votes but lost seats and lost control of the government. The differing regional strengths of the Canadian parties make Gallup's record there all the more impressive. In only two of the twelve general elections between 1945 and 1974 did it fail to get within 2 percentage points of the Liberal and Conservative share of the votes.[6] In Italy, the accuracy of the polls has traditionally been hampered by the reluctance of Communist supporters to reveal their political sympathies to interviewers. Recently, however, it is voters on the right who seem to be wary; in 1976 the polls overestimated the Socialist vote by 4 points on the average and understated the Christian Democrats' strength by 5.2 points.[7] Pollsters are usually careful to poll to the last day in order to avoid a repetition of the polls' disastrous failure to forecast correctly the outcome of the 1948 American presidential election. But the allocation of the undecided voters and adjustments for differential voting turnout are matters for subjective, not scientific, judgement.

Fairly or unfairly, opinion polls are widely judged by the accuracy of their forecasts. In Ireland in 1977 the opinion polls defied the conventional wisdom: they correctly anticipated the handsome victory of Fianna Fail against the predictions of the mass media, pundits, and bookmakers. The result greatly improved the polls' standing. According to Garret FitzGerald, the new leader of the opposition party, 'Perhaps the result of the election will encourage all concerned to take these polls more seriously in the future'.

Candidate Visibility and Support

A good rating in the polls may promote a person's candidacy even if he is not officially in the race. For reasons mentioned above, the best illustrations are found in the United States. Eisenhower before 1952 and Edward Kennedy in 1979 are obvious examples of this effect. Nelson Rockefeller tried to exploit his favourable standing in the polls in 1968 to persuade Republican convention delegates that he would be a more successful standard-bearer than Richard Nixon. A good standing in the polls is also useful to show electoral appeal, gain endorsements, and raise funds. It may help persuade contributors that a declared candidate can win a nomination or an election. American private and public polls are concerned to find out which candidate is in the lead and how different candidates or combinations of candidates run against others.[8] In France opponents of Francois Mitterrand in the Socialist party used and abused opinion polls to promote the rival candidacy of Michel Rocard. In the United States polls can be used to kill a candidacy; this is what happened to George Romney, who withdrew from the race before the primaries in 1968, and to Walter Mondale before the primaries in 1976. Hubert Humphrey's campaign in the California primary in 1972 was seriously damaged by the California Field poll showing him twenty points behind McGovern a week before the election – which he actually lost by a margin of only five points.

Election Timing

Where prime ministers have discretion in calling or not calling an election for a particular date, they usually take account of polls and

other portents. Lord Hailsham has suggested that it is rare for
governments in Britain to lose elections; by timing economic booms
to coincide with the run-up to an election and reading the opinion
polls, the prime minister has a formidable set of advantages.[9] In
fact, however, in Great Britain since 1945 the parties in power have
won only five of the ten general elections, and in 1951, 1970, and
February 1974 they clearly got the dates wrong. The Conservatives'
private pollsters advised an early dissolution in January 1974; Edward
Heath's decision to delay the election by three weeks to February
28 probably cost him the victory. There is still some dispute about
the attention James Callaghan paid to public and private polls in
deciding not to call the expected election in the autumn of 1978.
The recent volatility of voters, especially in Britain, makes leaders
more wary about reading too much into the polls. However, the
Irish government's voluntary dissolution in 1977 was taken in
defiance of the polling evidence, and the government was resound-
ingly defeated.

Presentation

Survey findings influence campaign presentation in various spheres.

1 *Presenting policy.* In most countries polls are extensively used to
  test campaign slogans, posters, and themes, but it is difficult to
  pin down actual cases of polls' influencing policy. According to
  Humphrey Taylor, who was a pollster with the Conservative party
  in Britain for four general elections, his task was 'communication
  of already decided policies and the presentation of the party
  itself'. He claimed 'only a marginal influence on the Conservative
  party'.[10] The difficulty in discerning the influence is that it is
  probably wise for a pollster who wishes to have a long-term
  relationship with a party not to emphasise his influence on
  politicians. He may be blamed if things go wrong subsequently.
  The politicians also will not wish to publicise the relationship.
  Taylor's private polls certainly contributed to the Conservative
  government's decisions after 1970 to boost old-age pensions and
  to introduce pensions for people over eighty, to sell council houses
  to tenants, and to accept comprehensive education in spite of the
  opposition of many party activists.
2 *The personal style of candidates.* With elections now being fought
  more than ever before through the mass media, in particular

television, which is a 'low intensity' medium, personality is important.[11] Polls are now extensively used to monitor the impact of broadcasts on television. It is difficult to generalise in this area, for the kind of television image desired is probably a cultural variable, even though the same tool – the opinion poll – is used to measure it.

3 The use of more direct and colloquial language in communications. Politicians are more concerned than in the past to speak in everyday language to the public, and polls may help by showing them whether the language they use is having the desired effect.

Manipulation

All parties and candidates want to guard against the impression that they will suffer a landslide defeat or score a landslide victory. The temptation is to misuse the polls, particularly private polls, where methods and findings are rarely open to public scrutiny. But there have been surprisingly few scandals concerning opinion polls and elections – cases of 'doctored' data or misleading reports; two such affairs may have taken place in the United States in 1978 in the campaigns of Senator Dick Clark in Iowa and Governor Lamar Alexander in Tennessee.[12] More common is the selective release of private polls. The best safeguards against these abuses are conformity with an approved code of practice and competition from public polls.

Another problem is the possibility that a candidate, by timing and targeting his campaign efforts, can influence the polls' findings. It has been claimed that President Nixon in 1972, knowing in advance the pollsters' sampling areas and interview schedules, made it a point to concentrate his advertising and workers in those areas in time for the poll.[13] A campaign organisation may also play back purported findings about public opinion in the hope of influencing voters. In Britain in 1979, Tommy Thompson, former chairman of ORC, raised funds from industry to carry out a series of polls in marginal constituencies on the issue of nationalisation. They showed that the majority of Labour voters were hostile to further nationalisation, in contrast to official Labour policy. Similar polls on attitudes to trade unions were sponsored but, following protests from trade union leaders and the Conservative party, publication of the results was delayed until after the election.[14]

Information

Parties conduct 'quickie' private polls during elections to check voters' reactions to issues, speeches, broadcasts, and themes. Speed is essential for this research to have any impact; because of the pace of events in an election campaign a survey can be out of date within a day or two. The information can reassure the party or candidate about new developments and help them decide whether or not to react. In 1960 Kennedy was encouraged by the polls to confront directly the worries some voters felt about his Catholicism, and in 1968 Nixon decided to ignore rather than attack the candidacy of George Wallace, who attracted many voters sympathetic to Nixon's point of view on many issues. In the first 1974 election in Britain the Labour party was reassured as the 'Conservative' issues declined in salience and Labour's preferred issues became more important. The changes in the agenda of the campaign presaged a shift in voting intentions, to Labour's advantage.

Targeting Voters

Targeting voters is particularly important for campaign advertising and broadcasts. This aspect of campaigning is usually left to market specialists, who commission voter surveys in elections as they do consumer surveys in their nonpolitical work. Rarely, however, are the target voters homogeneous, and rarely are they receptive to a single issue or appeal. The 'target voter' tends to differ across countries and elections. In the United States he usually is to be found in large states and key social groups. In Britain target voters are found in the hundred or so marginal constituencies and, again, in particular social groups; both parties emphasised the skilled working-class or blue-collar voters (32 per cent of all voters) in 1979. In France the main parties focus on the support for the 'proximate' candidates who were eliminated in the first ballot. In general the target voters are those who would seem to be likely to defect from one's own side or likely to be attracted from the opposition.

Affecting Voting

The foregoing features deal with the effects of polls on campaign managers and candidates. But what about the mass electorate? Terms like 'bandwagon', 'backlash', and 'boomerang', are increasingly used to describe those effects, but the fact is that there are no conclusive findings on the impact of polls on voters. Several possible effects suggest themselves:

1 The polls may help small parties gain momentum; for example, the Progress party in Denmark or the British Liberals in the Orpington by-election in 1962.
2 They may encourage tactical voting; for example, where the polls forecast a close result, there may be a shift from the smaller to the bigger parties.
3 They may tell voters something about the effectiveness of their votes; for example, poll results may encourage voters to vote for a minor party if they are committed to it or, alternatively, discourage them if they are only temporary protesters against the major parties. Thus the Liberals in the February 1974 British election saw their share of the votes increase considerably as the campaign proceeded.

Explanation of Electoral Change

This is most effectively done through panel studies. By interviewing the same group of voters at successive stages, a panel measures changes in individual voters' attitudes. In Sweden and West Germany panel studies are conducted between elections. In France, Britain, the United States, and Australia they are held during the campaign for both political and scholarly purposes.

THE INFLUENCE OF PRIVATE POLLS

Private polls want not only to convey information to their clients, but also to ensure that it is absorbed and understood. Though they will often deny it, most private pollsters want to have some influence on campaign strategies. In general the private pollsters' influence seems to depend on such variables as the following:

Whether the Party or Client is in Government or Opposition

Not only are ministers busy but they are usually more concerned to implement and justify existing programmes than to test new policies for their electoral acceptability. In Britain, the closeness of the private pollsters to a party's strategic thinking has varied with the party's position as government or opposition; a party's position in office usually downgrades its professional organisers as well. The incumbents' attention usually turns more readily to electoral strategy as the election date nears. With the shorter electoral cycle and the proliferation of primaries and general elections in the United States, it is not surprising that American presidents are attentive to the polls.

The Pollsters' Involvement with the Party

The more the pollster knows about the party's plans, policy options, and priorities, the more he is likely to exercise influence. A useful guideline here is the extent to which politicians involve themselves in selecting the areas for research or leave the initiative to the pollsters. Wolfgang Ernst used to have monthly meetings with Chancellor Willy Brandt to discuss his survey findings. In Britain and the United States the private pollsters regularly attend campaign strategy sessions of the main parties or candidates. The British Labour party keeps its pollsters more at arms length than the Conservatives when it comes to the formulation of strategy. Issues of the structure of the campaign organisation, personalities, and political values affect this relationship.

Some pollsters identify very closely with the politics of the parties and the party leaders for whom they are working. Indeed, they may well be strongly identified with a particular ideological position or a power group within the party. Others retain a much more distant, professional relationship. In general, pollsters who get too closely identified with a particular leader or faction or point of view tend to lose their relationship with the party when those with whom they have been associated lose power in the party. This seems to have been the case with Mark Abrams, who was closely associated with the Gaitskellite faction of the Labour party in the early 1960s.

The Salience of the Issue and the Extent of Disagreement Within the Party

It is almost impossible for a pollster to sell a course of action where the party leadership is set on a different policy. Where the leadership is divided, polling information is a tool which a faction may use in intraparty debates on policy or personality. Again, where an issue is relatively 'open' from the viewpoint of the party's ideology, the pollster may have more influence. The important question is: what is the partisan self-confidence and determination of the leaders? According to Bob Worcester, the Labour party's pollster: 'I characterize the responsibility I have as one of bringing witness to the ripples, the waves and the tides. If the Labour party leadership wants to swim against the tide of public opinion, that is their responsibility. I see my role as telling them which way the tide is running and how strongly, and then I stop'.[15]

Consonance With Other Cues

Polls are only one sort of information for campaigners. To be influential, the import of the polls has to be consistent with other information and pressures. Survey material in the late 1950s coincided with electoral setbacks and social and economic change to help the revisionists in the Social Democratic party in West Germany and the British Labour party. In an effort to adapt to social change and reach out to the less politically oriented floating voters, both parties reversed their traditional emphasis on public ownership and made appeals to all social classes.

Whether the Party is Programmatic or not

Attention to the polls is also affected by the nature of the party. Parties do have interests, traditions, and widely shared values which they are reluctant to abandon. Again, the useful if crude distinction seems to be between the United States and Western Europe. Western European parties are generally regarded as having a more programmatic function than American parties. The American parties are more decentralised, less disciplined, have less control over the recruitment of candidates, and, at the national level, may be taken over by a new candidate for the presidency every four years.

Accordingly, because American parties are less institutionalised and have less ideological baggage, the private pollster may have a larger rôle in suggesting and refining policy positions. For all the opportunism and development of 'catchall' trends in pursuing voters in recent years, the main Western European parties, by comparison, still appear less flexible.[16]

Reasons why the private polls have little or no impact on a party's strategy are not hard to find. Much of the information offered by the polls prompts the candidate to ask the question, So what? Surveys may show that voters want apparently inconsistent policies – less unemployment and less inflation, or lower taxes and more state services. Slight alterations in question wording on a substantive issue produce notable differences in responses. In Britain, this has been true when questions substitute 'public ownership' for 'nationalization', 'the EEC' for 'the Common Market', and 'devolution' for 'a separate Scottish Assembly'. The data may point to actions or to policies which a party considers to be 'politically impossible', in the short term anyway; for example, a left-wing party getting tough with trade unions or a party promising the restoration of capital punishment in Britain. Alternatively, the party may lack the organisation and will to use survey research; in 1963 Mark Abrams commented that survey findings would not lead anywhere in the Labour party because there was no effective machinery to shape political propaganda.[17]

Polls are not the only source of information or pressure operating on a candidate. The candidate has to appeal to activists who may have very different interests and issue preferences from those of less involved voters. In 1972 one reason why McGovern felt that he had to make further speeches on the Vietnam issue (on which Democratic voters were split) was its usefulness in raising money from activists.[18] In 1968, Humphrey, though urged by pollsters and advisers to protect himself against charges of being 'soft' on the law-and-order issue, found it personally embarrassing to be seen to deviate from his traditional stance. The growing importance of the 'purist' outlook in the United States has been reflected in the campaigns of Barry Goldwater (1964), Eugene McCarthy (1968), and George McGovern (1972). This approach emphasises the importance of the candidate's sticking to his principles, regardless of electoral consequences. The purist is more interested in moral crusades than in compromise or conciliation of the opposition; compared with the traditional 'professional' politician, he is less oriented toward winning the election. The supporters of Goldwater and McGovern were able to capture their party machines, but their presidential candidates were routed in the general elections.[19]

There is also a tendency for politicians to dismiss the polls when their tidings are gloomy or fail to show what practical steps can be taken to reverse the likelihood of electoral defeat. In Britain and France the private pollsters tend, quite undeservedly, to be enveloped in the sense of failure that follows a party's defeat. In the United States in mid-October 1964, Dean Burch, the Republican National chairman, cancelled the ORC polls for Goldwater. The last straw for the campaign teams was the pollsters' failure to find the latent or 'secret' support for Goldwater that the team believed was there. They had hoped, paradoxically, that the polls would confirm their belief in a 'hidden vote' waiting to be mobilised. McGovern, by contrast, continued to rely heavily on Pat Caddell in 1972 in spite of his depressing reports.

Finally, poll findings may be compatible with quite different interpretations. If a party's strong issue is of less salience than others, strategists may as readily interpret this finding as a basis for emphasising as for ignoring it. And, as politicians are quick to complain, information about the grievances and concerns of voters is rather dispiriting without suggestions for what to do about the situation. 'Polls are not very good on the "what to do" consequences of their research', was a revealing, if unfair, comment made by one British politician.

In some countries – for example West Germany, Japan, and the United States – enormous sums are spent on private polls. It would be surprising if much of this was not, literally, 'wasted', if considered in terms of how much of the pollsters' data were absorbed and acted on by campaign strategists. A party or politician should have a clear idea of what is wanted from the polls. John Kennedy and Harold Wilson were reputed to be particularly shrewd and critical readers of polls. But some polling is commissioned simply because others are doing it, because people like information for its own sake, and because it just might prompt an election-winning idea or theme.

There is another value in having the private pollsters in close and regular contact with party strategists. They do bring some objectivity to what is essentially an in-group and partisan gathering. Because they also work for commercial clients, they provide other perspectives during the election. They are professionals at gathering evidence, and they are trained to assess it calmly.

OBJECTIONS TO THE POLLS

Most complaints centre on the claim that polls have undue influence on elections. According to the Australians Murray Goot and Terence Beed, because polls are reported frequently and help the media to portray an election as a horse race, candidates spend more time reacting to the latest headlines, trends, and forecasts.[20] Between the 1966 and 1970 general elections in Britain the number of lead stories in the British press during the three-week campaign periods which dealt with the polls increased from a tenth to a third.

Polls may also affect campaign workers' morale, particularly when they forecast victory by a large margin for one side or the other. The polls certainly had this effect on the Goldwater and McGovern organisations, the British Conservatives in October 1974, and the Australian Labor party in 1975. Polls which report a large lead for one side over the other make the outcome appear inevitable, and the media may switch their attention to the consequences of defeat for the losing party.

More debatably, it is sometimes claimed that the publication of polls affects the outcome. Claims of bias or unfairness by the media and pollsters are a staple of campaign exchanges. An IFOP 'quickie' poll, conducted immediately after the first TV debate between Giscard d'Estaing and Mitterrand in the French presidential election of 1974, was very favourable to Giscard and prompted an official complaint from Mitterand. In 1974 also, the French polls and papers observed a self-denying ordinance against publishing poll results in the last week of the election. It was later made a statutory rule, and during the 1979 campaign for the European Parliament in France, the polls were barred by law from publishing their findings in the latter stages of the campaign. In West Germany in 1969 the pollsters did not publish their findings in the last week, but the London *Times* commissioned a poll by Marplan and broke the ban. A similar ban is still in force today whereby the polls report the current strength of the German parties without making forecasts. As Max Kaase notes, the pollsters' distinction between presenting their findings and not making forecasts escapes most of the public.[21] In New Zealand until 1978 the Heylen organisation did not publish its election polls, fearing that they would influence voters. In the 1978 election, Labour accused Heylen of attempting to mislead the public by not publishing a poll taken a week before the election that showed the National and Labour parties evenly matched.

Heylen intended to release the poll after the election, but Labour went ahead and leaked it to the media on the eve of the election.[22]

There is probably no easy way to accommodate the sensitivities and allay the disappointment of politicians; they are interested parties. But there is no good evidence bearing on how, if at all, the polls influence voting behaviour. In order to believe that polls do have an influence, one must assume that voters (1) are aware of other voters' first and second preferences, (2) know how other voters will react on election day in the light of poll findings, and (3) assume that the net changes will not cancel out. It is possible that some voters calculate how they can most effectively cast their votes in the light of poll findings but, as far as I know, it has not been clearly demonstrated that in fact they do so. In the 1964 American presidential election, the National Broadcasting Company commissioned a study by Market Dynamics of the effects on voting in the West of computer forecasts that were based on New York returns and released before the polls closed in the western time zone. Comparisons of the behaviour of groups who saw the forecasts and groups who did not showed only slight differences.[23]

In Britain there is some circumstantial evidence that polls may affect voting behaviour. In four successive general elections between 1966 and 1974, the party that was ahead in the immediate pre-election polls did less well than predicted in the election itself. Some observers attribute this to the 'reverse bandwagon effect' of the opinion polls' findings: voters wavering in their support for the party in the lead, or fearing that it might receive too large a majority, voted for the party said to be behind.

In the 1979 British general election, the polls again reported a narrowing of the Conservative lead until the weekend before the election. In the last few days, however, there was a boomerang effect, and the Conservative lead increased again. Observers speculated that this time the voters had reacted to the prospect of a deadlocked parliament. There is clearly no general or consistent effect of the polls on voting behaviour. Any hypothetical effects need to be set against the impact on voters of events and political activities reported by the media in the last days of the campaign: the polls may be merely reflecting these changes. If many voters decided to vote tactically, the result of their separate calculations might be an indeterminate election. Moreover, voters may be influenced in different ways without voting tactically. But, insofar as the polls provide more information for the voters and enhance

their awareness of the significance of their votes, they are surely no
bad thing.

   Banning polls or their publication hardly seems an effective answer
to the problem – if there is one. An obvious check against abuse is
competition between independent polling organisations. Parties or
interest groups are self-interested users of poll findings. In West
Germany, for example, the willingness of the mass media to
commission polls means that the voters are no longer exposed to
selective leaks by the parties; the public polls act as an external
check. It is also difficult to ban polls effectively in a free society.
As the German case shows, if foreign media commission polls and
publish them overseas, the results will be transmitted back.

   A different complaint is that where the mass media are the main
suppliers of the polls and are bitterly partisan, this may lead to
doubts about the status of the polls – even when the pollsters have
little control over colourful and misleading press coverage. In
Australia in 1975, the Murdoch papers conducted such a vitriolic
press war against the Labor party that the impartiality of the polls
they commissioned was questioned.[24]

CONCLUSION

There are several common trends in campaigning across the
industrialised liberal democratic countries. The growth of opinion
polls is only one factor to set beside the rôle of the electronic media,
the spending of large sums of money, and the declining importance
of traditional party campaign activities. It is possible to suggest a
number of consequences of the growth of the opinion polls.

   First, the polls have probably led to more informed reporting and
analysis of campaigns, issues, and personalities. One can now use
evidence where once one relied on hearsay or other impressions.
Sustained exposure to public and private polls has improved the
capacity of politicians and campaign managers to read the evidence
with a discerning eye.

   Second, the polls may influence the political agenda. By asking
voters to indicate which issues *are* important and which *should be*
important, the polls may spotlight issues that are neglected by elites
but bother voters. It is understandable that much attention is paid
to the polls as tools for predicting voters' behaviour. This, we have
seen, is a risky enterprise. A more important rôle of opinion polls,

between as well as during elections, is to tell politicians what people think and what issues concern them.

Surveys are also indispensable for evaluating a winning party's claim to have a mandate for a general programme or a particular policy. Public polls carry much of this information, showing issue preferences broken down by party or social class. In fact, the number of issues that decisively affect voting behaviour are few; parties are, for one thing, cautious about taking clear-cut positions.

But sophisticated analysis of elaborate surveys invariably takes time to filter through. Later interpretations of Eugene McCarthy's good showing in the New Hampshire primary in 1968 revealed that his was not, after all, primarily an anti-war vote.[25] Analysis of McGovern's defeat in the 1972 presidential election shows that it had as much to do with voters' assessments of the candidate's competence and personality as with his issue stands.[26] Academic analysis of Labour's two 1974 election victories shows that they were gained in spite of the electorate's growing hostility to major planks of the party's platform.[27] Again one can contrast the more complex analyses that students of electoral behaviour now offer with the rather simple judgements which were made of election outcomes in the not too distant past.

There is no clear relation between the growth of opinion polls and the decomposition of parties (a largely American phenomenon, anyway) and the trend away from programmatic parties to catchall parties. It can be argued that opinion polls, insofar as they report a lack of ideology and partisanship, do provide evidence against the ideological elements in political parties and weaken the rôle of the local activist as an opinion former in the party. These trends have been noticed in the main parties in West Germany, Austria, Italy, and France, affecting even the large Communist parties in the last two countries. But in Britain (since 1970) and the United States the patterns are more complex. In Britain, the Labour and Conservative parties have reacted to electoral defeat by adopting a more ideological stance in opposition (in Labour's case, the extra-parliamentary wing is important in exerting this pressure). In the United States the parties appear to be decaying as organisations, while change in issues and in the formal structure of the parties have enhanced the rôle of the ideologue. The rise or decline of partisanships, or of attachment to political parties, probably has little to do with the increasing use of polls.

Polls are regularly attacked and praised as surrogates for direct democracy. They may offer a check on the mediating or representative claims of parties, pressure groups, and mass media. It is also the case that where they are centrally commissioned, local candidates resent them as yet another instance of the centralization and nationalisation of campaigning. They may therefore strengthen the position of leaders within the parliamentary parties, and the parliamentary parties against the mass members. Such claims may invite a sceptical 'So what?' Used with care, however, opinion polls remain an important feedback device for decision makers and citizens between and during elections.

References

I have drawn heavily on the *At the Polls* series for information about polling operations in various countries. Other useful sources include:
Berrington, Hugh *Public Opinion Polls, British Politics, and the 1970 General Election*, Political Studies Association paper (Edinburgh, 1972).
Hodder-Williams, Richard, *Public Opinion Polls and British Politics* (London: Routledge & Kegan Paul, 1970).
Mendelsohn, Harold, and Crespi, Irving, *Polls, Television and the New Politics* (Scranton, Pa.: Chandler, 1970).
Noelle-Neumann, Elisabeth, 'Uses of Survey Research for Decision-Makers in the Social-Political Sphere: A Case Study, The German General Election 1976, (mimeo).
Taylor, Humphrey. 'The Use of Survey Research in Britain by Political Parties and the Government'. *Policy Analysis* (Winter 1977) pp. 75–84.
Teer, F., and Spence, J D, *Political Opinion Polls* (London: Hutchinson, 1973).
Stoetzel, Jean, and Girard, Andre. *Les sondages d'opinion publique* [Public opinion polls] (Paris: Presses Universitaires de France, 1973).
Webb, Norman. 'The Democracy of Opinion Polls', unpublished paper, Social Surveys (Gallup Poll) Limited, 1979.

NOTES

1. Lawrence Le Duc, 'The Measurement of Public Opinion', in Howard R. Penniman (ed.),*Canada at the Polls: The General Election of 1974* (Washington, DC: American Enterprise Institute, 1975) p. 210.
2. Terence Beed, 'Opinion Polling and the Elections', in Howard R. Penniman, (ed.), *Australia at the Polls: The National Elections of 1975* (Washington, DC: American Enterprise Institute, 1977) p. 222.
3. See Richard Rose, 'The Polls and Election Forecasting in February 1974, in Howard R. Penniman, (ed.), *Britain at the Polls: The*

Parliamentary Elections of 1974 (Washington, DC: American Enterprise Institute, 1975) p. 119.

4. Alain Lancelot, 'Opinion Polls and the Presidential Election, May 1974', in Howard R. Penniman, (ed.), *France at the Polls: The Presidential Election of 1974* (Washington, DC: American Enterprise Institute, 1975) p. 175.

5. In contrast to the monthly Swedish Institute of Public Opinion Research poll sample, the sample used for the prediction consists largely of people who were interviewed at the election three years earlier, though it is stratified by previous vote.

6. Le Duc, 'The Measurement of Public Opinion', p. 217.

7. See Giacomo Sani, 'The Italian Electorate in the Mid-1970s: Beyond Tradition?' in Howard R. Penniman, (ed.), *Italy at the Polls: The Parliamentary Elections of 1976* (Washington, DC: American Enterprise Institute, 1977) p. 88.

8. In 1968 Nixon commissioned polls to see how he would fare with different vice-presidential running mates in eighteen key states.

9. 'Elective Dictatorship', *Listener*, 21 October, 1977.

10. Humphrey Taylor, 'The Use of Survey Research in Britain by Political Parties and the Government', *Policy Analysis* (Winter 1977) p. 78. Few pollsters have achieved the influence and intimacy which Pat Caddell has with President Carter.

11. Marshall McLuhan, *Understanding Media* (New York: McGraw-Hill, 1964).

12. 'Polls Watcher Wanted', *Economist*, 13 January 1979.

13. Michael Wheeler, *Lies, Damned Lies and Statistics* (New York: Dell, 1976) p. 131.

14. David Butler and Dennis Kavanagh, *The British General Election of 1979* (London: Macmillan, 1980).

15. 'Rasmussen interview with Robert Worcester', *British Politics Newsletter*, no. 8 (Spring 1977) p. 8. For discussion of relations between the parties and private pollsters, see David Butler and Dennis Kavanagh, *The British General Election of October 1974* (London: Macmillan, 1975), chap. 8, and *The British General Election of 1979*, chap. 13. For a full discussion of the role of private polls in British politics, see my 'Political Parties and Private Polls', in R. Worcester (ed.), *Political Communications and the 1979 General Election* (London: Macmillan, 1981).

16. On the concept of 'catchall' parties, see Otto Kirchheimer, 'The Transformation of the Western European Party Systems', in Joseph LaPalombara and Myron Weiner (eds.), *Political Parties and Political Development* (Princeton: Princeton University Press, 1965).

17. Mark Abrams, 'Public Opinion Polls and Political Parties', *Public Opinion Quarterly*, vol. 27 (1963) pp. 9–18. After Labour's electoral defeat in 1959, the party's National Executive refused to sponsor a survey into the reasons for defeat; it was financed instead by a magazine, *Social Commentary*. See Mark Abrams *et al.*, *Must Labour Lose?* (London: Penguin, 1960).

18. On the McGovern campaign, see Theodore H. White,*The Making of the President, 1972* (New York: Atheneum, 1973).
19. Nelson Polsby and Aaron Wildavsky, *Presidential Elections*, 4th edn, (New York: Scribners, 1976).
20. Murray Goot and Terence W. Beed, 'The Polls, the Public, and the Re-election of the Fraser Government', in Howard R. Penniman (ed.), *The Australian National Elections of 1977* (Washington, DC: American Enterprise Institute, 1979) pp. 41–84.
21. Max Kaase, 'Public Opinion Polling in the Federal Republic of Germany', in Karl Cerny (ed.), *Germany at the Polls: The Bundestag Election of 1976* (Washington, DC: American Enterprise Institute, 1978) p. 210. Some countries deliberately restrict the publicity given to the findings of opinion polls. In Australia there is an embargo on radio and television coverage of them after midnight on the final Wednesday prior to the Sunday general election. In Britain the broadcasting authorities are forbidden to carry election news on polling day.
22. See Howard R. Penniman, 'Preface', in Howard R. Penniman (ed.), *New Zealand at the Polls: The General Election of 1978* (Washington, DC: American Enterprise Institute, 1980) p. x.
23. For a useful discussion, see Harold Mendelsohn and Irving Crespi, *Polls, Television and the New Politics* (Scranton, Pa.: Chandler, 1970) chap. 5. For an earlier study, see Donald Campbell, 'On the Possibility of Experimenting with the Bandwagon Effect', *International Journal of Opinion and Attitude Research*, vol. 5 (1951).
24. Beed, 'Opinion Polling and Elections', p. 234.
25. Philip Converse *et al.*, 'Continuity and Change in American Politics: Parties and Issues in the 1968 Election', *American Political Science Review*, vol. 63 (1969) pp. 1083–1105.
26. Warren Miller and Teresa Levitin, *Leadership and Change* (Cambridge: Whinthrop, 1976).
27. Ivor Crewe *et al.*, 'Partisan Dealignment in Britain, 1964–1974', *British Journal of Political Science*, vol. 7, no. 2 (1977) pp. 129–90.

Index

adversary politics 58, 127–8, 266
affluence 106
agenda, political xiv, 60–1, 332
Alliance, Liberal-SDP xv, 92, 96, 98, 115, 127–3, 282, 283
  1983 election 128–9
  1987 election 131
Almond. G. 197
  and Verba. S. 193–4, 205, 208
Alt. J. 54, 57
Amery, L. 220
Attlee C. 23–4, 183, 248
  government 248
authority, political 299, 300, 301

Bagehot, W. 188–90, 219–20, 287, 292, 301, 302, 309–10
Baldwin, S. 67, 95, 161, 248, 276
Beer. S. 197, 234
Benn, A. 13, 33, 177–87
  consensus and 183
  deputy leader contest (1981) 179
  and diaries and 177, 184
  leadership contest (1988) and 179
  1983 election and 183
  political thought 184–5
Berlin, I. 134
Bevan, A. 149
Bosanquet, N. 83
British Union of Fascists (BUF) 157
Brittan. S. 54
Bulpitt, J. 75, 80
Burke, E. 65
Butler, D. x–xi, 1, 2, 3, 9
  Stoker, D. and 93, 108, 201
Butler, R. A. 67, 164
Butskellism 47

cabinet system 27–8, 174, 222
Callaghan, J. 32, 123, 181, 255–6

Castle, B. 96
Central Policy Review Staff 262
Chamberlain, J. 123, 165, 174, 248
Chamberlain, N. 136, 137, 141
charisma 134–62 *passim*
  defined 134–6
  see also leadership
Churchill, Lord R. 147
Churchill, W. 67, 134–62, 174, 248, 259
  character and 137, 147–9
  charisma and 139–52
  party and 137
  as prime minister 149
  public opinion and 140–6, 150–1
civil service 224–5, 262
Clause IV 64
Clemenceau, G. 159
coalition government (1940–5) 45, 139
Commonwealth Immigrants Act (1962) 169
comparative politics 208–10
consensus
  breaking of 49–50
  defined 40, 41–2
  effect of Mrs Thatcher on 51, 56–7
  post-war 46, 48
  public opinion and 42, 57, 58
conservatism 65–7
Conservative party 16–37
  collectivism in 46–7, 93–4
  conference and 28, 29
  election of leader 28, 29, 257
  opinion polls and 322
  recruitment and 254–8
constitution 220, 221
  interpretations of 199
  reform and 178
Cosgrove, P. 82
Cox, N. xi

337

move to the left 31–4, 35
National Executive Committee
26–7, 30, 181
policy review (1989) 98
recruitment xviii, 249–54
revisionism and 31
trade unions and 25, 33, 35,
98–100, 111
working class and 111, 112–13,
118
labourism 45
leadership xix, 134–62, *passim*,
192, 246–69
recruitment and 153–4, 155–6,
195, 267
style of 247, 258–63, 268
Liberal Party 125–8, 131
see also Alliance
Lijphart, A. 194
Livingstone, K. 97
Lloyd George, D. 149, 150, 156,
158, 160–1, 248
local government 100
loony left 97
Lowell, A. L. 223

managerialism 262–3
MacDonald, R. 181, 248
Mackenzie, W. J. M. 22–3
Macmillan, H. 137, 166, 174, 248,
255, 277
government 259–60
Maxwell-Fyfe reforms (1949) 254
McCallum, R. B. x, 2
McKenzie, R. xii, 16–39, 200, 209
Members of Parliament 174
Mendès-France, P. 159
Michels, R. 19–20
Middlemas, K. 45
Militant Tendency 97
Mill, J. S. 190
Minkin, L. 26
monarchy, the xix, 153, 191–2,
286–314
Mosley, O. 123, 156, 157, 158,
174

nationalized industries 73
'New Class' 86–7
New Right 68, 76

Nordlinger, E. 200, 209
Northcote-Trevelyan reforms 224
Nuffield election studies x–xi,
1–15

Oakeshott, M. 66
opinion polls 280–2, 283, 315–36
influence and 330–4
1979 election and 331
political parties and 326–9, 333
Owen, D. 130–2

permissiveness 76
pluralism 21
political agenda 332
political change 231–2
political culture 154, 206, 207–8,
218, 228–31
political parties 43–4, 90, 123–4,
225–6, 333
convergence of 48–9, 263
outcomes and 58–60
see also two-party system
polls *see* opinion polls
Powell, E. xvii, 68, 163–76, 183
1970 election and 170, 172
1974 election and 171
EEC and 171, 172
political thought 167–8
race and 168–9, 171, 173
Ulster and 170
Prime Minister 149, 161
privatisation 79
professions, the 72
Progressive Alliance 126–7
public opinion 102, 116, 117,
280–2, 284, 286–314 *passim*
see also opinion polls
public ownership 47, 64

Queen *see* monarchy

race 173
see also immigration; Powell
realignment 178
referenedum 178
revisionism 30, 55, 107
Robertson, D. 49, 58
Rose, R. x, 52, 59
Runciman, W. G. 194, 204–5, 209